BUD

BUD

An Autobiography

David L. Furman

To the memory of:
   My mother: Mary Elizabeth Furman
   My grandparents: William David and Jennie Kembel Furman
   My uncle: Richard Kembel Furman
   My grandparents: Rhodolphus and Eva Potter
   My grandmother-in-law: Hazel (Grams) Phykitt
   My father-in-law: Washington Lee Matney
   . . . they will "dwell in the house of the Lord forever." (Psalm 23:6)

To Dr. Toni Stevens, counselor and friend.

Contents

Preface ix

I.	In the Beginning	1
II.	Life in Our House on the Loop	14
III.	World War II through the Eyes of a Boy	24
IV.	Another Move, Another Cottage	41
V.	Bad Days, Glad Days, Sad Days	50
VI.	There Is More to Bathrooms Than Meets the Eye	61
VII.	Pit and Me	67
VIII.	Three Memorable Casts	78
IX.	Cars, Freedom and the Price I Paid for Both	87
X.	The Ups and Downs of My Sex Education	100
XI.	Vices or Virtues: The Choices Were Mine	113
XII.	Hitchhiking to California: A Thumbnail Sketch	127
XIII.	A Year Like No Other: 1952	136
XIV.	Summer, 1954: An Unusual Mixture of Events	142
XV.	Sports: One Moment of Glory	151
XVI.	California, Here I Come Again	175
XVII.	Our Truck/Camper: A Status Symbol	197
XVIII.	Vas Valves: A Noble Medical Project	210
XIX.	Europe: A Dream Come True	215
XX.	Tent Camping: Wet, Wild, Wonderful	241
XXI.	Tragedy then Assurance: They're with Jesus	256
XXII.	There's More to Jobs Than Money	262
XXIII.	Driving Limousines in New York City	287
XXIV.	Working and Playing in the Grand Teton National Park	317
XXV.	Diets: I Could Write My Own Book and Get Rich	346
XXVI.	The Hitchhiker: Drifter or Convict?	350
XXVII.	Epilogue	354

Preface

For several years, relatives, fellow employees, and close friends encouraged me to write my autobiography. They all knew bits and pieces of the first fifty-five years of my life but not the entire story. They felt my life had been unique in many ways, and that they and others would enjoy reading about it. Therefore, a little over two years ago, I took their encouragement and prodding to heart and began writing. I soon found it to be both an enjoyable and difficult task—difficult because I wanted authenticity throughout the book and would not settle for less. I believe I've accomplished this goal.

As you prepare to read my autobiography, keep in mind that I did not want it to be a moment by moment, month by month, year by year account of my life. Therefore, only where dates seemed necessary were they included. I did, however, arrange the chapters in somewhat of a chronological order, although some overlap others.

I would like to thank Jean Edwards, Patricia Furman, Rose Marie Hess, Marilyn Kinnison, and the *Oswego Palladium Times* for their time and effort procuring pieces of information I needed.

I trust you will enjoy reading *Bud*.

BUD

Chapter I
In the Beginning

My birth certificate states that I was born on April 7, 1933 in Elmira, a manufacturing town on the beautiful Chemung River in the southern tier of New York State. Elmira's claim to fame is not the fact that I was born there, although I wish it were. Rather, it was the home of Mark Twain while he was doing his greatest writing. Twain's study and burial site are both interesting places to visit in Elmira. I have no recollection of anything that happened to me in Elmira, since my family moved to Little Falls, New York, while I was still very young. However, I do recall living in Little Falls.

Little Falls is near the Mohawk River. It's built primarily on hillsides and rather steep ones. When I was young, it was a manufacturing town. We lived in a third floor apartment across the street from sets of railroad tracks and the train station beyond. One could get to the station by walking through a tunnel under the tracks. One entrance to the tunnel was near our apartment building. Behind the buildings that fronted our street were manufacturing plants, although I never learned what they manufactured. Besides our apartment building, there were two food stores: The Hole in the Wall and Ignasis; plus a few other stores and a couple of saloons.

Our apartment was small. However, we could go out onto a roof adjacent to it and get a nice view up and down the railroad tracks and beyond the station. Spring and fall were the prettiest times of the year, since there were so many flowering trees and bushes in the spring and colorful leaves in the fall. It was in this apartment that I suffered through scarlet fever, a disease that left me with 20/200 vision in my left eye. Thankfully it didn't affect my right one. Thus, with 20/20 vision in only one eye, I began wearing glasses at an early age and have worn them ever since. Scarlet fever affected my mother's hearing as a young girl, so the disease was not new to us. In those days, there was little doctors could do. Today such a malady can be treated and cured.

If I had to describe our family with one adjective while growing up, that adjective would be poor. Many little things that happened became big things because we were poor. One day someone bought me an ice cream cone at the Hole in the Wall. I was so excited, I came running down the sidewalk to share my joy with my mother. Wouldn't you know it, I stubbed my toe. I can still see that ice cream flying through the air as I hit the concrete. My bloody knees and hands hurt, but my loss hurt more. We didn't get ice cream very often, and there mine lay melting on the hot sidewalk. I know my mother felt badly too, because she had no money to replace my delicious loss, just words of advice, "Buddy, walk, don't run when carrying . . ." Before I finally learned to do so, I tripped and broke a jar of mayonnaise my mother had sent me to the store to buy. I came home with mayonnaise all over me mixed with blood from my hands and knees. But I finally learned my lesson.

One day I was walking past one of the manufacturing plants near our building. It was lunchtime and four men were sitting on a ledge a couple of feet above the top of my head. One asked me if I'd like a hard boiled egg. I said, "Yes, please." He said, "Catch," and dropped it. I didn't catch it. It hit me in the face, broke open, and to his surprise and mine, it was raw. They laughed, I didn't. I had egg running down my face, neck, and stomach plus a mess on my shirt. I knew my mother would be upset, and I couldn't blame her. But a hard boiled egg would have tasted delicious that day, and who knew it was raw? Surprisingly, once my mother heard my tale, she laughed and helped me clean myself. However, I never saw the humor the others did. But victims rarely do.

I only remember one Christmas time while living in Little Falls. I was six and finances were worse than usual. My dad had gone to Oswego, New York, to work on a steam power plant being built. We were left behind and money became scarce. Why? I don't really know. Christmas eve was approaching, and I knew my mother was worried. She had little money for the bare necessities of life let alone for presents. All of a sudden, I had an idea. I went to the local Sears Roebuck store, took a pile of their Christmas circulars, walked to a busy street corner and tried to sell them for five cents each. By the time I left for home that evening, I had made thirty-five cents. Imagine the pride I felt, as I dropped seven nickels into the lap of my mother. It wasn't much, but every penny helped in those days, especially since welfare assistance meant a bag of cornmeal and a bag of flour. At least that's what Mom brought back, the day she went there for help.

One beautiful spring Saturday, a friend and I went to our school to play. We climbed to the top of the school's fire escape, and there we found a bird's nest containing three blue eggs. Three stories below sat an open garbage can. I wanted to play bombardier, my friend didn't. So I played alone carefully sighting my target and dropping the eggs one by one. I felt great joy hitting the bull's-eye once out of three tries. Deep down I knew what I had done was wrong, but the urge to "bomb" the can overcame whatever else I was feeling at the time.

Soon after I arrived home, my mother gave me a grocery list and some money. I opened the door to our apartment and began descending the enclosed two flights of stairs leading to the sidewalk. All of a sudden I saw a bird flying wildly in the enclosed stairwell. A horrible thought raced through my mind, *The mother of those three eggs had come to get me!* Panic overcame me. I quickly turned, raced up the stairs, threw open the door, ran in, slammed the door behind me, and only then breathed a sigh of relief. However, as I turned to go into the living room, I came face to face with my mother. She was only four feet nine inches, but at that point, she looked much taller. In response to her question, "What's the matter?" I answered, "Nothing. I just need to go to the toilet." Half of my answer was correct. Once I reappeared and refused to go to the store, my mother began questioning me. Finally I broke down and in tears told her what I had done, and now the mother bird had come to get even. I knew it! I knew it! I was a goner for sure!

After calming me down and talking to me, Mom went into the hall and down the stairs. Returning soon after, she agreed a bird was trapped, but it was not the mother of the eggs. She assured me a robin had laid the blue eggs and the trapped bird was a sparrow. What a relief! I was saved from sure death at the hands of an angry bird. However, the entire episode gave me an early respect for other living things including eggs in nests. One other incident cemented that respect to this day.

When I was in the seventh grade, Jackie Sawyer, a classmate and good friend, received a BB rifle with a telescopic sight for his birthday. He brought it to school and had it on the playground before school began. Since no one in my family had any kind of gun, I was curious. Like a typical kid, I asked Jackie if I could handle it. He agreed and handed it to me. We were standing under the branches of a tall tree. I raised the gun to my shoulder and pointed it up into the air. As I looked through the telescopic sight, I saw a bird sitting on a limb. I took aim, slowly pulled the trigger, and fired. For a brief moment, the bird didn't move. Then it fell at my feet. It was dead. Instead of elation, I felt awful. Without saying a word, I gave the gun back to Jackie, slowly picked up the bird, quickly buried it under a bush, and vowed never again to shoot anything else.

Years later, during my junior year of high school, my friend, Neil MacDonald, took me hunting for rabbits. He loaned me a rifle and gave me ammunition for it. It was winter, and we spent an hour or so hunting together with no luck. Then he suggested that we separate and go in different directions to see if our luck would change. I quickly agreed, turned and began trudging through the snow as silently as possible. I soon came upon a large rabbit. As I slowly raised my rifle to shoot, my thoughts raced back to the vow I had made after shooting the bird with Jack's BB gun. Instead of pulling the trigger, I exclaimed, "Scat! Get out of here!" Immediately the rabbit darted away to safety, and I lowered my rifle and continued walking. This same scene happened three times that afternoon. When I rejoined Neil, he was all smiles. He had bagged two rabbits, and he felt sorry for me for having bagged none. I didn't feel sorry at all but didn't let him know it.

It's ironic in a way as I think back to that day. I love to fish and don't mind catching, cleaning, and eating them. But to this day, I don't hunt.

My two other recollections of Little Falls center on the railroad tracks. One day after school, I was told that a man had deliberately walked into the path of a train not far from the station. By the time a friend and I reached the area of impact, only bits and pieces of flesh remained. At that moment I don't recall if I was more disappointed or relieved. I do remember asking my mother why any man would do such a thing. I don't recall her answer, but I know I felt sorry for him.

The second concerns a train wreck that occurred not far from our building. A passenger train had jumped the tracks on a curve, sending some of the cars into the river and others next to it. The local paper was full of pictures and articles. By the time we were allowed to go and see the wreck, any known dead had been removed. On the day we went, the engine was righted, and the body of the engineer was discovered under it. It took several days to remove the badly damaged cars, the engine and debris, plus clean up the area and return it to normal. From our roof I saw several of the damaged cars as they passed our apartment building atop flatbed railroad cars. As a young boy the trauma of this accident cured me from wanting to ride on trains or become a railroad engineer. However, after riding in a train a few years later, my fears disappeared.

In early July 1940 we moved to Oswego and left Little Falls with all its memories, good and bad, safely tucked into our hearts and minds. By then, our family consisted of five children, my mother and father. I was the second oldest at seven and already had lived quite an exciting life.

After weeks of anticipation, the morning finally came when I would see this body of water that my dad had mentioned and compared to the local swimming pool during one of our last days in Little Falls. "That's the biggest, bluest, prettiest lake I've ever seen. Why, all those people, who cram into the pool up in the park, wouldn't be a drop in the bucket in Lake Ontario." I tried to imagine such a lake during our final, hot, summer afternoons when we, with everyone else who could take the time, tried to find a spot in the town's only pool and felt victorious standing with so many others. Of course no one swam, there wasn't room. No one dove, no one floated, no one did anything but stand. That morning I woke up early, hopped into my shorts, grabbed a wrinkled shirt, and quietly tiptoed out the screen door of the small three-room cottage that we had moved into after dark the night before.

As I stepped into the bright world outside our cottage, the scene that met my young eyes was more beautiful than I had imagined. Mighty Lake Ontario in all its splendor lay patiently before me. It was as blue and as pretty as my dad had said, but its size was so much larger! I walked across the road to the edge of a high bank that sloped gradually up from the shoreline and looked down into the water, so sparkling clear, I could see fish swimming. The lake's vast expanse met the sky at the horizon and to the left and right ripples of water wafted lazily onto the rocky shore. After drinking in the beauty of the lake for several minutes, I noticed the rest of my surroundings.

The shoreline extended in both directions as far as my eyes could see. To my left, far off in the distance, it gradually curved forming an arc. I noticed the woods; green, green grass; many other cottages along the bank; a dirt road with puddles here and there; beautiful butterflies; my first, graceful, lake gull. As I stood there silently, I could hear the joyful sounds of birds welcoming a new day.

This new world I had entered was like a fairy tale wonderland, only it was real and it was my new home! Gone were the dirty streets, the railroad tracks so near to our home, the factories and the third-floor flat. In their place was this scenic paradise.

A slight breeze ruffled my red hair and leaves on several tall trees nearby moved gently, approving of the breeze's presence. As the hot sun beamed down on my face, the breeze was welcomed. Suddenly a squirrel scampered by clutching its breakfast between its teeth. I jumped when I saw it. In Little Falls I had seen many dogs knocking over garbage cans in search of food. And cats were everywhere, chasing mice and rats that lived in factories, stores, and tenements. But never a squirrel. I watched this new creature scurry up a tree and lose itself amidst the leaves.

I had gotten up soon after the first rays of light shattered the darkness of the cottage. Everyone else was still asleep when I quietly left. Now I heard footsteps and excited voices. Turning around, I saw Corky, Rose Marie and Marilyn running toward me. Arriving, they stood and enjoyed what I had already been drinking in. Corky finally summed up his feelings, "It's like being stranded on the beautiful island described in the book Mom recently read to us." We agreed.

After breakfast Corky and I helped Dad unload the remaining furniture and boxes on the truck. Where to put everything was a problem. With only a small kitchen, one small bedroom, a medium-sized third room and the screened porch for seven people, space was tight. Therefore, several boxes were piled along one wall until their contents were needed. The third room became our storage room, dining room, living room and bedroom for four of us kids. Baby Paul (Paddy) slept in his crib in our parents' bedroom. Therefore, each evening four cots had to be set up, then made up, and taken down the following morning, the bedding folded and stored in other boxes along the wall.

Since there was no plumbing, water had to be carried from a community well down the road. We washed in the kitchen and used water was emptied into a covered cesspool. An outhouse was our toilet.

Our cottage was far smaller and had fewer conveniences than our apartment in Little Falls. However, it was nice to be out of there with its musty apartments and dusty stairs. We loved being in the country where we could run and play unhampered by traffic, railroad tracks and buildings. In Little Falls our windows opened onto the roof with its chimneys and smoke. Here our windows opened to the lake, the woods, the sky, the whole world. What more could we ask for?

Much of that summer Corky and I spent countless hours learning to swim and relaxing on the rocky beach. In the beginning there were a few times when we thought we would drown, but we soon learned not to swim out from but along the shore and never over our heads. The lake was our bathtub, and we brought soap, that would float, with us everyday.

When we needed to rest, we carefully walked out of the water over wet, often slippery rocks and onto the rocky beach. At first we found it difficult to walk on the rocks even though they were smooth and roundish. They would wiggle and jiggle as we walked on them, and we fell a few times.

However, we soon learned how to cope with their movements and could walk and run over them without falling.

As we sat or lay on the warm rocks, we talked, sang, whistled, and tossed rocks at objects in the water. We soon discovered that small, flat, rounded stones would skip across calm water if thrown similar to a side-arm pitcher throwing a baseball. This discovery afforded us many hours of pleasure, as the supply of skipping rocks never seemed to diminish.

One morning Corky and I were stretched out on the rocks enjoying the soothing heat from beneath and the warmth of the sun from above. We had our eyes closed and lay there dozing in the early morning sunlight. As I lay there, something tickled my arm. Figuring it was Corky fooling around, I ignored it. But after feeling it several times, I ordered him to cut it out. "Cut what out?" he asked. "You know. Don't act so dumb," I countered. Corky denied having done anything, so I waited until I felt it again then quickly opened my eyes hoping to catch him in the act. Instead of Corky's hand tickling me, a small, black spider was crawling on my arm. I yelped, quickly sat up and flicked it off. It darted between two rocks and disappeared. By now Corky was sitting watching me. I told him what happened, and then we sat quietly and waited. Soon we saw many spiders cautiously advancing from their hiding places in the rocks. They were tiny and fragile but moved as though they were jet propelled. We watched in fascination and soon noticed that our slightest movement caused them to retreat instantly into their nooks and crannies.

In the days that followed, as we watched the spiders, we began to see other insects here and there among the rocks on the beach. Each was unique, yet each had the same flawless alert system that was triggered by our slightest movement. We had discovered a marvelous science lab.

We also took many walks through the woods as far as Three Mile Creek and sat quietly watching other people fish. Whenever anyone got a bite, we felt the same excitement he did. One evening at the supper table I mentioned wanting to go fishing not knowing what to expect. To my surprise Dad laughed in approval and agreed to take Corky and me fishing the following Saturday. However, we had to dig for worms and have at least fifty by Friday night. A piece of cake, or so we thought.

The next day we borrowed a shovel from Mrs. Reed, our next door neighbor, and tried digging for worms in a large, bare spot behind our cottage. To our dismay, every time either of us tried to force the shovel into the ground, we'd hit a rock. We soon learned rocks were not limited to the beach, they were everywhere we dug. By the end of the afternoon we had more blisters than worms and saw our fishing trip in danger.

At supper, in answer to Dad's question about worms, Corky told our sad tale and then we both held up the palms of our hands so he could see our blisters. Upon seeing them, Mom got upset, but my father remained calm and said, "At least you tried. I guess I'll have to show you how to catch night crawlers after dark."

After supper Mom doctored our blisters ignoring our pleas for leniency. She did what she had to do, painful or not, to prevent infection.

Darkness finally came and Dad kept his promise. He took his flashlight in one hand and an empty coffee can in the other. We quietly followed him out the door and into the darkness. Once outside he whispered, "Walk with me and watch closely." Commands given, he turned, flicked on the flashlight and began walking ever so quietly through the moist grass all the while shining the light on the grass and slowly moving it back and forth. Seconds later he stopped and quickly motioned for us to do likewise. Then, while we watched in awe, he slowly bent over, reached out his arm, quickly opened his hand and slammed it down on the grass and immediately closed it again. When he slowly raised his arm, dangling partly below his closed fist was the largest worm I had ever seen! He stood, showed us his catch up close then dropped it into the can Corky was holding. All I could say was a quiet, but excited, "Wow!"

Dad repeated the process several more times. Soon three pairs of eyes searched the grass for more worms and when sighted, Dad, with lightning speed, grabbed each before any could retreat into the ground. Eventually, Dad let both Corky and I try our luck. It looked so easy, we were eager to try. However, we both failed miserably. Time after time the worms retreated to safety leaving us empty handed. Then on my last try, I grabbed one and not wanting it to escape, I pulled too fast and too hard. To my horror the worm broke in two, but after my initial shock, I triumphantly dropped my half into the can. Once inside the cottage, Dad put some moist coffee grounds into the can and then explained how to keep night crawlers from dying before being used as bait.

The next two nights Corky and I tried our luck with minimal success. However, we knew we'd eventually master the art, my Dad was so adept at. And we did.

Years later, as an adult, one of my ten-year-old students taught me an easier way to catch night crawlers. He instructed me to, "Take a few pans of good soapy water out into the yard, spray it on the grass and wait. Soon plenty of night crawlers will appear, and you'll have easy pickins." One night I tried it, and he was right. "Out of the mouth of babes . . . " (Psalm 8:2)

That Friday when Dad came home, he was carrying three, eight-foot bamboo poles and a paper bag containing a spool of fishing line, some hooks, sinkers, bobbers, and a stringer.

Saturday morning we went fishing. Once again Dad was our teacher, we were his pupils. After teaching us how to cut a small slit in the top of our poles then how to tie some fishing line on, using the slits, he taught us how to add bobbers, sinkers, and hooks to our lines. Soon he was ready to teach us how to bait our hooks. "Ugh!" was my first reaction watching Dad do it. Then I tried, but I soon found it was almost impossible to put a whole night crawler on my hook. Thus, I had to cut one in two and use half. What a mess I encountered as I followed my Dad's instructions. As I forced my hook through the worm, the worm forced much of its insides onto my fingers. At this point I wasn't sure I'd like fishing.

Again I followed Dad's instructions and soon had my line far out into the creek. I watched my red and white bobber intently with my eyes while visions of catching a whale-sized fish flooded my mind. Soon my bobber moved slightly, then it began to bob rapidly, and finally it disappeared under the water. I stood there watching as in a trance. Finally my dad's words brought me quickly back to reality. "Bud, you've got a fish on your line. Pull it in!" With that command, I pulled back on my pole and out of the water came my first fish, a sunfish about six inches long. Even though it was not large, at that moment, I was both ecstatic and hooked for life on fishing!

Several more times that summer and early fall, Corky and I went fishing. Usually we caught lots of sunfish, which we threw back and a few large bullheads, which we kept and took home. It wasn't long before Dad taught us how to clean fish, even bullheads, using pliers to pull the bullhead's skin off. At first, cleaning fish was as distasteful to me as baiting my hook with half a night crawler. But I knew I had to do it, since neither of my parents would, and Corky would only clean his own catch. However, I soon grew to love the taste of fresh fish prepared so deliciously by Mom and decided cleaning them was little price to pay for such delicious feasts.

One evening, arriving home with an empty stringer, I angrily flung my pole toward the ground next to the side of the cottage. It flew, but only for a second. Almost immediately it stopped, and at the same instant I felt a terrible pain in one finger on my left hand. The pole fell to the ground, and I quickly looked at my hand. My eyes opened wide as I saw that the hook on my line had gone into my finger at one spot and out another exposing the barb. One look and I knew I was firmly hooked. There was no way I could pull the hook out.

Soon my cries for help were answered. Corky came out, saw my predicament, and retreated to get Mom. Both hurried out and stood there, neither knowing what to do while I stood there holding my injured hand with my other, cursing under my breath and trying not to cry. But it really hurt and neither did anything to help the situation.

As luck would have it, at the moment when all seemed lost, Dad came walking into the yard and over to us. Quickly sizing up the situation, after looking at my injury, he turned and walked into the cottage. He soon reappeared with a knife and a pair of pliers. Without saying a whole lot, he cut the line near the hook. Then he held my injured hand with his left, and with his right, using the pliers, cut the fishhook behind the barb. Immediately the part containing the barb fell to the ground. Then, as I grit my teeth, he carefully pulled the rest of the fishhook out of my finger. As soon as Dad finished, Mom took me into the kitchen, washed my wound, and applied a good dose of iodine. The sting caused me to dance and shout like a wild Indian. Finally she bandaged my finger. I don't recall what my mom or dad said after things quieted down. However, I had learned an important lesson: Fishhooks can be dangerous to one's health, humans included. Therefore, I treated fishhooks with respect from that time on and still do.

Life in our cottage was fairly peaceful after the fishhook incident until Labor Day. All of us kids were pretty excited. Dad was going to march in the parade in town, and we were going. We hadn't seen a parade before but had heard from Mom that parades were colorful, full of music from marching bands and exciting. So we anticipated having a great day.

Since everyone was ready to go except Dad, we were all out in the yard waiting for him to finish dressing. It wasn't long before we kids heard noises coming from inside. Mom, being so hard of hearing, hadn't heard a thing. There was a mixture of noises, some coming from my dad's loud voice and others from objects hitting the floor and walls. As the noises continued, Corky and I decided to investigate. Fearfully we walked across the porch and into the main room.

Devastation lay before us such as we'd never seen before. Boxes and dressers had been emptied and their contents strewn across the room. From where we stood, we could see the same had occurred in the bedroom. And there in the bedroom stood our father swearing a blue streak as he emptied yet another box. As we stood there frozen in our tracks, he turned, saw us and yelled, "What the hell do you want? When I'm ready, I'll come out. Right now I'm looking for my damn blue vest!"

"But Dad," Corky replied timidly, "You're wearing your blue vest." Immediately my dad looked down at his stomach and saw what he had been looking for while making a shambles of our cottage. Without showing any signs of embarrassment or remorse, he instantly cooled down and said, "I'll be out in a minute."

Corky and I kept the secret to ourselves not wanting to upset Mom and spoil her day. Thus, we all enjoyed the parade and waved to Dad as he passed by. However, Corky and I didn't wave as enthusiastically as the others.

We arrived home happy but tired late that afternoon. We all had enjoyed ourselves, but now Corky and I knew our Labor Day would soon begin. Seeing the mess, my mother gasped, said something I didn't hear and then cried. My sisters followed her lead and did the same. Paddy was too young to react negatively. Instead, he sat down on the floor amidst the mess and began playing with his surroundings. Dad didn't say a word. He simply walked into the kitchen and made a pot of coffee as if nothing had happened.

Mom and the four of us kids worked far into the evening to restore order out of chaos in our cottage. When I finally crawled under the covers on my cot, I was more than tired, and I fell asleep quickly only to be awakened by a heated argument between Mom and Dad. Eventually things quieted down, but I knew, from what I had heard, that all was not well between them.

As I lay there waiting for sleep to return, my mind reviewed the events of the day. Granted I was only seven, but I found myself wondering how or why my dad could have put on his vest and then forget he had it on. Didn't he look at all into the mirror atop the dresser in the bedroom during his search? How could he not? And if he had, why didn't he see himself wearing it? Too many questions to ponder at such an early age and too tired . . .

Years later, as a college student, I learned that one's mind and senses can play tricks on oneself. I learned that seeing is not the same as perceiving. In other words, at times a person can look at something and not be aware of what he's looking at. There are reasons for this, an unfamiliarity with the object or a lack of attention when looking are two. As I sat there during that particular lecture, I thought back to the vest episode. I finally realized that my dad had probably looked into the mirror at some point during his search, saw the vest on himself but did not perceive it. In other words, for some reason what he saw did not register on his mind. Therefore, he frantically continued searching, making the mess he did.

One morning in 1977 while dressing for church, I had put on the tie I had chosen to wear. However, I was interrupted by a lengthy phone call and then by someone at the door trying to sell me something. When I finally returned to the bedroom, I went to my supply of ties hanging in my closet and began looking for the one I wanted to wear. However, I couldn't find it and soon became quite upset. When Shelley entered the bedroom, I asked her, "Have you seen my blue tie with the gray stripes? I can't find it."

"You mean the one you have on?"

Immediately I turned and looked into the mirror. Sure enough, there was the tie hanging neatly. And then I recalled having put it on before the interruptions. As I stood there, for some reason my thoughts raced back many years to my father, the vest, Labor Day, 1940. Another of the questions I had asked myself that night as a seven year old had finally been answered.

When I was fifty-five, I arrived in Norfolk, Virginia, to visit my sister, Rose Marie, and her husband, Paul. We had gotten our wires crossed, thus I found myself sitting in my truck waiting for them to arrive home from Florida. It was raining, quite cool and getting dark. Finally I walked to their next door neighbor's house, borrowed a spare key they had to Rose Marie's home and let myself in.

Having already eaten supper, I went into the room my mother had occupied before her death to watch TV. Entering the room, I saw no television set just some other furniture including a small settee, framed pictures and photos on the walls, and some others on an object in one corner. I took time to enjoy all the pictures and photos even those on top of and below the object on the stand in the corner. I turned off the light and left the room figuring Mom's TV set had been put elsewhere.

A thorough check in the other bedrooms, living room, and dining room proved negative. I then returned to Mom's former room again and checked the closet to see if the TV had been stored there, but it hadn't. Again I stopped and looked at some of the photos on the stand in the corner and even picked a few up to see them up close. Satisfied I turned, walked back across the room, turned the light off and left.

I finally decided to sit on the enclosed porch (their den) and watch the large TV there. However, it was too cold, and I did not want to run the portable heater. So I again returned to Mom's former room, put on the light, opened the top of their large stereo to see if it was a combination stereo and TV, but it wasn't. I took a final quick look around the room, saw no TV, turned off the light and headed for the kitchen to watch the small, black and white set there.

Shortly Rose Marie and Paul walked in. After warmly greeting each other, Rose Marie asked, "Why aren't you watching the color television in Mom's old room instead of this little one?"

"There is no television in that room. I know because I looked three times."

Hearing my words, their facial expressions suddenly changed to more serious ones, and Rose Marie countered, "Then we've been robbed! Come on, let's go see." The three of us hurried down the hall and into the room. Rose Marie arrived first, entered and flicked on the lightswitch. As soon as I entered, she pointed to the stand in the corner and said, "There's Mom's television." And to my amazement, it was there! On top of it were the several photos including the ones I had handled, and underneath the TV were others I had looked at.

I was too embarrassed to say much, so I half-heartedly laughed it off. However, if I had been a witness in a court of law at a future date and was asked, "Before your relatives arrived home that particular night, did you see a television set in your mother's former room?" I would have had to swear, "No, I did not!"

As I sat there watching the "set that wasn't there," I suddenly mumbled to myself, "My gosh! I saw the TV but never perceived it. Just as my dad did his vest forty-eight years ago."

Chapter II
Life in Our House on the Loop

In October 1940 we moved into a larger two-story house next door and nearer the lake. On the main floor it had a kitchen, an alcove eating area with bay windows, a living room, two small bedrooms off the living room, a screened front porch and an enclosed back porch. There was one large bedroom on the second floor over and the same size as the living room. Since this house was larger, it had many more windows through which we could enjoy the never ending beauty of the lake, woods and sky.

Like our cottage, our new house had no plumbing. Thus, water had to be carried from the well, used water emptied into a covered cesspool and our toilet was an outhouse. Once the lake was too cold for swimming and bathing, we washed and took pan baths in the kitchen.

The house was not insulated or finished off inside. Whenever we looked at the outer walls, the two by four studs looked back. To make matters worse, there were no storm windows or doors. Being so close to the lake, we soon realized how ferocious the storms coming off the lake could be. Thus, we soon appreciated the two wood-burning stoves: a range in the kitchen for cooking and heating and a potbellied one in the living room.

As winter set in, the storms began coming one after another. The wind and snow buffeted our house unmercifully. And even with two stoves glowing red hot, the bedrooms remained quite cold. During the worst storms when the chill temperatures would often dip to fifty degrees below zero, my mother would stay up all night feeding the fires and praying for our safety. It was also during such cold spells that all five of us kids slept crosswise on one bed in a bedroom downstairs. Dad did his part by keeping an ample supply of firewood on hand all winter.

In the spring, on the evening of the very day when the fire in the living room stove was finally allowed to die out, a leg on the stove broke. It immediately fell over with a crash and spewed its cold ashes across the old wooden floor. At that moment we knew my mother's prayers had been answered.

During the cold winter months, there were few sunny days. However, each was a welcomed treat. The blue sky; the even bluer lake with countless white ice floes; the tall, white, crystallized masses of ice extending out from the shore; and the undisturbed snow everywhere brought to our squinting eyes a beauty not easily surpassed. Since there were few such gorgeous winter days, Corky and I would often bundle up and play outside as long as the weather permitted. At times we'd pester two older teenage girls who lived nearby, and sometimes they'd chase us. On those occasions we'd hightail it to the bank along the lake and escape their grasp by jumping off and landing in the deep snow many feet below. Lucky for us the girls never followed.

Since there were no hills for sleigh riding nearby, we'd often take our sleds, descend the bank, walk carefully out onto and across the built up masses of ice and snow, slowly crawl up those the farthest from shore and the highest, and peer down into the icy water several yards below for several seconds. Then we'd turn back toward the shore, lie on our sleds and fly down the ice while steering the best we could and hoping to come out alive. We always did, but our sleds took a terrible beating. We saw what we did as thrilling, adventurous, and fun, and it was. However, as I reflect back now, what we did was very dangerous. We could have been badly hurt or even killed. But once again the god who watches over foolish little boys was with us. However, I wonder if he enjoyed those rides as much as we did.

As the days became warmer signaling the approach of spring, nature began doing its job of rebirth. Soon the evidence could be seen everywhere bringing utter joy to our hearts. Early one morning while eating breakfast, we saw a fawn walk slowly out of the woods, approach a puddle of water in the dirt road near our house and begin to drink. After watching this beautiful animal a few seconds, Corky and I decided we'd like to have it for a pet. So we quickly gulped down the rest of our food, hurried to the back porch, grabbed two pieces of rope, went out the door, ran around the side of the house away from the lake and stopped behind some lilac bushes not far from the fawn.

While catching our breath, we made a quick plan of attack and made lassos from our ropes. Finally we were ready. At the count of three, we stood up and ran toward our prey while whirling the lassos over our heads. Immediately the fawn stopped drinking, looked up and ran down the dirt road toward the woods. We pursued the fawn, as true cowboys would, but never even got close enough to attempt to lasso it. Were we discouraged? Not one bit. In the days that followed, whenever a young deer came to drink, we'd try our best to lasso it but never did. Finally we realized it was a lost cause and gave up. However, we did not give up on the idea of having a pet.

One night at supper the topic of a pet came up. For some reason I piped up that I'd like to have a collie dog, and the other kids agreed. However, I can still hear my mom's words in answer to my plea for a collie. "There'll be no dogs in this house! We can't afford to feed one, and I won't have dog hair all over the place!" Case closed.

We understood, but we were still disappointed. Any dog in our house would have received more tender loving care (TLC), than one could imagine. We had lots of love to give a pet, and no pet to give it to.

Early that June a stray cat meandered into our yard, came over to where the four of us kids were playing and meowed softly. We stopped what we were doing and looked at the cat. It was skin and bones, and its gray fur was matted. However, we took turns stroking it, and soon the cat began to purr its approval, bringing smiles and giggles to our faces. Marilyn disappeared into the house and soon returned with a small dish of milk, which the cat devoured eagerly. I don't recall who had the idea first, but we all agreed that this mangy-looking cat would be our long awaited pet. We knew Dad wouldn't mind, but Mom would. So we began making what we hoped would be a foolproof plan.

As we sat in a circle around the cat, lo and behold if Mom didn't appear and ask, "Where did THAT come from and whose is it?" I meekly responded and told her all I knew, which wasn't very much. Then Rose Marie had the courage to ask Mom if we could keep it for our pet. A bold move indeed! Somehow the cat must have sensed at that moment that its future lay in the hands of my mother. Thus, before she could answer, just as "fools rush in where angels fear to tread," the cat walked over, rubbed its body against Mom's leg, looked up at her, as only a cat can do, and meowed the most pathetic meow possible. Mom looked down at the starving creature, and her compassion, buried so deep for so long, surfaced. She looked at our four hopeful faces and agreed we could keep it as long as no one came by to claim it, and if it stayed on the back porch and not in the house. With that she turned toward the house then turned back and commanded, "Come on, cat. I'll give you something to eat." The cat promptly followed her into the back porch. And thus began a warm, caring relationship between my mom and the cat. Watching them go, we whooped and hollered in delight. We had our pet! Yippee!

Days passed and no one claimed the cat. By now Mom had informed us that our pet was a female. And it was gaining weight and looking healthier. After a week we knew she was ours, thus we had to name her. Johnny Cash in his song, "A Boy Named Sue," makes it clear that he hates that awful name. And what boy wouldn't. However, since our pet had been called 'cat' for seven days and now answered to it, we decided to call her Cat. Maybe in her own cat's way she would hate it, but we gave her that awful name anyway.

During the next few months, Cat received much TLC, not only from us, but from a tomcat, who lived somewhere nearby. We noticed that she was getting fatter and fatter and finally Mom told us Cat was going to have kittens. We kids were ecstatic at the news and waited excitedly for Cat's big event.

One morning Rose Marie and Marilyn were on their way out the back porch when they were stopped in their tracks by a few faint meows. At that instant they knew the blessed event had occurred and came screaming back into the house to tell us. Immediately Mom, Corky, Paddy, and I followed the girls to the porch. Once there we could hear the meows but didn't know where they were coming from. Eventually we pinpointed the location and realized it was above our heads and in a storage loft. Corky put a ladder in place while I ran for a flashlight. He stuck the light in his pocket and climbed up to see how things were. Using the light to pierce the darkness, he soon reported proudly that Cat had three kittens. With that news our celebration began. Kool Aid and cookies all around! However, Mom instructed us not to bother Cat or her kittens for a few days. Therefore, Corky moved Cat's food and milk dishes to the loft and made sure they were full. We wanted to see our three new pets, but we knew Mom's word was law, so we resigned ourselves to waiting for the right time—whenever that would be.

Early the next morning on my way through the back porch to the outhouse, I spotted something tiny and black on the floor near the ladder. Examining it, I soon realized it was a dead kitten. In tears I reported my discovery and soon everyone but Dad, who had left for work, shared my remorse. After Mom soothed our grief, she directed Corky and me in preparing a place for Cat and her family in a box on the floor of the porch. Once the box was ready, we moved the two remaining kittens there. Cat followed. Later that morning Corky and I dug a hole in our rocky back yard, and with everyone present we buried the kitten.

As the two remaining kittens matured, their fur grew long and silky, similar to that of Persian cats, and they were beautiful! We all loved and enjoyed playing with our pets. Even Mom and Dad enjoyed having them around, especially since the cats kept the field mice away. One day we noticed our beautiful white cat was missing, and to our sorrow he never returned home. We searched everywhere and asked all our neighbors if they had seen Taffy. But none had. Mom consoled us somewhat by saying Taffy had probably been taken by some older person, who was lonely and needed some company. After several sad days we accepted the fact that he was gone and gave the remaining two cats more love and attention.

Someone has written, "Blessings come in bunches." And were we ever blessed the following July 1942. Within a few days Cat and her daughter each had six kittens and all of them lived. Every one of us kids thought having twelve kittens and two cats was the greatest thing that could have happened to our family. However, Mom didn't share our happiness as she was now struggling alone to keep our family safe, secure, and healthy. And with twelve more mouths to feed, she knew each food dollar would have to be stretched even further, something she might not be able to do. She knew we loved our pets, but she loved us more, and we came first in her life.

In August we took a train to Pennsylvania and visited her parents, our grandpa and grandma Potter, in Mildred. Upon our return, all fourteen of our cats were missing. As soon we entered the house, Mom sat us down and, as lovingly as possible, explained our financial situation and her decision that the cats had to go. Thus, while we were away, she had arranged to have a man from town come and take them. She assured us that each would be given another home. Yes, she would miss them too, but it was a decision she had to make, and she made it.

Of course we cried as she spoke, but as her words penetrated our young minds and hearts, we began to understand our situation and tried to accept our loss. In the days that followed, we missed the companionship of the cats and the fun we had playing with them. But as children usually do, we found other ways to amuse ourselves and gradually the loss of our pets didn't seem so tragic.

During the cat era and beyond, other events affected our lives. Some were very important, some less.

In September 1941 I entered third grade. Part way through the first morning, the door opened and the principal entered followed by a new, tall boy for our class. He introduced George Pitluga, Jr. to our teacher, Miss Wright and to us. Then he turned and left. Miss Wright welcomed George to our class, and then she had each of us stand and say our name. Once this ritual was completed, she led George to a desk, and we returned to the business at hand.

During our bathroom break prior to lunch, three of the boys quietly commented about George's right hand, something about his fingers that I hadn't noticed. Luckily George hadn't come in yet, so he didn't hear them, but I had, and when George entered, I made it a point to wash next to him and see his hand. The boys were correct. His hand hadn't developed correctly; it had fingers and a thumb with no joints.

After lunch during our playtime outside, I heard some of the boys taunting George by yelling, "little fingers," and "stick fingers," at him and then running away. George just stood there bewildered. I was not raised to do such things, so I quickly took his side. Together, we caught each of the boys and convinced him to stop, or else he would have to answer to both George and me, and if necessary, Miss Wright. Each got the message and ceased. During the rest of the playtime, George and I talked. His father had just joined the science department faculty at the college, thus their move from New York City to Oswego. He was an only child, but he wished he had at least a brother to play with at home. From that first playtime on, George and I became the best of friends, and we still are.

That fall everyone in my class had his or her eyes tested, and soon I was wearing my first pair of glasses. In the months and years that followed, I went through several pairs and countless visits to Dr. Joseph Riley's office to have the current pair fixed. Glasses or not, Corky and I or George and I would be fooling around or wrestling, and my glasses would often emerge the loser. However, in a short time, Dr. Riley would have them as good as new and not charge us.

On December 7, 1941, World War II broke out. Because of the magnitude of this war, I've devoted a chapter to it entitled, "World War II through the Eyes of a Boy."

During the winter of 1941, the construction job finished at the steam plant, and my dad went to Rome, New York, to work and came home weekends. Arguments between him and Mom often flared up and each time became more intense, which horrified us kids. Eventually, with gas rationing in effect, Dad had problems getting home weekends, so in the spring, 1942, Mom went to Rome seeking a place for us to live.

While she was gone, our grandfather Potter came and stayed with us. Having him as our sitter was going well, until the first morning he made our lunches. He always seemed to have a pipe full of tobacco in his mouth, even though it was often unlit. On this morning, as he leaned over to make our sandwiches, bits of tobacco fell out of his pipe and onto the potted ham he was spreading on the bread. He didn't seem to notice this, but I did and said nothing. However, I could taste the tobacco at lunchtime and endured it, refusing to swap half a sandwich with any of my classmates. The next morning I managed to hide Grandpa's pipe, while he made our lunches. It solved our problem, but left him wondering where he misplaced his pipe. Before leaving the house to catch the bus, I suddenly found it and graciously accepted Grandpa's thanks.

When Mom returned from Rome, she was very upset. She said very little to us, except she didn't think we'd be moving.

A few days later Grandpa returned home, and a few weekends later Dad came home on a Friday night. After we went to bed, a terrible fight between Mom and Dad woke all of us kids. I could hear them yelling, then Dad hitting Mom and her screams. The other kids lay paralyzed in fear, but not me. I jumped out of bed, hurried to the partly closed door of their bedroom and in a loud voice pleaded with Dad to stop. However, my words only seemed to anger him more, and he continued. I returned to my bed, put my hands over my ears and cried myself to sleep.

The next morning Dad was his normal self and acted as if nothing had happened. Mom, on the other hand, looked like a truck had hit her. She had swollen black eyes and most of her exposed body was black and blue. Seeing her, I felt terrible, absolutely terrible, and terrified at the thought that I was partly responsible for the beating she received.

The rest of the weekend passed quickly, and soon Sunday evening rolled around. Dad packed his small bag, bade us all good-bye and walked out the door. Soon after he left, Mom broke down and cried uncontrollably, as she raised her arms and pounded her fists against the door. We all sat and watched, not knowing what else to do. Finally, one by one, we got up, walked over, wrapped our arms around her bruised and battered body and stood there crying with her. Somehow, I knew in my heart, that Dad would not be coming back.

Without Dad being home, certain changes came about. Once our wood supply was almost gone, we began using coal, which Corky and I dragged home on our sled, a bag or two at a time.

Together, Corky and I could carry a pail of water, so we added that to our chores, making two trips to the well before the school bus came and two more early in the evening. Believe it or not, we survived on four pails of water a day.

Since money from Dad now came sporadically, we shopped the A &

P in town for rationed items but bought most of our groceries and other items at Bradway's General Store in Fruit Valley. Lucky for us, Mom could charge them and pay, as she was able to do so. Depending on the weather, Corky and I would walk the mile and a half to Bradway's and either carry the groceries home or pull them home in boxes on a sled. On the back of Bradway's bill of sale was a poem I've never forgotten:

> You need your money, and I need mine;
> If we both have ours, it will sure be fine.
> But if you have yours and hold mine too,
> What the hell am I going to do?
> THINK IT OVER

During the late spring and early summer, Corky and I landed our first paying job to help Mom out financially. Mrs. Reed hired us to cut her large lawn for fifty cents a time. Together, Corky and I were able to push her reel-type, hand lawnmower. Mrs. Reed was the person who taught us how to cut grass correctly. She instructed us to cut a swath about two-thirds of the width of the mower at a time. According to her, this would insure a perfect job every time and prevent narrow, uncut ridges of grass. She was correct, and her lawn always looked really nice after we finished.

She was a gracious employer and served us cookies and cool drinks as we labored in the hot, humid weather. Sometimes, during the hottest weeks of the summer, she would say, "I'm so proud of the job you've done today, I'm paying you seventy-five cents!" I'm sure she knew Mom could use all the money we could earn.

A few years later, my expertise as a grass cutter paid off. I landed a job caring for the lawns and flower gardens at Mulcahey's Cabins by the Lake. Using a reel-type, hand lawnmower, I worked forty to fifty hours a week at fifty cents an hour cutting the lawns around twenty-two cottages and cabins plus a few other buildings. I also weeded several flower gardens. Even though I gave my earnings to Mom, I enjoyed the physical labor involved and felt proud when compliments came my way.

Wild blueberries, blackberries, and strawberries grew in abundance around our house, near the woods and along the country roads. Thus, as each kind ripened, Corky, Rose Marie, Marilyn and I often picked enough to fill our tummies at the moment, plus some for our cereal the next morning and maybe enough for dessert at suppertime. Paddy was still too young to pick, and Mom was usually too busy doing other chores, such as washing clothes by hand.

As Christmas 1942 approached, I knew it was going to be a sparse one, and presents were going to be very few in number. However, I knew a nice tree would brighten things up, once it was decorated. As we had no money to buy one, Corky and I took Dad's small crosscut saw, some rope and our sled late one afternoon and headed for a row of beautiful, young, pine trees. They were growing on some property across the road from John Dowie's farm on Snake Swamp Road. We trudged the one and a half miles through the snow, using a route that took us by the lake bank for awhile, then through some woods, up a dirt road and finally across the rear of the property on which the trees stood. It was getting dark when we reached our destination, so we had to hurry. We quickly chose a tree the right height, cut it down, roped it to our sled and returned home over the same route. When Mom asked where we got such a beautiful tree, we nonchalantly responded, "Oh, in the woods." Luckily she believed us and didn't pry further.

The next day, John Dowie, a long-time friend of our family, stopped by to chat with Mom and see how things were going. Before he left, he took me aside and spoke seriously, "I saw you and Corky steal that pine tree yesterday. But don't worry, I covered up your tracks, so no one can follow them here. And if asked, I won't tell my neighbor who took it. But don't ever steal one again. Do you understand?" While he was saying all this, he must have seen the fear reflected in my eyes and on my face. For when he had finished, he smiled, placed a kind hand on my shoulder and murmured, "That sure will make a pretty Christmas tree! Enjoy it." As soon as he left, and Corky came home, I told him, and we both breathed a sigh of relief.

Mr. Dowie was correct. Our Christmas tree that year was the prettiest one we'd ever had, and it would be the prettiest tree we would have for several years to come. For the longest time after that, whenever I'd pass that property and see that tree stump, I'd smile happily to myself. Then I'd remember Mr. Dowie's words of warning. We never stole another tree from anyone.

As predicted, that Christmas gifts were few, even fewer than I anticipated. Corky and I shared one gift to play with, a Ping-Pong set. We got four paddles, a net and a tube of four balls. However, we did not receive a Ping-Pong table. So we propped the net up the best we could on the floor and played our special version of Ping-Pong there. Sad to say, a Ping-Pong table was never delivered to our home. However, a few years later, I learned to play table tennis very well at the YMCA in Oswego, and to this day, can hold my own against most opponents.

Raising five children alone in a rather primitive environment was difficult for Mom. Being an only child, raised in style and well educated, she was not equipped in many ways to deal with situations that arose in our family of six. For one thing, she was always afraid that one or more of us would get hurt or sick. Then what would she do? We had no phone, and we lived too far from any doctors and the hospital. That worried her. And, on the financial side, we had no insurance and little money to pay any medical expenses. One evening, she faced such a situation.

Paddy got a large marble caught in his throat and couldn't breathe. Mom, not knowing what to do, hit him on the back several times, hoping to dislodge the marble. No luck! As Paddy was beginning to turn blue from a lack of oxygen, using strength I never knew she had, she lifted him up, held him upside down by his feet with one hand and reached into his mouth and down his throat with the other. Somehow she managed to grasp and pull the marble free and out of his mouth, giving him back his life. The task completed, she slumped into a chair, held Paddy close, and they both cried. Mom had faced this life-threatening situation and had emerged victorious. However, it would not be the last one this four foot, nine inch giant-of-a-mother would face.

Chapter III
World War II through the Eyes of a Boy

Sunday, December 7, 1941, was a typical, cloudy, cold, windy, snowy day, where we lived on Lake Ontario. Corky and I were sitting on the cold floor playing a game. Music from our small radio filled the air. I was eight at the time, living in a child's world, which encompassed my family, my friends, the woods, the lake and my third grade class. Suddenly the music stopped and solemn words, spoken by President Roosevelt, exploded in our ears. The Japanese had attacked Pearl Harbor! We were at war! None of us, especially us children, could fathom the seriousness of his words at that time. Yet, the full impact would affect our lives for several years to come. Several minutes later, the talking stopped and music once again filled the air. However, my parents continued to talk, and I could tell by their facial expressions, that they were worried. Not me. I returned to my world and continued the game we had been playing.

At first, life remained pretty much the same for our family. School, motherly chores, my dad's construction job and fatherly chores kept us all busy. Evenings my dad checked his muskrat traps. I often went with him, anxious to see the "catch of the day." As we moved across the ice on Three Mile Creek, checking each trap, some yielded a catch, others didn't. Now and then only a muskrat's leg would be found secure in the trap. In its efforts to get away, the muskrat would chew its own leg off only to face death elsewhere.

Once all the traps were checked and reset, we'd carry the catch home. Dad would skin each and hang the pelts up to dry, until he could get to town and sell them, usually on Saturdays.

Some evenings during the week and on weekends, Dad would throw his ax over his shoulder, carry his small, crosscut saw in one hand and head for the woods. Corky and I trudged behind him pulling our sled. After a tree had been cut down, trimmed and cut into logs, Dad carried one on his shoulder, and we transported others on our sled back to our yard. Then Dad would cut each log into usable lengths and split them into pieces. Corky and I carried the pieces to the enclosed back porch and stacked them. Our two wood-burning stoves consumed lots of wood, but Dad made sure there was always plenty available.

Now and then, while walking through the woods, Dad would discover a tree with a large hole some distance up its bole, in which bees had stored honey. While he was cutting it down, not only for the honey, but for the wood, I'd run home, fetch a pail and return to enjoy the delicious taste of raw honey and beeswax. We'd take a pailful home. Then my dad would tell the few nearby neighbors where it was, so they, too, could enjoy it. Once the honey was depleted, he'd cut the tree into logs, and we'd sled them home for firewood.

Other times, Dad would tap maple trees, collect the sap, and Mom would boil it down into maple syrup, a delicious treat we enjoyed on hot pancakes or french toast.

At first the "big war" didn't penetrate my world, but as the months passed, slowly but surely, it crept in. My dad, needing work, went to Rome, New York, to help build Griffiss Air Force Base. Soon marital problems arose, splitting my parents. They separated legally but did not divorce. We stayed by the lake, he stayed in Rome.

Money became scarce, and Mom waged her own war, trying to get Dad to send enough to sustain us. After all, he was our father, our hero, the main man in our lives. We were his children. How could he turn his back on us, as though we didn't exist? Not only did he not send enough money to sustain us, he never even sent any of us a birthday card to let us know he cared the least bit. Then, to top it off, he soon fathered another son by another woman and named him—DAVID! On his TV sitcom, Bob Newhart had brothers Daryl and Daryl. In real life my family has David and David.

As the war effort continued, rationing began, and rationing stamps became a common household commodity. We always had enough stamps but not enough money. Thus, we seldom wore shoes during the summer months. We had to save them for school. The soles of our feet soon became tough as leather, giving us the freedom to run and play to our heart's content.

One week in July, a road crew sprayed tar on our road, and then scattered crushed stone hit or miss over the tar. The next day I walked to town in order to see the weekly serial episode of *Batman* at the Strand Theater. Try as I might, I couldn't keep from getting tar on my feet. Arriving back home, I had the two blackest feet in the county and the angriest mother as well. Little did I know that soap and water don't take tar off, gasoline and kerosene do, and gas was rationed. To my chagrin, no one in our neighborhood had either, or so they said. Thus, it was several weeks before my feet were free of the tar, and even longer before I was free of the embarrassment associated with it.

Several food items were rationed including three of Mom's favorites: meat, sugar, and butter. Since we had no car, and no one to drive one, if we did, early each Saturday morning, good weather or bad, Corky and I walked to the A & P in town and lined up with everyone else waiting for the store to open, hoping one or more of the rationed items would be available. If we came home with one of Mom's favorites, she was happy. If two, she was elated, and if three, she was ecstatic and would do her special dance of joy. However, it was seldom that more than one or two were available. After all, we were at war, and the armed forces came first and rightly so.

One food item Mom could not stand was oleomargarine. Oleo came in pound packages. It was white. A small package of yellow coloring dye came with it. The two would be mixed together at home. We kids ate oleo. My mother would never eat it and hated it until she died in 1988 at age eighty-seven. Any time we brought home a pound of butter, she'd hoard it for herself. Meat and sugar she'd share but not her butter.

One morning, while standing in line at the A & P, I saw an older woman with no nose, only a triangular hole where her nose should have been. She also had a purple growth on her neck below one ear. I'm sure I stood there open-mouthed, staring. After all the word cancer was seldom heard then, although people probably had it including this lady. Needless to say, the sight made a lasting impression me. I couldn't wait to get home and tell everyone what I had seen.

Buying food, even rationed items, was easy compared to carrying it home, especially during the long, harsh, winter months. Oswego is known for two things: its number of taverns and its winters.

Winter storms blowing in off Lake Ontario cause wind chill factors as low as fifty degrees below zero. And the snow accompanying them stings any exposed body parts so painfully, that one has to walk backwards into the wind and snow to escape the brutality of it all. At times, even though I wore heavy winter clothes, I thought I would freeze to death, as I battled such storms while carrying one or two shopping bags full of groceries. Arriving home, icicles would be hanging from my eyeglasses, and I would spend several minutes thawing out by a stove in our living room.

It was during one such storm that several coastguardsmen and lighthouse keeper, Karl Jackson, drowned in the Oswego Harbor. They were returning to shore after taking Bert Egelston and Carl Sprague to the lighthouse to relieve Karl. En route the engine quit and the boat drifted and soon hit the east breakwall. A few of the coastguardsmen managed to get up on the wall. The others drowned. Bert watched the entire accident through binoculars and later developed angina as a result of it.

Some of the bodies were still missing the following spring, and those people living along the lake were alerted to watch for them. One day, while playing along the shore near my house and three miles from the harbor entrance, a friend and I spotted what we thought was one of the missing bodies. It was about fifteen feet from shore. As we slowly waded toward it, my heart beat rapidly and several thoughts raced through my mind. Arriving at the spot we looked wide-eyed at the large object almost submerged below us. Using a hefty wooden stick that had been floating in the water nearby, we managed to turn the body over to get a better look. We realized it was a body but not a human one. It was a drowned pig. I guess we were both relieved and disappointed.

Eventually all the bodies were recovered. Karl Jackson was found floating in the St. Lawrence River. Bert was able to identify him by his belt, the only thing left on his body.

Not long after this tragedy, Bert Egelston retired. He died a couple of years later. Some said he died of a broken heart. Knowing the kind of man this neighbor of ours was, I wouldn't doubt it.

Fertilizer was another scarce item. We never grew a garden, so we didn't miss it. But John Cochran, our neighbor, did. However, he soon thought up a plan for fertilizer that also put money in the pockets of us kids.

Each winter, small ocean fish, we called mooneyes, swam down the St. Lawrence River into Lake Ontario. They'd soon die in the fresh water and in the spring and early summer would wash ashore and decay, stinking up the entire, rocky shoreline. At times, we couldn't sit on the beach or swim due to the odor and the flies drawn to the rotting fish. By August, thing were back to normal with only traces of the fish noticeable.

One spring Mr. Cochran decided to use dead mooneyes for fertilizer. So he paid us a penny for each ten mooneyes we delivered to him. It was still too early in the spring for the mooneyes to have begun rotting, so there was very little odor, only a few flies to contend with. I'm not sure how much I made during the years we sold him mooneyes. But I do know Mr. Cochran's garden flourished that year and in the years that followed, as the mooneyes enriched the soil. As a boy, it was hard for me to understand how rotting fish could make plants grow and produce such abundant harvests. Understand or not, I enjoyed the vegetables he gave our family each year.

There was other money to be made apart from our mooneye business. Milkweed grew in abundance in the fields near our home. One day we learned that we could make money filling cloth bags about eight feet long with milkweed pods. It took a long time to fill one bag, but we were doing our part for the war effort and making some money to boot. Once I heard, they were used to make stuffing for life jackets and vests. However, I never heard anyone confirm it.

As the months slowly passed, the reality of the war was more and more evident even in Oswego. Sirens wailed periodically, signaling another air raid drill, plunging the entire city and surrounding area into blackness for several minutes. Whenever I stayed overnight at George's, I relished the air raid alerts. For it was during these blackouts that we enjoyed the beauty of the star-studded sky, while sitting quietly on his porch or lawn.

Although few people in Oswego ever expected the city to be bombed, there were good reasons for the enemy to do so. Army soldiers were being trained at Fort Ontario on the east side of town. Air force cadets were being trained at the college on the west side of town. And tank hulls were being manufactured in a converted boiler factory near the center of town. Every so often, a train load of hulls would pass slowly in front of me, as I stood near the railroad tracks close to the factory. Having seen many newsreels about the war and many war movies at the local theaters, I could envision these tanks in battle. It made me proud that they were partially made in Oswego—so proud, in fact, that I often wished I were old enough to join the army and serve in one of those tanks. "I'd show those miserable enemies a thing or two!"

Living near the lake and some woods, we often had contact with both the soldiers and cadets. Twice daily the cadets were required to run several miles, completing a loop course over rural roads that began and ended at the college. En route, they would pass our house and, if any of us were outside, several would yell, "Join the air force and run!" I never understood why these men, who were going to fly war planes, had to run so much. I just had to assume it was part of their physical training, or officers getting even with them for poor class performance, or both.

On Sundays, when the weather was sunny and warm, both soldiers and cadets brought girls to the lake and woods for a time of relaxation. Of course, many used the woods as a secluded place to make mad, passionate love.

One Sunday afternoon, Corky and I were walking through the woods toward Three Mile Creek to do some fishing. We soon came upon a couple really going at it. Evidently they hadn't heard us coming, since their actions continued hot and heavy. Having never seen such behavior, we were spellbound. Finally, the cadet saw us, and in no time at all, had given each of us a quarter to "Get the hell out of here!" As we turned and walked away, we looked at each other with a smile on our faces. If we had made one quarter so easily, could we not make more? We were eager to give it a try.

From that Sunday on, quietly strolling through the woods, stopping and staring here and there was far more profitable than fishing had ever been. However, after a lucrative summer and early fall, business dropped off drastically, as cooler, wetter weather came to stay. Soon there were more bare trees than bodies.

In 1944 George left to be with his dad, who was in the navy. I was sorry to see him go and knew I would miss him. Unlike so many other males, who had already left or would leave Oswego for the war and wouldn't return, I knew my best friend would. However, I was concerned for his dad's welfare.

My father is the oldest of sixteen children born to my Grandmother Furman. Two died in infancy, leaving fourteen to feed, clothe, shelter, and nurture. By the time the war broke out, several were old enough to serve and did so with honor. At one time or another, each sent us a large photo of himself, dressed in his finest uniform. We were proud to have so many uncles serving our country. The last one to enter the service was Richard, an eighteen year old eager to serve.

The summer after Richard entered the army, we rode the train to visit Grandma and Grandpa Furman and our aunts and uncles still living at home. They lived in the Sunbury/Northumberland area of Pennsylvania near the coal mines where Grandpa worked. While there, we had a great time and played to our heart's content with aunts and uncles our ages.

On the morning we were to leave and return home, a telegram arrived, informing everyone that Richard had been killed in battle in Europe. At that instant, I realized more than ever how terrible the war was and wished it would end. I wondered how much further it would penetrate my world, and the thought scared me. What if more of my uncles were wounded or killed. Through a boy's eyes, I finally saw the war for what it was, and I didn't like what I saw. We left for home with very sad hearts.

REFUGEES

In September 1944 Mrs. Eleanor Roosevelt made an historic visit to Oswego. She spoke at the college, outside of Sheldon Hall, to a large crowd including the upper grades of the Campus School. Being a sixth grader, I was there, although I didn't pay too much attention. It was too nice a day. She was talking about the war and the refugees from Europe that had come to Oswego and were living at the refugee shelter at Fort Ontario. I perked up when she mentioned the possibility that the refugee children would be attending the schools in Oswego.

I had to think that over. I had lost an uncle in Europe, and I knew, from all the gold stars displayed in the windows of my Grit paper route customers, that many had lost sons and daughters in the war—some in Europe and others in the Pacific. Now refugees from Europe had come to my hometown, and refugee children might come to my school, to my classroom! At that moment, I wished I had listened very attentively to all Mrs. Roosevelt had to say. Sad to say I hadn't, and it would be many years before I learned of the terrible holocaust they had lived through.

One day our classroom door opened and in walked the principal and eight refugee children. I looked at each and was amazed. They looked just like us, although most looked older than we did. Of all the characteristics I noted, the one that stood out the most in my mind, was the fact that all eight were thin, not one was at all overweight. Funny I would notice that, but I did.

The principal introduced them to us, although he stumbled over some of their last names. Then we stood, one by one, and introduced ourselves to them. Introductions over, we set about getting to know our new classmates. We were surprised at how well they all spoke English, plus two or three other languages.

In a few days, it was evident that most of them were quite smart and could "run circles around" some of my American classmates. It didn't take long to assimilate them into our class and accept them as classmates and friends. It also didn't take long for them to feel a part of us, and soon, some were fooling around and getting into trouble with our teacher, Miss Angel.

When they first came, none ever smiled or laughed, but this all changed in a short time. We American boys enjoyed telling the refugee boys our favorite jokes during recess periods outside. Of course, they didn't understand all the jokes, giving us something to laugh about. Before long, a couple of the boys and one of the girls became close friends of mine, something I didn't expect would happen when I first heard they were coming to our school. But I was happy it did.

Prior to the coming of our new friends, softball, played without gloves, was our favorite outside sport, whenever the weather was favorable. However, soon after their arrival, they began playing soccer. One by one, we opted to try this new sport, and our new friends were good teachers. But we Americans suffered physically, since our teachers showed no mercy during each game.

I clearly remember the first time I tried hitting the soccer ball with my head. As the ball came down toward me, I bent down and then straightened up to hit the ball with my head. However, I did not leave the ground, and kept my feet firmly planted. When the ball and my head met, the ball felt like a cinder block hitting my head. I thought for sure my head and neck would be driven down into my chest. They weren't, and I survived, but I learned then and there to leave my feet when "heading" a ball.

As we became better and better at soccer, it became more and more fun, and I lost more and more of my "pot," something softball never did for me. Soccer soon replaced softball as our favorite outside sport.

Each noon hour we'd choose up sides and begin a game. Almost without exception, Merco, a refugee, would come out late and want to play. His playing would make uneven teams, but time after time, we let him join one team, even though there was no one else to put on the other team. One day we told him he could not play unless he found another player to keep the sides even. Instead of finding someone, he went to Miss Angel and complained. She immediately came over, stopped our game and ordered all the American boys to the classroom. We could tell she was angry.

Once we were seated, she shut the door and then paced back and forth in front of the room for several minutes. Finally, she stopped, turned to us and, with fire in her eyes, said sternly, "And you call yourselves Americans! Bah!" I don't recall what else she said, but I do recall that it made all of us boys very angry. After all, we really hadn't done anything wrong, Merco had. And we were being scolded, not him.

The next noon hour, we Americans got together and secretly agreed to challenge the refugee boys to a game, and if they agreed, we'd play as dirty as we could within the rules. We challenged, they accepted, and we did. Oh, did we ever! Not for one game, but for several, and Merco got it the worst. Yet, none of the "enemy" ever complained or retaliated. They just kept playing, and we just kept playing dirty. I don't recall how many games we won, but we definitely won the "war." One day we decided to choose up sides again, and the "war" was over. However, Merco was never any trouble after that, and he was often the first one on the playground waiting to choose up sides.

As the school year progressed, Miss Angel's carefully planned program of studies paid off. Our room became the "melting pot" for our refugee classmates. Through the academics, the socials, and the physical activities, including industrial arts and physical education, their scars were healing rapidly, and they were rapidly becoming Americanized. Our class became very close.

Finally the end of the school year arrived. When final report cards were given out, to everyone's surprise, the few older and academically brighter refugee students had been promoted from the sixth to the eighth grade. And to my complete surprise, when I received my card, I looked at it and on the bottom of the first page, I saw the words, "Promoted to the eighth grade."

As the summer days passed, I wrestled with the decision whether to take the double promotion or to enter seventh grade with my long-time classmates and three close refugee friends. I guess in the end, it was an easy decision to make. I entered seventh grade in September. I wanted to be with my friends, all my friends. Later I was glad, I had made such a decision. Unknown to me at the time, by the beginning of the eighth grade, our refugee classmates would be gone.

Eventually the refugees were allowed to leave Fort Ontario, to resume normal lives and eventually to become American citizens. When this occurred, most of them left Oswego including my three close friends. I often wonder what became of all eight. Ironically, the only one I've ever met since they left, is Merco in 1954 in Newark, New Jersey.

In 1986, columnist Mark A. Stuart wrote an article entitled, "America's Terrified Guests." It appeared in the *Bergen* (N.J.) *Record* newspaper. This article sheds light on the refugees that came to Oswego so many years ago. The following has been gleaned from his article.

The army troopship Henry Gibbins brought one thousand frightened, emaciated refugees from Nazism to Hoboken (N.J.). From there the refugees took a ten-hour train ride to Fort Ontario in Oswego. The one thousand on that ship were an unusual group; the only refugees from the Holocaust brought to this country by the U.S. Government during World War II. For years, although Allied governments had clear evidence of Germany's extermination policies, no country offered even a temporary haven to Nazi victims. The U.S. quota for Europe was less than half filled, yet no official gesture was made to harbor refugees.

Finally, after months of pressure from Congress and some members of his own cabinet, President Franklin D. Roosevelt created a "free port" at an abandoned military base in upstate New York where a token number of refugees, the one thousand on that troop ship, could be accepted. They'd come from camps inside the Allied lines. The Roosevelt order had one proviso; as soon as the war was over, the thousand in Oswego would have to promise to return to their old countries.

After the ship docked in Hoboken, those aboard were escorted into an empty, dimly lit waiting room. They were being assigned to coaches on the train, that sort of thing, but the fear they were feeling was reflected in their eyes. They were coming to the land of the free, they thought. And here they were being herded by soldiers into rooms for processing. Was this just another cruel transport to yet another concentration camp? The fear was the result of uncertainty. It didn't help matters for the refugees to see the ship first tie up to a New York pier covered by a shed labeled "Hamburg-American Line" before proceeding to the pier in New Jersey.

The sick, the elderly, and a few pregnant women were put aboard an army hospital car, but the people in the waiting room couldn't see that. All they knew was that the most vulnerable had been separated from the group. It brought back fear-filled memories.

Time to get on the train finally came. It was the old Delaware Lackawanna line that snaked its way through several counties in New Jersey, then wound its way through New York State until it arrived in Oswego. When the refugees finally arrived at Fort Ontario, the fear returned. It was an old-style army camp, surrounded by barbed wire designed to keep people out, not in.

Those in charge tried to reassure the refugees, but they were so frightened that they were being taken to still another concentration camp, it was difficult. That August, the thousand refugees from Hitler found they were "guests" in a country that didn't know what to do with them, so they lived behind barbed wire.

As mentioned earlier, after eighteen months and additional pressure from Congress, the refugees were allowed out of the camp to assume normal lives that led eventually to citizenship.

In 1986 the New York State Museum in Albany opened a permanent exhibit, "Bitter Hope from Holocaust to Haven," to tell the story of the thousand. Someday I will visit that museum to see that exhibit and learn more of what my eight refugee friends went through.

THE END OF THE WAR AND ITS AFTERMATH

April 12, 1945, was a good day for fishing. Even though the weather was still quite cool, and patches of snow lay here and there, I couldn't resist digging up some worms and heading for Three Mile Creek for a relaxing afternoon. As a Chinese proverb states, "No man is wasting his time who is fishing." So off I went not wanting to waste my time. As I walked along the path through the woods, the springtime sights and sounds helped me forget about school and the war still being waged. I didn't want to think about it, even though America was slowly, but surely, winning. I even found myself whistling a happy tune now and then in answer to the ones the birds were singing. I soon reached the creek, and I walked around its shoreline until I reached the short bridge that spanned the narrow road and under which the creek flowed.

I sat down on a large rock nearby, baited my hook, cast my line into the water and waited expectantly for the bobber to signal me that a fish was taking the bait. I was not disappointed and soon had three nice-sized bullheads on my stringer and was preparing to cast my line in again. As I cast it out, a teenager, riding a bike, stopped and asked how the fishing was. I responded affirmatively and then showed him my catch. After a bit more talk about fishing, he turned to leave, then turned back and remarked, "Pretty sad about President Roosevelt dying, ain't it?"

"President Roosevelt died?" I questioned excitedly. "When?"

"Earlier today. They've been announcing it on the radio."

We exchanged a few more phrases, then he turned, hopped on his bike and was soon out of sight.

His news ruined my appetite for fishing, so I packed up my gear, lifted my stringer of fish out of the water and headed home. As I walked, my thoughts were somber, and I didn't whistle one tune. After all, President Roosevelt had been President since before I was born, and he had recently been reelected to his fourth term. He was the Commander in Chief of our Armed Services, in a sense he was our emperor during this terrible war. Now he was dead. I wondered how my mother was taking the news. She and all her lady friends were staunch Democrats and idolized Roosevelt.

Perhaps she hadn't heard yet, since our only radio was in a repair shop being fixed.

As I entered the front door, Mom looked up from her chair and complimented me on my catch. I soon said, "I suppose you've heard by now that President Roosevelt died earlier today."

Being very hard of hearing, she asked, "What did you say?" I repeated loudly, what I had said. She immediately became very upset and said something about President Roosevelt's death giving new hope to Hitler, the Nazis, and the Japanese. Then she ran out of the house, down the stairs, and across the road to Mrs. O'Leary's home. Why? I wasn't sure. Maybe for consolation. At any rate, she eventually returned with a borrowed radio under one arm. I could tell she had been crying. The radio was quickly plugged in and turned on. From that moment until late in the evening, she stayed "glued" to the radio.

Shortly after President Roosevelt's death, Vice-President Harry S. Truman was sworn in as President. Now, as Commander in Chief of the Armed Forces, he was leading our country in this terrible war. Surprisingly, President Roosevelt's death didn't seem to make any difference. Under Truman's leadership, we continued to forge ahead in Europe and in the Pacific. My mom's fears were unfounded.

Unknown to everyone at the time, President Truman turned out to be a "tough old bird." He had a placard on his desk that stated, "The buck stops here," and it did. He made the agonizing decision to drop the first atomic bombs on Japan. In the 1948 national elections, he upset the heavily favored New York Governor Thomas E. Dewey and won reelection. He fired General Douglas MacArthur during the Korean conflict. Truly, he lived up to his placard.

As the history books will tell you, the war in Europe ended on May 8, 1945, V-E Day, and V-J Day finally came on August 15, 1945. There was some celebration when the war in Europe ended, but it was nothing compared to the celebration when the Japanese surrendered marking the end of World War II. V-J Day had finally come! And, as with all Americans, we celebrated! We joined our neighbors out in the road. We whooped and hollered, until we were hoarse. We hugged and kissed each other. And we banged on pots and pans with spoons until our muscles ached. But the hoarseness and muscle aches were worth it. We had won the war, a terrible war, and now it was time to celebrate. And we did, far into the evening!

The next morning I walked to town for some groceries. Reaching the "forks in the road," a few blocks inside the city line, I noticed a large sign in front of the first gas station. It stated, "OUT OF GAS." As I continued walking, all the stations had similar signs. Evidently, as soon as gas rationing had ended, many, who still had cars that would run, had happily filled their tanks. No more five gallon limits and no more rationing stamps to get it. Had I been one of them, I would have been just as excited. I'm sure in the days that followed, many families took long-awaited joy rides and/or trips to visit relatives in distant towns and cities.

In fact, all rationing soon ended, making Mom's life much more enjoyable. However, rationed items did not suddenly appear in abundance, but gradually they did appear. Thus, Mom knew for sure, she would never have to eat oleo, and that assurance brought many-a-smile to her face.

Soon after the war ended, Georgie and his family returned home. He was still my best friend, and we spent many happy hours catching up on each other's experiences while separated. Even though I had many, including the coming of the refugees to our school, his experiences sounded a lot more exciting. However, I was too naive at the time to realize some of his so-called experiences were only stories he made up. At any rate, I was happy he was back home, and looked forward to any new adventures we might cook up together.

Not long after George returned, I went to spend a few days at his home. We often walked the two miles down country roads to Lake Ontario to swim. On one particular day, as we neared the lake, we decided to sneak across some fields ready for harvesting. As we carefully moved forward, we spotted some POWs (prisoners of war) working in the distance.

These men were former enemy soldiers, who had been brought from Europe to America to work in the fields. Hoping to get a better look at some of our former enemies, we inched our way across the field, until we were quite close. Then we stopped and examined each one with our eyes, until we had seen enough.

Still keeping low and quiet, we turned and headed for the lake. En route, we came upon several canteens of cool water. Realizing they belonged to the POWs, we had a sudden surge of patriotism, even though the war was over. We gathered up all the canteens, took them to the high bank overlooking the lake, flung each as far out into the lake as possible and smiled as each one sank.

As twelve-year-olds, we were getting a little even for all the heartaches these, and all other POWs, had caused our country. We should have known that the canteens had been issued to the POWs by our own military, but we didn't. Once this dastardly deed was done, we felt exhilarated and thoroughly enjoyed the afternoon swimming, lying in the warm sun and talking to our heart's content. Life was good that day!

In September 1946 I entered eighth grade at the Campus School. By now the college was humming again, since so many veterans were taking advantage of the GI Bill and enrolling as freshmen or re-enrolling as upper classmen. Temporary barrack-like quarters for married couples were built near the lake and became known as Splinter Village. Other temporary buildings were erected for classrooms, science labs, gyms, offices and the like. Rooms in homes all over Oswego and the surrounding areas were being opened to help house the influx of students. Everyone pitched in and helped in any way they could. I'm sure among the happiest were the coeds, starved too long for affection. Even though conditions were not the best, they were far better than any foxhole had been. I never heard one veteran complain.

Early into the school year, both sexes came into our classroom to observe and participate as part of their teacher training preparation. During the year, I got to know many of them quite well and in my eighth-grade yearbook, I still have their comments and signatures to remind me of any who limped, any who had an artificial arm or leg, any who had only one eye and any who came back seemingly in one piece. They had come back and were now preparing for the future as teachers. In my own way, I was very proud of each one. Now, over forty years later, I wonder how their lives turned out.

For four years in high school, I sat next to veterans, now older and wiser, coming back to finish high school, so they could go on to college. I knew several who had dropped out of school, not to join the service, but out of boredom. Now here they were, veterans, some with families, determined not to get bored again but determined to finish high school and go on to college. Even though I could never fully repay any veteran for what he or she had done for me, I found some satisfaction in helping a few academically over some rough spots in some of our courses. They, in turn, taught me some valuable lessons about life.

In 1951 after returning from my venture to California, I landed a job at the Marathon Corporation, a paper mill and carton finishing plant. During my tenure there, I met several veterans. Some I worked next to, others were my bosses. Some were "thorns in my flesh," others became good friends even though I was somewhat younger. Space does not permit me to write about all of them. However, I would like to write about three, each having served his country well and each having been wounded.

Richard (Dick) Burke was drafted into the army in 1942 soon after his high school graduation and nineteenth birthday. During his thirteen weeks of basic training as a commando, he escaped a spinal meningitis outbreak so severe the entire camp was quarantined after some recruits had died.

His training completed, Dick looked forward to some time at home with family and friends. However, the army, fearing Dick might be carrying the virus, denied him leave and shipped him overseas to fight, first in Africa, where he suffered from malaria, then in Sicily and more malaria. After some time in England to recuperate, he fought in France, Belgium, and Germany. In the famous Battle of the Bulge, he was part of a machine gun outpost. On January 1, 1945, he was found wounded, unconscious, almost frozen to death and the lone survivor of the outpost.

In the hospital, the doctors thought they might have to amputate Dick's left leg, since gangrene had begun to set in. However, his condition improved over the next few days and his leg was spared. From that time on, Dick experienced poor circulation, tenderness and pain in both legs, but he was determined to live with the pain and continue serving his country. After leaving the hospital, Dick was sent to England, where he helped train troops for the Pacific offensive against the Japanese.

When Dick returned home in December 1945, he soon visited the YMCA. He wanted to box, play basketball and volleyball, as he had done so many times prior to entering the service. However, he soon realized his athletic activities had to stop. The pain in his legs became unbearable, plus they would begin to bleed during such physical torture as running and jumping. Accepting his fate, Dick was glad to be alive and in one piece.

As my boss, Dick was a real "thorn in my flesh," yet he taught me a valuable lesson. During much of my tenure at Marathon, I was attending college full-time and working a 3:30– 11:30 P.M. shift on the wax line. One week out of three, he was my boss. Whenever he and I were on the same shift, he would make it a point to join me daily on one or more of my breaks in the cafeteria. He would usually sit across from me and soon ask me some question about current events in the news. Since I had so much to do, and so little time to do it, I did not keep up on current affairs. Therefore, I usually could not answer it. Then, in front of everyone at my table, he would make such comments as, "You stupid redhead! Here you are going to college, and you can't even answer a simple question about world, national, or local affairs. What the hell's the matter with you? What good is a college education, if you don't know what's going on in the world?" Then he'd give the answer, smile in triumph, and everyone else would laugh including me. I would be too embarrassed to do otherwise.

Eventually I made time to read a daily newspaper and listen to the news on the radio. Once I began answering his questions, I could see the disappointment on his face, and soon the harassment ceased. However, to this day, I keep up on current affairs: world, national, and local. It's a rewarding habit, one Dick goaded me into over thirty-five years ago.

Donald (Don) Drake was my supervisor on the wax line one week out of three. He was happy-go-lucky most of the time, laughed a lot and often quoted Scripture verses from the New Testament. When he became angry, he would usually talk to himself in Italian words and phrases. Whether Don was swearing or not, no one knew, unless the hearer understood Italian, and I did not.

During breaks, Don almost always had some new joke to tell those at his table and would usually laugh along with the others, as if he were also enjoying the joke for the first time. I usually sat with him not wanting to miss any joke I could tell to my friends at another time.

During my years on the wax line, I learned from Don that he had enlisted in the marines early in the war and soon found himself in heavy fighting in Guadalcanal, after which he helped drag out his buddies, who were either wounded or dead.

Don also volunteered for another mission and ended up serving with Merrill's Marauders in heavy fighting in Burma, China, and India. During these campaigns, bad food and not much rest gave him ulcers and some nerve damage. Thus, he returned to the U.S. aboard a hospital ship in 1944 with a fifty percent disability.

Once I asked Don where he learned so much Scripture. He replied, "In the service. I read the New Testament quite often. Believe me, there are no atheists in a foxhole."

One evening, during our lunch break, Don told me about a "Dear John" letter he had received from his wife several months after he arrived overseas. In it she mentioned the birth of a son, whom she named John. Even though Don knew he could not be the father, he did not stop John from keeping Drake as his last name. Of course the "Dear John" letter tore Don up inside. He had left the woman he loved to help fight a war. But being so far away, there was nothing he could do at the time but accept it. However, Don was sure this event contributed to his ulcers and nerve damage. Even so, Don claimed the war did give him a better outlook on life, because there were so many who didn't come home and get a second chance for happiness.

Besides his happy-go-lucky personality, I remember Don's serious moments during our talks and his ability to play just about any song on his harmonica. On several occasions, I visited a tavern Friday evenings after work just to hear Don, who was part of a combo and soloist, play his harmonica.

In 1945, Don married his present wife. Writing to me in 1988, he stated, "I'm forty-three years with my present spouse and couldn't be happier." And I'm happy for both of them.

Howard (Chip) Vincent was a forklift operator in the carton finishing plant. Thus, I often had contact with him, whenever he brought a pallet of something to the wax line. Since he had wide mood swings, I said to him one night, "Chip, some nights you're the nicest guy I know. On other nights, you're a real dog. How come?" Chip looked down at me from his seat and asked, "Do you really want to know?"

"Of course I do. Tell me."

Chip hurriedly related to me that he had served during the war in Germany. In one battle, he had been injured in the forehead by enemy shrapnel. During the operation to correct his injury, the surgeons had inserted a small, steel plate in his head, using it to replace some damaged bones.

Some nights at work, when only a certain number of machines were running, he felt fine. However, on nights when too many machines were running, the plate in his head would vibrate and almost drive him crazy. Once I heard his story, I never again questioned his Dr. Jekyll-Mr. Hyde behavior. However, I did become his friend and learned to sense when too many machines were running. On those nights, I said very little to upset him.

In conclusion, whoever stated, "War is hell," hit the nail right on the head.

Chapter IV
Another Move, Another Cottage

World War II was still being waged in June 1943. I was finishing fourth grade and looking forward to the "lazy, hazy, crazy days of summer." However, Mom had other plans as to how I would spend much of my vacation in early July. One evening, she broke the news that we were moving to the large, beautiful Smith cottage about a block down the road. Even though it meant many hours of work for everyone, I received the news exuberantly. "The Smith cottage! Wow!"

Our new house was a Cape Cod style beauty and much larger than our previous one. The outside was painted white with red trim. A nice-sized lawn surrounded the house, and trees of various kinds and heights rimmed the outer edges of the lawn. The lake, though no longer across the road from us, could be seen from the windows and porches on the western side of the house. A few cottages lay between the lake and our house, but we could still enjoy the beauty of the lake, especially the unparalleled sunsets.

Inside, the first floor had a large living room, a dining room, a small kitchen, a tiny closet and large, screened porches front and back. Upstairs, there were four average-sized bedrooms off a hallway, each with a small closet, and two gable-style screened porches, one in front and the other in the rear.

The inside was insulated, finished off with Masonite paneling and freshly painted downstairs but not upstairs. All the floors, except those on the four porches, were made of hardwood. However, new linoleum covered the beautiful oak floors in each room downstairs but not upstairs.

There were plenty of windows to brighten every room even on the darkest days. When we were inside, the windows were our "eyes" to the scenic world outside. Usually the opened windows facing the lake provided us with all the fresh air we needed. Otherwise, the summer heat and humidity would have made life unbearable. For we owned no fans, had no money to buy any, could not have afforded the cost of electricity, if we did own any, and air conditioning was a comfort yet to come.

As in our two previous houses, there was no plumbing, so we gained nothing in that department. In fact, we didn't even have a sink to dispose of used water. Therefore, used water was emptied into a pail on the floor, carried to the backyard and sprayed onto the high weeds that grew beyond the lawn and trees. We soon discovered that our disposal method was the same as that used by several nearby neighbors, whose cottages also backed up to this unkept area of no man's land.

This house came partly furnished, including a large icebox that sat on the back porch just outside the kitchen door. Between the furniture already there, and the few pieces we moved in, each room had enough furnishings to make the house comfortable. We even had an out-of-tune, upright piano, so Mom, who loved music, would play all her favorite tunes as often as she liked, and the neighbors would enjoy them as the music wafted through the open windows. Often, we kids would invite friends in for a sing-along. At such times, Mom was in her glory, as she played song after song from memory.

There were rustic chairs and a table on the front porch, a picnic table and benches on the back porch, and two iron, double-decker bunk beds on the back porch upstairs. Corky and I often slept on these beds on hot, summer nights and enjoyed the cool, fresh air that gently moved inland from the lake and wafted over our scantily clad bodies.

Corky and I shared one of the two bedrooms that faced the lake, and Mom shared the other with Paddy and his crib. Rose Marie and Marilyn shared a third, and the fourth room over the kitchen was used for storage. Why for storage, when we had so little to store? And why wasn't it used as a playroom instead of a storage area? The answer to both questions follows. Since Mom didn't want her kitchen contaminated by dust and dirt falling from the kitchen ceiling, any prolonged movement on the floor above had to be prevented. In her mind, walking on that floor, playing on that floor and dropping objects on that floor would loosen dust and dirt on the kitchen ceiling allowing it to fall. Therefore, the room was used for storage and entered very infrequently. Her reasoning never made any sense to me, but it did to her, and her word was law.

A few months after moving in, Mr. Smith told us the story of Emma. According to him, Emma had been born, and had lived and died in our house, and then returned as a ghost to continue living there. After hearing his tale, we gladly gave Emma that storage room to live in, hoping she would enjoy it and not bother us in any of the other rooms. To this day, if you ask her, Rose Marie will swear up and down that she once saw Emma's ghost in that room late one night, while passing its doorless entryway on the way to her bedroom. However, I never saw Emma nor heard her walking about.

In our bedroom, there was a double bed with boxsprings and a mattress with holes in it; a small dresser with three drawers, one of which was broken; a rectangular table we used as a desk; and one chair. The closet contained a few hooks for hanging clothes. By today's standards, our room would be too small for one preadolescent, but for us, with our few clothes, games, and other items to store, it was adequate. To top it off, we had an unobstructed view of the lake.

The stove in the kitchen and the space heater in the living room both used fuel oil (a type of kerosene), thus our days of hauling bags of coal from town ended. A fifty-five-gallon drum, used to store the fuel, was kept on the back porch as far away from the icebox as possible to prevent the contamination of any food by dust, dirt, or fumes being emitted from the drum. During the winter, an oil truck often came to refill the drum. Thus, we always had to keep the driveway shoveled, even though we didn't own a car.

Once we were settled in, as we had time, Corky and I began to enjoy various summer activities with our new friend, Jimmy O'Leary, whose family had recently moved from Rochester, New York, to a cottage nearby. We swam, skipped rocks, fished, played flies and grounders in the road with our only bat and beat-up softball, made campfires by the lake and roasted marshmallows while talking or singing, and teased the girls who lived in cottages around ours. Whenever we found enough discarded soda and beer bottles to make it worth a trip to Mulcahey's Fish Fry stand, we'd cash them in for two cents each and use the money to buy fish fries and sodas. Apart from our daily chores at home and odd jobs elsewhere to make money Mom needed, life was good during our leisure time, and we enjoyed every minute of it.

One evening, Corky, Jimmy and I decided to build a raft, so we could go fishing in the lake instead of the creek. We figured, we could catch larger and more fish in a shorter period of time. Using much of our leisure time for the next few days, we cut down several trees seven to eight inches in diameter that stood at the edge of the bank. We made sure each fell over the bank and onto the rocky shoreline. Then we trimmed away the branches and cut each trunk into seven foot lengths. Once we had enough logs, we lashed them together. Then we built a floor on top of the logs using some discarded rough lumber. To finish it off, we erected a four-foot flagpole made from a broom handle and attached a flag we had created to identify our vessel.

The night before our raft was to be launched, I lay in bed enjoying the visions I had of us happily floating on the lake, catching tons of fish, and, in general, sailing our "high seas" to adventure.

The next afternoon, we arrived at the beach in high spirits ready to launch our raft. However, we soon realized, it was too heavy and launching it would be no easy task. Using our ingenuity, sweat, and three sturdy poles as pry bars, we moved it inch by inch over the rocky shoreline to the water's edge and finally into the water. Our task accomplished, we patted each other on the back but only for a brief period of time.

In disbelief, we looked and saw that our raft floated so low in the water, only the top of the floor remained above the waterline. Holding our makeshift oars, we boarded it. Immediately the floor slipped below the surface of the lake, leaving us ankle deep in water. After all our blisters, sweat, and labor, the raft was a failure, but why?

As we stood on the raft, pondering the answer to our question, Skunk Roberts, a local fishing and hunting legend, happened to walk by en route home after fishing at the mouth of the creek. He stopped, looked at all the branches on shore, then at us, the raft and smiled.

Skunk lived in a small, one room shanty on the shoreline of the lake beyond Mulcahey's stand. Skunk had built many rafts to fish from. Therefore, we waded to shore and asked his advice. "Too green," he said. "Your logs are too green. You need to use logs that have been around awhile and have had a chance to dry out; the kind you find along the shoreline, such as that one down there," pointing as he spoke.

As we fired one question after another at him, he answered each in his slow, deliberate manner, and we understood his answers. We not only learned how to make a raft that would float, we received an interesting science lesson about trees. And from a man, who seldom bathed or shaved, thus his nickname. Yet a man, who possessed knowledge about nature, hunting and fishing few others could surpass.

Using Skunk's information, we spent parts of the next several days gathering logs that had "been around awhile" and built a new raft but flying the same flag on the same flagpole. We launched it, and it floated beautifully. We cheered long and loud, as we hopped aboard for its maiden voyage.

During the weeks that followed, we spent many happy hours aboard our raft. We used it for fishing, diving and sunbathing. When fishing from it, just as we had anticipated, we caught larger and more perch and bullheads in a shorter span of time. And we caught them easier. Because the lake was so clear, we'd find a school of fish, slowly lower our baited hooks among them and watch as they took the bait. Once hooked, we'd pull our catch out of the water, deposit it into a pail, rebait our hooks and start over. Thanks to Skunk Roberts, we enjoyed many delicious fish dinners and a great deal of fun the remainder of that summer.

Maybe it was because I was getting older, or maybe I just hadn't realized it before, but I began to notice that Mom was becoming more and more eccentric. For example, she'd wash her hands many times a day as thoroughly as a surgeon, scrubbing for an operation, would. And she expected us to do the same, after touching or before doing anything, where germs were concerned. Having no sink and no running water, Mom always kept an empty food can, filled with warm water, handy to complete the "sterilization process" on herself or on one of us. This ritual alone helped fill the used water pail many times each day. But, oh how the weeds thrived on so much water being sprayed on them!

Another of Mom's eccentricities surfaced, once Corky and I could carry a pail of water alone. This one centered on bringing pails of clean water from the well to the house. If I were going, I'd follow her ritual, and she would supervise me. First I'd wash and "sterilize" my hands. Then I'd carry the pail to the well and rinse it out. Next I'd fill the pail, then grasp the handle and lift the pail into the air, using the same motion, as one flexing one's muscles would use. With the pail in this raised position, I would walk the short distance down the road, across our yard and into the house. If a car passed me, while I was walking down the road, the water in that pail would only be used for washing, since it was a little contaminated. If no cars passed, the water would be considered drinkable and would be used for cooking and drinking. That pail of water would be covered with a piece of waxed paper. Any time I delivered a pail of clean water, Mom would smile. A pail of "contaminated" water would make her frown.

Like it or not, Corky and I had to use her system, even on mornings when the school bus sat waiting for us. All eyes on board would watch me, as I walked past the bus with the pail held high. It was embarrassing, but Mom insisted on clean water whatever the consequences in getting it. On the positive side, I'm sure her method of carrying the pails so high helped build up my arm muscles if not my ego.

With such an inadequate kitchen and no plumbing, I'm sure Mom looked for ways to circumvent these inadequacies. Thus, it was no surprise to me, when paper plates and cups replaced our glass dishes except on

Thanksgiving and Christmas, or whenever bowls were needed for Mom's thick, hearty soup or her delicious stew. However, it was a surprise to me, when pieces of waxed paper were used, whenever the paper plates ran out, and a new supply hadn't been purchased. After Mom realized that paper cups could be rinsed out and used over, our names were written on each new cup before being placed on the table. The number of flatwear pieces used at a meal was determined by the food to be eaten. At times only a spoon, at times a spoon and a fork and so forth. Knives were usually shared, unless everyone felt a need to have his or her own.

Since plastic coated paper plates and cups and styrofoam plates and cups had not yet appeared in the stores, the ones we used were porous, thus, poor substitutes for glass ones. However, using them cut down on washing dishes and boiling water to sterilize them. Therefore, in Mom's eyes, the positives outweighed the negatives, so we continued using paper plates and cups for many years.

Since there were no laundromats and no wash-and-wear clothing, laundering clothes was also difficult. Everything had to be hand washed in tubs, hung to dry, taken down and folded. Clothing that needed to be ironed was set aside and later pressed with a heated flatiron and a damp rag. Since each of us had few clothes for school or play, Mom did laundry several days a week.

Once knickers and high socks went out of style, my wardrobe for school consisted of one striped polo shirt, one pair of chino pants, a belt, two pairs of socks and one pair of shoes, but no underwear. My play clothes consisted of a few used clothes, that were wearable but not for school. For colder weather, I had a parka, wool hat, mittens and buckle boots. I changed from school to play clothes immediately after arriving home on the bus. Thus, if any school clothes needed washing, Mom would wash them that evening and have them ready for me the next morning.

I'm sure fellow students noticed me wearing the same clothes every day, but no one ever said anything to me until one day in the eighth grade. From the beginning of fourth grade, when she entered our class, I had a crush on a cute blonde named Patricia Salander. Her dad had a well-paying job at the college, thus, she always came to school nicely dressed. On that particular day in front of several classmates, she said to me, "Why do you always wear the same clothes to school?" My face turned red, and I wanted to crawl into a hole and pull the dirt in over me. I meekly answered her question honestly then returned to the task at hand. However, my crush melted away. Why? I didn't really know. But it did.

Since I wore no underwear, I often wondered what I'd do, if I ever ripped the seat of my pants in school. When I finally did during a lunch hour on a mild, spring day in high school, I cut my afternoon classes, used my polo shirt to cover the large tear, and walked home. The next day, Miss Cullen, the Vice-Principal, gave me three days of jail (an hour after school) for not reporting to her prior to leaving. I told her, I was too embarrassed to do so, but my plea fell on deaf ears, so I served my time.

Now that we had a bedroom upstairs away from Mom's domain, Corky and I assumed we were safe from her wrath if we wrestled on our bed now and then. During our first wrestling match, Mom felt the vibrations downstairs, even though she didn't hear anything. Quietly mounting the stairs and reaching our room, she flung open the door and stood there, a "giant" holding a doubled-up light cord in one hand. "I've told you fifty thousand times not to wrestle on your bed!" Mom often exaggerated certain statements, and that was one. "I'll teach you to disobey me!" And with that, she began hitting us on our lower bodies. The light cord not only hurt, it stung, and we danced a jig as we cried. Her wrath vented, she stopped, barked, "Let that be a lesson to you," and left. Even though Corky and I were now twelve and ten and getting taller and stronger, we were still no match for our four foot, nine inch mother, especially when she was armed with her light cord.

The first winter in our new home proved to be colder than we bargained for. Even though the house was insulated, it had no storm windows or doors, and the oil burner was no match for the bitter cold air, that often enveloped the house, especially the second floor. Many mornings that winter, when Corky and I woke up, we could see our breath when we exhaled, and we found snow on the inside of the windowsill. On such mornings, we hated to get up, but Mom's famous call, "Are you up, or do I have to come and get you up?" was all the prodding we needed. Once dressed, we'd brush the snow onto a piece of cardboard and dump it into the pee pail in the hall. Luckily for the girls, the stove pipe passed through their room en route to the chimney connection. The heat, radiating from it, kept their room quite warm. Mom and Paddy survived the cold by sleeping downstairs, she on one sofa, he on the other.

On those days, when the weather was at its coldest, Mom hung a folded blanket over the entryway to the upstairs and, in doing so, managed to keep the downstairs warmer and livable. In the evenings, a little before bedtime, the blanket was removed, allowing some heat to reach our bedroom, but not enough, believe me, not nearly enough.

To make matters worse, on full moon nights, the bitter cold penetrated the entire house and forced us all to sit in the closed-off kitchen and keep warm from the heat generated by all four top burners and the oven going full blast. On such nights, Corky and I slept on the floor in the girls' room. Mom and Paddy remained downstairs and used the only extra two blankets we owned.

Three times a week, bottles of pasteurized, but not homogenized, milk were delivered by Siver's Dairy before dawn and placed on the porch table near the front door. By the time we fetched them, their contents would have frozen and expanded, pushing the bottle caps and the cream on top about two inches out of the bottle. Once inside, Mom would cut the exposed frozen cream off, put it into a jar to melt for later use in her coffee, recap each bottle, let it defrost and then put it into the iceless icebox for later use.

It was years later in my high school physics course, that I learned why the milk expanded, pushing the cream out of the bottle. I also learned that the homogenization of milk would usually prevent this from happening. From the time homogenized milk became commonplace, Mom lost her source of cream. Since she would not use milk in her coffee, she had to drink it black or spend extra money on a pint of cream now and then.

As each winter storm rolled in off the lake, blinding snow accompanied the wind. The two often caused massive snow drifts in front of our house. After one such storm, snow had gradually drifted upward from the top of our front porch stairs, across our lawn, the road, the neighbor's lawn and over his ranch house, creating a marvelous hill to sleigh ride down. Ignoring the cold, bleak, dismal day, Corky and I bundled up, grabbed our sleds and climbed to the top of the hill on the hard-packed snow. Arriving, we looked over the edge and saw that the snow had not covered the rear of the house. Therefore, its occupants could open the back door to let fresh air in and themselves out. Turning our sleds around, we boarded them and followed one another down the hill and onto the porch, using the bare, wooden floor as our brakes. What a glorious time we had as ride after ride carried us through the afternoon. When Mom finally called us to come in for supper, we were exhausted.

We were up early the next morning hoping to get a few more runs in, before a snowplow arrived cutting our hill in two. After braking for the third time and heading back up the hill, we heard a noise and looked toward the loop in the road, where we used to live. Coming around the bend as fast as possible and with all blades in place, a huge snowplow came barreling down the road. It cut a swath through the snow, sending mounds of it and a few mailboxes flying through the air in its effort to clear the road. A second plow followed, continuing the cutting process the first had begun. Soon both plows returned from the opposite direction and completed the task. We watched in awe, as the plows created huge piles of snow on both sides of the road, once again opening civilization to our neck of the world.

Once the road was plowed, Corky and I reluctantly swapped our sleds for shovels and began the monumental task of shoveling our driveway. But our task was small compared to our neighbors across the road. It took the father an entire day just to shovel a path from the rear of his house to the road, so he could walk to work.

Spring 1944 finally came. We had faced another terrible winter and had survived. However, before the next one rolled around, Mr. Smith had storm windows and doors ready to put on the house at the first signs of winter. These made a difference during the next several winters, but our home was never overly warm or cozy during winter storms.

In the years since, *The Saturday Evening Post* magazine once featured a centerfold article and picture entitled, "Digging Out." It began, "Great, flat flakes began to fall on a Friday night last winter and six days later, Oswego, New York, lay under an accumulated six and a half feet of snow . . . " The accompanying picture showed a snowplow at work and, nearby, a man shoveling out his buried car.

In 1965, I was living in southern California. Rose Marie sent me a picture she had cut out of her Norfolk, Virginia, newspaper. The picture showed the main intersection of Oswego, Under the picture were these words, "OSWEGO PARALYZED: Snow drifted as deep as thirty feet in the Oswego business district. This scene in the city, near Lake Ontario, shows West First Street. Lower windows across the street are on the second floor."

Having experienced such storms in my youth, I was not surprised at either of these articles. However, after reading each and looking at the pictures, my mind drifted back to that one particular storm, when Corky and I sleigh rode down the hill that God and the weather had created for our enjoyment. Then I smiled to myself.

Chapter V
Bad Days, Glad Days, Sad Days

Soon after World War II ended in 1945, plenty of meat became available to satiate the appetites of meat lovers including my mother. However, in Mom's case, with abundance came pickiness. She knew she no longer had to accept whatever the butcher pushed our way at the meat counter. In no time at all, she became very hard to please.

Since Corky and I were still the grocery shoppers most of the time, we took the brunt of Mom's wrath, if her instructions were not followed. Therefore, we made every effort to follow her instructions exactly as she gave them to us.

One day she sent me to the A & P for some groceries including "six lean pork chops." At the meat counter, I repeated Mom's exact words to the butcher. When I arrived back home, Mom opened the wrapped meat, took one look at the pork chops and complained angrily, "I told you to get six lean pork chops. These are not lean. Take them back and tell the butcher, I want six lean pork chops." With that, she rewrapped the meat, put it into a bag and thrust it at me. I took the bag, left the house, complaining under my breath, and walked back to the A & P three miles away. At the meat counter, I told the butcher what Mom had told me and handed him the package.

Without saying a word, he opened the wrapper, trimmed all the fat off, then rewrapped, reweighed, and repriced them. Before leaving the counter, I answered his questions about who I was, where I lived, who else in my family shopped, and so on. He concluded our conversation with a request, "Whenever you or your brother come to buy meat, ask for Joe."

I arrived back home in the late afternoon. Mom, oblivious to the extra miles I had walked, examined the meat, smiled and exclaimed, "Now those are lean pork chops! Let that be a lesson to you. Always get what I order."

After that, whenever Corky or I went to the A & P for meat, Joe would weigh the meat first, write the cost on the butcher paper, then trim all the fat off and wrap it. If I was shopping, as he handed it to me, he'd wink, give me a sly grin and say such phrases as, "You won't be bringing that meat back." And he was always correct, I never had to. However, both Corky and I knew that Mom was still paying for any fat on the original meat, but she didn't know it, and we never told her. The one positive outcome of such experiences taught both Corky and me to be careful shoppers, a quality we still possess.

Once I had my first car in 1951, Mom began to shop regularly, and soon all the A & P personnel knew her and treated her with kid gloves, lest the wrath of Mom would fall upon them. She wasn't nasty, just overly picky and determined to get exactly what she wanted come hell or high water. This determination permeated every aspect of her shopping, even to where and how each item was bagged, making sure bars of soap were not put in the same bag with meat or vegetables, and so forth.

Once the groceries arrived at my car, the bags had to be placed on the rear seat and nowhere else. Bags placed in the trunk or on the rear floor meant contaminated food, and Mom would not stand for that. Once we arrived home, the bags remained in my car until she unlocked the front door of the house. Then they were carried in and placed on the kitchen or dining room table. Finally, before putting anything away, her hands had to be washed and "sterilized."

During my growing up years, I often suspected that Mom's eccentricities were abnormal, but I never voiced my suspicions seriously. Oh, Corky and I kidded about them now and then, but we knew Mom would never change, so we continued to carry out her rituals.

Several years later, I read an article about obsessive-compulsive disorders (OCD) caused by a chemical disturbance in the brain. After finishing the article, I classified Mom as one suffering such a disorder. In OCD the patient has obsessions that he cannot stop. In Mom's case: fear of germs. The patient also feels compelled to repeat endlessly the same rituals. In Mom's case: handwashing and others. After all the intervening years, this article proved that my boyhood suspicions had been valid. Now I could accept Mom's eccentricities and feel sorry that she suffered so many years with them.

That fall, 1945, Mom made a deal with Mr. Smith to buy his cottage. The terms: no money down and twenty-five dollars a month until the twenty-five hundred dollar selling price plus three percent interest a year were paid. Why he sold it to her was a mystery then as it is now. I did know that he was a Professor of Education at Syracuse University, some thirty-five miles away, and had used his cottage only during the summer months.

Whatever his reason, Mom seemed happy to buy it and felt a little more secure owning her own place. The nicest thing was, once Mom began to pay on the cottage, it became known as the "Furman house," replacing the name, "Smith cottage."

As all homeowners soon learn, with ownership comes the responsibility of upkeep, and Mom knew this. However, with an almost new roof and exterior paint job and no plumbing to worry about, she figured the upkeep would be minimal at least for a while. Besides, she knew Corky and I were learning many skills in our weekly, industrial arts classes at school. And these skills could be applied when doing simple home repairs. She was correct. We did make needed repairs under her close supervision for several years.

By the spring of 1953, the exterior of our house badly needed painting. Even though I was working full-time at the Marathon Corporation, I figured I could paint it before leaving for college in early September. A friend, who painted for a living, came by, looked at the house and told me it needed two coats, once the bad spots were scraped, sanded, and ready for painting. He gave me a list of items to buy: twelve gallons of white paint, a gallon of gray for the porch floors, a quart of red for the trim, brushes, brush cleaner, paint scraper, sandpaper, and a sturdy extension ladder that would reach the peaks.

I took his advice, bought everything on my list, paid for it with my money and transported it home on a friend's pickup truck. Mom knew nothing of my plan until I arrived home and put everything on the back porch. Then she started in with all the reasons why I shouldn't paint the house, including her fear that our property taxes would be raised if the house were newly painted. I ignored her reasons and remained determined to do it.

After a few days into my task, I began to think Mom was correct, that I had bitten off more than I could chew, but I kept at it and made slow but sure progress. Eventually I was ready to start scraping and sanding the eastern side of the house, so I placed my ladder up to the peak and climbed it with materials in one hand. As I neared my starting point, I soon realized that wasps had taken over the peak and were determined to keep me away. Seeing that the odds were against me, I quickly descended the ladder and chose another area in a safer zone to scrape and sand.

That evening at work, I mentioned my wasp problem to Murphy Piazza seeking his advice. Should I spray them or what? Before giving me any advice, he informed me that wasps don't fly in the dark but stay in their nests. Thus, he had a foolproof method for getting rid of them. As he spoke, I wrote down each step in order, thanked Murphy, stuck the paper into my pocket, returned to work, and counted the hours and minutes until my shift ended.

I hurried home and found Mom asleep on the sofa near the large picture window on the same side of the house as the wasp nests. Quickly, but quietly, I gathered all the necessary materials and placed them where needed. Once this was done, I was ready to attack the wasps.

Following my list, I placed a large, wooden box on the ground next to the house and under the peak above. Next I crumpled up several pages of old newspapers and tossed them into the box. Finally, I sprayed some gasoline onto the crumpled papers. Once this was completed, I hurried to the front porch, grabbed a long pole and a flashlight placed there earlier, quietly tiptoed across the living room floor, up the stairs and to the window in the girls' bedroom. I opened the window, leaned the upper part of my body out and, with the pole in one hand and flashlight in the other, I looked up toward the peak and took a deep breath. Then I turned on the light and saw several wasp nests filled with wasps. Using the pole, I managed to dislodge each nest and, as a true bombardier would, prayed that each would hit the target; in this case the inside of the box below. All nests dislodged, I hurried back to the box.

Arriving, I lit a match and threw it into the box. Immediately the contents burst into flames rising several feet into the air. Instantly realizing I had forgotten a step, I quickly grabbed the end of the box and pulled it away from the house but right in line with the picture window.

At that moment, while the flames were at their highest, Mom woke up, saw the flames, assumed the house was on fire and let out a scream the entire neighborhood could hear. Hearing her desperate scream for help, I rushed in and quickly assured her that the house was not on fire, just some newspapers in a box. I then returned to the burning box and stayed there until the fire burned itself out.

Once I returned to where my mother was still sitting and shaking, I tried to explain what I had done and why. However, she would not listen. Instead, she let me have it with both barrels until she ran out of breath. Once the barrels were empty, I tried again to tell her and succeeded. Even though she listened, I'm sure she didn't forgive me for almost scaring her to death. In a way, I couldn't blame her.

Early the next morning, I checked the peak for wasps and found none, nor did any return to attack me that day, or any day that I worked in or near that peak. Murphy had been correct. His plan was foolproof even though my one little error had almost given Mom a heart attack or stroke.

By early September, I had completely finished the front and both sides of the house but had no time left to do the rear. The day I left for college in Rhode Island, Paddy assured me he'd get busy and paint it. And he did, in 1980.

Corky and I were out of bed early on Thanksgiving Day, 1945. The day before, Hart's Poultry had delivered a large, fresh, cut up chicken ready to be cooked. However, Mom, following another of her eccentricities, had to wash the chicken several times to make sure it was clean before cooking it. This ritual meant extra pails of clean water had to be carried from the well, and extra pails of used water dumped. Apart from carrying water in and out, we stayed out of the kitchen to avoid getting in Mom's way and upsetting her as she cooked and baked in a kitchen ill-equipped to do either. However, the delicious meal we would enjoy at the end of the day was well worth it.

As the tantalizing aromas increased, and the time for our feast drew nearer and nearer, the girls put a beautiful, but worn, white lace tablecloth on the dining room table. To add a little class to the table, they placed a bouquet of old, but resurrected artificial flowers in the center. Glass dishes, a three-piece set of silverware and a traditional Thanksgiving Day napkin at each place completed a banquet table setting fit for a king, or so we thought.

Everyone responded quickly to the "Come and get it," order by Marilyn. Hands washed "with a lick and a promise," we all sat down around the table. Corky asked the blessing, and then Mom began bringing in and serving the food. We gladly would have helped but, in her eyes, our hands were never clean enough to do so. Juicy pieces of chicken, mounds of real mashed potatoes, tasty yellow gravy, Mom's special dressing, peas, cranberry sauce, hot rolls, cold milk and large pieces of pumpkin pie with whipped cream for dessert was the bill of fare, and everything tasted delicious. As she usually did, Mom served and sat with us but did not eat with us. Once we were finished, she would eat alone in the kitchen. I was never sure exactly why. As kids often do, we may have eaten too fast for her, since she chewed each mouthful innumerable times to aid in her digestive process.

While eating, each of us gave at least one thing we were thankful for. Among those mentioned were the end of World War II, Mom buying the house, no serious sicknesses or injuries, Dad sending money more often, and of course mine: the safe return of the Pitluga family, my joining the "famous" Troop 11 under the leadership of Scoutmaster Henry Shurr, and the job I now had, helping to deliver the *Palladium Times* newspaper on a rural route while riding in a truck with an adult driver.

Once the feast ended for us and Mom, we cleaned the table, but she faced the tasks of putting leftovers away and washing all the dishes, silverware, pots and pans. Even though she was very tired by then and her legs were killing her, she felt none of us was capable of doing the dishes and scalding them properly. So we played games, listened to the radio or read while she worked far into the evening.

Once Thanksgiving passed, everyone, especially the store owners, knew that Christmas was around the corner. Even though most people enjoyed the hustle and bustle, the music, the special church programs, the shopping, the anticipation and all else that made Christmas a joyous holiday, I didn't.

To me, as a young boy, it meant getting a tree Mom would like, having little money to buy gifts and walking to and from church on a cold, winter night. Once home again, Corky and I faced the arduous task of trimming the tree, making sure every candle-shaped, bubble light on the string was placed strategically and vertically. Then putting together any items that needed to be assembled and arranging everything just so under the tree. While doing all this, Mom supervised from her chair and often dozed off. Rose Marie, Marilyn, and Paddy slept happily with visions of Christmas gifts filling their dreams. Worst of all was working until three or four in the morning to get everything ready, and finally going to bed only to be awakened at the crack of dawn by screams of jubilation. Finally, it meant getting very few gifts compared to the younger ones, since Mom always explained to us in advance, "Since you two are the oldest, and I only have so much money to spend, you won't be getting many presents. You understand, don't you?" I didn't, but I shook my head up and down anyway.

The Saturday before Christmas, Corky and I walked to the woods, looked at the tops of many tall pine trees and finally saw one we wanted for our Christmas tree. In order to cut it, we climbed almost to the top of the tall pine then topped it with our saw. We then climbed back down as carefully as we had climbed up, cutting some extra branches as we descended. Once back on the ground, Corky stood the tree up, and we both agreed it was a beauty, one that should certainly please Mom.

We put the tree on the sled, the branches on top the tree and tied both securely to the sled. As we walked home on the crunchy snow, pulling the sled behind, we agreed we had cut the perfect tree and enough branches to make decorations for all the windows and doors downstairs. Shortly after we arrived home, Mom inspected the tree and looked at the branches. She agreed with us and smiled happily.

Christmas Eve soon arrived and melted into the wee hours of the morning before Corky and I fell into bed dog tired. As I lay there, a thought I had made me smile, so I turned on my side and whispered, "You know, Corky, in a few hours, people all over America will be madly opening presents, flinging bows aside and tearing wrapping paper to pieces. At the same time, many store owners will be gathered in the back of their stores happily counting their money and singing the hymn, 'What a Friend We Have in Jesus.'" Corky saw the humor and laughed with me. Then we fell asleep without another word.

Christmas morning came too soon, and, as promised, my gifts were few. However, I found my joy looking at the beautifully decorated tree with every bubble light standing tall and glowing. And on top, the angel, Gabriel, ready to proclaim, if only he could, "Peace on earth, good will toward men."

When my class entered the eighth grade in September 1946, we did so joyfully. Not only were we new teenagers, we were now the kingpins, the top dogs, the ones every other kid in the school looked up to. After this final year, we would leave the Campus School, but for now, we were at the top!

As seniors, we published and distributed the monthly edition of the school newspaper, *The Campusette*. We were the ones who made marionettes in shop, wrote a long script, produced and presented a lengthy puppet show to the entire student body and to many college students. It was our class, who planned and painted a series of historical murals and hung them on the walls around our room for everyone to see. We were the ones who studied the United Nations, a peace organization new to the world, and gave illustrated talks to the upper grades. This final year, our class made a total commitment to produce our own hardcover, class yearbook complete with photos, class history, and class song. We were the big shots, and we reveled in everything we did.

In the fall, we boys challenged male college students, who came to observe our class in action, to games of tackle football without any protective equipment. To tackle their ball carrier, we threw ourselves in front of his legs, tripping him up. I injured my left foot in one such pileup.

During the winter, it was our basketball team that represented our school at games both home and away. And when the college's annual, winter, ice carnival came along, we were the class that created a large, colored-ice model of a dinosaur to represent the Campus School.

As eighth graders, it was our turn to have dances and parties in school and in various homes of our classmates. Unknown to parent hosts, it was our delight to play kissing games such as spin the bottle and chocolate wink. On one occasion, we were the ones who drank a large decanter of wine that we mixed with our apple cider, only to have the hostess, upon discovering the empty container, tell us it was only grape juice, but Sam Giambo knew better. Believe me, life that year was everything a senior year should be and more, much, much more.

However, we were also the class that tried to drive our teacher, Irene Eisele, crazy but failed. Whatever we did, she'd smile, keep her cool and persevere. We were the stinkers who frequently ignored the bell after lunch on warm, spring days, hid out in the pine woods near the lake and dared our student teacher, Mr. Keach, to come and find us, if he could.

Life was good that year, too good and too fast. Soon we were on the stage being handed our graduation diplomas as our teachers looked on with broad, relieved smiles while our parents looked on with tears in their eyes. On that day, the worn, faded curtain fell closed, ending that part of our lives. However, we all knew that a fresh, new one would open in September, promising new adventures to us lowly freshmen as we entered Oswego High School.

Several years before we moved by the lake, a long, concrete retaining wall had been built parallel to the road partway between our house and Mulcahey's stand. Its purpose was to prevent the lake, during storms, from washing away the remaining land that separated the lake from the road. As hoped, it was preventing erosion. However, during any major storm, large waves would smash against the wall one after another, sending an endless spray across the road and beyond. During such storms, all vehicles and pedestrians passing over this section of the road were at the mercy of the spray. In warm weather, the spray felt refreshing but not so otherwise.

When the weather was cold enough, the spray would freeze on the road causing dangerous, icy conditions. Unsuspecting drivers, upon reaching this section of road, would suddenly face two dangers: ice on their windshields cutting their visibility and an icy road to contend with even though it may have been sanded. Such icy conditions often led to accidents: cars hitting cars, cars hitting trees, guard rails, or other objects and cars simply turning over and skidding along the icy road. Pedestrians, especially those wearing glasses, faced the same two conditions.

One afternoon during the winter of 1947–1948 I walked to town. The road was dry except for this section of the road. Even though a storm had passed, the waves were still acting up and sending plenty of cold spray over the road and beyond. It was not freezing, however, so it posed no problems.

Late that evening, I was walking home and noticed that the temperature had dropped considerably. As I walked along, singing to myself, Dave Mulcahey came along on his motor scooter, stopped, and offered me a ride home. I accepted and hopped on behind him.

As we approached this section of road, I yelled into his ear, "Water's spraying across the road at the wall. Maybe you'd better go a little faster, so we won't get so wet." He nodded and turned up the throttle, increasing our speed. Unknown to either of us, the road had become icy and cinders had been spread over the ice. As soon as we reached the ice, Dave began losing control of his scooter, and I began losing my grip on his waist. I soon slid off the back of the scooter onto the ice and cinders. We both continued moving forward, he on his scooter, and I on the seat of my pants. Once we had both stopped, he turned his scooter around and came back to where I was sitting in the road.

As I sat there, catching my breath and spewing out profanities bemoaning my fate, he asked if I was okay. Weakly, I rose to my feet, grimaced as I felt my rear end, and realized the cinders had torn my pants and flesh unmercifully. After a few more expletives, I assured him that I would live and would walk the remaining distance home. I knew I was in no shape to ride on anything. We bade good-bye, then he headed back toward his home, and I headed through the icy spray toward mine, being very careful not to fall again.

Soon after arriving home, Mom doctored me up, using plenty of iodine after washing my wounds. She ignored my painful yelps during the entire process and finally said, "In time, you'll be as good as new, if none of your injuries become infected. However, your pants will not be so fortunate. There's no way in this world I can fix them."

My injuries were almost healed, when I arrived early at the *Palladium Times*. It was a cold, winter day, and I was glad the circulation office was open even though the presses hadn't as yet began spewing forth the Saturday edition of the paper. So I took off my hat, gloves, and scarf, opened my parka, found an empty box, turned it on end, sat down, and waited for other carriers to arrive so we could chat a bit before the presses started. Soon Fred came through the door, stamped his feet on the large, rubber mat, took his gloves off and blew on his hands. Seeing me, he yelled a few words of greeting, swore at the weather and opened his coat to absorb the warm air. This done, he walked over to where I was sitting and said, "Too bad about your friend getting killed last night, isn't it?" "What friend?" I asked.

"Didn't you hear? Ray Forbes."

"Don't kid me like that, Fred. It isn't funny!"

"I'm not kidding, Dave. Since you haven't heard, you can read about it in tonight's paper."

"But how? What happened? Tell me whatever you know."

"The radio reported that Ray was riding his bike down a hill in Minetto after dark and skidded into the path of a car. Never had a chance."

Stunned, I sat there in silence for several seconds. Finally, I looked at Fred and in a quavering voice responded, "That's a shame. Ray was a nice guy. I just met him in September. He sat in front of me four classes a day, and we used to shoot the breeze a lot, especially over girls and sports."

Fred's news cured my appetite for further conversations apart from a "hello" here and a "hi" there as other carriers sauntered into the office.

Finally the presses started and soon a pile of 154, ten-page papers was handed to me. I turned from the conveyor belt, walked over to a large table and set the pile down. There, in front of my eyes, was Ray's picture and an accompanying article. I read it, took a long, sorrowful look at his picture, then put the papers into my carrier bag. I bundled myself up, slung the bag over my shoulder and headed for my first customer on Bridge Street, folding papers as I walked and thinking all kinds of thoughts.

When I reached the Coyers' house on Eighth Street, Jo Anne, the current girl of my dreams, was waiting, ready to walk part of my route with me as she often did. After talking about Ray's death, we walked in silence for a bit while I tossed paper after paper onto the porches of my customers. Once the silence was broken, we enjoyed our brief time together. Soon we arrived back on Bridge Street. Jo Anne turned and headed home in one direction while I headed the opposite way down Bridge Street and more customers.

As I walked and tossed, my mind drifted back to my first day in high school and the uncertainty I felt. My eighteen classmates from the Campus School were now scattered among this large student body, and I faced the task of making new friends. One of the first fellows I met that day was Bill Stone, who had sat in the desk in front of me in general science. When a pretty, young, shapely teacher walked in, Stoney turned around and whispered, "Hey, Dave! Look at the knockers on her!" Then he smiled and turned back. I agreed with his evaluation and gave her my utmost attention as she spoke, giving us important information and instructions. Before this first period was over, I was beginning to like high school, especially this class and our voluptuous teacher.

In second period, I met Raymond Forbes, just an ordinary kid like me. From our first meeting, we hit it off and became good friends. Now he was gone, But the empty seat in front of me four classes a day would remind me of him. Eventually I reached the home of a customer, who owed me for the paper. I returned to reality, climbed the stairs of his porch, rang the bell and collected the money due.

Someone has stated, "Time heals all wounds," and it was doing so, when one day, I was called to the office. Arriving, I was introduced to Ray's parents by the principal, Mr. Faust. He explained that Ray's parents had come for his personal things, and would I take the master key for the lockers and clean Ray's out since his was next to mine, and we had been friends. I took the key and the three of us walked silently to Ray's locker, and I opened it. There lay his textbooks, notebook, pencil case, and a few odds and ends on the upper shelf. His gym shirt, shorts and socks hung on hooks and his sneakers lay on the bottom.

As I began handing items to Ray's parents, tears began running down their cheeks, and soon his mom began to cry softly. As I continued, I felt a little eerie. When Ray left for home that Friday, he had every intention of returning on Monday. Thus, he left everything in his locker. Who would have guessed he would not be returning. Certainly not me. Yet, here I was, cleaning out his locker, knowing I would never see him again. Once I finished, I bade good-bye to the Forbes and headed back to the office, carrying Ray's textbooks. En route, a few warm tears slowly made their way down my cheeks. Before entering, I wiped them off with the back of my hand.

Apart from Uncle Richard, who had been killed in World War II, Ray was the first person close to me who had died. Little did I know then, that two more close to me would pass away before I graduated from high school. Knowing how sad I felt when Ray had died, I could understand Mom's grief and my sadness when her mother died in 1949 and her father in 1950.

Chapter VI
There Is More to Bathrooms Than Meets the Eye

Most people in America in this day and age probably take bathrooms for granted. Not so in my life. During my early years in Little Falls, our apartment had normal, indoor plumbing. However, when my family and I moved to Oswego, all that changed.

Our first cottage had three rooms and a path; the path leading to an outhouse equipped with two holes. Why two? I never knew, unless it was a poor man's excuse for a two bathroom house. Since rolls of toilet paper were not a common household item, ours was made from old newspapers and magazines torn page by page into usable sizes. For fun, Dad used to tell the following story, whenever the time was right, to fellow workers, friends and casual acquaintances.

"My wife, Betty, wrote to Sears Roebuck and asked them to send her ten rolls of toilet paper. Someone at Sears wrote back and said, if she would look on page 2,465 of their 5,000 page catalog, she would find their brands of toilet paper and could order accordingly. Betty wrote back and told Sears that if she had their 5,000 page catalog, she wouldn't need their toilet paper."

When we moved down the road into the Smith Cottage, we still had no indoor plumbing. Our bathroom was a small, closet-sized room on the back porch. To get to it, we had to go out the kitchen door onto the screened porch and then enter the bathroom. The toilet was a five gallon, empty, paint pail. Covering the pail was an inverted, wooden box with a round hole cut into the bottom. A toilet seat was placed over the hole. A small window vented the room. Used toilet paper was placed into a paper bag for burning.

There was a neighborhood dump by the lake not far from our house. The land along the lake, including the dump area, was elevated about thirty feet above the lake level. People threw garbage and trash over the bank at the dump, and eventually it washed into the lake or was eaten by wild animals in the area.

It became my chore to empty the toilet pail at the dump. One very windy night in late November, I carried the full pail to the dump. I lifted the pail, one hand holding its handle, the other gripping its bottom. Standing erect, I flung the contents out into the wind and darkness. As easily as I flung it out, the wind flung it back, covering me from head to toe including my glasses. What a mess I was!

As I walked back to the house, cursing all the way and dreading what Mom would say, I could hardly stand the smell. Once I was inside, Mom not only scolded me, she ordered me to leave my clothes on the back porch before taking a pan bath in the kitchen. Therefore, I undressed on the porch and was shivering by the time I was naked and ready to enter the warmth of the kitchen for my bath. The next day, Mom let me wash those clothes after I arrived home from school. I'm sure it was her way of reminding me to use more sense the next time I took the pail to the dump. Not long after this incident, the dump was closed, and we had to find another means of handling our waste.

Empty five gallon cans with covers were readily available in those days, so Mom decided we should bury full pails of waste in our back yard. Thus, whenever a pail was full, I'd put the lid on securely, dig a hole, lower the pail in and cover it with dirt. Grass would soon grow back over the disturbed area. Great system except during the winter months, when the ground was frozen and covered with several feet of snow. During those months, full pails, with lids secured on tightly, were stored in the bathroom until the ground thawed in the spring. Then several were "planted," each in its own hole.

Using our crude bathroom was okay except during cold weather. Both the back porch and bathroom faced the lake. Having to use the bathroom during winter months was torture, especially at night after awakening from sleep. Therefore, a pee pail was placed in the hallway upstairs at night. However, anyone using it for anything but urinating was in deep trouble. Each morning, the pail was dumped, rinsed out and left on its side outdoors with the opening facing the sun for natural sterilization.

A few times I used the pail wrongly and dumped aftershave lotion or some other fragrance that was handy into the pail in order to hide my "evil doing." Sometimes I got away with it, and sometimes I didn't. Now and then, when I didn't get the pail out early enough in the morning and the dreadful deed was discovered by Mom, I was scolded.

All five of us kids were guilty at one time or another, for who, in his right mind, would want to get out of a warm bed, bundle up, face a bitter cold night and sit on a freezing cold toilet seat? When nature called, we had to respond, but, oh, the agony of it all! The day I moved out of that house, was a grand day indeed, and if my intestines could clap, I'm sure they would have given me a standing ovation.

This bathroom and system of burying pails lasted for several years. Finally, my brother-in-law, Paul Hess, and I put in a crude, septic tank system for Mom, who, by then, was living alone. We also built a bathroom off the dining room using part of the back porch. We put a chemical toilet in it and connected the toilet to the septic tank. However, I still have visions of someone, someday, walking through the backyard and getting the surprise of his or her life as the lids, weakened through time and natural processes, give way.

Years later, when my own family and I traveled and camped along the way, we stayed at campgrounds. Many had outhouses. Using them brought back many memories of my boyhood days. Mark usually didn't mind them. At times Shelley didn't either, but Bonnie hated them. She would rather hold it in or use a spot behind a bush or tree than enter an outhouse, unless it was almost odorless, bugless, and clean. Me? I could stand any outhouse I entered.

In the summer of 1974, we traveled to Banff National Park in Canada. One day, we hiked to Victoria Glacier at beautiful Lake Louise about four miles from the main lodge. Before beginning our trek back, we enjoyed the tea house offerings, the icy cold well water, and the outhouse.

The outhouse was clean and odorless, and the waste matter went into a holding tank and not into a deep hole as in the case of so many outhouses. This outhouse sat on two runners. I asked the tea house proprietor about this, since I was curious. He informed me that when the holding tank was full, the outhouse was moved forward on the runners, baring the tank. A helicopter, hovering overhead, would lower a cable. The cable would be connected to the tank and air lifted to wherever full tanks were taken. Soon an empty tank would arrive and be lowered to the spot. Then the house would be pushed back into place, resecured and reopened for use. Talk about protecting the environment! I was both impressed and envious as I thought back to my earlier days in Oswego and the dump.

During the summer of 1975, we decided to take a camping trip to historic Boston, the areas around Boston and then along the Atlantic Coast to Nova Scotia. Since 1976 was the Bicentennial, we opted for 1975 to escape the huge crowds expected everywhere in the Boston area. Things went smoothly for the first few days and then panic time arrived.

It was a Sunday morning in early July. We had visited Boston, Lexington, and Concord, Massachusetts, all key, historic, Revolutionary War areas. We were preparing to leave the Lexington-Concord area, taking bathroom breaks and getting drinks. Shelley and Bonnie went into the ladies' bathroom building which contained three pit toilets and three sinks. Shelley came out first and hopped into our minibus, joining Mark and me. Soon Bon came out crying. I asked her why she was crying. She responded that she had felt sick, had gone into a stall to vomit, and while doing so, her retainer had come off her teeth and had fallen into the pit toilet.

Immediately two options presented themselves. One was to drive the 250 miles back to New Jersey, get a new retainer from her dentist to protect her beautiful, straightened teeth, then continue our trip. The second option was to try and rescue the retainer. I opted for number two. I told Bon to go back to the stall she had used and not let anyone else use it. Then I got my flashlight and fishing pole and headed for the bathroom with Shelley and Mark. Once I knew the bathroom was empty except for Bon, I posted Mark outside to keep females from entering. Shelley and I entered and walked directly to the correct stall. We entered, knelt on the floor, lifted the toilet seat and, with the flashlight's illumination, peered into the hole. Luckily, there was more solid waste than liquid.

Slowly moving the light, we searched for some sign of the retainer. A few minutes passed without success. Then Shelley suddenly exclaimed, "Hold the light there! Is that a shiny object?" I responded, "Maybe yes, maybe no, but let's check it out." I took my fishing pole, slowly lowered the line into the area of the hole Shelley kept lit with the flashlight, and began "fishing." After several near misses, I finally hooked what proved to be Bon's retainer and carefully reeled it in. I let Bon take the "catch" off the hook and told her to wash it in hot water. We left the bathroom triumphantly, put the light and pole away, hopped into the bus and headed toward our next destination. That evening we sterilized the retainer in boiling water and, squeamishly, Bon put it into her mouth to protect her teeth from shifting.

In the early summer of 1976, Shelley and I sold our bus, then decided to take an extended trip in our large, Chrysler sedan without the kids. I slept on the front seat, she on the back.

One leg of our trip took us to Maine. It was an especially hot summer. One night we decided to stay near Bar Harbor. Early in the evening, we parked our car in a parking lot, walked around the town, had supper, and finally returned. Leaving the lot, I mistakenly drove off the curb and banged the bottom of the car. I immediately checked for damage but found no visible evidence of any.

As it began to get dark, we drove up a spiraled road leading to a large parking area on top of Cadillac Mountain (1530′) in Acadia National Park. It was much cooler there, the views in every direction were delightful, and there were portable toilets nearby. It was a perfect place to spend the evening and the night. Apart from the loud radios and even louder teenagers who frequented the area, our decision to spend the night was a good one.

When I arose the next morning, I walked to a bathroom, took a few minutes to enjoy the early morning splendor then headed back to the car. As I neared our "hotel," I saw a puddle under it.

Since it hadn't rained during the night, I immediately recalled driving off the curb and figured something related to the car was leaking, but what? I got on my hands and knees, reached under and stuck a finger into the liquid. I quickly smelled it then put a little on my tongue in an effort to determine what it was. The first test told me nothing, so I tried a second then a third. Still no conclusions. Finally, I decided to circle the car and look under at various places to see if anything was leaking. At the rear of the car, I again knelt down, peered under, saw nothing leaking and began to stand up again, when I saw something tucked into one corner of the rear bumper.

I assumed it was paper, and after pulling it free, found that I had assumed correctly, only it was not any kind of paper, it was toilet paper. I asked myself, "Where did this come from, and why was it tucked into my bumper? Could it have been put there by a teenager? And, if so, why?" Suddenly, the realization of the entire matter hit me like a bolt of lightning. Only I needed verification of what I suspected from Shelley.

She confirmed it. Yes, she did get up to go to the bathroom during the early morning hours. However, she didn't feel like walking in the dark to one of the portable toilets, so she went behind the car and put the toilet tissue where I found it. No wonder I couldn't identify the liquid. It had trickled under the car and stopped, leading me to believe it had come from the car. For a few moments, I vacillated from being angry at Shelley to being relieved that the car was okay. Finally, I saw the humor in what had happened and tucked away the memory of it for future remembrances of our camping days gone by.

It's easy to see, by now, why I appreciate modern bathrooms. When I began working at a large hotel/casino in Stateline, Nevada, I was taken on a tour and shown two of the standard hotel rooms. Each had two complete bathrooms. In each was a small TV and a telephone. As I gazed upon the second, I exclaimed to myself, "They've come a long way, Davy!"

Chapter VII
Pit and Me

From that first day in third grade, when George Pitluga Jr. (Pit) and I took on the other boys for calling him "little fingers" and "stick fingers," we became close friends. Since he was the only child and needed someone to play with at home, I was often invited to spend one or more nights.

These overnight visits were happy times for both Pit and me. Not only did I enjoy playing with him, I enjoyed being in a house with plumbing, and one that was always warm in colder weather. And, to top it off, I enjoyed the quiet mealtimes, the polite conversations, and the meals served on glass dishes.

Coming from my world, I relished each overnight visit, even those times when we'd get into trouble for not going to sleep after lights were out, or calling the fat lady next door names, or knocking over a floor lamp or some other piece of furniture while wrestling in their living room. Usually, we'd get a talking to for inappropriate behavior. However, at times, I'd get the talking to and Pit would get a spanking. Even as a young boy, I never felt that was fair and would have gladly shared his spankings, but his parents never changed their methods of discipline. Unknown to them, I soon "adopted" Pit's parents as my own, especially his dad.

By the time we entered fourth grade, the Pitlugas had rented a house nearer to the college and next to a large vegetable farm. The following summer, Pit and I were hired by Mr. Bokeno to pick green beans for ten cents a basket. At first, we were happy with the job and savored each dime. However, in a short time, we realized how long it took to fill one basket and the glamour soon faded. But we stuck with it and one morning, we picked our last green bean and made our last ten cents.

Now that we were unemployed and had time on our hands, we decided to walk the short distance to Otis Field and snoop around the carnival being set up for its opening that night. Our presence amid the busy workmen was not welcomed, and soon we were ordered to "Get the hell out of here before you get hurt!" We took the hint, retreated to a safer spot outside the carnival, then stopped.

Looking around, we noticed that the backs of several game booths had not been secured and were flapping in the gentle breezes. Since we had been so rudely treated inside the grounds, we decided to investigate the booths from the outside. Moving carefully to avoid being seen, we reached the first rear canvas, carefully raised it and saw nothing of value. We moved stealthily to a second, then a third, and we hit the jackpot. There, on a nearby table, was an unopened pack of cigarettes and a small box of matches. Agreeing to the heist and without being detected, we soon had them in our possession and slowly retreated to the safety of several large trees some distance away.

Opening the pack, we lit up and smoked our first cigarettes, trying to inhale now and then but ending up choking and coughing. Since the first one gave us pleasure, we tried a second, then a third. Halfway through my third, I had inhaled several times and was now very dizzy. Therefore, I passed on a fourth and just sat on the ground trying to regain my equilibrium and keep from vomiting. Eventually, I felt somewhat better so we walked back to his house, hid the rest of the pack and chewed some gum so neither of his parents could smell cigarette smoke on our breath.

That evening, Dr. Pitluga gave both Pit and me some money for the carnival. Eager to ride everything, we hurried to the entrance, walked inside and bought tickets for the first ride we came to, the bumper cars. After several minutes of practicing our driving skills along with several smashups, we exited it and headed for the Ferris wheel and the fun of seeing all the lights from high above the carnival. From there, we continued to work our way around the grounds, taking each ride in stride. Finally, we boarded the one that would do me in. It spun around and around, faster and faster before stopping. Once the spinning stopped, I got off the ride, staggered to an out-of-the-way area, and vomited.

Since Pit was feeling fine, and I was not, we agreed to part company. He headed toward the next ride, and I headed back to his house. Before reaching my destination, I felt so sick, I decided to lie down on some cool grass and rest a little. However, I fell asleep.

By the time I woke up and reached the house, Pit was already home, and everyone there was worried for my safety. In fact, they were considering their options for locating me, when I ambled in alive and well. I told them where I had been and apologized for not coming straight home. Then I excused myself and went to bed. As I stretched out under the sheet, I promised myself that I would never board such a ride again.

I didn't until 1987 at Knotts Berry Farm in southern California. Shelley and I had just finished eating their famous chicken dinner and were walking around when we came to the ride, Montezuma's Revenge. As we stood in awe watching it, I hemmed and hawed over whether or not to ride it. Finally, with some prodding by Shelley, I got in line, and she took a seat nearby to wait for me.

When my turn finally came, I boarded my assigned car and seat, laid my glasses on the platform as directed and hung on to the bar in front of me for dear life. Without warning, the short string of cars was suddenly propelled forward and soon made a 360-degree loop. It then continued onward and ascended a high ramp. When it reached a point near the top of the ramp, it paused for a second then covered the same track backwards, passing the original starting point at ninety-three miles per hour. Again it ascended a high ramp, paused and came flying back to its starting point and stopped abruptly. The ride lasted two minutes. When I climbed out of my car, I put on my glasses and staggered to the exit. Shelley laughed when she saw me coming, but I didn't. I was too dizzy and my stomach was too upset to even smile slightly.

As we drove home, I had mixed emotions. On one hand, I was glad I took the ride for my ego's sake. On the other hand, I didn't like the physical discomforts caused by the ride and vowed, once again, never to succumb to the temptation of taking any ride that could make me dizzy or upset my stomach. Enough was enough after two such experiences.

Like our family, the Pitlugas moved twice in a few years after coming to Oswego. Their final move was to a farm they bought west of the city on Hale Hill Road off route 104. Their spread consisted of a large, old, farmhouse, a toolshed, a chicken coop building, a large barn, and several acres of fruit trees. Surrounding their "country estate" were acres and acres of woods and open fields with only a sprinkling of houses here and there. Thus, Pit and I could hike and explore to our heart's content without being ordered to "Get the hell our of here!" by irate adults or threatened by vicious dogs. However, just as Pit and I were beginning to enjoy this new found freedom, his dad left for the navy, and the rest of the family soon joined him.

Shortly after the Pitlugas returned in 1945, my overnight visits became more frequent and lasted longer. When the weather was foul and forced us to stay indoors, we'd work on Pit's stamp collection, build model airplanes, play games, wrestle with his two dogs or with each other, scrub our sailor hats with our toothbrushes to get them as white as possible, or lie on his bed and talk. However, whenever we could be outdoors, we were.

The warm months were the best. A few times during Pit's first summers in the country, we tried camping near a pond about a mile from his home. After gathering together our supplies, we'd hike to the pond; erect a tent out of a blanket, short poles, stakes and ropes; then make our bed inside the tent. Next we'd stash our bag of food in a safe place outside the tent and stick our bottle of milk in the water near the edge of the pond to keep it cool. Finally, we'd gather some rocks to make a fireplace and some firewood. Once all this was completed, we'd spend the rest of the afternoon swimming, ignoring any cattle that came to drink, and keeping a watchful eye out for any snakes passing by.

For supper, we'd eat our sandwiches and cookies and drink some of the milk. Then we'd build a campfire, roast marshmallows, sing a few songs and chat far into the evening. After putting a stack of logs on the fire to keep animals away, we'd crawl into bed with our clothes on and soon fall asleep.

Cattle, coming to drink at the crack of dawn, would awaken us. We'd crawl out of bed and soon have a fire ready to cook breakfast over. However, upon checking the "safe place" for our food, we'd discover the bag ripped to shreds and most of its contents gone. Animals, attracted by the smell of our bacon, would have easily found our bag and helped themselves to its contents. Only our eggs would be spared. Finally, after tasting our milk and finding it sour, we'd spend a few seconds cursing our misfortune. Then, in anger, we'd pick out a tree some distance away, use our eggs for ammo and see who could hit it.

Once "breakfast" was over, we'd take our tent down, pack up our gear and head for home, arriving a little after 6:00 A.M. While Pit's parents slept on, we'd make breakfast, eat, put everything away, wash up, and be gone again.

Even though we often swam in the pond, we found Lake Ontario more inviting and would often hike the two miles each way. Besides swimming and sunbathing, we'd often climb and traverse the dangerously steep, dirt cliffs that towered above the shoreline and ran along it for some distance. After completing a climb, we'd return to the cool, refreshing water, swim out to a large, flat, elevated rock and lie there, letting the hot sun dry us off.

One day, Pit took a pack of cigarettes from the carton in the refrigerator. I knew Mom would "kill" me if she caught me smoking or even smelled smoke on my breath. I hadn't smoked one cigarette since the carnival episode. But that day, I smoked a few while walking to and from the lake and even inhaled a few times without choking or coughing. What started out as a lark soon became a regular occurrence. Even though Pit got our supply from the cache in the refrigerator, neither parent ever noticed a shortage, so we continued smoking to and from the lake.

One dismal, rainy afternoon, even though we couldn't go swimming, we ran to the empty chicken coop building and lit up. Between puffs, we chatted and laughed about all sorts of things. We sat there enjoying ourselves while the rain continued to fall heavily on the roof and beat against the windows.

Somehow our conversation turned to smoking, and one of us raised the question, "How many cigarettes could either of us smoke at the same time?" Coming from a family whose father was a scientist, Pit didn't want to guess the answer, he wanted to experiment and see the results. After further discussion, a coin was flipped, and the lot fell upon me. Pit inserted cigarettes between my lips from one side of my mouth to the other. Then he quickly lit them, and I puffed as he did so. Using the first two fingers on each hand, I was able to take the cigarettes out en masse in order to exhale the voluminous smoke after each drag.

Once I gained the confidence that I could smoke all the cigarettes at once, I tried inhaling a few times. I got more than I bargained for. By the time I had stamped out the final butt and the smoke cleared, I was both dizzy and nauseated, and I staggered around like a chicken with its head cut off. Pit found enough humor in my condition to laugh but stopped abruptly when I threw up on the floor, and some of my vomit spattered onto his bare legs and sneakers.

After everything in my stomach had escaped and was covering much of the floor, my head cleared enough for me to make two decisions. The first led me away from the stench and out into the fresh, moist air. As I looked up, allowing the rain to pepper my face and glasses with its freshness, I made the second. It was far more important and longer lasting than the first. I vowed never to smoke again.

As Pit became older, his interest in pets widened. Two large dogs were not enough. He eventually turned his attention to white rats and soon had one for a pet. Had Pit kept it in a cage, I wouldn't have minded, but he didn't. Except for school, Pit and his rat were almost inseparable. Even though I hated rats, white included, I accepted Pit's with the philosophy that if my best friend wanted a white rat for a pet, he could have it, and I could live with it. Therefore, when summer came, the rat, sitting on Pit's shoulder, accompanied us to the lake and even swam with us to our favorite sunbathing spot far out in the water.

On one such swim from the rock back to shore, our eyes and attention became focused on some kids climbing the cliffs. When we finally made it to shore, Pit looked around for his rat, but it wasn't there. He immediately panicked, but I remained calm. After all, it wasn't my rat. Together, we reswam our route to the rock and back again, looking down into the clear water for any signs of the rat, but we came up empty. Arriving back on shore, we sat for the longest time scanning the water and shoreline but to no avail. Pit's rat was gone, and where it went was a mystery we never solved.

The loss brought sadness to Pit, but relief to me. However, my relief was short lived as a new, white rat soon replaced the first. Only its name was different, and this rat hung around for a long, long time.

One summer we became small-time entrepreneurs. Since there were ample cherry trees on Pitluga's acreage, we approached his dad with our desire to pick several quarts of cherries and sell them door to door in Oswego. Even though many people came, picked their own and paid Dr. Pitluga so much a quart, he agreed to our plan, He even agreed not to charge us for the cherries, neither the baskets nor the transportation. Thus we knew we'd make a hundred percent profit on each quart sold, so we began picking eagerly, eating a few along the way. By the end of the first afternoon, we had picked twenty quarts and were both tired of picking and sick of eating cherries.

The next morning, Mrs. Pitluga drove us to town and in a short time, we had sold all our cherries and had the money in our pockets to prove it. However, after three days of picking cherries in the hot sun and three mornings of selling them, our desire to become millionaires soon faded, as the thoughts of swimming in the clear, cool lake increased. Thus, our days as entrepreneurs came to an end.

Since neither of us had bicycles or horses to ride, we had to scout the vast amount of land adjacent to the Pitlugas on foot. Thus, whenever I came to stay any length of time, we'd take one or more hikes. In the summers, most were to the lake, to swim, and back. However, during the rest of the year, we'd hike in many different directions, anxious to see what lay behind the next field or clump of trees. In the spring and fall, when the weather was at its worst, we'd often hike to the cliffs along the lake and climb, oblivious to the danger that the wet, slippery dirt afforded us. And, as we descended lower and lower, the icy spray from the waves, beating against the shore, warned us not to come any closer, lest we be soaked to the skin and face a long walk home chilled to the bone. But our adventurous spirits beckoned us to such places at the worst of times, and we returned again and again defying the odds.

In the winter, we'd often hike to Snake Swamp and carefully cross sections of it on the ice, hoping, with each step, that the ice would not break. Had the ice broken, sending us waist deep into the cold, dark, foreboding water, we were sure, we'd either freeze to death, or snakes would soon wrap themselves around our legs and slowly pull us under, snuffing out our last breaths. In either case, we'd be goners. Even in the face of such dangers, we continued going there and hiking across the perilous swamp. Lucky for us, the ice never broke, so we never experienced what our imaginations conjured up.

However, early one spring day as we trudged across some ice-covered muck, my left boot suddenly crashed through the ice and disappeared beneath the black, wet soil. Before I knew it, my leg was submerged above the top of my boot and sinking deeper. Pit, seeing what was happening, came to my rescue and with his help, I was eventually able to pull my leg out. However, my boot slid off my foot and remained under the muck. After a few choice words of disgust, I took my coat off, rolled up my shirt sleeve and knelt carefully on the ice. Bending over, I reached down into the icy-cold muck, searched a few seconds, felt my boot, grasped it as firmly as possible and slowly pulled it out. After a few more choice words, I cleaned my boot, my arm, and my hand the best I could. Then I put my boot back on my foot, trying to ignore the cold, wet feeling.

After rolling down my sleeve, putting on my coat, and buttoning it up, Pit and I headed for home. As we gingerly backtracked across the muck to the road, we agreed it was better, I had gone through the ice covering the muck than the ice covering the swamp, but this realization did not make walking in my left boot any more enjoyable.

Arriving home, I explained to Mrs. Pitluga why I was in the shape I was in. She smiled, told me to take off my dirty clothes and hop into the shower. By the time I had finished, my clothes were being laundered, and Pit had cleaned my boot inside and out, getting it ready for another day of hiking to the lake, the swamp, the muck, or wherever else we chose.

By the time we became teenagers, we were allowed to walk along route 104 to Bradway's General Store. Whenever we had money, we'd go there to buy candy, soda, and other goodies. Walking the same route going and coming, we soon knew who lived in each house by the name on each mailbox that lined the road.

One day we bought several sticks of black licorice. On the way home, we began spitting black saliva onto the road, pretending it was tobacco juice. As we had done so often in the past with regular spit, we soon realized that if we rolled our tongues up and fired, we could send our black spit quite a distance. Now that we had the ammo, we needed a target smaller than the road and soon found one, a mailbox several feet ahead of us. Looking at each other for approval, we nodded and slowed our pace, all the while getting a large dose of spit ready. Pit fired first, and I followed. His hit the target, slowly ran down the side of the box and dripped off. Mine missed and fell harmlessly on the dirt below the box. "Bull's-eye!" Pit exclaimed triumphantly as he smiled, baring his licorice-stained teeth. I slapped him on the back and spouted, "Nice going!"

As we continued walking, we continued our target practice, using a different mailbox each time. After each hit, we'd congratulate each other, pop more licorice into our mouths and continue priming our skills to higher and higher levels of accuracy. By the time we turned into his driveway, we had left several mailboxes behind with our calling cards dripping slowly off their bottoms and onto the ground below. In the days and weeks that followed, our accuracy increased to such a degree that boredom set in. Therefore, we began looking for a new thrill to occupy our time while walking to and from Bradway's.

One evening, as dusk was slowly giving way to darkness, Pit and I were returning from Bradway's. As we walked along the shoulder of the road, kicking small stones into the air, the new thrill that we were looking for suddenly emerged. Pit stopped, bent down, picked up a handful of small stones, then jumped into the dry, drainage ditch nearby, motioning for me to do the same. Once I joined him, Pit said, "Watch this."

Presently, a large truck came barreling down our side of the highway. As it passed, Pit flung his handful of stones at the side of the trailer, scoring several hits. However, before we felt the thrill of victory, we almost faced the agony of defeat. To our horror, the vehicle just behind the truck was a highway patrol car. Immediately, the officer slammed on his brakes and pulled onto the shoulder. At the same moment, I dropped my stones and we hightailed it across the field behind us, running as fast as our legs would move, and then jumped into a ditch some distance from the road.

As we crouched there, listening to our hearts pound, we were scared to death! After doing such a stupid thing, we were getting a thrill we never expected. Before we could catch our breath, the officer turned on his car's spotlight and was searching the field, slowly fanning the light back and forth. As the light passed over us, we held our breath in fear and hugged the bottom of the ditch. After what seemed like an eternity, the light was turned off and the car left. We didn't leave the ditch until it was out of sight, heading in the opposite direction that we had to walk. By then, we had regained our composure and our breath. Feeling it was now safe, we climbed out of the ditch and headed home, thankful we had escaped the agony of being arrested and who knows what else.

After such a frightfully close call, one would surely assume that we would have stopped throwing anything at any vehicles forever. Well, we did for quite some time. Then on a boring Saturday afternoon, we took four raw eggs from a carton in the refrigerator and headed toward route 104. Arriving, we stood at the top of a high, sloped bank overlooking the highway pass below. Partly concealed by hay, we waited until a tractor trailer came chugging slowly up the hill below and to the left of us. As it passed, we each threw an egg and both splattered on the side of the trailer. Then we crouched down amid the hay and congratulated each other. Soon another truck appeared, two more eggs flew through space and two more direct hits. Again we crouched and swapped smiles of satisfaction.

Now that we were out of ammo, we decided to hike through the woods on the other side of the highway. Our trail eventually led us to the outer edge of a harvested field, and there we spotted a pile of discarded, slightly damaged, ripe tomatoes. I don't recall who had the idea first, but soon we were backtracking and carrying several tomatoes. As we walked, the anticipation we felt was overwhelming. Tomatoes for ammo. Great!

Arriving back at our original position overlooking the highway, we took turns hurling our tomatoes at the sides of passing tractor trailers, panel trucks, and vans without a miss. When we finally exhausted our supply, we turned homeward, relishing the fun we had and agreeing that tomatoes were definitely the best ammunition yet.

Having an almost unlimited supply of tomatoes waiting for us, the next afternoon, we took two, large, heavy-duty paper bags to our "ammunition dump" and filled each. Then we headed to our "turret" overlooking the "enemy pass." After several hits, we decided the sides of trailers, panel trucks and vans were too large and trucks moved too slowly. We needed a smaller and faster target in order to improve our accuracy. So we chose the only other vehicles on the road, cars and station wagons. Thus, we began targeting them and soon found our percentage of hits rapidly decreasing.

However, these new targets increased our determination to improve our aim and accuracy over a period of time.

Late in the afternoon, one of us made a direct hit on a black station wagon. Shortly thereafter, as we were about to shoot at the next target, we saw two men running through the hay toward us. Since they were still some distance away, we turned in the opposite direction and began running for our lives. However, this time it was still light out, and there was no ditch to hide in.

As the distance between them and us narrowed, Pit and I came to a barbed wire fence about four and a half feet high. Without missing a stride, Pit grabbed the nearest wooden post and vaulted over the fence. In doing so, he caught the front of his shirt on the top strand of wire and ripped both his shirt and his flesh in the process. Ignoring his wound, he continued running to safety.

Being much shorter than Pit, I was not able to jump or climb the fence in the time I had. Therefore, I changed directions and ran along the fence, hoping to outrun my pursuers. But I was not that fast and soon found myself in the clutches of two very angry men. Had they been dragons, fire would have belched from their mouths several feet into the air, and I soon would have been burned to death. Lucky for me, they were not. Instead, angry phrases, punctuated with swear words, flowed from their mouths as they led me back to their parked vehicle on Hale Hill Road.

Once we arrived, I saw immediately that it was the black station wagon we had hit, and one tomato had splattered on the windshield, cutting the driver's visibility to near zero. Besides the two men, their wives and five children had been in the wagon. Sizing up the situation, I realized our little game could have been responsible for a serious accident, and who knows what the outcome would have been. No wonder the men and their wives were so shaken and angry.

When they asked my name and where I lived, I lied and gave them false information. However, when they decided to take me home and tell my parents, I recanted what I had told them and then lied a second time as to who I was and where I lived. Again they ordered me into their wagon, and again I recanted what I had told them. I was playing for time and praying that they'd eventually let me go. After all, I wasn't sure I could face Mom's anger and verbal abuse as I stood before her, guilty of such wrongdoings. Just as I was about to give them a third, fictitious name and address, Pit yelled from a distance, "Furman, are you all right?"

Immediately my cover was blown. They now knew my last name, and it wouldn't take them long to find out where I lived. Seeing the odds piled against me, I tried the only other method of escape I knew. I began to cry and while doing so, I apologized for what I had done and promised I'd never do it again if they let me go. The men never budged in their determination to take me home. However, the women did, and they soon persuaded their husbands to release me, since they felt I was sincere in my apology and promise. By the time I was running out of tears, one of the men chewed me out some more and warned me again of the dangers of such folly. Then they set me free.

I turned and ran down Hale Hill Road toward the Pitlugas. When I had put a safe distance between us, I turned and looked back. They were still outside their wagon, cleaning their windshield. Venting my pent-up emotion, I yelled one, long, derogative sentence filled with obscenities. Then I ran toward Pit's house, meeting him on the way.

Once home safe and sound, Pit's mom accepted his story as to how his shirt and flesh got torn. Then she doctored the long wound with iodine, a most painful remedy, but he took it like a man and never said a word.

Once his mom finished, we went to his room, and I filled him in on all the details of my short, but frightening, incarceration. After hearing me out, he and I decided never to do such a potentially dangerous thing again. We had had some fun and excitement, but we now realized that it was a foolish way to entertain ourselves. Thus, we never again returned to our "ammunition dump." However, we did return to our "turret" a few times and stood there, recalling the enjoyment it had afforded us.

Chapter VIII
Three Memorable Casts

By the time late spring of 1949 came along, I had given up my paper route and returned to a new job with the Mulcaheys. By now, I had climbed three steps up their "corporate ladder." My first job, a few seasons earlier, consisted of cleaning up around the outside of the fish fry stand and the adjoining parking areas. Each day for fifty cents, I picked up discarded paper plates, napkins, empty soda and beer bottles and other debris and deposited it into barrels for burning or into empty bottle racks. From that job, I moved up the ladder and began cutting grass and weeding flower beds around Mulcahey's Cabins by the Lake and earned fifty cents an hour. Then, on rung three, I was working in their ice-cream stand for fifty cents an hour. In a year or two, I would climb the final step and work in their fish fry stand and earn a whopping sixty cents an hour. Since each of these jobs was seasonal, and Mom always needed as much money as I could earn, I worked more than forty hours each week, except the year I cleaned around the stand.

One Saturday in September, since my hours had been cut at the stand, I had time to pick pears at an orchard in Fruit Valley. I spent much of the day standing on a wooden ladder, reaching for the fruit on the higher branches, and praying that the rickety ladder would not break, sending me flying. By the end of the day, I was exhausted. However, I had given my employer an honest day's work for an honest day's pay and was satisfied with the ten dollars I earned.

During the afternoon, my left foot began to ache. By the end of the day, it ached severely. Not wanting to worry Mom, I did not mention it when I returned home and gave her the money. I figured it would stop hurting in a day or two, and it did but not for long.

After that Saturday, the first time I wore sneakers at my scout meeting, the pain returned. By the time the meeting had ended, and I walked home, my left foot was killing me! Just before going to bed, I put some Mennen aftershave lotion on it, hoping the cooling effect would help deaden the pain until I fell asleep, and it soon did. However, as I lay there, I knew something was wrong, very wrong with my foot, but what?

This ailment continued, but the resulting pain did not stop me from wearing sneakers to the scout meetings, at the YMCA, in gym at school during physical education classes, and wherever else sneakers were required. Whenever I arrived home in agony, I'd kill the pain with aftershave and fall asleep. Believe me, I had the best smelling foot in the school.

One day, while sitting in the library, I happened to read an article in a sports magazine. The article talked about sprains and stressed the importance of having any sprain, especially sprained ankles, cared for immediately or face a more serious ailment in the future. After finishing the article, I thought back to the fall of 1946, when I injured my foot playing football. I must have sprained my left ankle and was paying for it now, since I hadn't received medical attention then.

However, at the time of the injury, I knew Mom would get very upset if I came into the house on crutches with my foot bandaged and told her I had sprained my ankle. She would have ranted and raved about the medical bills to pay, who'd care for me, my inability to help with the chores, Corky having to do them alone and on and on and on. So, I didn't go to the school nurse and have my ankle cared for. Now I was paying the price.

Eventually, Corky told Mom about my foot, and how I'd use aftershave to deaden the pain. Mom never mentioned much about it to me until one day, she informed me that I had an appointment to have my foot examined at the free medical clinic in town. Since I had been suffering with this pain for over six months, I was relieved that she finally knew and had made the appointment.

I went alone to the clinic across from the high school. When my turn came, I was ushered into a room and soon an orthopedic doctor appeared. During his examination, I informed him about my football injury in 1946, about my picking pears in 1949 and the terrible pain that ensued from being on the ladder that day. He listened attentively, asked some related questions and made another appointment for me the following week. Before leaving, X rays were taken, and the nurse gave me a white appointment card and requested that Mom come with me. When I arrived home, I repeated everything the doctor had told me while Mom cupped her ear with one hand and leaned forward to hear every word I spoke.

The doctor's oral report was given to Mom and me the following week at the clinic. The X rays confirmed what he had suspected after his initial examination of my foot. In brief, he reported the foot was damaged and needed to be placed in a plaster of paris cast for six months to correct as much of the damage as possible. When Mom heard this, she looked concerned. However, once we learned we would incur no medical bills, her countenance changed, and a date was set to have the cast put on.

The Monday morning of my Easter vacation week, 1950, a neighbor drove Mom and me to the University Hospital in Syracuse, and I was admitted. As I lay in bed, waiting for the operation to take place, I had mixed emotions. On the one hand, I was finally getting my foot corrected. On the other hand, the annual youth basketball tournament was beginning that day, and I would miss it. I played on the Senecas, and we were favored to win the intermediate-level championship. Only now, I wouldn't be a part of it. Once again, I resigned myself to the fact that if it "wasn't for bad luck, I'd have no luck at all."

All went well in the operating room. When I woke up in my bed afterwards, I saw a cast covering the area of my leg below my knee and my foot except for my toes. The area of my cast below my foot was thicker than the rest. I learned later, this thickness, plus a rubber heel attached to it, would allow me to walk on the cast after a few days on crutches.

During my first, unsteady walk down the hall on my crutches, I peered into several rooms and saw others wearing casts on various parts of their bodies. After seeing one little girl, who was almost covered with plaster of paris and lying in a prone position, I didn't feel so sorry for myself for missing the tournament. Only one part of my body needed correcting, not several, as in that little girl's case. On my return trip, I stopped in and talked to her. I could tell by her laughter that she enjoyed our chat, and I left, exhilarated.

On the day I was discharged, I caught all the correct buses and arrived back in Oswego just as Mr. Dowie pulled up in front of the bus station to take me home. En route, I filled him in on all the details of my brief stay in the hospital, including my visit with the girl encased in plaster. As I thanked him and prepared to get out of his car, he said to me, "Bud, no matter what your circumstances, there's always someone worse off than you. Remember that." And I have.

Several days later, I kicked the crutches aside and began walking on my cast. Life almost returned to normal. In a short time, my cast was covered with writing, some of it was positive and some was negative, some was clean and some was dirty, but I couldn't tell the inscribers what to write. I just made sure Mom never spent much time reading it.

Before I knew it, six months had passed, and I was on the bus to Syracuse to have the cast removed. Arriving, I waited until my name was called then followed the nurse to a large room and sat down. Soon my doctor entered and after a few words of chit chat, he lifted a saw off a table, took a position on a chair in front of me, placed my leg in the position he wanted and began cutting. Soon the cast came off in two pieces and fell to the floor.

As I looked at my shriveled-up lower leg and foot, fear came over me. Shaking inwardly, I asked myself, "Is that the way my leg and foot will look forever?" Before I could ask the doctor the same question and others, he was checking my foot, nodding up and down as he did so. Finished, he looked at me, smiled and then began speaking. He soon answered my unasked questions and gave me a few instructions that would help to keep the foot as normal as possible.

When he finished, I thanked him, rose to my feet to leave and began walking toward the door. As I did so, every time I took a step with my right foot and prepared to take one with my left, I raised my leg way up in the air before setting it down. Walking this way embarrassed me, so I returned to the room and asked the doctor why I was doing it. He smiled and assured me it would not last. He called it learned behavior.

Since I had been walking for six months with a heavy cast on my left leg and foot and exerting much more muscle power to lift that leg with each step, it became part of my behavior. Now that the cast was gone, I would continue the behavior until I unlearned it. In the meantime, I would walk in that manner, automatically lifting the left leg into the air before setting the foot down. His final words were, "Don't worry, Dave, the goose step will cure itself in time." And, in time, it did, but until that occurred, I was one embarrassed walker.

By the time my cast had been removed in early November, I had completed my junior year of high school, had worked long hours all summer and early fall as a cook in Mulcahey's Fish Fry stand and was now two months into my senior year. Like many high school seniors, I was overly involved with too many activities and often struggled to keep my head above water. But in the back of my mind, I knew a list of all these activities would take up a lot of space under my senior picture in the yearbook, the *Paradox*, as well as make an impressive addition to any college applications I filled out.

To keep the wrath-of-Mom from falling on me, I continued to maintain an honor roll average. In my heart, I knew I could do much better scholastically. I had done so during my first two years, but the desire had slowly died, due to Mom's comments, each time I'd bring my report cards home.

In those first two years, I'd usually bring home four ninety-fives and one ninety covering my five major courses. Proudly, I'd hand Mom the cards expecting to be congratulated for doing so well. However, she'd look at the cards, then at me, and say, "These grades are good, but why isn't that ninety a ninety-five?" By the end of my sophomore year, I had much less desire to excel academically, except to make the honor roll, not only for her sake, but more, for mine.

In the end, I would graduate tenth in my class of two hundred eighteen and feel satisfied. However, Mom let me know several times that I could have graduated first or second in my class, had I studied harder. Little did she know, she was the main reason I hadn't.

Thanksgiving vacation that year was extra long and extra special. Pit and I were allowed to miss a few days of school before vacation officially began. Thus, on Monday, we traveled by train to New York City to visit his grandparents. Dr. and Mrs. Linton lived in Manhattan on Morningside Drive near Columbia University, where he taught. Besides our visits to Central Park, our days were full of activity.

On Tuesday morning, since Pit had a lot of talent and was considering a career in commercial art, Dr. Linton took us to the well-known and highly respected Pratt Institute. He felt Pit could look the place over as a potential school to get his training.

We arrived, sat through certain formalities with the admissions officer and were then given a tour of the facilities.

Just about the time I was beginning to get bored, our guide opened the door to yet another classroom, allowing us to observe these students and their work. I looked at the almost completed painting on the first easel and saw a beautiful, nude, blond-haired woman. Keeping my eyes glued to his work, I watched in awe as the student continued, adding a dab of paint here, a dab there, and so forth. Finally, I moved to another easel, and my eyes fell on another painting of a beautiful, nude woman, only this one was dark and lying on her side. Having never seen paintings of nude women before, I stood motionless, as in a trance, enjoying what I saw. As Pit's poke jolted me back to reality, he pointed subtly in two different directions. I looked both ways and saw the two nude models that were being painted. Being very naive at seventeen and having never seen naked women before, my mouth fell open, my eyes bulged, and I became sexually aroused, as I stared at each model, first one then the other and back again.

Minutes later, our tour continued, but nothing I saw on the rest of it could compare to that class. Now I could see why Pit was leaning toward art school, and I couldn't blame him one bit. Had I his talent, I would too.

Wednesday we spent the day marveling at the countless exhibits in both the Museum of Natural History and the Metropolitan Museum of Art. We filled our minds with as much science and art as they could absorb but realized, we would need to spend several days in each to really see everything thoroughly.

Thanksgiving Day we stood with thousands of other as the Macy's Parade slowly passed by, band after band, giant balloon after giant balloon, float after float, until the last band signaled the end. Tired and hungry, we were truly thankful for the delicious dinner that awaited us upon our return home. However, once we had eaten and were revitalized, Pit and I walked around Harlem, without fear, and later took in a movie before returning home.

The next morning the Lintons had more exciting plans for us two hayseeds from Oswego. Undaunted by the threat of a storm hitting New York City later that day, Dr. Linton, Pit and I rode the now infamous subway to Battery Park, paid the five-cent fare and boarded the Staten Island Ferry. A ride to and from Staten Island would give us a chance to see the historic Statue of Liberty; Ellis Island, the gateway to America for countless immigrants in times past; the famous Manhattan skyline, and other sights in the Upper Bay.

The ferry plowed through gusty winds and choppy waters and finally reached its destination. We debarked, walked into the terminal, looked at the schedule board to see when the next ferry would return to Manhattan and headed for the correct embarkation pier. As we walked, we looked out some windows and saw the beginning of a storm as waves beat against pilings and the ferries began to rock. Soon an announcement came over the loudspeakers, telling everyone the storm that had been working its way up the coast, had arrived, and its fury would lash the area for several hours. Therefore, no ferries would operate until the storm passed.

Resigned to our fate, we stood looking out windows and watched the dark, ominous clouds, the rain beating against the panes, and the huge waves, driven by the high winds, batter the piers and ferries unmercifully. Soon the electricity went off, leaving us, with so many others, stranded in a dark terminal with no way to escape.

As the storm raged on through the afternoon, Dr. Linton became more and more concerned for his wife. Not being able to phone her, he knew that she would be sitting at home alone worrying about our well-being. We shared his concern, but there was nothing we could do to alleviate it.

Eventually, Dr. Linton expressed a second concern to us. It was a surprise, but one in danger of not coming to pass, so he told us. He had gotten tickets for all of us to see the long-running, Broadway play, *Mister Roberts*, starring Henry Fonda, that evening. Unless the storm subsided soon, allowing the ferries to resume service, we would miss this treat.

From that moment on, both Pit and I offered up silent prayers. We prayed that the storm would soon pass, allowing the ferries to resume service in time for us to make the opening curtain for the play.

Don't tell me that God doesn't answer prayers. He answered ours and five minutes before the curtain was due to rise, we settled into our seats at the Alvin Theater, ready to be entertained.

And entertained we were. I laughed and laughed. At the end, I joined everyone else and gave the cast a standing ovation.

It always amazes me how time flies when you're having fun. Before we knew it, Pit and I were on a train heading back to Oswego. As we sat watching the scenery pass by, we relived verbally our many adventures in New York City and vowed to return for more.

Unknown to us at the time, the storm, packing hurricane winds over one hundred six miles per hour, lashed the entire area east of the Appalachians from Maryland to Massachusetts. In the East, the wind storm raised tidal waves, ripped houses apart, overturned cars, blew small craft onto beaches, destroyed power and phone lines, wrecked planes and hangars, and silenced radio and TV stations. It was called the greatest land storm on record in the northeast United States. It covered twenty-two midwestern and eastern states, killed two hundred ninety-five people and did an estimated four hundred million dollars worth of damage. The storm's fingers reached into upstate New York, bringing havoc to rural areas, quiet little towns, and cities. However, on Monday morning, schools in Oswego were open as usual even though the cleanup was continuing.

When I walked into my trigonometry class, my teacher, Miss Glann, was not there to greet us as she always did. I took my seat and looked at the side chalkboard. Sure enough, there was her new proverb for the week, "Good, better, best; never let them rest, till your good is better and your better, best!" I took out a pencil, copied it down on a sheet of paper containing several other proverbs from past weeks and waited for her to appear. Soon after the bell rang, another teacher came into the room, announced that Miss Glann was absent, and said we could use the time to study. Having been out for three days prior to the vacation period, I copied a friend's trig. notes, then sat there studying them.

The next day, Miss Glann returned, but she seemed very upset. Finally, she could contain herself no longer and told us what was bothering her. She had gone away for the vacation period, could not get back on time due to the road conditions and, thus, had to miss her first day of teaching in over thirty-seven years. And this bothered her? What dedication!

As spring approached, so did the tryouts for the senior play, "We Shook the Family Tree." As a lark, some of my friends and I auditioned, figuring none of us would ever land a part. A few days later, Edith Dell posted the list of cast members and a schedule of rehearsals outside her room. I passed by, saw the list, and stopped to scan it. When I reached the fourth name, I paused. It was mine, and it was next to the name of a major character in the play.

Immediately, feelings of grandeur surged through my body. I was going to be a star! I, David Furman, the only kid in high school who wore the same clothes everyday. The person known as "four eyes" to some classmates, "Red" to others and "Finney" to a few, was destined for greatness! I looked again to make sure my name was really there. Then I headed down the hall, head up, shoulders back, and a lilt to my step.

At first the rehearsals were boring, and I asked myself many times, "What are you doing here?" But as we learned more and more of our lines, my boredom evolved into elation, and acting really turned me on. As the final dress rehearsals approached, the cast became a little apprehensive, but a pep talk by Miss Dell calmed our nerves.

In one scene of the play, I was supposed to come into the house, holding a large fish by the tail behind my back, approach my mother excitedly and spout out a line similar to, "See what I caught fishing," and immediately produce the large fish, holding it up near her face. During the dress rehearsals, I used a realistic-looking, cardboard fish. However, late in the afternoon of opening night, I stopped by a local fish market in town and talked the owner into giving me an uncleaned fish about two feet long. He wrapped it in white, butcher paper, handed it to me and remarked, "Knock 'em dead!" When I arrived at the school's auditorium, I hid the package behind the stage and told no one about it.

The play was going well, and soon that particular scene began. When it came time for me to enter, I did so. Holding the fish behind my back, I excitedly approached my mother, blurted out my line and produced the fish, holding it as close to her face as possible. Startled, she screamed, jumped back and almost fainted. Of course the audience, thinking it was all part of the play, burst into prolonged laughter, and I enjoyed every second of it. However, I could tell by the look my mother gave me, once she recomposed herself, that if looks could kill, I'd be a dead man. Even so, my prank would have been worth it.

Once the laughter died down, the play continued to its conclusion. Once the final curtain closed and the applause ceased, I hurried to the boys' dressing room and celebrated with all the other guys. As we removed our makeup and changed our clothes, we agreed the play was a success.

Soon we were headed for the cast party to continue the celebration. Soon after arriving, my mother, Claire Downes headed my way. Since there was no place for me to run, I stood my ground but feared for my life. She came as close to me as possible, looked me square in the eye, and without the slightest smile, snarled, "I should have known, you'd pull a stunt like that." Seeing the hurt on her face, I melted and apologized. She accepted, we hugged each other and remained good friends.

Even though I enjoyed acting in that play, and the excitement I felt on stage, I never seriously considered acting as a career. After all, according to my Campus School and high school yearbooks, my ambition was to become a surgeon. In the years that followed, I became neither an actor nor a surgeon, but a teacher.

Early in my teaching career, I realized a successful teacher must often be a good actor and assume many different roles in order to motivate his students to learn. And when his students do learn and absorb more than anyone expected them to, a teacher's reward is far more satisfying than the applause given to an actor in the live theater. For a teacher's reward is eternal, while an actor's reward is only temporary.

Chapter IX
Cars, Freedom and the Price I Paid for Both

It was a '37 Ford, two-door beauty. Outside, it was white. Inside, the decor was red including red-plaid seat covers. The entire car was in mint condition.

I was a senior soon to graduate from high school in 1951. My dream car sat in front of a small, candy store-luncheonette across the street from my school. The owner of the luncheonette also owned the car. For almost four years, I had walked past that car at least twice everyday when school was in session. And many, many times, I stopped and admired it, inside and out. One day in the fall of my senior year, I told the owner how much I liked his car, and that I would be interested in buying it, if ever he decided to sell. He listened, but his answer didn't give me much hope of ever owning it. But day by day, I'd admire the car anyway as I walked by.

One day in April, I was in the luncheonette buying some candy. The owner came over to me and said he wanted to see me in his "office." We sat in the last booth near the rear of his store. With a little small talk out of the way, he got right to the point. He told me he had begun some door-to-door selling of cleaning products, and his two-door car was not handy for his new adventure. He needed a four-door car with a trunk. Therefore, did I still want to buy his present car? You bet I did, but I didn't let him know how much I wanted to. I acted cool and after the negotiations ended, I had agreed to buy it for one hundred fifty dollars. A handshake cemented our deal, As I walked back to school, I leaped into the air three times as a sign of victory and joy similar to what people do today in certain foreign automobile commercials on TV. I was going to get my dream car! Hallelujah! I leaped again.

That evening at home, Mom made it clear she was not in favor of my buying this car or any car. So we had quite a verbal battle. Finally, I said I was going to buy it, whether she liked it or not. After all, I was working and making money. "But," she argued back, "you're working to earn money for college. A car will keep you broke." At that point, her words were falling on deaf ears. I wanted that car, and I was going to have it.

Two weeks later, I walked into the luncheonette with my payment and came out with the keys and bill of sale. Next, I walked to the Motor Vehicle Office, plunked down the fee and received my license plates. Back to my car and soon the plates were bolted on. Now only three things remained to be done. The first was to learn to drive a car. The second was to get my driver's license. The third was to get auto insurance.

The summer before, a friend named Bob gave me a one-hour driving lesson in his 1938 Packard. Since then, I had no other lessons. Now I owned my dream car, and I had to drive it three miles home through much of Oswego and then out a two-lane road along Lake Ontario. Both Bob's Packard and my Ford had floor shifts, so I knew a little about shifting.

I sat in my car quite awhile getting up my nerve to start the engine and face the unknown for three, long miles. Finally, I turned the key and the car lurched quickly forward and stopped. I turned ashen. Luckily, there were no cars parked in front of me, so no damage was done. In a few moments, I realized I had failed to push in the clutch before turning the key.

After calming down, try number two began. I pushed in the clutch, held my breath, turned the key and started the car. Once I knew the street was completely clear of other moving cars, I slowly pulled away from the curb and headed home. It was not a smooth ride but one more like riding a bucking bronco, especially whenever I had to shift. But slowly I covered the three miles, and once I was safely in the driveway, everyone, including Mom "oh'd" and "ah'd" over my dream car. I was on cloud nine.

After work that night at the stand, Jack Mulcahey, the owner's son, agreed to give me a driving lesson. From 1:00–2:00 A.M., he instructed me while drinking bottles of beer in the passenger's seat. Other lessons followed, and two weeks later, I took and passed my driver's test and received my license.

I loved my car! It ran well. It gave me the freedom to come and go as I pleased. It allowed me to sleep later on school days since I didn't have to be up early to catch the school bus. It meant no more walking or hitchhiking to town or home from town. And I could take Mom shopping and let her select her own vegetables, fruit and meat, a welcomed relief for me.

The only problem I had was the braking system. The car had mechanical brakes, not hydraulic as cars do today. Mechanical brakes did not stop a car as fast as hydraulic brakes do even when new, and mine were far from new. Second, when the emergency brake was pulled on, the brake pedal was pulled to the floor. Both were on the same system. Third, there was very little drag, if a car was driven while the emergency brake was on, and the brake pedal pulled to the floor.

One day in May, even though my brakes needed an overhaul, which I couldn't afford at the time, three friends and I decided to take the afternoon off from school and drive to Syracuse. It was my first time at playing hooky, but it was such a beautiful, spring day, I couldn't resist. We had a pleasant ride there and had fun in the city cruising the streets. However, by 3:30, we headed home, since I had to be at work by 5:00.

I was cruising north on route 57 between Syracuse and Fulton. The four of us were singing and having a ball. All of a sudden, a long line of traffic somewhat ahead of us quickly slowed down. I put on my brakes, but I didn't quickly slow down. I kept moving closer and closer toward the first car ahead of us. As we got nearer and nearer, Pit had his door open and was ready to jump. My two friends in the back seat just sat there, hands over their faces, waiting for the crash. Me? I looked quickly to see if any traffic was coming the other way. None was, so at the last moment, I pulled into the oncoming lane and passed the first three cars to my right, before my car finally stopped. Then I pulled back into the north lane and continued the trip home. By the time we arrived in Oswego, my body had stopped shaking, but my first-ever undershorts were a bit soiled.

The day after our jaunt, we were called into the vice-principal's office. An English teacher, who knew all of us, saw us drive back into Oswego and turned us in. Our pleas for mercy went unheeded as Miss Cullen gave each of us one hour of "jail" each day after school for a week. She was a tough, old bird, so we accepted our punishment and served our time.

Needless to say, I had the brakes fixed a few days later. I also decided it was time to buy auto insurance. It was costly, but not as costly as an accident would be. I paid $186 a year for $5,000–$10,000 liability and $5,000 property damage. Mom was right. My car was keeping me broke.

The remaining weeks of high school quickly passed, and graduation night arrived in late June. It was a hot, very humid night, and without air conditioning, the auditorium reeked with sweaty bodies, especially those wearing caps and gowns. Even though I thought the ceremony would never end, it finally did, and freedom for me had arrived in another realm.

After taking Mom home, I picked up my friend, Neil, and our dates: his steady girlfriend and her sister. A party, we were to attend, was in

Minetto, a few miles away. We headed out the Fifth Street Road. We were about halfway there, when it began to rain, then pour. My headlights searched out the road, and my windshield wipers did their best to clear a path for me to see. Even though driving became very difficult, we kept moving.

To get to the party, I knew there was another road we had to take that went left, off the road we were on. So I began straining my eyes watching for it. Finally, I thought I saw it, so I made a left turn. The rain continued to pour down.

A few seconds after my turn, I noticed muddy water on my windshield and in the air. I remarked to Neil, "I don't remember this road being dirt, do you?" He said he didn't and neither did the girls. Had I turned onto the wrong road?

I was still moving slowly forward, when the headlights, piercing the darkness and rain, pointed out some weeds then the side of a barn. "My gosh," I thought, "Where am I?" The answer came quickly. I hadn't made a full left turn, and I was driving through a field heading for someone's barn! Panic time inside, keep cool outside. My brain said, "Keep moving, don't stop now. There's a way out of this at the barn." So I kept cool and hoped my date plus the couple in back wouldn't see my hands shaking on the steering wheel.

An eternity later, I thought, I saw a dirt driveway leading to the barn, so I made a slight turn and headed for it. I was correct, and soon we were on the long, dirt driveway heading toward Fifth Street Road. Everyone began breathing normally again.

Neil and the girls couldn't believe that we made it through that field in the rain. We wouldn't have if the snow tires, that were on the car when I bought it, weren't still on it.

This time with the rain abating a little, we made the correct turns and soon arrived at the party. As we got out of the car, we could see evidence of our detour everywhere. I hoped the rain would continue to wash it away. When we returned to the car hours later, it had.

June faded into July. I quit my job at the stand and went to work on a construction job for more money. I operated a jack hammer for a few days and then pushed wheelbarrows full of concrete from concrete trucks to the construction area. It was hot and humid, and the work was very physical, but I stuck to it.

Evenings and weekends I enjoyed my car, my friends, and the activities available to us: swimming, tennis, cruising and movies. Little money was saved, so I decided not to go to college that fall, much to the chagrin of Mom. However, I promised her I'd go the following fall, and that appeased her somewhat. Once that decision was made, I was free to continue enjoying life, only more so. However, the construction job was taking its toll on me physically. I was losing a lot of weight and not getting enough sleep to keep up the pace expected of me, so I quit.

The following Monday morning, another friend and I decided to drive to Fulton and seek employment at a company that made paper and paper products. At the edge of Oswego I stopped at a gas station, pulled my emergency brake on, got gas, checked the oil and put water into the radiator. After paying, we headed for Fulton. It was a beautiful summer day, and the ride along the Oswego River added to the beauty.

As we approached Minetto, we began climbing a gentle hill behind another car. Without warning, a farm tractor, pulling a farm machine of some sort, pulled out onto the road and into our lane heading in the same direction that we were. The car ahead slowed rapidly, and I, too, put on my brakes, only I didn't have any. My pedal was to the floor, since I had forgotten to release my emergency brake before leaving the station.

I quickly looked to my right at the ditch along the road and saw three boys playing in it. Then I quickly looked to my left and the other lane. A bus was coming. So I gripped the wheel, saw my life flash in front of my eyes, and my dream car rammed into the rear of the car in front, pushing it into the farm machine. The entire incident took only a few seconds.

We all stopped, got out and looked. My car was ruined! The radiator was bashed in, the fenders badly damaged, the bumper ruined and the headlights broken. The other car and farm machine weren't too damaged, and no one was hurt.

After exchanging the necessary data, the others left, leaving my friend and me with a car unable to move under its own power. We pushed the car onto the shoulder of the road, walked to a nearby house, called my friend, Bob, and waited for him to come in his Packard to tow my dream car home. While waiting, it's hard to describe how badly I felt over my loss, but anyone who has been in similar circumstances would understand.

That afternoon, I contacted my insurance company with the bad news. Several days later, my insurance man told me the other driver collected for every dent he had in his car and not just for the damage I had caused. I felt badly about this, but I was only eighteen and a high risk to insurance companies. Thus, the older driver got what he wanted, since I rear-ended his car. I got nothing but heartache.

At the time I didn't realize my car could have been repaired cheaply using parts from a junk car dealer near Fulton. However, a student, majoring in industrial arts at the college, did. Only he didn't tell me. Instead he gave me a big line about how much it would cost to repair the car and offered me nine dollars to "take it off my hands." Like a sucker, I took his offer. He towed it to the auto mechanics shop at the college, bought used parts, put them on and then painted the entire car. Once he finished, the car looked like new.

For the next two years, I often saw it here and there around town. Every time I did so, I got a lump in my throat. That was the only dream car I ever owned. I couldn't bear the pain of having another.

MY MAFIA CAR

A couple of days after I smashed up my Ford, I landed a job at the plant in Fulton. I rode with another employee from Oswego and paid him for doing so. The rest of the time, I returned to walking and hitchhiking. One day in August, I was out joy-riding with Bob in his '38 Packard. I was telling him how miserable I felt without a car. He interrupted me and said he would soon be returning to Cornell University for his senior year and, since he could no longer afford his car, did I want to buy it. I didn't give him an answer that day. However, I eventually bought it for $135, partly because he needed to sell it, and partly because I needed a car.

My "new" car was a large, heavy, four-door one with a powerful eight cylinder engine and a large trunk. It was black outside and inside. It had running boards and a wheel well in each of the front fenders for spare tires. It was a true Mafia car if ever there was one. And, to top it off, it would cruise at seventy miles per hour with no strain on the engine.

My friends and I enjoyed riding in this car more than in the Ford. There was more room, the seats were more comfortable, and it gave us a smooth ride even on the bumpiest roads. However, it took more gas, and it burned oil, taking even more money out of my pocket. Would I ever get to college?

One late afternoon on my way home, I was passing another car on route 104. Like most roads in those days, it was only two lanes wide. Suddenly, a car ran a stop sign, pulled out from a road ahead of me on the left and began making a right turn in my direction. Before I could complete my pass and get out of the car's way, it hit my left rear fender with its front bumper. I stopped and the other driver stopped. He was more upset than I, and began shouting that it was my fault, my fault! However, he denied having run the stop sign.

Once we finally swapped the required data, I returned to Oswego, made one report out at the police station and another at my insurance office. Several days later, I learned from my insurance agent that the other driver had no insurance and, more important, had recently been released from a mental institution. Therefore, he suggested I not pursue a claim against the man.

Being a stubborn German, I didn't listen to his advice. One day, while one of my uncles was visiting our home, he and I drove to where the other driver lived near Fulton in an old, run-down house with an unkempt lawn and junk all around. I was determined to talk to him, and, if possible, get some compensation for my dented fender. My uncle stayed in the car and waited for me. He was my back-up man in case I needed him.

I walked to the front door, knocked loudly and waited. Presently the door opened and there he stood—dirty, unshaven, and half dressed. He invited me in. The house looked worse than he did. Once he shut the door, I knew I was a prisoner in his domain, and my bravery began to wane.

However, he was pleasant, so I began to relax and sat in his kitchen talking with him. Our chit chat soon turned to the accident and whose fault it was. I don't recall everything we said to each other. However, I remember making the comment, "You probably didn't stop at the stop sign, because your brakes were worn out." I no sooner got those words out of my mouth, when he went berserk ending our discussion.

He jumped up, walked to a drawer near the sink, pulled out a large butcher knife, turned and headed my way. I jumped to my feet, dashed through the living room and was out the door in seconds, all the while calling to my uncle for help. Luckily, the man didn't follow me out the door but continued cursing at me and waving his knife, as I ran to my car and jumped in. There sat my back-up man, legs stretched out, head back against the seat, eyes closed, listening to the radio and oblivious to my shouts and to what had just happened. Some back-up man! I could have been killed, and there he sat!

I did not pursue the matter further. However, I did report what happened to the proper authorities and a couple of months later, I was informed that my attacker had been readmitted to the same institution. After hearing this, I breathed a little easier.

Except for two months, when I was away, I enjoyed my Packard until the following spring. In early June, I discovered it had a cracked block, and the cost to repair it was more than I could afford to pay. So I sold it to a fellow for twelve dollars. Cars were definitely keeping me broke.

MY MIRACLE CAR

When I sold the Packard, I was working at Marathon and needed another car to get to work, so I bought a 1941 Chevrolet four-door sedan. It ran well, did not burn oil and drank less gas than the Packard. However, it didn't have the room, the comfort or the class the Packard did. It was just a plain, old, dependable Chevy.

As the summer of 1952 wore on, I realized I couldn't attend Hamilton College due to a lack of money, so I enrolled at the state college in Oswego. I attended classes days and worked 3:30–11:30 P.M. at the plant. Thus, my car was now more of a necessity and less of a luxury. This realization changed my whole outlook on cars; an outlook I still have today. I've given up the desire to own a Mercedes, Rolls Royce, or B.M.W. Just give me a car that runs well, is comfortable to drive and economical, and I'm happy.

Some important events occurred in my life that year, leading me to transfer to Providence Bible Institute in the fall of 1953. I drove the four hundred miles to Providence, Rhode Island without incident. My three passengers and I, plus all our luggage, fit into the car. Considering two of my passengers were girls, I called that a miracle.

I left a college that cost little to attend, and a job that paid well, to attend a school that cost much more, and jobs that paid much less. So I had to make a tight budget and stick to it. My budget limited my use of my car even though gas cost only seventeen cents a gallon.

Two new friends I made at the college were Dick Thomassian and Larry Doyle, both upper classmen. Both had steady girls, but none of the four had a car. So the two fellows would often borrow mine on a weekend night and double date. The next morning, I would notice that the gas tank was full. This tank of gas would last me until they borrowed my car again, and then I'd have another full tank to use. I know how much they appreciated using my car, but I doubt they ever knew how much I appreciated their using my car. They kept me in oil and gas almost all of that year.

My second year, I lived on the Barrington campus, where all sophomores were housed. However, I still had some classes at the

Providence campus about seven miles away. Every time I knew I was going to the other campus, I'd put my name on the message chalkboard by the switchboard in case other students were in need of a ride to the other campus. Usually there were, and I'd take them. However, no one ever offered me any money. I soon realized I was becoming a free taxi service, something I couldn't afford.

To correct the situation, I made a small sign and taped it on the back of the front seat for all riders to see. It stated, "This car runs on faith plus gas. I furnish the faith. Guess what part you play?" From then on, every rider got the message and contributed freely. Their donations got me through the second year as far as gas and oil were concerned. But I still had to find ways to pay for other auto expenses, since most of the money I earned at my jobs went toward paying my college bill.

Late that October, I learned that my car's rear axle needed to be replaced. All the money I had at the time was an unknown amount in a jar into which I tossed my loose change each night when emptying my pockets. The garage owner, where I took the car, promised he'd try to buy a used axle, put it on and trust me for the cost until I could pay him. He did as he promised and called me when the car was ready. I took my jar to the garage with me, planning on paying part of the bill from its contents. I can't recall the exact amount of the bill, but it was somewhere between twenty-five and thirty dollars. I do recall, however, opening the jar and counting its contents. When I finished counting every last penny, I had the exact amount of the bill, nothing more, nothing less. Some people would call that a coincidence, some a miracle. I called it God providing for my needs.

Later that year, I had a problem with my taillights. They weren't working. My friend, Anthony, a fellow with more nerve than know-how, convinced me he could fix them. In doing so, he put a toggle switch on the dashboard and hooked the taillights and dashboard lights together. Thus, one flip of the switch, and I had both. "Great job, Anthony!" I said when he finished.

A few days later, I was on my way to see a sick friend some miles from the college. As it got dark, I put on my lights. It was then I noticed how bright the dash lights were. As they were connected to the toggle switch, I couldn't dim them. To solve the problem, I reached over and shut off the switch, killing both the dash and taillights. Since there was so little traffic on the road, I assumed it would be safe to drive without taillights.

I was singing and having a good time as I drove. All of a sudden, I saw trooper's lights in my rear view mirror. I pulled off the road, he pulled in behind me. I knew why he stopped me. He got out of his car and began walking toward my door. Once he passed the rear of my car, I quickly reached over and pushed the toggle switch to the on position.

As he arrived, I rolled my window down, gave him a cheery greeting, and waited for him to respond. Once he had my license and registration, he asked in a stern, official voice, "Do you know you have no taillights?" I responded, "Really? Are you sure? I wasn't aware of that." Then he answered back, "I didn't see any, but, just a minute, I'll check again." As he walked to the rear, I smiled a smug little smile to myself and murmured, "You're bad, Furman, really bad." When he reappeared at my window, he reported, "You have lights now. There's probably a short in the system." Then he wrote out a warning ticket, explained what I had to do, gave everything to me and left.

According to the ticket, I had to have the problem corrected, have the ticket signed by the person who did the repair, and then mail it back to his station. I knew Anthony would sign it with pleasure. He enjoyed putting his name on anything where people could see it. Shortly after arriving back on campus, Anthony redid his repair job, and, as I thought, gladly signed the ticket, which I mailed the next day.

On all my trips home and back again to the college, I needed help with my car expenses. Therefore, I signed up other students who needed rides and who lived along the routes I would take. Some, who lived close to Oswego, became steady riders and paid me eight dollars for each round trip of eight hundred miles. At times, I sensed a few thought the fare was too high, especially at those times, when I had four riders paying me a grand total of thirty-two dollars. However, on a trip home one Christmas vacation, my heater broke and had to be repaired, and a tire needed to be replaced. These two problems silenced my critics for good.

One fellow, who rode regularly with me for two years, lived in Syracuse. One night Bob Hammonds and I were driving from Schenectady to Syracuse on route 5. All my other riders had been deposited at their homes, leaving just the two of us. Bob was relaxing in the front passenger's seat, dozing off quite frequently. I was very tired and every so often, as I drove, I'd see a tractor trailer not too far in front of my car. I'd slam my brakes on, then regain my senses and see a large billboard at the side of the road and no truck. My mind was playing tricks on me. I soon realized the danger of driving under such tired conditions, but with little money to spare, a motel was out of the question. So I continued on.

The radio was on and, at one point, I reached down to change stations.

Bob was asleep. In the few seconds that followed, I heard a loud bang and felt a severe jarring, another bang and another jarring. Before it occurred a third time, Bob was wide awake. Simultaneously, he yelled and hit me on the arm. I had fallen asleep with my eyes open and woke up, when he reacted as he did.

Once awake, I realized the driver's side of my car had climbed the curb-high, sidewalk-wide divider in the road and the wheels on that side were periodically dropping into spaced, grate-covered, drainage areas cut into the divider. Thus, the noise and jarrings. I also saw that we were heading for a large, concrete, overpass support. Quickly, I turned the steering wheel, came down off the divider, pulled to the right off the road, and shut off the engine.

We sat a few moments to calm down. Then we got out to assess the damage. A good portion of my exhaust system had been torn off and was in pieces along the divider. Other than that, we saw no visible damage. Once we picked up the pieces and put them into the trunk, we were ready to continue on to Syracuse. Since Bob was now so wide awake, and I was so tired, I let him drive, and I slept until we reached his home. Looking back on that night, I believe it was a small miracle, I arrived home safe and sound.

My dependable Chevy carried me into my senior year, but there were signs along the way that it was on its last leg. One day in the fall of 1956, I had several errands to do. I left the dorm, walked to the parking lot, hopped into my car, turned the key and nothing happened. I got out, opened the hood, pushed this, wiggled that, doing what all stranded drivers do in similar situations. Did it work? Of course not! Does pushing and wiggling ever fix a car? Not usually. But doing so is a tradition among drivers.

After closing the hood, I did the second thing usually tried when stranded in a manual shift car that won't start. Two other fellows and I pushed the car out of the lot and down the street to the top of a small hill. As the car began to pick up speed on its downward movement, I jumped in, turned the key, depressed the clutch, put the transmission into second gear, let out the clutch, and started the engine. The car wasn't repaired, but it was running, so I began my errands. At each place I had an errand to do, I parked where I could roll the car forward, jump in and start it, as I had done the first time. Everything was going well thanks to standard transmissions and small hills.

My last stop was in downtown Providence to have my picture taken for graduation and the yearbook. I parked near an intersection where three streets crossed, fed the meter, walked to the photographer's studio, had my picture taken and returned to my car. I unlocked the door, put the transmission into neutral, released the emergency brake and began pushing it down a slight incline toward the intersection.

As I neared it, the red traffic light in my lane changed to green. I thought, "Great! I'll make it." However, just as I got the car rolling fast enough to jump in and start it, the light turned red again, and I was only part way through the intersection. I jumped in anyway, started the car and made a left turn. A motorcycle policeman, parked on the next street and shielded by buildings, didn't see anything I had done except go through the red light. He caught up to me and pulled me over.

With my car idling, I gave him my license and registration and then explained my problem. He listened politely then ordered me to "Turn the engine off." I did so. Then he said, "Now try to start it again." I turned the key, assured that it wouldn't start, but to my horror, it did! We looked at each other and then he started to write a ticket. While he wrote, I turned the engine off and waited. He completed the ticket, handed it to me with my credentials, started his motorcycle and rode away.

Disgusted, I threw the ticket on the seat next to me, put my license and registration away and turned the key to start the car. This time the car wouldn't start, nor would it on the next three attempts. I was furious and was sure my blood pressure had risen several degrees. How could my trustworthy Chevy do this to me? I got out, pushed it, jumped back in and started it.

My next stop was not on my list. It was to the police station. With license, registration, and ticket in hand, I stormed in and asked for the person in charge. I was soon escorted into his office and sat down facing him. I explained what had just happened, not leaving out one detail. He must have sensed that I was telling the truth. For when I finished, he took the ticket and stated that he would take care of it. I thanked him, breathed a sigh of relief, returned to my car and pushed it to get it started. Not wanting to face a similar situation, I had the car repaired the next day.

I kept my Chevy until late August. By then, I had to carry several gallons of water in containers in the car and stop every twenty-five to thirty miles to put some of it into the leaking radiator. Plus the tires were bald, the belts were worn, the engine coughed and wheezed and the brakes needed relining. Therefore, I decided to trade it in on a 1954 Chevrolet. My miracle car had served me well, but time makes all things expendable, especially cars.

Over the years, as I've grown older, my cars have become newer. I've owned many good ones including trucks. However, the nostalgia I felt for my first three cars still remains in my heart. I cannot say that about the rest. In fact, I remember very little about them.

Chapter X
The Ups and Downs of My Sex Education

At times, when I hear or read of a child or teenager being sexually abused, I think back to my boyhood and the close calls I had. One spring day while walking home, I stopped at a gas station to use the men's room. Shortly after I had entered a stall and was sitting on the toilet, I heard the door open and the sound of footsteps. After he used the urinal, I heard other noises and assumed he was washing his hands. Before he finished, I finished and was about to pull up my pants when the door to my stall suddenly opened.

There he stood looking at my private parts, and there I stood looking at him, embarrassed and becoming frightened. He assured me that he meant me no harm. Then, in his next breath, he propositioned me. In one short vulgar sentence, he offered me five dollars if I'd allow him to perform anal intercourse. I immediately refused and was prepared to yell as loud as I could and kick him in his private parts if he made one step toward me.

For whatever the reason, the fear in my eyes, my refusal, or the nearness of others in the station, he finally turned and left. I soon followed and left the station without saying a word to anyone. In fact, I never told anyone about this, yet, when I close my eyes and think back, I can still see the station, the bathroom, and the man's face looking at me.

On another occasion, I was successful in hitchhiking a ride home to our house on the loop. All the way, the driver and I had a pleasant conversation. However, as soon as he stopped to drop me off, he said, "Wait a minute." I turned, looked at him and saw his stiff penis protruding from his pants and a smile on his face. His next words were, "I'll give you a nickel if you'll kiss it." Without answering, I quickly threw open the door, jumped out, slammed the door behind me and breathed a sigh of relief as he drove off. Again, I didn't tell anyone. Why? I don't know. Perhaps I figured Mom had enough to worry about without me adding to it.

Shortly after quitting my job, riding in a truck delivering newspapers on a rural route, I read that the driver had been arrested for sexually abusing the boy who took my place. After finishing the article, I leaned back in my chair, closed my eyes and thought of times when Dick had made suggestive remarks to me or had patted my bare, upper leg while smiling over some remark he had just made.

He had always been pleasant to me and had never made any threatening advances. Therefore, I never had reason to fear him, especially in sexual ways. Had I not taken my own paper route in town, I could very well have been the boy Dick molested. Luckily, I was not.

Weeks later, after reading that he had been sent to prison, I had mixed emotions. On the one hand, I felt he got what he deserved. On the other hand, I felt sorry for his wife and children, as they now faced life without a husband and a father.

While "splinter village" was being constructed behind the college, Pit and I met a carpenter named Charlie. We soon found ourselves sitting with him during the noon lunch breaks. We'd meet on the bleachers at the athletic field across from the college president's home, eat lunch and enjoy Charlie's homespun stories and jokes.

As eighth graders, we felt grown up enough to hear, understand and enjoy the dirty stories and jokes that spewed from his mouth. However, we were not prepared to indulge in certain sexual acts, Charlie eventually suggested, kiddingly at first but more seriously later on. Once we were sure he was serious, Pit told his dad, and soon Charlie was gone from the construction job. We learned later that he, too, had been arrested and sent away.

In all four of these incidents, I escaped physical harm and sexual molestation. However, I still remember each one vividly as if it happened yesterday. Therefore, I can readily identify with anyone who carries the scars from sexual abuse.

During a recent television news broadcast, a sex education program being given to second graders in Livingston, New Jersey, was reported on. Near the end of the segment, the reporter asked a boy, "What did you learn today?" Without any hesitation, the seven year old replied, "When I have sex with a girl, I should use a condom." I found humor in his answer. However, I also realized anew the importance of sex education beginning early in a child's life. This is especially true, now that the threat of AIDS looms so prevalently in our society.

After the broadcast ended, I turned off my TV and thought back to my sex education. Not long after an unwed, teenage mother, her baby, and her parents moved into a cottage near ours, our two families became friends.

Soon after their arrival, Mom gave Corky and me her teachings on sex education. Simply put, she instructed us to, "Have respect for girls. Don't do anything to a girl that you wouldn't want a boy to do to one of your sisters." It was short, to the point, and very effective.

To that point in time, bits and pieces of my sex education had come from different sources. I had seen couples making love in the woods near our home. I had walked past parked cars along the lake at night, had seen legs protruding from them and had heard grunts and groans. Finally, my peers and I had swapped juicy bits of information, swearing on "my grandmother's grave," it was true, although none of us could prove any of it. But, to be honest, I was still very ignorant about sex.

Then one summer morning, during our early adolescent years, Dr. Pitluga sat down with Pit and me. Using scientific terminology and diagrams, he gave us a lengthy discourse on the "birds and the bees, and how they make honey." As he spoke, carefully choosing each word, I sat in awe, taking it all in and storing it in my mind for future reference. I had never heard most of what he was teaching, just bits and pieces.

That afternoon, Pit and I grabbed our bathing suits and towels and headed for the lake. As we walked, our conversation centered on what we had heard that morning. Soon we were comparing our heretofore synonym for each of the terms Pit's dad had used, including breasts, vagina, penis, scrotum, condom, sexual intercourse, semen, and ejaculation. Our synonyms for his terms were mostly one syllable, four or five letters long, more commonly used among our peers, and thus easier to understand in everyday conversations about sex.

Dr. Pitluga's words sounded so foreign to us, we soon became giddy as we took turns pronouncing each and then saying our corresponding synonym. However, once we assimilated the vocabulary and could express what we had heard correctly, we were able to take conversations about sex out of the gutter and discuss it on a higher plane with our peers. And, like Socrates, we found great satisfaction in doing so.

When it came to girls and girlfriends, I guess I was as normal as any other boy my age. I had several "dream girls" and envisioned myself hugging, kissing, and whispering words of love into their ears. However, none of them ever became reality for some reason or another. They simply remained girls that I knew, and none ever became my girlfriend. This sorry state of affairs followed me into my high school years, where it continued to haunt me.

I often tried to analyze myself by asking such questions as, am I too shy, too poor, too poorly dressed, too self-conscious or what? I could ask plenty of questions but could never come up with concrete answers. Therefore, I continued having "dream girls" but never the real things.

One Sunday evening during the latter part of my sophomore year (1948–1949), our Presbyterian Youth Group had a joint meeting with the youth group from another church across town. When they arrived, I met Shirley, a very pretty brunette with large, sparkling, brown eyes and a smile that would melt anyone's heart.

During the entire meeting, I had trouble keeping my eyes off her, and when she left, she became the new "girl of my dreams." But that's as far as it went, since I didn't know her last name, and I never bumped into her at school. Maybe it was just as well, since I never could have gotten up the courage to call her and ask her for a date.

One evening in 1953, during Corky's spring break from college, he asked me to drive him to Syracuse so he could visit his fiancée, Judy Hammonds. I agreed and on the way he asked me if I'd care to double date and take Judy's sister bowling with them. After twisting my arm a bit, I agreed. After all, I was no Romeo to begin with and had never gone on a blind date before. But I figured one date wouldn't hurt, and if she was a nine or ten, that would be a plus. If she wasn't, well, it was only one date, and I would survive.

When we arrived, Judy was waiting anxiously to see her beau and gave him a big hug and kiss. Then, after meeting me, she introduced me to her family, but her sister was not among them. Soon Corky whispered something into her ear that made her smile. Judy excused herself and went upstairs. When she returned a few minutes later, her sister was trailing behind her.

As soon as I saw her sister, my heart skipped a beat and my brain began flashing, "A 10, a 10, a 10!" There, before my eyes, stood Shirley, the girl I had met almost four years before at the youth meeting. She stood there smiling at me, and I'm sure she was as surprised as I was. After all, what were the odds that something like this could happen? Yet it had, and I felt like shouting "Glory! Hallelujah! Praise the Lord!" But I didn't. I was too bashful to do something that rash. Instead, I spoke calmly and uttered the only other words that came to mind, "Gee, it's nice to see you again."

I've often heard the adage, "Time sure flies when you're having fun." Well, that's exactly what happened that evening, and soon we were back at the Hammonds' saying good night to our dates, Corky with a hug and a kiss, and I with a verbal utterance and a smile.

On the drive back to Oswego, Corky fell asleep, giving me time to relive the wonderful evening I had just experienced. As I did, I realized that Shirley had proved to be as delightful a person to be with as I had hoped. It was a shame her family had moved to Syracuse the summer after we first met. Had I gotten to known her at school, just maybe I would have found the courage to have asked her for a date. If I had, and she had accepted, who knows where our relationship would be by now. However, at the end of my thoughts, all I could say was, "Que sera, sera," (What will be, will be) and continue on with my life.

My senior prom was approaching and like all the other dances during my high school years, I hadn't planned to go for three good reasons. I had no date, no extra money, and I didn't know how to dance. Many times in my dreams during those four years, I had envisioned myself dressed in the latest fashions, dancing like Fred Astaire with my current dream girl and treating her like a princess. But they were just dreams, nothing more.

One day, while Bev Moulton and I were working on the next issue of the school newspaper, *The Murmur*, she seemed upset. Responding to my inquiry, she confided in me that her boyfriend might not be able to get home from the service to take her to the prom. And since she was one of the candidates for Prom Queen, she really wanted to attend. Hearing her tale of woe and knowing I had not intended to go, something I had recently read suddenly came to mind, "Life without a risk now and then is no life at all." Spurred by this maxim, I found myself saying, "If Beaver doesn't make it home, I'll take you to the prom. However, you'll have to teach me to dance once we get there."

Hearing my words, she turned to me with a relieved look on her face and responded, "You would? I'd really like that." After absorbing her generous smile into my soul, I asked her to let me know as soon as she knew, and with that, we returned to the task at hand.

The following week, Bev broke the news I had been waiting for. Beaver was not coming, so I had a date. I'm sure I looked pleased as she told me, because I was. After all, we were good friends and had often worked and laughed together on *Murmur* assignments. Therefore, why shouldn't I take her to the prom and feel at ease doing so? So what if I didn't know how to dance. Big deal! I was sure plenty of the other fellows at the prom wouldn't know how to dance either, so I'd be in the same boat with them. Besides, Bev promised, she'd teach me once we got there, and I believed her.

I left the newspaper office that afternoon excited, yet a little apprehensive. Bev was pretty, very popular among her peers, active in several clubs and in general, the all-American teenager. And she was going with me, a hayseed from the other side of the tracks. How lucky could I be!

By the time the evening of the prom arrived, I had worked extra hours at Mulcahey's and spent the money on a new set of clothes, bringing my appearance out of the Dark Ages into the twentieth century. And, to top it off, I had shaved early and had managed to stop all the nicks from shedding blood with a styptic pencil. Thus, there were no little blood stains on the collar of my white shirt. The last ritual I did, before leaving the house, was splash an ample amount of aftershave lotion on my face, just in case my deodorant didn't live up to its promise on the container. Once I was ready, I came downstairs, endured the wolf whistles from my sisters, enjoyed the compliments from Mom, took the corsage box out of the ice box and headed out the door, ignoring further comments from my sisters and Paddy.

As I walked up the Moultons' sidewalk, everything I had on was so new, I felt like a mannequin fresh from the window of the leading men's store downtown. Her dad answered the doorbell, introduced himself, then invited me in. After meeting her mom and chatting a bit with both parents, I heard someone coming down the stairs. Bev made her grand entrance, dressed in a beautiful, blue gown, and looked more lovely than I had imagined. As she stood there, smiling at me, I suddenly became ecstatic that Beaver couldn't make it home and smiled back. Then I gave her the wrist corsage, which matched her gown perfectly, and she gave me a boutonniere.

As we were heading for the door, her parents wished both of us a nice time, then her dad, as dads often do, admonished me to drive carefully. Drive carefully? You bet I would and slowly too! I wanted this evening to last as long as possible, knowing my Cinderella wouldn't change back into a pumpkin at the stroke of midnight.

The gym at the high school was a virtual garden of Eden. It had been transformed from an arena permeated by the smells of sweaty bodies into a garden paradise with the fresh scent of flowers drifting silently into every nook and cranny.

When the band began to play, Bev began my dance lessons, teaching me what she called the box method. Soon I could do a decent fox trot and a waltz without stepping on her toes too often. Once I knew what my feet should be doing, everything else came easily, and I enjoyed holding her close, swaying to the music and inhaling the scent of perfume emanating from behind her ear. For the first time on my life, I was in "seventh heaven," two words Corky had often used after returning home from a dance, and now I knew what they meant.

When the time came to reveal and crown the Prom Queen, spotlights illuminated all the candidates and their dates. Each couple was introduced and after the final applause died down, the envelope was opened as each girl held her breath in anticipation. "The Prom Queen is Evelyn Boyer." Hearing these words, I'm sure Bev was disappointed, but she didn't show the slightest sign of it. We both clapped heartedly for Evelyn as the crown was placed on her head.

Following the coronation, the Queen and her date danced alone in a circle of light, while everyone else watched and clapped sporadically. Following this, the Queen's Court was invited onto the dance floor to join them. Smiling, I took Bev in my arms, looked into her sparkling eyes, waltzed her around and around, as sweat ran down my back, and only stepped on her toes a few times.

After the last morsel of food was eaten and the last dance danced, we left our paradise and headed for the inn at Mexico Point, where the festivities would continue. However, a new ingredient would be added, alcholic beverages. As I drove, Bev sat close to me, put her head on my shoulder and fell asleep. When we arrived, I parked, then nudged her gently. She woke up, our eyes met, and then she kissed me—a warm, tender kiss on my lips, and I didn't mind one bit.

More dancing, more food, and a glass of champagne later, the inn closed, and we slowly walked back to my car with another couple that was riding with us. It was now 2:00 A.M. and, as far as I was concerned, the night was still young. Therefore, once our dates were in the car, Bob Fancher and I agreed to a plan before we joined them. I'd drive toward Watertown until three while he and his date sat in the back and enjoyed themselves. Then they'd change places with Bev and me, and he'd drive back to Oswego.

The plan went without a hitch, and I spent a marvelous hour and a half petting with Bev, yet keeping in mind the admonition Mom had given me years before concerning the treatment of girls on dates. Therefore, I did not become what girls often described as an octopus, using my hands to explore unfamiliar territory. Rather, I remained a love-starved teenager and enjoyed the affection received from kissing and holding Bev in my arms.

Once Edith and Bob were safely home, I sadly returned my Cinderella to hers, enjoyed a final, good night kiss, then headed home. As I passed the church, where my Boy Scout meetings were held, the scout oath came to mind, and I began reciting it, "On my honor I will do my best . . . to keep myself physically strong, mentally awake and morally straight." The last two words hit me right between my eyes. In her own way, that's exactly what Mom had instructed me. And that's the way I had remained with Bev.

I undressed, and I was glad I had worn underwear. A biological function, something Dr. Pitluga had warned Pit and me about during his sex education talk, had taken place, and my briefs bore evidence of it. Even though I had biologically "boiled over," I had controlled my sex drive, had enjoyed a marvelous time, and had taken a giant step toward becoming a man and leaving the teenager I knew behind.

Even though I now had my first real date under my belt, I was still quite ignorant when it came to petting. My ignorance surfaced on my next date in late June. My friend, Jack, his girlfriend, my date, Lori, and I were returning from a fun-filled evening in Syracuse. Lori and I were in the back seat, and with nothing better to do with our time, we began to kiss. Right away, I noticed that she kissed with her mouth open. *How odd*, I thought to myself, but I didn't stop kissing. I simply adjusted my open mouth to hers. I didn't say anything to her for fear she might become embarrassed or angry and stop. At this point in my young social life, I needed all the practice I could get. So I continued enjoying each kiss even with our mouths open.

After we had dropped our dates off, I didn't mention anything to Jack about my date's weird style of kissing. In fact, I didn't say anything to anybody. Many years later, I was introduced to French kissing. Immediately, my mind reran the memories of that night, and then, I was sure I knew why Lori had refused a second date with me. I suppose to her, I was a real jerk when it came to making love, even the kissing part.

One night, shortly before I quit working at the fish fry stand, business was slow. As we waited for each customer to appear and order, Jack Mulcahey and I had a talk, sprinkled with humor, about women and sex, since these two topics were on both of our minds much of the time. From what I said, Jack must have concluded that I was still a virgin and eventually, he put the question to me. I answered in the affirmative. Then, as he often did upon hearing choice bits of information from me, he laughed out loud, then took another swig or two of his beer. Finally, he looked me square in the eye and promised to get me "laid." And I believed him. After all, he was a lady killer and had the notches on his belt to prove it. Many times in the past, I had listened to blow-by-blow accounts of his conquests. And, if what he had related so often was true, why couldn't he help me do the same?

As he sat there, giving me a step by step by step, fool proof method for such a conquest, I was etching each step in my mind. When he finished, he reached into his pocket, pulled out a condom and handed it to me with the instruction, "Be sure you use this, or you might be sorry."

On my next night off, I had my prey in my car and was parked along the lake. I had chosen a girl who I knew had a big crush on me. Thus, I had asked her for a date, and she had accepted. Now, after a movie and a stop at the stand, we were parked. I was armed and eager to begin my step by step conquest.

Within a reasonable length of time, I had worked my way through Jack's first three steps and was fast approaching the twilight zone. As step four came to the forefront of my mind, it collided head-on with Mom's admonition, bringing any further advancement to a screeching halt. As Jean and I continued kissing, I began to have second thoughts about step four and the others that followed. Should I or shouldn't I? That was the question I had to answer internally while steaming up the car's windows externally. Finally, many kisses later, the battle ended, and I proceeded passionately to step four.

As we continued kissing, I slowly slithered one hand toward her voluptuous breasts and soon made contact. Instantly, Jean reacted faster to my stimulus than Pavlov's dogs to his, and she pushed my hand away. Then she spoke cruel words, put space between us and returned to her side of the seat, leaving me embarrassed and defeated on my side.

Obeying her command to "Take me home!" I headed that way. Feeling ashamed, I apologized, and she accepted. Before getting out of my car, she made it very clear that she was not "that kind of girl." I knew what she meant, and in return, I assured her that I was not "that kind of guy," but had let my emotions get away from me. I don't think she really believed me, and she had a good reason not to.

Even though I had failed in my first conquest attempt and felt guilty, to boot, over my behavior, I stopped at the stand on my way home and filled Jack in on the details of my defeat. As I spoke, instead of consoling me, he saw plenty of humor in my words and laughed repeatedly. Once my last detail had been aired, he stopped laughing and simply spewed out one long sentence, "There are plenty of fish in the sea, eventually you'll begin to catch your share." At that point, I wasn't sure I wanted to, but I kept the condom just in case.

Later that summer, Pit and I double-dated. Since he had his dad's car, he drove. Thus, my date and I sat in the back seat. After a full evening of food, fun, and fellowship, I volunteered to drive back to Minetto, so Pit could neck with his date, but he refused. Since I was not in the mood to pet with my date, I was sorry he had. Why such a mood? I guess it was because I didn't know my date that well.

Pit took a long route, drove slowly and kissed his girl at each red light, while I chatted with mine. When we finally arrived in Minetto, we were on the wrong side of the river. Therefore, Pit drove onto the two-lane bridge and took his foot off the gas pedal, figuring the gentle, downward slope of the bridge would allow the car to continue moving. And he was correct in his assumption.

Then he took his eyes off the road and his hands off the steering wheel. He turned, embraced and kissed his girl. As he sustained his kiss, the car began to slowly drift to the left. Seeing this, I calmly reported it to Pit, but my words fell on deaf ears. As the car continued drifting, I continued to warn Pit, and he continued to ignore my words.

Just as the car was about to hit the left curb of the bridge's sidewalk, I panicked and yelled a final warning to Pit. Before he reacted, the left side of the car mounted the curb and headed for the protective railing and the river below. At that second, realizing the imminent danger we were in, the girls screamed, I held my breath, and Pit quickly grabbed the wheel and spun it to the right, narrowly escaping from the jaws of death and a watery grave.

The car missed the railing by a coat of paint, turned sharply, came off the sidewalk, slammed back onto the road and headed to the right. Keeping cool, Pit managed to control the direction of the car and soon had it heading in the right direction. By then, we were all shaking.

After getting off the bridge, Pit pulled into the nearest parking lot and turned off the engine. As our nerves settled down and our shaking decreased, we became giddy. Soon we were laughing at whatever any of us uttered, humorous or not. I suppose psychologists would call this normal behavior. Normal or not, it continued for several minutes.

Once both girls were safely home, Pit and I headed back to Oswego. During our conversation, Pit agreed with me that what he had done while driving was stupid. He had definitely learned an important lesson.

He had, too, except for one other night, when he was going too fast on an icy road. The rear end of his dad's car skidded on a curve and knocked over several concrete, guard-rail posts. After that incident, I thought twice about riding with Pit and letting him drive. Was I a coward? Not on your life! I just wanted to see the sun come up the next day, that's all.

During the early part of 1952, I was born again during evangelistic meetings at the Baptist Tabernacle in Oswego. Following my conversion, I attended church there and sat enthralled as the Reverend Earl Leiby preached the Word and exhorted his flock to apply the Bible's teachings to each of their lives. I began doing that and soon my teenage outlook on life began to change.

One Sunday, Pastor Leiby invited me to join other teenagers from the church and attend a weekly youth fellowship meeting in Fulton with Christians who lived there. I accepted and drove to Fulton the following Friday evening with my car full of young people. During the game time, I met Dorothy Adams, a pretty high school senior from Fulton. Since I enjoyed being with other Christians about my age, and the meeting was worthwhile, I decided to continue going.

As I became better and better acquainted with Dorothy, I began to like her more and more. I often drove her and her younger sister home after the meetings just to be with Dorothy a little longer. Eventually, her mother heard about me. After I met her, she subtly treated me as if I had the plague. And no matter what I said or did or how nicely I treated Dorothy, she didn't want me driving her daughters anywhere. In her mind, I was from the wrong side of the tracks and definitely not worthy of Dorothy.

The following fall, I began a year of studies at the college in Oswego and became involved with the Inter-Varsity Christian Fellowship on campus. At its first meeting, I met Walt, one of Dorothy's two older brothers. He was a very likable chap, and we soon became good friends much to the dismay of his mom. Now I had two strikes against me, but I took Mrs. Adams' negative feelings toward me for what they were and ignored them. Perhaps, if her husband had still been alive, her outlook toward me might have been different. Playing two roles was taking its toll on her.

Early the next spring, the I.V.C.F. had a party and invited any and all college students to attend. I was in charge of the entertainment. I put together the "Fantastic Foolish Farmaceutical Follies" using talent within the organization to fill the follies with funny folks, and I was one of them.

When it was my turn to perform, I presented a magic show and did several bona fide tricks. Once I had the audience believing in my ability as a magician, I called for a volunteer, wearing a tie, and chose Walt from among several men, who had raised their hands. Unknown to the audience, I had seen Walt the day before, had given him one of my ties, had asked him to wear it to the program and go along with whatever happened to it during my magic show. He had agreed and now came to the stage, when chosen.

As he stood there, I complimented him on his tie, and he responded, telling the crowd it was a gift from a good friend, and he really liked it. I then told the audience, I was going to perform my famous tie trick.

While Walt continued to wear the tie, I had him stand, facing the audience. I took a piece of newspaper and, with my back to the audience and facing Walt, I wrapped it tightly around the tie. Then I reached out and took a large pair of scissors off the table next to me. As the audience became attentively quiet, I held the wrapped tie in one hand and cut through the middle of it with the scissors in my other. When I finished, I placed the scissors and the lower half of the cut portion on the table. Then I moved to the side of Walt, turned, faced the audience, confidently shouted, "Abra cadabra!" pulled the newspaper off the tie around his neck and bowed before the audience.

The audience, seeing only half a tie, knew I had blown the trick and began to laugh hilariously as Walt stood there stonefaced. Seconds later, I turned back to Walt, saw half the tie and acted as if I had goofed, causing the onlookers to laugh even louder. We both waited patiently until the laughter died down. Then I apologized to Walt and assured him that I would replace his gift tie with a new one. Then, while the audience clapped, Walt returned to his seat never to reveal our secret.

Before Walt's next visit home, word reached Mrs. Adams that I had ruined one of his favorite ties. Try as he might, he could not convince his mother otherwise. My dastardly act was her last nail in my coffin, and I was not allowed to date Dorothy again.

Sixteen years later, I was hired as an assistant professor in the elementary education department at the college in Oswego. I was assigned to teach one of the two fifth grades in the Campus School. During my tenure, classes of college students, majoring in elementary education, often came to observe and/or participate. As one group of students entered my classroom, I was surprised to see Dorothy among them.

Seeing her brought many pleasant memories to mind. When I had a chance, I spoke to her. After several years of marriage and motherhood, she had decided to return to college and become a teacher.

As I walked home later that afternoon, I thought again about my past relationship with Dorothy. Presently, her mother came to mind, and I laughed. The kid from the wrong side of the tracks, the one who would never be good enough for her daughter, was now one of her daughter's college professors. How ironic!

After my fling with Dorothy, I had many dates with many girls. I went steady a few times and fell in love twice. However, adding Biblical principles to Mom's admonition provided me with a strong set of values in determining all my actions. Thus, I still had the condom Jack had given me several years before and used it the night I married Shelley.

Chapter XI
Vices or Virtues: The Choices Were Mine

Whenever Mom caught a cold that kept her from breathing through her nose, she'd send Corky or me with a note to the stand or store for a pack of cigarettes. Once we returned, she'd light up, begin puffing and try to exhale the smoke through her clogged nose. I never learned whether or not her remedy worked. However, I do know she was the only person I ever met who smoked cigarettes for medicinal purposes. Even though she did this, she was vehemently opposed to any of us kids smoking for any reason. Therefore, I limited my smoking to those times when I stayed overnight at Pit's.

When I was in the seventh grade, several of us guys would often troop to Dashner's Soda Shop near the college, occupy a booth in one corner, buy milk or soda, and eat our bag lunches. One day, after we had finished eating, Mike Shurr pulled a pack of chewing tobacco from his shirt pocket and put some into his mouth. Then he offered each of us some, as he happily chewed away, spitting now and then into his empty milk carton. Even though I was a bit startled at Mike's new habit, I followed suit as the pack made the rounds. Surprisingly, none of us got sick, and when we headed back up the hill to school, we enjoyed trying to out spit each other as our tobacco juice flew through the air and onto the snow.

The next day, the scene was repeated, only this time, the tallest, strongest, most macho boy in the eighth grade, or so he thought, came into Dashner's and eventually over to our booth. Soon Mike offered him a chew, and he greedily accepted, popping a large wad into his mouth.

Since our booth was full, Bob sat in the adjacent one, with some other eighth graders, and continued chewing, as their conversation grew louder and coarser. All of a sudden, Bob got up, turned and looked at us for a split second, then quickly headed for the door. I assumed from the look on his face that all was not well, and it wasn't. Bob managed to get outside, but before he could reach an area away from the two large, plate glass windows, he threw up, and everyone inside saw him. Talk about his reputation being tarnished! Word traveled fast among the students that we seventh graders could chew tobacco and not get sick. Yet, Mr. Macho threw up during his first chew.

After that incident, Bob was never the same person, and neither were we. We soon realized, we had elevated our position among our peers, not only in the seventh but in the eighth grade as well. And this knowledge gave us a feeling of superiority unequalled in our previous years in school.

I'm sure Pit had this feeling when, two days later on our trudge back to school, he packed a hard snowball and threw it at a male college student, hitting him in the back of his head and knocking his hat off. In times past, we had thrown our snowballs at others more our size and age. However, this time Pit chose someone much larger and older.

After hitting his target, Pit smiled, but the smile was short lived. Soon after he was hit, the man replaced his hat, turned and headed our way. As he neared, he stopped on the sidewalk, faced us, stretched his arms out to the side, and blocked our forward movement. Then, in an angry tone of voice, he asked, "Who threw the snowball that hit me?" Without hesitating, Pit answered in a cocky tone of voice, "I did, so what?" Hearing Pit's confession, the man quickly reached out, grabbed Pit by his coat collar, dragged him to a pile of snow nearby, and proceeded to wash his face with handfuls of snow. While doing so, he spewed obscenities at Pit and us and warned us not to do it again or else.

The entire incident was over in a short time, yet the effects lasted much longer. A college student had dared to touch one of us Campus School students and had gotten away with it. If he had, could others? And if so, wouldn't it be wiser not to mess with any of them again? These and other related questions were discussed the next day at Dashner's, while we ate lunch and chewed tobacco.

One afternoon, as we were getting ready to head back to school, Mr. Dashner came over to us and asked, almost apologetically, if we were chewing tobacco in his shop. With tobacco in all our mouths and spit building up, we confessed that we were and headed for the exit. He beat us to it, turned, and with his back blocking the door, told us we could not come there to eat unless we agreed to stop what he called, "this nasty habit." Without waiting for a reply from any of us, he stepped aside, and we left.

On the way up the hill, everyone had something to say, but in the end, we agreed to Mr. Dashner's ultimatum. To be perfectly honest, I was glad things turned out as they did. I really didn't enjoy chewing tobacco and knew Mom would really let me have both barrels if she found out. And with two sisters and a brother in the Campus School, I would have been living on borrowed time, had I continued.

With the desire to smoke and chew tobacco behind me, a third vice would soon raise its ugly head and be more difficult to overcome. It began during one of our eighth grade parties. This particular one was at Pit's home. The usual gang was there and the Pitlugas had provided plenty of food and a keg of fresh, apple cider before retiring to the upstairs.

At some point in the evening, either before, during or after our kissing games, Sam Giambo noticed a large decanter on the dining room buffet near the food-laden table. Taking a whiff, he smiled, poured a little into a glass, and drank it. Satisfied that it was wine, very good wine, he poured half a glass and began sipping it.

I don't recall the chain of events that followed. However, in a short time, most of us had sampled the wine and some began mixing wine with cider eventually resulting in some giddy teenagers. Once the decanter was emptied, it was placed back on the buffet, but no one thought to replace its top.

As the hour approached, signaling the end of the evening's festivities, Pit's mom came downstairs, saw the top of the decanter and soon realized we had drunk the wine. However, to save face in the eyes of the parents, she laughed and insisted that it was not wine, just decorative grapejuice. Sam, blurry-eyed by now, smiled and responded, "It sure tasted like wine to me!" Again, Mrs. Pitluga insisted it was not, and soon the guests were filing out the door, each thanking Pit's mom for a nice evening.

Once the last one had been picked up, Pit's mom turned and faced Pit and me with a stern look on her face. She confessed that the grapejuice had really been an expensive wine given to her by a close friend that morning. She had emptied the contents of the bottle into the decanter expecting to drink a little of it over several days. Now it was gone, and she was very upset.

She scolded both of us for allowing her gift to be consumed when a keg of cider had been provided. She made us feel very guilty and for good reason. We both apologized, but we still went to bed feeling guilty. However, in the eyes of our classmates, that party at Pit's was eventually voted the best one all year, especially by Sam.

After that party, Pit and I limited our drinking to milk, soda, hot cocoa, and an occasional cup of coffee loaded with cream and sugar. Even though we didn't really like coffee, such delicious doughnuts as headlights or taillights could only be fully enjoyed with a cup of steaming hot coffee at a diner on cold, winter days. However, during the second half of our senior year in high school, the lure of alcohol returned.

Once the basketball season ended and winter began to loosen its grip, Pit and I found ourselves looking for something to do on Friday and Saturday evenings. On one such evening, after some Ping-Pong at the YMCA, Fritz Adelman, Pit and I headed for a small, dimly lit bar on Utica Street that sold nickel beers. Even though I would not turn eighteen until April 7 and Pit on April 8, Fritz was already eighteen and had his draft card to prove it.

We shed our outer clothes and sat down at a table in one corner. Fritz took out his draft card and waited. When the owner/bartender sauntered over and asked for our order, we each asked for a nickel beer. Requesting to see some identification before serving us, Fritz flashed his draft card then quickly passed it under the small table to Pit. After Pit flashed it, he passed it to me, and I flashed it. Seeing, but not examining the "cards" up close, the bartender nodded approval, turned, and walked back to the counter. Returning, he placed three beers on the table before us and collected his fifteen cents.

Even though I had worked at the stand, where beer abounded, I had never tasted it. Now I had a glassful staring me in the face. Once the foam settled down, I raised the glass to my lips and took a sip. Yuck! Such a terrible taste! How could anyone like beer? However, I did not let my friends know my true feelings and went on drinking, a little at a time. I allowed plenty of time to pass between each sip. Finally, I finished, but before I knew it, another full glass had been placed in front of me. I cringed on the inside but thanked Fritz on the outside for treating me. Thus, I slowly began sipping my second beer, hoping to nurse it through the rest of the evening.

Fritz and Pit were enjoying their beers and were on their third when Fritz suggested we play "Beep." After explaining the rules, Pit wanted to play. I didn't, but not wanting to be a party pooper, I went along with them. At first, everyone "beeped" when they were supposed to. As the numbers grew, a "seven" here and there instead of a "beep," resulted in full glasses of beer being downed without stopping. As the game continued, I prayed silently that I would escape the sheer torture of downing a beer without stopping, but my prayers were not answered, and I soon fell victim, not once but three times. By the time we had spent our last nickels and the game came to an end, I felt a little dizzy and my stomach was upset. However, both Pit and Fritz were feeling no pain and were becoming a bit too loud vocally.

When Pit's dad finally dropped me off at home, I ate handfuls of snow, hoping to kill the smell of beer on my breath. I did not want Mom to find out I had been drinking. Once I had consumed enough to freeze the insides of my stomach for a long time, I entered the house and found Mom sound asleep in her favorite chair with the *Pall-Times* opened on her lap, and the TV blaring away. Seeing her, I knew my secret was safe and tiptoed up the stairs to bed.

In the months that followed, I went to the bars with Pit and other friends and even played "Beep." Try as I might, I could not acquire a taste for beer. On the other hand, Pit enjoyed it and found great satisfaction in downing a few whenever we went out on the town alone or with dates. I found my satisfaction in a cold soda.

One Saturday evening in July, Pit and I were doing what all red-blooded American teenagers do at one time or another, cruising the streets of one's home town. We were in my '37 Ford. As we passed the A & P on First Street, we noticed two girls walking toward Seneca Street. I immediately slowed down and pulled over to the curb.

As I continued driving at their walking speed, Pit struck up a conversation with them. Soon they accepted his invitation to join us. Once they were settled in the back seat, we continued cruising while the four of us talked, laughed, and enjoyed the cool breeze coming through the open windows.

Presently, we approached a car parked next to a curb. Seeing it, the girls quickly whispered something to each other. As we passed the car, one stuck her head out and yelled some obscenities while making an obscene gesture at the car's two occupants. Immediately, the car left the curb and began to follow us.

I continued driving, looking every so often in my rear view mirror. The girls confessed that the guys in the car behind us were their boyfriends. Earlier that evening, the four of them had an argument. In a fit of anger, they had gotten out of the car, slammed the doors, and were walking home when we came along. Since they were still hot-under-the-collar at their boyfriends, they did not want to rejoin them. They preferred to ride with us, and in so doing, make their boyfriends even angrier as well as jealous. So we continued cruising, as night settled down around us, and no moon appeared.

Once it was dark, I winked at Pit then asked the girls if they'd like me to lose their boyfriends. Without the slightest hesitation, both replied, "Yes," so I headed for Snake Swamp Road eager to lose "dem bums." I knew all the dirt roads in that area for miles around, and if I couldn't lose that car, I'd be very disappointed. Once we turned onto Snake Swamp Road, I slowly increased my speed, churning dirt and gravel into the air behind me and increasing the distance between us and them. However, they kept coming, determined to get their girls back. The chase was a merry one for all, until I flew over a rise on one dirt road and sent an empty soda bottle and a tennis racket that lay on the ledge behind the rear seat into space.

The bottle struck one girl on the back of her head and the tennis racket the other. Both immediately screamed in pain and felt their heads. Neither was bloody, but both felt "goose eggs" rising at the points of impact. I apologized profusely, as I continued barreling over one dirt road after another. Try as I might, I could not shake the car behind.

Finally, I had a new plan and immediately put it into operation. I increased my speed, putting more distance between us and them. Then I turned off all my lights and flicked on my spotlight. Using this to see, I continued on, snaking through the maze of dirt roads. Finally, at one intersection, I slammed on my brakes, turned the steering wheel to the right, skidded around the corner, and headed down another road.

Before the other car turned, I saw a place to pull off the road and drive between two rows of fruit trees. I quickly did so, turned off my spotlight and waited. The enemy car soon sped by, and its occupants never saw us. While we waited for the dust to settle, we reveled in our victory. Then I backed out onto the road and headed back to town.

Once we deposited the girls at their homes, we headed for Buckland's Bar and Grill, a local institution, at the forks of the road. While there, I bumped into a friend who was home on leave from the army before being shipped to Korea. He asked me what I was drinking. Embarrassed to say, "7-Up," I uttered the only alcoholic drink I could think of, "seven-seven." Immediately, Norm signaled the bartender and ordered one for me. By the time it arrived, I had finished my soda and took a sip. It tasted really good. I took a liking to it and bought the next round.

By the time Pit and I left, we both had had too much to drink. I had never been drunk in my life, but I was now. Yet, I climbed into the driver's seat of my car and headed toward the center of town. Lucky for us, there was little traffic on the streets and fewer police cars. When we reached the main intersection at Bridge and First Streets, I stopped my car in the middle of it and pulled on the parking brake. Then we got out and peed on the base of the sign there, laughing as we did so and ignoring the few cars that slowly passed by. Once we had finished, we climbed back into my car, turned around and headed for the stand.

I parked the car, then we walked unsteadily to the counter. Seeing our condition, Jack laughed and asked us for our order. We ordered two fish and chips, a bottle of beer for Pit and a chocolate milk for me. While we ate, we both acted obnoxiously, but Jack acted more amused than aggravated by our behavior. Once we had consumed the last crumb and drunk the last drop, we bade Jack good night and stumbled back to my car.

As I drove to Pit's home, I began to feel sick to my stomach but didn't say anything to him. I soon dropped him off and headed back toward my house. Halfway there, I suddenly became very nauseated and pulled off the road into the driveway of a closed fruit stand. I quickly parked, got out and spent the next several minutes vomiting the entire evening's entertainment onto the dirt below.

As I did so, I began to realize getting drunk was no fun at all if it led to this. Soda never did this to me. Maybe I should continue drinking it and leave the booze alone. Once I had turned my stomach inside out, I wiped my mouth and blew my nose. Finally, I reentered my car and drove on home. Miraculously, I arrived in one piece.

Since the downstairs lights were still on, and it was now after two o'clock, I figured Mom was still up waiting for me. I knew I couldn't face her in my condition and live, so I didn't enter. Instead, I managed to walk around the outside of the house to the back yard. Soon I returned, carrying the remains of our wooden ladder.

I positioned it against the front of the house and began climbing toward the upper porch. Twice I tried stepping on rungs that weren't there, and twice I almost fell. Each time, I realized that a man in my condition should not be climbing a ladder, especially this one and in the dark to boot.

My persistence paid off, and I reached the torn screening safe and sound. After I wiggled my body through the hole and landed on the floor of the porch, I stood up, reached through the torn screening and pushed the ladder away, sending it crashing onto the lawn. Then I flopped onto a mattress covering one of the iron bunk beds and fell asleep.

Later that morning, I woke up with a terrible hangover. It felt as if tiny elves were inside my head bowling and getting strikes with each ball thrown. Somehow, I managed to get downstairs without falling and into the kitchen, where Mom was waiting for me. After washing my face and hands in a basin of water, "sterilizing" them and wiping them dry, I answered all of Mom's questions and managed to sidestep the drinking I had done and its consequences. I finally told Mom that I had come home at a reasonable hour, had seen her sleeping in her favorite chair and had gone to bed without waking her. I figured one little white lie wouldn't hurt. Much to my relief, she believed me. I was going to live after all, but with my head pounding, I wasn't sure I wanted to.

That night on the town convinced me that alcoholic beverages were not my cup of tea. Therefore, I returned to drinking soda whenever Pit and I visited a local tavern. However, he enjoyed drinking and continued downing wine, beer and whatever else suited his fancy at the moment.

One night a few weeks later, Pit and I were alone at his house with little to do except shoot the breeze and drink. He was drinking a bottle of cheap wine he had bought, and I, a bottle of Coke. We were slowly running out of conversation and wine, when Pit rose from his chair and headed for the buffet in which his parents stored their alcoholic beverages. After opening the door, he took out a bottle containing a little whiskey. He opened it and drank its contents in record time. Then he wiped his mouth with the back of his hand, belched, and handed me the empty bottle for disposal.

Bending down again and looking into the buffet, he spotted another partial bottle, reached in and took it out. This one contained more than the first, so he returned to the living room, sat down and began drinking its contents, getting drunker with each swallow. A half hour later, he handed me a second empty bottle and returned to the buffet. Finding a third and final bottle almost empty, he polished it off as well.

By now, he had downed all the liquor in the buffet, yet he ignored my suggestion that he had drunk enough and kept insisting he wanted more. Walking unsteadily to the kitchen, he opened a cupboard door and began reading the labels on every bottle and can. He soon took a bottle of vanilla in his hand, read its contents and seeing the word, "alcohol," he smiled, grunted something I didn't understand, opened it, and took a few swallows. After replacing the cap on the bottle and the bottle on the shelf, he continued his search. Finding nothing else in any cupboard containing alcohol, he took a can of soup, opened it, dumped it into a pan on the stove and turned on the burner.

Next, Pit went into the bathroom, leaned into the shower stall and turned on the cold water. Once he had completed his "shower," he dried off the best he could and headed back to the kitchen. As he exited the bathroom, he spied a bottle of bleach on a shelf in the hallway just opposite the bathroom door. He reached out, took it off the shelf, opened it and drank two swallows. Satisfied, he recapped it and put it back.

His next move was back to the kitchen for his soup. He took the handle of the pan, raised it to his mouth and drank the warm soup. After putting the empty pan into the sink, he staggered back to the living room and sank down into an easy chair. While observing all this, I had to bite my tongue several times to keep from laughing.

As we sat there, I knew Pit was in no condition to hold any kind of conversation, so I just watched his movements. Finally, I suggested he go to bed, and he agreed. Rising from his chair, he immediately lost his balance and landed on the floor. From there, he crawled across the room, up the stairs, into his bedroom and onto his bed. In seconds, he was out like a light.

Having no reason to stay up, I got ready for bed, turned the light off and crawled under the covers, praying silently that Pit would be all right. The first time I woke up during the night, I smelled a stench stronger than I had ever smelled before. Quickly turning on the light, I looked over at Pit, and there he lay, snoring away in the middle of a sea of vomit. Sizing up the situation, I decided the best thing for me to do was not disturb him. So I opened the window near my bed, turned the light off, crawled back under the covers, and once the cool, fresh air replaced the stench in my nose, fell back asleep.

When Pit finally awoke the next morning, all hell broke loose. He had a terrible hangover to start with. Then both his parents bawled him out unmercifully and finally, he had to clean the mess off his bed and wash the linen in a large tub before putting it into the washing machine.

Even though Pit was my best friend, I decided to let him do it by himself. While he did so, I gave his parents a blow by blow account of the previous night's activities. His dad found it amusing, but his mom almost fainted in disgust. And I, having been there and seen it all, etched it into my memory forever.

On January 2, 1953, Uncle Sam paid the military to give me a complete physical. Even though I have only one good eye (Examiner: "You only need one good eye to shoot a rifle.") and one good foot (Examiner: "The army will supply you with very sturdy boots."), I was classified 1-A. Since several of my former high school friends had already been inducted, I figured my number would soon come up, even though I was attending college. Therefore, this possibility played on my mind and kept reoccurring every so often.

The following Saturday night, Pit and I stopped at a bar for a few drinks. As I nursed a glass of soda, I meandered through the crowd and ended up by a table occupied by David Place, his girl and another couple. After a few words of greeting, I asked kiddingly, "Hey, Dave! When are you going into the service and serve your country?" I did not get the response I expected. Instead of a smile and a friendly retort, his face lost its color, and a mean look came over it.

Before I knew what was happening and why, David rose from his chair and came at me, ready to knock my head off! Since I was sober, and he was not, I pushed him away. He lost his balance and crashed against a table and the wall beyond. Before he could regain his senses and attack again, Ducky Dowd, one of David's closest friends and a very tall, strong fellow, saw what had happened. He immediately came to David's aid.

He came up behind me, put his right arm around my throat, cutting off my air supply, lifted me off the floor, and carried me across the room away from the fray. The more I tried to release his arm, the tighter he held it around my throat. I thought I was a goner for sure and was about to lose consciousness, when he let go of his grip, and I fell to the floor gasping for breath and shaking from fear. The entire incident was over in a few minutes, yet I had almost lost my life.

After settling my nerves with two whiskey sours, I went over to David's table and apologized. After hearing me out, he left the table and took me aside. Softly and almost ashamedly, he confided in me that he had been classified 4-F and, therefore, could not serve in any of the armed services. He was very disappointed because of it. That's why he became so upset when I had badgered him earlier. After hearing this, I apologized again, put my arm around his shoulder and the two of us returned to his table smiling as if nothing had happened.

Once Pit and I left the bar, I filled him in on all the details of my near miss with death. Like the prophet, Daniel, I had seen the handwriting on the wall, and I didn't like what I had seen. Therefore, I promised myself that I would not enter any bar, saloon, tavern or any other "watering hole" for a long time. Thus, Pit and I enjoyed fewer and fewer evenings on the town together.

As it turned out, I was not drafted and sent to fight in Korea. Therefore, I continued going to college days and working at Marathon in the evenings. Even though I was very busy, life was good.

That summer, I attended the annual Marathon clambake. I arrived early, so I could enjoy all the activities. The softball game, pitting the blue collar workers, like me, against the management, was scheduled for the late afternoon. By then, I had won the horseshoe pitching championship and had enjoyed my share of clams and other delicious food items. I left all the beer for others to enjoy, and by the time the game began, most of the players on both sides had consumed too much beer and not enough food.

The game began, and I was playing second base. Inning after inning, I saw lots of action and had even turned a few double plays. As we slowly built up a lead, some of the beer-filled, opposing players became a bit hostile.

During the last half of the final inning, we were still ahead by three runs. Mark Potter, a mountain of a man, who loved to drink and had the stomach to prove it, hit a single and was on first base. The next batter hit a slow grounder up the alley toward me. The ball and Mark arrived almost at the same time.

As I bent down to field the ball and touch second base ahead of Mark, I saw him barreling toward me. He deliberately belted my head with his stomach and sent me flying. A few seconds later, I regained consciousness. I still had the ball in my glove, Mark was lumbering across home plate, the other batter was on third, and everyone, both on and off the field, was laughing hilariously. I was still a little groggy when the next batter came to the plate, but I was determined to stay in the game. It soon ended on a pop fly, and we won by one run.

As I sat at my table, waiting for the evening banquet to begin, I thought back to the game and the knockout punch Mark had laid on me. Normally, Mark was a pussycat and wouldn't hurt a flea. Yet, with several beers in him, he became a tiger, ready to "eat up" anyone on the base path. I came to the conclusion that too much alcohol really affects people in many different ways, and not all of them are pleasant.

This conclusion was underscored near the end of the dinner when Bill Mentor, normally a quiet, soft spoken, stick-to-himself kind of guy, climbed up on his table and danced by himself for several minutes much to the delight of everyone there. After seeing him and enjoying his antics as much as everyone else, I thought to myself, "Furman, had you drunk as much as he, you might be on your table dancing, too. Aren't you glad you stopped?" And I could only answer, "Yes."

A final vice I had to deal with, as a young person, was gambling. I was still a seventh grader, when I was introduced to craps, a gambling game played with dice. Several of us boys would play it outdoors before school began, and I'd use my milk money to get in the game. Some days I'd win a few nickels and rejoice. On other days, I'd lose and eat my lunch dry. But

I was hooked and played as often as I had a nickel in my pocket, and a game was in progress.

During the summer between the seventh and eighth grades, Jimmy taught me how to play poker using match sticks for chips. However, no money was involved, thus the chance factor was zero, and I soon became bored. One evening, a mixed group of us played strip poker and the pleasurable expectation returned. By the end of the evening, I had seen parts of a girl's anatomy heretofore unseen, and that was worth far more than the monetary gain of a few coins.

Once I entered high school, I was introduced to two, illegal, five cent, slot machines in a poolroom not far from the school. They were tucked away from the eyes of the law in a small room by themselves. Whenever I had a few nickels, I'd play them, winning a few coins now and then, but losing a few coins more often. However, win or lose, the thrill of anticipation was always present.

One day, the slot I was playing went "berserk," and winning combinations kept coming up, and coins kept dropping into the tray. I was ecstatic and kept putting coins into my pants pockets until both were full, and it was time to return to classes. The next time I visited the poolroom, the machines were gone, and my enjoyment had been snatched from me.

At least one carnival came to Oswego every summer. I'd usually go one evening, amble around, gawk at everything and enjoy a ride or two. That's why I was there one summer evening after completing ninth grade. However, on this particular Saturday evening, I had stopped in after completing my paper route and had my week's earnings in my pocket.

After sauntering from one area to another, I stopped at a booth offering money as prizes and took a chance. I won, not once but three times in a row, and I was smiling in glee. Then the tables turned, and I began losing. Soon stupidity replaced common sense, and I kept playing, hoping desperately to recoup my losses. As my perspiration increased, my money decreased, and finally I had lost my last quarter.

Shattered, knowing how much Mom depended on that money, I left the carnival and slowly walked home, carrying the weight of the world on my shoulders. How could I ever face Mom? What should I tell her? The truth? How would she react if I did? These and other questions raced through my mind as I continued on.

When I finally stood before her in utter humiliation, I informed her that I had lost all of the money, but I didn't tell her where or how. With a worried look on her face and searching eyes, she began questioning me. I managed to sidestep most of her questions. Soon the trial ended, but the whole truth lay buried deep within me never to be revealed to her. However, that loss plus the subsequent half confession burned within my soul for a long time and left a scar that still exists today.

After that incident, the glamour of gambling faded and has never really returned to haunt me. Once it raised its ugly head during the summer of 1985. I was vacationing in the beautiful Lake Tahoe area, Now and then, I'd play one of the ten, penny, progressive, video-poker, slot machines at Harvey's Casino. To my surprise and joy, I hit the royal flush five times in two months and won a grand total of $350. Since then, the penny machines have been taken away. Now I play a few nickels in similar slot machines whenever I visit a casino, but I rarely win.

Even though I gamble very little, I do tell others to know what they're doing before they begin. I've learned this from my own experiences and from watching others. For example, my son, Mark, played blackjack (twenty-one) at various casinos for over two years before he knew that an ace could be counted as an eleven or as a one. When I finally informed him of this, he was embarrassed. Up to then, he had always counted an ace as an eleven, never as one. How much money he lost over the years due to this lack of information is a question left unanswered.

No matter what a person gambles on, I believe sheer luck is the main ingredient. When I was driving limousines, I had a friend who was a part-time driver. He loved betting on horse races and would pore over the daily racing forms before making each bet. One afternoon, he stopped at the Meadowlands Racetrack in New Jersey and bet the trifecta (the bettor must select the first three finishers in exact order) in the last race that evening.

While driving to his next pick up, he took the ticket out of his pocket and looked at it. It was then that he realized the clerk had made an error and had given him the correct numbers but in the next to the last race. Disgusted, he put the ticket back into his pocket, knowing he had no time to return to the track.

That evening, the three horses corresponding to the numbers on his ticket won, not in the last race, but in the next to the last race. The next day, he went to the track and soon had $750 being counted into his hand. That evening upon entering the chauffeurs' waiting room, he shouted, "Gentlemen, this is my lucky day!"

Another example of sheer luck happened one evening while I was having dinner at Karl's Casino in Sparks, Nevada, with my son, his wife, and his daughter, Melody. Mark took a keno slip out of the rack and let Melody point to seven numbers. Being only three years old, Melody didn't know the numbers she was pointing to. Once Mark had circled the seven, he turned it in with thirty-five cents. When the winning numbers were displayed, Melody had picked enough winners for a $20 payoff. Since then, neither Mark nor his wife, Kim, have ever won at keno.

I'm sure if I were a gambler, I'd often lose my shirt. Therefore, I'm glad I learned early about the agony of defeat. It has saved me a lot of heartache through the years.

Chapter XII
Hitchhiking to California: A Thumbnail Sketch

It was a cold, rainy night in late September 1951. I was working the graveyard shift outside at a paper mill in Fulton on a machine that takes bark off logs before the logs can be used in making paper.

During the summer, I had worked inside supplying various machines with packing cases into which finished ice cream containers or milk cartons were packed. Then in late August and early September, I had worked days outside unloading boxcars filled with debarked (peeled) logs each about three feet long.

I used a tool called a hook. It was similar in size and shape to a sickle but designed differently and stronger. With it, I could hook a log and pull it out of the boxcar onto a conveyor belt. The belt carried it to the top of the wood pile. Those who did this job were called hookers. Our foreman made sure we were fast hookers.

As the pile grew, the belt was extended higher and higher, and water was sprayed on top of the pile. Thus, it would remain slippery allowing logs, coming off the end of the belt, to slide a bit down the pile keeping log jams from occurring. Enough wood had to be stockpiled before winter set in so that the paper mill could continue to operate until the following spring. By late September, the boxcars stopped coming. However, a mountain of logs towered high above the tracks nearby.

Trucks carrying unpeeled logs continued to arrive daily. I was assigned to the machine that peeled the logs after they were cut into three- to four-foot lengths. My job was to put a log into a v-shaped trough on the left side of the machine then push the start button. The machine would slowly spin the log and move it forward.

As operator, I took the long handle of a cutting device that, when lowered to the spinning log, would peel the bark off. However, as the bark flew off in pieces, some of it hit me in the chest, stomach, face, arms, et cetera, and it hurt. Once peeled, I took the log off from the right side of the machine, put it on a pile nearby and immediately started the process over again. This job was not to my liking, but it assured me of a weekly paycheck.

On that particular night, I was wearing a rain hat, raincoat, boots and protective goggles. I was standing in several inches of water and being pelted by the flying bits of bark as I worked. I thought to myself, "There has to be a better life somewhere . . ."

On my two o'clock lunch break, I remarked, in jest, to a fellow worker, "This job is for the birds! I think I'll quit and go to southern California for the winter. I hear it's really nice out there."

"You're all talk, Furman," was his reply. "You'll never quit this job. It's not like you."

"I know, but there's no future here. I could go to California, get a job, go to college and get away from this lousy job and lousier weather."

"You're right, Furman. I hear the weather in southern California is great, but you'll never do it. You ain't got the guts!"

At first I agreed with his last statement. However, during the rest of my shift, I argued with myself and finally made up my mind to go, to "chase the impossible dream." I left work that morning whistling a happy tune.

Arriving home, I sat down and had coffee with Mom. During the course of our short conversation, I broke the news to her.

"Mom, I've decided to hitchhike to southern California and live out there."

"That's nice," she responded in a calm voice. "When are you leaving?"

"Tomorrow morning if I'm ready, the day after if I'm not."

After sleeping a few hours, I drove to Fulton for my pay, bought a small suitcase, returned home and packed. Besides clothes and my seventy-eight dollars, I put in some white, twelve by eighteen inch pieces of thin cardboard and a black crayon.

By late afternoon, I was ready, having completed all my necessary business. Therefore, I decided not to go to work that night. Instead, I would go to bed early and start my venture the next morning, a Thursday.

By seven thirty, I was ready and eager to begin. I hugged and kissed everyone good-bye, picked up my suitcase and sang a few bars of "California, Here I Come!" as I walked out the door, down the porch stairs and across the lawn to the road. I turned, waved to everyone, and they waved back.

With that, I began my journey west, an eighteen year old reaching for the stars. I hadn't walked far, when a neighbor, Louise Mulcahey, picked me up as she had done so many previous times when I had been hitchhiking. She was driving to her teaching job in Fulton.

Seeing my suitcase she asked, "Where are you off to?"

Trying to act nonchalant, I answered, "Oh, I'm hitchhiking to California."

"You're what?"

After I repeated what I had said and expanded on it, she smiled and wished me good luck. During the remainder of the eleven-mile trip to Fulton, we chatted about several things, none of which was important. As I got out of her car on route 57, she wished me good luck again and made me promise to send her a postcard from Hollywood.

In a couple of minutes, I had written "Syracuse" on one of my pieces of cardboard. I held it in front of me with one hand and hitchhiked with the other. Using this method, I managed to cover three hundred miles and checked into the YMCA in Erie, Pennsylvania by day's end. I was tired but excited.

Day two began early. I took a quick shower, dressed, ate a quick breakfast, and caught an early city bus that would take me to the outskirts of Erie and U.S. Highway 20 West. Since the Interstate System of Highways was still a dream and not a reality, U.S. 20 was one of the main highways that ran from the east coast to the west coast.

Exiting from the bus, I quickly positioned myself, held up my "Cleveland" sign and stuck my thumb into the air. I soon had my first ride, then my second and a third. In no time at all, I was through Cleveland and was waiting for the next person to pick me up. My new sign read "Toledo."

Luck was with me again. I soon had a ride with a man and his son. The man reminded me of an undertaker, gloves and all. He was pleasant and quiet in his speech and manners.

As we were driving along, the man passed a car then pulled back into the right lane. The car ahead of us had California license plates. Seeing the plates, we commented about them. The man remarked, "Maybe you can get a ride to California with the driver of that car."

"That would be terrific, but it would take a small miracle."

"Maybe not," he said, and with that he suggested I make one of my signs and pass it to his son, who was sitting in the back seat. I made the sign "California? Will help drive." As he passed the car, I passed the sign to his son. Once the pass was completed, his son put the sign in the rear window and waited.

As soon as the other driver saw the sign, he shook his head up and down. Therefore, I quickly made another sign that stated, "Norwalk, stop." Soon we pulled off the road into a large parking area on the outskirts of Norwalk and stopped. The other driver did the same.

After we met, Dan, the driver, agreed to try it for the rest of that day to see how well I drove. I agreed and after thanking the "undertaker" and his son, joined Dan, and off we went.

Dan was on his way to his home in San Francisco. He had been involved in some governmental business in Washington, D.C. Now he was in a hurry to get home to his wife. She was pregnant and close to her delivery date.

That Friday, we made it to Ames, Iowa, some 757 miles from Erie. However, in Illinois we left U.S. 20 and picked up U.S. 30. He allowed me to drive much of the day, so I assumed I passed his test, especially since he slept soundly now and then. By the time we checked into a hotel in Ames that night, I was very tired but elated over the distance covered.

As I lay in bed waiting to fall asleep, I reviewed the day's trip in my mind. Apart from the many cities and changing geographical features in each state we drove through, I became enthralled with certain billboards we passed. Several times we passed one showing two men in a canoe on a river and the words, "Harold's Club or bust! Reno, Nevada," blazoned across the top. Another, that was repeated several times, was advertising Little America in Wyoming. Each billboard was the same except for the mileage. Finally, we passed countless Burma Shave signs stretched along the road and each with a delightful, short poem advertising the product.

Even though we went to bed late Friday night, we were up and on the road again early Saturday morning. We drove through the rest of Iowa, across Nebraska, and into Wyoming as far as Laramie, some 660 miles in all.

As we neared this wild west city, we were riding at a high elevation and could see its lights far off in the distance. We could also see snakes in the road, some alive and others killed by passing motorists. Dan informed me that many were rattlesnakes that had crawled onto the road to enjoy the warmth generated by the macadam pavement giving off its stored heat from the daylight sunshine. Not knowing much about snakes and their ways, I believed him. I also politely refused his invitation to stop and cut a rattle from one of the dead snakes. With my luck and poor eyesight, I probably would have messed with a live one and gotten bit. And I knew rattlesnake bites are often fatal. Arriving in Laramie, we stayed at a real western hotel with real cowboys, a thrill for this teenager from upstate New York.

Sunday morning came early, and soon we were heading toward Rawlins and points beyond. Two interesting events etched themselves into my mind that day. First, the New York Giants baseball team under Manager Leo Durocher, came from thirteen and a half games back in early August to tie the Brooklyn Dodgers on this final day of the regular season. A single, playoff game would be played later that week. The second event was finally passing Little America about thirty-five miles west of Rock Springs, Wyoming.

Leaving beautiful Wyoming behind, we drove through Utah and into Nevada. That evening, we stopped in Elko for the night. Before checking into a hotel, we bought gas at a local service station and had supper in a local diner. It was a shock to me to see slot machines everywhere including the gas station, the diner, and the hotel. Seeing them took me back to my slot playing days in Oswego. But that was a far cry from what I saw in Elko. And the machines were legal! Temptation overcame me. I tried a few nickels in one machine, lost and quit.

Monday morning, we began our last lap. It was raining and cold as we entered northern California on U.S. Highway 40. We soon began crossing the Donner Pass. Our progress was slow, partly due to the weather and partly due to all the trucks and other traffic on this two-lane road.

Once we made it over the fog-shrouded pass, we descended into the valley. At three o'clock, I bade Dan a fond farewell in Sacramento. He continued toward his destination and I took a bus south to the city limits and route 99.

It was raining as I stood hitchhiking with no luck. As it began to get dark, I finally decided to let two more cars pass. If I didn't get a ride with either, I would check into the motel near where I stood. Two cars sped by and neither stopped. I picked my suitcase up and turned to walk to the motel, but out of the corner of my eye, I saw the second car backing up on the shoulder of the road toward me. At last I had a ride after trying to thumb a ride for over an hour.

Ted had a new Studebaker and was very proud of it. He was on his way to southern California and had to drive all night to be on time for an appointment early in the morning. What a break for me! Another few hours and I'd be in beautiful, southern California and my new home.

Before long, Ted asked, "Do you know that this car will do over a hundred miles per hour?" I confessed I didn't, but even if I did, he was very eager to show me. He did, it did, and I froze in fear.

As we drove into the night, Ted picked up a serviceman who was hitchhiking. I volunteered to sit in the back seat hoping to get some sleep while they talked. It wasn't very long before Ted was showing his new passenger how fast his car would go. I closed my eyes and prayed that I would get to see southern California after coming so far. Before I finished my prayer, I fell asleep.

I woke up when Ted stopped to let the serviceman off, and I woke up again when he picked another up. I stayed awake until the hundred mile per hour ride was over. Twice more, Ted picked up hitchhikers and twice more extolled the merits of his car. Why Ted was never stopped by a police officer is still a mystery to me. I continued napping and praying as the excitement sporadically continued.

By 6:30 A.M., we were in the San Fernando Valley. Ted dropped me off at a bus stop then sped away in a cloud of dust down a dirt road. A bus soon came along and eventually deposited me in downtown Los Angeles. It was a warm, sunny, clear, Tuesday morning, and I was here just five days after leaving home. I felt terrific!

I don't recall how much of my seventy-eight dollars was left, but whatever the amount, it had to last me awhile. Therefore, I had to be very frugal. I rented a room at the YMCA on Hope Street for seven dollars a week. It was an inside room, one with no windows and not very large, but it was now home to me. The weekly rent also covered the use of the gym, pool, and other facilities. That was a nice plus to living there.

It didn't take me very long to unpack my small suitcase, so I was soon on my way to the employment office. After filling out a form, I got in a line and handed it to the clerk when my turn came. She looked it over, spoke with me a few minutes then handed me a card with the name and address of the Cadmium and Nickel Plating Company on Long Beach Boulevard.

After asking a few people directions, I boarded a trolley and soon found myself being interviewed for a job as a shipping clerk. I confessed to the interviewer that I had just arrived in Los Angeles that morning and didn't know a thing about Los Angeles or the towns and cities around it. In fact, I told the man that I still wasn't sure why the clerk at the employment office had even sent me to be interviewed.

His response surprised me. Instead of sending me away, he pointed to a large map of the area and declared, "Here's a map you can use. Each morning you'll set up the deliveries for our five trucks. The rest of the day, you'll answer the phone. You can do that, can't you?" I assured him I'd give it my best effort. He hired me and told me to report at 7:00 A.M. Thursday. I was elated getting a job so quickly and walked out of his office on air.

The rest of the day and much of the evening I spent walking around Los Angeles and relaxing in Pershing Square. I was too excited to sleep, even though I had been up since early Monday morning, some thirty-seven hours, not counting my catnaps in Ted's car.

I soon learned that Los Angeles was very safe as most cities were in those days. One didn't have to worry about coming or going after dark. Therefore, people of all ages enjoyed the evenings outside. Some window shopped, others sat in the park, some walked their dogs and others did a variety of relaxing activities.

When I did finally go to bed, I planned on getting up to watch the Giants-Dodgers playoff game on a small TV in the YMCA lounge. However, I failed to leave a wake-up call at the front desk. The next day, when I got up, I showered, dressed and came down to the lobby. I looked at the first clock I saw. It was 3:00 P.M. (6:00 P.M. EST), the game was over, and the Giants had won! I had slept through it and was very disappointed.

Later that day, I read about Bobby Thompson's game winning home run in the ninth inning, giving the Giants the pennant and the right to play the New York Yankees in the World Series. That evening on the TV news, I saw a film of Thompson hitting his "shot heard 'round the world." It eased my disappointment but not entirely.

The Yankees would go on to win the World Series in six games. But it would be rather anticlimatic in the minds of many baseball fans, especially those rooting for the Giants.

I enjoyed my job and learned a great deal about the entire area very quickly. Therefore, on weekends, I took bus rides to many of the towns and cities around L.A. There was virtually no smog. There were countless orange, grapefruit, lemon, and lime groves. The entire area was a paradise, a true garden of Eden. I enjoyed immensely the sights I saw, the smells I smelled, and the tastes of the delicious fruits I ate.

I also spent many hours in Hollywood standing in lines in order to get into live radio and TV programs. Among those I enjoyed were Jack Benny's and Phil Harris's radio programs and Red Skelton's TV program.

In those days, all programs were aired live, none were taped. No canned laughter was used, and all TV programs were aired in black and white. Since all programs were aired live, a program being shown on TV in New York City at 8:00 P.M. was being presented to a studio audience and being aired in Hollywood at 5:00 P.M.

Mistakes were aired to the listening and/or viewing audiences and were not edited out as they are today. TV programs, especially, showed the human shortcomings of entertainment personalities. However, what went awry was often funnier than what was supposed to be said or done. Good or bad, that was the price of live broadcasting in those days, and I loved it.

I didn't spend much time in stores. However, there was a large department store across the street from the YMCA. Every so often, I'd walk through and look at everything interesting to a male: men's clothes, sporting goods and pretty saleswomen. One day on the main floor, I noticed a fancy, new car on display. I stopped and stood there admiring its beauty and drooling covetously.

As I did so, two men came along and did the following demonstration. One got into the car and started the engine. The other lit a cigarette and stood it on end on the hood of the car. Then the man in the car revved the engine. To my amazement and to the amazement of all those watching with me, the cigarette did not fall over nor did the smoke, rising straight up, waver.

What a car! I don't remember what make it was or if it was made in America. One thing I do remember. I wished I could have bought it right then and there.

The entire Los Angeles area was great, but I began to miss my family and friends back in Oswego. So I decided to return home in late October and leave the wonderful, southern California climate behind, a decision I would regret many times.

I looked in the classified section of the *Los Angeles Times* newspaper under *Travel-Transportation: Riders Wanted*. I saw one by a fellow driving nonstop to Chicago, Illinois, a couple of days later. The price was right, so I called. His father answered the phone, and after a short conversation, he took my name and address. Before hanging up, he mentioned another couple was going as well.

The morning Sam picked me up, I discovered he was stone deaf! Even so, I decided to ride with him. After all, what possibly could go wrong? After picking the couple up, we headed east on U.S. Highway 66.

Early into our trip, our written pleas to let us help with the driving fell literally on deaf ears and a closed mind. Sam made it clear that he was the driver, and we were his passengers.

Talk about a wild ride! Sam was oblivious to tires squealing, horns honking, and many other noises associated with traveling a long distance in a short time on two- and three-lane roads. But we weren't. I bit my nails much of the time and didn't sleep much the entire trip. However, the patron saint of deaf drivers was with us, and we arrived safely.

Sam dropped me off on U.S. Highway 20 before Chicago. I said my good-byes and watched as his car disappeared into the night. Then I picked up my suitcase and my bronze-colored, five quart, oil dispenser that I was given at my job, and walked to a lighted spot to begin hitchhiking. Using my educated thumb and buses, I continued my trip home.

I arrived back in Oswego on Halloween night. Ghosts, goblins and other costumed trick or treaters were everywhere. I began my trek home. It was a cold, dark, overcast night. The wind blew dead leaves all around me as I walked. But I didn't care. I was home. Back where my family was. Back where my friends were. Back where my roots were. I felt great. I didn't mind the three-mile walk at all.

With a big smile on my face, a gift for Mom and a heart full of joy, I walked into the house. Mom saw me and, without showing the least bit of joy, asked, "What are you doing home?" At that moment, I wished I had not returned.

Chapter XIII
A Year Like No Other: 1952

For as long as I could remember, Mom had used her "drip method" to instill a desire in me to go to college. She often stated such phrases as, "When you go to college . . . " or "After you go to college . . . " She just assumed that I would go, and I grew up assuming it also. However, in the spring of 1952, I began to talk of not going and had several good reasons. Even then, Mom continued using her "drip method," undaunted by my statements to the contrary.

One evening, while reading the *Pall Times*, I spotted a large want ad for draftsman trainees at the General Electric Plant in Syracuse. The job sounded interesting, the pay and benefits were good, and I realized that I met every qualification listed. So I decided to apply. However, I kept my decision to myself. Once I was hired, I would tell Mom. Otherwise, I would say nothing.

Early Saturday morning, I drove to Syracuse, found the plant and was soon seated, with many other hopefuls, in the personnel office filling out a long application form. Wherever a phone number was called for, I put Mrs. O'Leary's number. Since we had no phone, she had often taken messages for us in the past. Even though Jimmy and I had a heated argument recently, I didn't think that would matter. After all, the argument was between her son and me and did not involve her. Thus, I felt secure using her number.

Besides the initial application, there were other written and oral parts to the application process that dragged on forever, or so it seemed. Finally we were informed by the personnel manager that a certain number of us would be hired. Those who were would be notified by phone sometime during the following week. He concluded by making it very clear that anyone, not receiving a phone call, should assume that he was not hired. With his final words ringing in my ears, I left the plant and drove home, feeling sure I would be called.

Each day the following week, after arriving home from my job at the Marathon Corporation, I checked with Mrs. O'Leary to see if a call had come. Each day she said, "No." By Friday evening when I heard the fifth "no" from her lips, I knew that door had been closed. I was disappointed for a while, but eventually I got over it and kept my job at Marathon.

That fall, I entered my freshman year at the local college and began my education leading to a career in teaching. Ten years later after working my way through college and graduate school, I had earned my B.A. and M.Ed. degrees and had five years of teaching experience under my belt.

While in Oswego visiting Mom, I decided to pay Mrs. O'Leary a social call. As we sat and chatted over coffee and cookies, she suddenly said to me, "Bud, there's something I have to tell you. Do you remember the week you were waiting for a call from General Electric in Syracuse, and each day I told you no call came? Well, I lied. They called Tuesday of that week, and when they asked for David Furman, I replied, 'I don't know any David Furman,' and hung up. Your argument with Jimmy riled my Irish temper, Bud. That's why I did what I did. Please forgive me."

As she finished, tears were filling her eyes and a few were overflowing and beginning to run down her cheeks. Stunned by her confession, I sat silently for several seconds, thinking back to that time in my life and realizing the door had not been closed after all. But now, here I was ten years later, educated and involved in a profession of utmost importance. I took a final sip of coffee, assured Mrs. O'Leary that I forgave her and filled her in on all that had happened to me since that fateful week. As I was about to leave, she gave me a big Irish hug, and I gave her a big German one in return.

Shortly after walking back across the road to Mom's house, I related what Mrs. O'Leary had told me. Once I finished, Mom smiled and said triumphantly, "See, Buddy, I knew you would go to college! Mrs. O'Leary helped the Lord answer all my prayers for your future." And in a way, she had.

During the years I worked for Mulcahey's, another fish fry stand opened about a stone's throw down the road. Rudy's was not much competition at first, but gradually the two became more and more competitive. During Corky's summer vacations from Hamilton College, he worked long hours at Rudy's, and I did the same at Mulcahey's.

Along the way, we both built up strong loyalties to our employers and often had heated arguments as to which stand was busier, which had the better fish fries, and on and on. As it so often happened in the Civil War, it was brother against brother. Now we had our own "Civil War," brother against brother, Rudy's against Mulcahey's.

By Thanksgiving Day 1952, the feud should have been over. Even though Corky still worked summers at Rudy's, I had quit Mulcahey's in June 1951 to work construction. However, I remained loyal and continued to buy my fish and chips at Mulcahey's, insisting his were still the best.

On that particular Thanksgiving Day, Corky was home from college, and I had driven out from my room in town to enjoy dinner with everyone. For some nonsensical reason, Corky and I began badgering each other over which stand was better and why. Our "Civil War" began all over, harmless at first but soon becoming more and more serious.

Just as Mom put the final dish of food on the beautifully set dining room table, our tempers boiled over, and we began to fight. Ignoring Mom's pleas to stop, we continued. I soon had Corky in a headlock with one arm and flung him over my back onto the food-laden table with a crash. Dishes of food that Mom had spent so many hours preparing went flying, ruining the meal. The crash plus Mom's screams of anger was the noise "heard 'round the neighborhood," and the fight was over.

I felt terrible over what I had done to her meal. I apologized to her, then turned, walked out of the house, got into my car, drove back to town and had my Thanksgiving dinner at a diner.

After that fight, whenever Corky and I were together, neither of us uttered one word about the stands. Our "Civil War" had finally ended. Who won? I suppose, in a way, I did since I had ruined a delicious meal in a fit of anger. Which stand was better? To this day, that question, as far as Corky and I are concerned, ranks up there with such philosophical ones as, "Which came first, the chicken or the egg?" However, it's the only one we never debate.

In the early fall of 1952, I moved into a warm house in town situated halfway between the college and Marathon. Since I was going to college full-time days and working full-time nights, my room with a private bath was a godsend. I was not only surviving, I was getting enough sleep to boot. But I had to budget every minute of my time and stick to a close schedule.

One day a week, I had no classes between noon and two o'clock. Therefore, I would arrange with Mom to take her to town for groceries and whatever else she needed. Even though I stressed several times that I had a two o'clock class, Mom was never ready to go on time, and I was never on time for my class.

Week after week I'd arrive just before noon, and she wouldn't be ready. Before I could utter one word, she'd fly into one of her "fits," talking a mile a minute and waving her arms in the air, as if I were to blame for being on time. When she was finally ready to walk out the door, she would stop and go to the bathroom.

From this weekly experience, another of Mom's eccentricities surfaced. It was one I should have noticed sooner but didn't. No matter where she was going or with whom, she was never ready on time. Considering the poor washing facilities, I could have understood her lateness if she had to be ready at eight o'clock or nine o'clock in the morning and wasn't. But at noon or later?

For some reason, known only to the gods, she could not break her daily, morning routine and accommodate the person coming to pick her up by being ready on time. Therefore, everyone had to wait for her, and then she'd wonder why none of her neighbors would continue to offer her rides to town. I never figured her out, and she never changed.

The day she passed away on June 21, 1988, she hobbled into the bathroom at Rose Marie's home, sat down, went, then leaned against the wall and died. Later, in a lighter vein, my brother-in-law, Paul, commented to me, "You know, Bud, the last thing your mother always did, before going anywhere, was go to the toilet. And she even did it before she died."

As Christmas 1952, approached, the college closed for vacation giving me some time to play basketball at the YMCA, catch up on assignments and relax doing nothing. One afternoon on a cold but clear day, I took Mom shopping. As we walked past one of the large, furniture stores on First Street, she saw a new white refrigerator with a blue interior in the window. She oh'd and ah'd over it, then commented that its blue interior was exactly the right color for her "dream kitchen." Since she was still using the icebox on the back porch and hadn't had a refrigerator for twelve years, I could empathize with her feelings.

We also looked at some of the black and white televisions in another window of the store. Mom wished out loud a second time as if wishes could make dreams come true. She didn't find everything she was looking for, so I agreed to take her to Syracuse the following Saturday.

That evening at work, I kept thinking of the refrigerator and television Mom had enjoyed looking at. I finally did some figuring and decided that maybe I could make her wishes come true and bring some happiness into her boring life.

The next morning, I went to the store, spoke to the manager, bought the refrigerator, a 21-inch TV and an antenna on time and incurred a $1200 debt. After paying the down payment and signing some papers, I arranged to have everything delivered and the antenna installed on Saturday while Mom and I were in Syracuse. When the deal was completed, I walked out of the store whistling my favorite Christmas carol.

Saturday came and once Mom was ready, we headed for Syracuse leaving Paddy and the unlocked house behind. As I drove from one store to another, I prayed little prayers that my gifts would be waiting upon our return. Exhausted by late afternoon, we headed home.

As I drove, my thoughts and anticipation were getting the best of me. Would everything be there as promised? Or would the store foul things up as so often happens at Christmastime? What would Mom say? How would she react? Would she insist that I take the items back as she had a few times in the past? Could I meet the monthly payments? Questions, and more questions.

As I finally neared the house, my thoughts changed. There, on the roof, was a TV antenna signalling me that the men had come and delivered everything I bought. A few of my earlier questions had already been answered.

I pulled into the driveway and parked. I helped Mom with her packages then, arm in arm, we walked across the snow, up the stairs, across the porch and into the house. As soon as she saw the refrigerator with a large red ribbon and bow tied around it, she stopped in her tracks and stared at it for several seconds with her mouth open, but no words coming out. Then, looking to her right, she saw the television decked out with another red ribbon and bow. As I smiled from ear to ear, I yelled, "Merry Christmas!"

Her reaction to my gifts was not what I had expected. Instead of screaming with delight, she turned toward me and with tears streaming down her face, hugged me longer and harder than she had ever done before. And that made my $1200 debt worth it.

Once the initial excitement died down, Corky, Paddy, and I moved the refrigerator into place, leveled it and plugged it in. Even though it was spic and span inside and out, Mom still had to wash it with lots of hot, soapy water and rinse it twice. Then she turned it on, shut the door, stepped back and smiled. Finally, she declared, "It sure is a beautiful refrigerator and just the right color inside. At last, I've got the beginning of my dream kitchen."

That evening, Mom turned the TV on for the first time. We all sat and watched spellbound by each program with few commercial interruptions. Many of our neighbors had televisions before us, but we now had the biggest screen of any. The antenna was positioned perfectly and all three channels came in as clear as a bell. It wasn't long before neighbors were coming to our house to watch TV.

In the years since, I don't recall what Mom whispered into my ear as she hugged me on that eventful day. I only recall the hug and the warm feeling, it gave me, knowing that her Christmas was very, very merry.

Chapter XIV
Summer, 1954: An Unusual Mixture of Events

My second year of college was over, and I drove home from Providence anticipating a summer job at the Marathon Corporation. Since I had worked there full-time for almost two years before going away to college, and since summers were their busiest production times, I was sure they would hire me. However, soon after arriving home, my anticipation turned to disappointment, and I was not hired. Therefore, I had to look elsewhere for work, but jobs were scarce.

About the middle of June, I received an invitation to attend the high school graduation in Maplewood, New Jersey, of a cute, musically talented girl, I had met at college that year. As high school seniors often did, Marilyn Binns had come to visit on two different weekends to look the college over. I met her in a small lounge while playing Ping-Pong with Victor Anderson. We dated a few times and enjoyed each other's company.

Since I had her invitation and still needed a job, I decided to go to the Newark area, look for work and attend her graduation. Newark and the surrounding towns were much larger than Oswego. Certainly, there were jobs to be had there. The day before her graduation, I packed some clothes and other necessities. Early the next morning, I headed for the Newark/Maplewood area in a positive frame of mind.

In Hancock, New York, I phoned Marilyn and informed her I was coming. She was elated and agreed to meet me at the train station in Newark and ride with me to her home giving me the necessary directions. I arrived at the station early, parked my car, walked to the station and found a men's washroom. I took advantage of it and came out looking and smelling much better than when I had gone in. I even changed my clothes. Marilyn arrived at six o'clock, and soon we were in my car heading toward her home for supper.

The graduation exercises were typical. The auditorium was hot and humid, the speakers were windy, and before it was over, the smell of sweaty bodies wafted throughout the room. The graduation finally ended and we headed for a party at the home of one of Marilyn's well-to-do friends. The party goers were sedate at first but loosened up after drinking a few sips of champagne. Before we left, things got pretty wild, but isn't that the way graduation parties are supposed to be?

After a few hours of sleep and some breakfast, I said my good-byes to Marilyn and her mom and went looking for work. As luck would have it, I landed a job at an industry in Kearny beginning on the following Monday. Since it was only Friday, I was sure I would have a place to live by Sunday. However, in the meantime, I would have to sleep in my car.

Saturday I looked at several rooms for rent, but they were either too expensive, too run-down, too far from my job or in bad neighborhoods. That night I drove out near the plant, parked on a deserted side street, rolled the windows partway down and settled down for the night. I would look again the next day.

Before I could fall asleep, a car pulled up behind mine and soon red and blue lights were flashing. A police officer walked up and began questioning me. I answered his questions and explained to him why I was there. He was very nice but firm. He informed me that the area was too dangerous for someone sleeping in a car with the windows even partially open. Therefore, I could not stay there. But, if I wanted to, I could drive to the police station, see Officer Dick, and he would work something out with me. I accepted the officer's suggestion, asked for directions to the station and headed that way.

Officer Dick listened to my tale of woe then gave me two options. I could sleep in my car in the police parking lot, or I could sleep in a jail cell. I opted for the cell since it would be much cooler.

Following normal police procedures, I gave him my belt, glasses and watch then requested an 8:00 A.M. wake-up call. He laughed and said, "You'll be out of here by six o'clock." A short walk and the cells came into view. I entered one, the door clanged, the key turned, Officer Dick said, "Good night," then turned and left.

The cell was cool and damp, but as clean as could be expected. I stretched out on the cot and relaxed. There was enough light, so I could read what others had written on the wall next to me. Someone had kept track of time. A few had expressed anger and others hope. One had written poetry. Before I finished reading, I fell asleep.

The next sound I heard was an officer banging on the bars of my cell.

I awoke with a start, sat up, quickly gathered my thoughts together, rose to my feet and followed him out of the cell area. When I entered an adjoining room, I looked at a clock. It was exactly 8:00 A.M. I smiled to myself.

After I washed up and retrieved my things, I was given coffee, a doughnut, and the classified section of the Sunday paper. Officer Dick had left it for me with a note wishing me good luck in finding a room. I was, and still am, grateful to him for treating me so kindly. I thanked the officers, tucked the paper under my arm and left.

Before Sunday was over, I had found a nice room in a safe section of Newark at a price I could afford. I had unpacked everything and had room left over in both the bureau and the closet. I had enjoyed a large piece of cold watermelon while sitting in a park. Things were looking up.

Monday morning I reported for work. I was checked in, given a locker and taken on a tour. I saw what was made in each section and then taken to my work station and quickly trained. The plant was a refinery. Bones of animals, such as cows, were processed. The end products were laundry detergent, fertilizer, dog food, and some kind of oil. My job was to stencil addresses on fifty-five gallon drums of the oil for shipment to places all over the world. As long as the paperwork figure matched the number of barrels I stenciled for each order, things went fine. And the two usually matched.

The afternoon of my second day, several boxcars arrived near my station. Soon a fellow, riding a small tractor with a scoop bucket attached, arrived. He opened the doors of the first boxcar and began to unload its contents. The boxcar was full of rancid, bug infested, meaty bones that had been shipped from another state. I could hardly stand the terrible odor as it wafted my way. The bones were deposited on a long, conveyor belt that carried them to another building for processing. Boxcars frequently arrived at the plant and were unloaded near me. Try as I might, I never got used to the stench.

To get from my locker in one building to my work station in another, I had to walk past the outside area where the conveyor belt entered the first processing building. The stench was the worst in this area. It was so bad, I could not eat my breakfast and then make this trip, for fear of vomiting. Therefore, I carried my breakfast in a bag, walked to my station and then ate. Once at my station, I would not return to my locker under any circumstances until quitting time.

On certain mornings, as I quickly walked through "odor alley," I'd notice an older man sitting at a work station near the conveyor belt. He would be skinning all the dead dogs that had been picked up the previous few days and nights in and around the Newark area. After each was skinned, he'd scoop it up in his arms and deposit it on the moving, conveyor belt for processing into the various products.

To this day, whenever I use a laundry detergent, I recall my experiences there and, in a way, I can even recall the stench. I also recall losing several pounds that summer, not from being overworked, but from eating much less food.

My first payday finally came. With money in my pocket, I called Marilyn and asked her if she wanted to go to the Dodgers' baseball game in Brooklyn that evening. She accepted. I told her to be ready at 5:30, and I'd be there to pick her up.

On the way, I got lost and arrived forty-five minutes late. I apologized, but I don't think she really heard me. She complained that she had gone without her dinner to get ready, and on and on and on. I finally murmured, "Marilyn, I'm sorry I was late. But there's nothing I can do about it now. So please, let's forget it and leave for the game. Since you know the way, please give me directions."

She gave me direction after direction, and soon we arrived at the entrance to the Holland Tunnel. She told me not to go through the tunnel but to stay in New Jersey and head north on routes 1 and 9. I did as she ordered and crawled for seven miles stopping at traffic light after traffic light and dodging large trucks that appeared from everywhere. We finally reached the Lincoln Tunnel.

Following her instructions, I drove through the tunnel under the Hudson River and exited in New York City. Her next directions put us on the West Side Highway heading south. Several minutes later, we passed a large sign, "Holland Tunnel Exit Ahead." I looked over at her, she looked at me and remarked in a haughty tone of voice, "Now are YOU aggravated?"

Aggravated? Was I aggravated? We were already late, she deliberately took us fifteen miles out of our way, and she had the nerve to ask if I was aggravated? Of course I was; wouldn't anyone be at that point? But I didn't act aggravated, and I'm sure this made her even angrier inside.

We finally arrived at Ebbets Field. The game had begun, and we could hear cheers. But I couldn't find a parking place. As I continued to look, Marilyn began needling me. I finally stated, "You don't really want to see this game, so I'm taking you home," and headed that way. My words silenced her all the way to the Brooklyn Bridge. We were stopped by a police officer for a minor infraction and given a warning. Once the officer left, she began needling me again. I couldn't believe this cute, talented girl could be so nasty.

This time I went through the Holland Tunnel. A sign outside the tunnel directed me to turn off my headlights. When I exited on the New Jersey side and pulled the light switch to the on position nothing happened. I had neither headlights nor taillights.

As I pulled off the first exit ramp to check out the system, Marilyn started in again. By now I was boiling mad inside, but I was determined to control myself. I soon found a blown fuse in the fuse box under the dash, replaced it and headed as fast as the speed limit would allow for Maplewood.

En route, we saw a Howard Johnson's Restaurant. Since I had made Marilyn miss her dinner, I decided to "rub salt in her wound," and stopped for something to eat. After being seated, Marilyn whined, "I'm so hungry, I'm going to order the biggest steak on the menu!" I finally boiled over a little and responded, "I don't give a hoot what you order!" And with that, I headed for the men's room. Upon returning, I ordered, and when the food was served, the orders were almost identical: cheeseburgers and french fries. Only our drinks were different. Why she hadn't ordered a steak was beyond me. Maybe she had a heart after all.

As I left her at the door of her home, I was very relieved. Walking back to my car, I mumbled to myself, "Good riddance, Marilyn. I hope I never see you again." But fate stepped in and Marilyn entered PBI that fall. In time, she, Shelley and I became good friends. Marilyn majored in voice and cello. When Shelley and I were married on December 27, 1957, Marilyn performed beautifully during our ceremony and at our reception.

As the summer progressed, I realized I needed to make additional money. So I began reading the *Help Wanted* section of the classified ads in a local paper. The second day, I spotted one that interested me. I called and made an appointment to see the man who ran the ad. We were to meet in his hotel room. When he opened the door, I didn't see anyone at first, but his greeting quickly caught my attention. I looked down and there he was, an older man with no legs, just stumps protruding from his torso.

We sat down, exchanged some pleasantries, I answered some questions, and then he explained the job. He needed someone to come early each morning, Monday through Saturday, use his car to drive him to a section of the area in or around Newark, and drop him off. Around 6:00 P.M., he was to be picked up at the preestablished rendezvous and returned to his hotel.

As we continued talking, I learned that Peter was a World War I veteran who had lost his legs in combat. He was a proud member of the VFW (Veterans of Foreign Wars) and loved his country, his medals and his old, army uniform. To earn a living, he sold pencils, shoelaces and other items to small stores or to individuals on the streets.

To do this, he had a simple cart on which he could carry a selection of merchandise and still have room to sit. He could propel himself using his arms and hands. He had special blocks for his hands that reached the sidewalk's surface. Thus, as he swung his arms and hands back and forth, the blocks made contact with the sidewalk, and the cart was moved forward. What he needed now was an honest chauffeur, and the pay, he offered, was good. Therefore, I accepted the job, since it would fit into my work schedule at the processing plant.

The first morning, I went to his hotel room for the keys to his station wagon. I told him that I would get his wagon from the garage and meet him in front of the hotel. Not having talked at all about his wagon, I expected to find an old, beatup piece of junk. *After all*, I thought, *How much money can he make selling pencils, laces and other cheap items?*

When I reached his assigned spot, my mouth fell open. There stood an almost new, beautiful, blue, station wagon. "What do you know!" I exclaimed in surprise. I opened the door on the driver's side and slid behind the wheel. I started the engine, adjusted the mirrors and seat and turned my head around toward the rear.

One look and I could see that the wagon was crammed full of merchandise and clothes including his old, army uniform. What I saw told me, he was not a very neat person, but how could he be with his physical limitations. I assumed he expected his chauffeur to keep the contents of the wagon in some kind of order, and I soon found out, he did.

I pulled up in front of the hotel, just as he was coming out. To walk, he had thick, leather pads strapped to the ends of his stumps. Using the blocks in his hands, he swung himself forward landing on his padded stumps. He had mastered this procedure, and with a little help from me, he was soon on the passenger's front seat. I dropped him off as directed, and once he was ready to begin his day of selling, I left him and drove to my other job.

I picked him up at six o'clock, stopped at a deli to buy him some food, drove back to his hotel and helped him out at the entrance. "Park the wagon," he ordered, "Then come to my room, and I'll pay you in cash for today." "Terrific!" I murmured to myself. "I can use the cash."

I parked the wagon and quickly walked to his room on the second floor. I knocked and entered after being invited to do so. Peter was on his bed and smiling. Spread out in front of him was the day's receipts, far more money than I ever expected to see.

Patiently, I waited while the money was counted and the total written in a small ledger. As he counted, I thought to myself, "Either this man is a super salesman or people feel sorry for him or both." At any rate, business must have been great that day if smiles were any indication.

Peter paid me. Then, before I left, we had a chat. Most of what we chatted about, I soon forgot. However, one thing he said stuck in my mind. He informed me of the amount of his wagon payment each month and with business so good, he was making two payments each month. I left with his words ringing in my ears. I soon learned to respect this man, this hard working, self-sufficient veteran.

I continued working both jobs most of the summer. However, in late August, Peter said it was time to move on and asked me if I would travel with him. He'd pay my way plus wages. We'd spend the cold months in the southern states and the other months in the northern. We'd travel all over the United States.

I took his invitation as a compliment. Having had many talks during the previous weeks, I knew Peter trusted me, liked me, and enjoyed being with me. He felt more secure with me than with any of his previous chauffeurs. It was a very tempting offer, but I graciously declined.

Once he hired another chauffeur, who seemed like an honest man, I helped Peter pack, loaded his wagon, bent down and hugged him good-bye. I had tears in my eyes as his wagon pulled away from the curb. I knew I'd never see him again, and I would miss his friendship. He was a great person and an even greater American.

One day, soon after Peter left, I saw an alluring ad for door to door salesmen of pots and pans for a well-known aluminum company. I couldn't resist answering it. My thoughts went wild. Here was my chance to get rich while still in college. No more cleaning dorms, working in the dining hall, cleaning houses, doing lawn work, et cetera. I was going to work a few hours each week selling and make enough money to pay my college bill, keep my car going, go on dates, buy new clothes and "live happily ever after."

When I entered the office where the interviews were being held, I saw about twenty young men all dressed in suits, and all looked sharp. I had on slacks and a shirt and didn't look sharp at all. However, I sat down between two fellows and struck up a conversation with one of them. I soon learned he had graduated from Princeton University with a major in physics. Now he needed to earn some money, so he could go to graduate school and earn his doctorate in physics. I was impressed.

Finally I asked, "What's your name?" His answer, "Merco Nussbaum." When my mouth dropped open in surprise, the expression on his face suddenly changed. I asked him if he had ever lived in Oswego, New York. He replied in the affirmative. Then, without pausing except for air, he went into the details of his being brought to America in 1944 after his liberation from one of the Nazi death camps in Europe during World War II. He was one of a thousand refugees that had been sent to Oswego to live until 1946. Then, when all of them were given their freedom and American citizenship, he and his surviving family members had left Oswego to escape the brutal winters.

I then asked him if he remembered attending the Campus School in Oswego and playing soccer during the lunch hours. It was then that he recognized me as a classmate during his years in that school. Smiling broadly, we both stood and hugged each other, just as his name was being called for his interview. This certainly was a joyous reunion for both of us, and I had so many questions to ask him. However, I was soon called for my interview, and when it was over, Merco was gone. I could have kicked myself for not getting his address.

My interview went well, and I became a salesman of aluminum waterless cookware. I studied the training manual and listened carefully to the pros in training meetings as they demonstrated procedures for selling the product. I practiced my spiel in front of a mirror, coordinating my words with my hands and showing the finer points of the pots and pans. While practicing this, I dreamed of the money I'd make on countless sales.

The day finally came when I set out to make my fortune. With my large, black suitcase full of cookware in one hand, a smile on my face and a positive attitude in my heart and mind, I knocked on my first door and waited. I won't go into details, but I soon realized my success and riches were washing out to sea.

I soon discovered that I was not a born salesman. In fact, I was not any kind of salesman, especially a door-to-door one. I managed to sell a few sets, but nothing like I had dreamed of selling. I was not a salesman, and once I came back to earth with this reality in mind, I stopped trying and stored my set of cookware until the day I'd return from my honeymoon. Then I'd let my "blushing bride" use these wonderful, waterless pots and pans and make me delicious, vitamin-filled meals. And I did.

I was near the end of my living and working two jobs in the Newark area when on August 31, hurricane Carol finally came ashore. It unleashed its fury from the mid-Atlantic states through New England. Winds topping out at 135 miles per hour caused five hundred million dollars worth of damage and caused at least sixty-eight deaths. In covering the hurricane, one paper reported that in Boston the storm toppled the steeple of Old North Church from which lantern signals in April, 1775, started Paul Revere on his famous midnight ride. Newark also suffered its share of damage but only made local headlines.

By the time the clean-up was well under way, I was packed and ready to return to Oswego. I needed a few days to relax, see friends and family, and pack in preparation for my return to Providence and college. I had enjoyed my interesting summer in the Newark area, but I shed no tears when I left.

While home, hurricane Edna struck from North Carolina to Maine and Nova Scotia adding to the damage of hurricane Carol. Even though I knew road conditions were bad, I left for Providence on the day I had planned. En route, I saw the extent of the damage: bridges out, buildings cut in two, power lines down, flooding, boats smashed into kindling and much, much more. I arrived safe and sound and had quite a tale to tell whenever anyone asked, "How was your summer?"

Chapter XV
Sports: One Moment of Glory

I was in the seventh grade the day Max Ziel, head coach of the college's basketball team, sat us boys down in gym and began teaching us the fundamentals of basketball. His willingness to do this impressed me, so I listened carefully to his instructions and later executed them on the court as well as I could.

The main points he emphasized about set shots still remain fresh in my mind. He began by pointing out the small, metal loops that hang at intervals around the bottom of any basketball rim on which a net is hung. As he stood facing one, he continued by telling us that the loop now directly in front of him divided the rim into two equal parts. Therefore, in shooting, we were to focus our eyes on a loop and not the entire rim. Once our eyes were focused, we were to shoot the ball, arching it over the loop and into the basket. After saying it, he did it. Then he began moving in a circular path fifteen to twenty feet from the basket, stopping in front of each loop, focusing on it, then shooting the ball, arching it over the loop and into the basket.

I was very impressed with his accuracy as he kept repeating the same words over and over and making basket after basket. When it was our turn to try, I had memorized his instructions. I did exactly what he taught, and it worked. I soon began making set shot after set shot with only an occasional miss.

As a kid I was thrilled! Being short for my age, I realized that if I could shoot from the outside with a high degree of accuracy, I could play basketball and score well.

By the time Coach Ziel's teaching sessions came to an end, I had the fundamentals down pretty well. However, I continued to practice them at every opportunity. As I got better and better, my enthusiasm for the game increased more and more. Eventually, I developed a passion for basketball, a passion that would last my lifetime.

But basketball was not the first sport I learned to play and enjoy.

Softball was. As a boy, I had been playing softball for as long as I could remember both at home and at school. All we needed to play softball was a bat, a ball, some markers for bases and a few players, male or female, for each team. Since few of us had gloves, we played without them enduring the pain associated with catching any ball coming our way until calluses formed on our hands.

Since we never had umpires, heated arguments erupted at times over close calls, but these were usually settled by our standard rule: close calls go to the runner. When arguments continued, the game often ended abruptly, and each player stormed off the field vowing never to play with any of the opposing players again. However, once tempers cooled down, the vows were forgotten, new sides were chosen, and a new game began.

For several years, I enjoyed playing the outfield, shortstop or second base. Then I became interested in learning to pitch after watching Raymond (Ducky) Drake, now a member of the Softball Hall of Fame, fast pitch several games over a period of weeks. In each game, Ducky struck out batter after batter with his sizzling fastball and an assortment of other pitches. His expertise amazed me. If ever there was an artist in softball pitching, Ducky was it.

Watching him pitch was all the motivation I needed. Since my sister, Marilyn, was the catcher on her eighth grade baseball team, she agreed to catch for me. I began pitching to her slowly and wildly at first. However, I became a tiny bit better with each practice. Once I could pitch fairly fast with accuracy, I began using diagrammed instructions from a library book about softball and taught myself how to throw various pitches.

After a year of practicing whenever the weather permitted, I felt I was ready to begin my legacy as a fast-pitch, softball player. Thus, one day, I challenged Marilyn, one of the best hitters on her team, to try and hit my pitches. She immediately accepted, ran and got our taped up, slightly cracked, baseball bat. She walked up to the "plate," swung the bat a few times, then hollered, "Ready!"

My first pitch was a fast ball right down the middle. She swung, connected and drove it almost into the lake some distance away. Seeing it go, she smiled, and I frowned. That one hit told me, I needed more practice. So I continued until I could strike Marilyn out more often than she could hit my pitches.

Even though I continued practicing, my official debut didn't take place until the spring of my freshman year in college. Pitching my first game in the men's, fast-pitch, softball league at the college, my years of practice paid off. I pitched a shutout.

Since then, I've pitched a great many games for a number of different teams and have won more then my share. However, I never became another Ducky Drake and to this day, he remains my pitching idol.

For many summers, a family named O'Gorman escaped the heat and humidity of New York City by coming to their cottage near the lake. Even though their son, Jack, was a year older than Corky, the three of us enjoyed many fun times together.

Since Jackie was a New York Yankees baseball fan, he often listened to their games on the radio. Mel Allen, the "Voice of the Yankees" for many years, made each game come alive and exciting through his colorful, inning by inning commentary. His words, "Going, going, gone!" still ring in my ears whenever I think back to those days with him behind the mike. Thus, Corky and I became Yankee fans during the era when such stars as Joe DiMaggio, Phil Rizzuto, Tommy Henrich, Joe Page, Yogi Berra, Bobby Brown, and Charlie Keller played for the Yankees. And we're still fans.

Once Corky and I began listening to Yankee games regularly, we wanted to play baseball and forget softball. However, we soon painfully discovered, we could not catch baseballs barehanded. Since we had no extra money to buy gloves, we returned to playing softball and only dreamed of playing the other. One spring a few years later, I scraped together enough money to buy a cheap baseball glove, and my dreams soon came true.

It was during my early teenage years. One June, several friends and I formed a team and entered the Recreation Department's Intermediate Baseball League for boys in our age bracket. Several poorly kept baseball fields were used. The Recreation Department provided a new baseball—which the winning team kept after the game—the bases and an older teenager to umpire. The teams provided their own bats.

There were no protective helmets in those days and no uniforms, not even T-shirts with logos. Most players wore sneakers since few could afford baseball shoes, and those who had neither, wore street shoes. There were no adult managers or coaches pushing us beyond our abilities and getting angry if we didn't meet their expectations. Since all games were played in the afternoon, few, if any, adult spectators ever came to watch, cheer, boo, yell derogatory remarks at the players, including their own, and complain to and/or threaten the umpire. Thus, we could play relaxed and, win or lose, have fun.

Every Saturday evening the box scores for all games the previous week and the schedule for the upcoming week appeared in the *Pall Times*. Every team was scheduled to play two or three games each week.

Even though everyone on our team had played a great deal of softball, none of us had played much baseball. Thus, many of our weaknesses surfaced during our first game. For starters, most of us had trouble hitting. Being long-time, softball players, the smaller size of the baseball and the speed at which it crossed home plate stymied us. Therefore, the opposing pitcher fanned fifteen batters in our seven inning game, and we lost ten to zero.

After losing our next two games as well, I visited Rupert McGrath (Rupie), an outstanding hitter on the high school's varsity baseball team. I asked him how he learned to hit so well. He smiled slyly then began telling me his secret.

"Using a piece of a broomstick for a bat, have someone pitch Ping-Pong balls at you from a distance close enough that the balls will remain airborne and cross the plate somewhere in or near the strike zone. Once you can hit those with any regularity, hitting a baseball will be a cinch."

After hearing his secret, I thought he was pulling my leg and told him so. He insisted he wasn't. But knowing how much Rupie enjoyed kidding people, I was still skeptical, but determined to try his cure-all method.

On the way home, I bought six Ping-Pong balls. The next morning I made my broomstick bat and a cardboard home plate. Marilyn agreed to pitch even though she scoffed at Rupie's advice. As she pitched ball after ball, I swung and missed every one. The movement on each ball was tremendous, and I had trouble just following the ball from her hand to the plate, let alone hit it. However, I didn't give up and after many misses, I finally hit one and danced for joy.

In the course of an hour, I managed to hit about ten and felt lucky doing it. However, that afternoon, we practiced another hour, and I hit between ten and fifteen. Marilyn was kind enough to pitch some more that evening and three more hours on Sunday. By Sunday evening, I had improved dramatically and looked forward to our first game of the new week on Tuesday afternoon.

Tuesday's opposing pitcher was very wild and narrowly missed beaning our first five batters. Thus, when my first turn at bat came, I entered the batter's box in fear and trembling. When I was set, he reared back and fired. As his first pitch barreled toward home plate, the ball looked huge. I swung and hit it past the infield for a single. As I stood on first base catching my breath, I figuratively patted myself on the back and whispered to myself,

"Thanks a lot, Rupie, you were right." And he really was. I went two for four that day thanks to him.

In the weeks that followed, I continued hitting Ping-Pong balls at home with my broomstick and hitting the "huge" baseballs at the games. In doing so, I raised my batting average a few percentage points each week.

During a game later in the season, our pitcher went home sick after three innings. Since we had no other pitchers, I volunteered. I figured I could at least throw the ball across the plate with some consistency and speed, even if I couldn't throw an assortment of pitches. At the bottom of the fourth inning, I took the mound, threw a few warm-up pitches then faced my first batter. I wound up and delivered. My pitch "flew through the air with the greatest of ease." Seeing the ball coming awry, the batter turned in an effort to get out of its way. However, he didn't escape and the ball hit him on the back. As he sat in the dirt groaning and cussing, I quickly walked to home plate and apologized.

By the end of the seventh inning, I had walked five, had given up six hits, and had only hit one other batter. Even though I was the winning pitcher, having seen the expressions of pain on the faces of the hit batters, the thought of pitching part or all of another game turned me off, and I never volunteered again.

After that initial season, my job at Mulcahey's and my chores at home didn't leave much time for playing organized baseball in a league. So I hung up my glove and retired from the game. However, I continued listening to Yankee games on the radio.

I returned to playing softball at home and at school. Whenever enough players gathered at our homemade field, we'd choose up sides and play a game. Otherwise, I played flies and grounders with whomever was available. A few years later, I saw Ducky Drake pitch, motivating me to follow in his footsteps. Thus, I continued to play softball for thirty more fun-filled seasons.

In the years since my brief baseball career came to an end, I've told Rupie's secret to many aspiring baseball players of all ages. Like the skeptics on my team back then, they've all looked at me as if to ask, "Are you crazy?" And immediately, they've shunned my advice. Thus, I tried to be Rupie's disciple but failed.

Since my various jobs at Mulcahey's were seasonal (April–September), I had time during the other months to play sports, and basketball was my favorite. During my final year in the Campus School, I practiced the fundamentals Coach Ziel taught me, played on our eighth-grade basketball team and sharpened my skills through both.

In the spring of that same year, Corky and I built a regulation-sized, basketball backboard from used lumber given to us. Once we finished bolting the backboard to the long, supporting post, we dug a hole in our backyard, mixed some concrete, and, with blood, sweat and tears, erected the pole, dropping one end of the post into the hole. While Corky held the post to keep it vertical, I shoveled the concrete into the hole around it. Then I braced the post on all four sides, and we left it that way for a few days.

Once the braces were removed, we bolted a rim that was given to us by a friend to the backboard, making sure it was exactly ten vertical feet from the ground. Once a used net was attached to the rim, only one thing was missing—a basketball. Luckily, Jimmy O'Leary owned one and often came over to play. Eventually the gym teacher at school gave me a ball that had a slow leak. From then on, we could play whenever we wanted, only stopping now and then to pump more air into our ball.

Soon after I entered high school, I joined the YMCA nearby. I made it my second home during the months when school was in session. As a member, I could play basketball to my heart's content, and I did. I played noon hours, evenings, and Saturday afternoons through four years of high school.

That winter I played on the Fightin' Five, a team Corky organized. We played in the Intermediate League of the town's Youth Basketball Program. We had a losing season, but I enjoyed every second of every game. I also took a giant step forward in learning how to lose graciously, since Corky did not appreciate technical fouls being called against members of his team.

During the basketball season of my sophomore year, I entered a five-man team in the Noon Basketball League at the Y. Much to my chagrin, the physical education director and referee for all games, replaced my team's name with another more to his liking and dubbed us, Furman's Flatheads. To overcome such an insulting name, we played extra hard and won all our games. I scored well in each, a lift for my bruised ego. By the end of league play, I had learned the hard way that he who sweareth out loud during a game, taketh an early shower and leaveth his team with only four players. However, on such days, I had time to dry off before dressing and, therefore, did not return to school sopping wet as I normally did.

In the Intermediate League that season, I played for the Methodist

Knights. Under the tutelage of our coach, I continued to improve with each game, much to the dismay of those on the opposing teams who guarded me. When the final whistle had blown ending the season, the Methodist Knights finished second. It would have been humorous in a theological sort of way if a team from the evangelical Baptist Church had finished first, but one didn't.

Basketball played a more dominant role in my life during my junior year of high school. I continued playing at the Y. I agreed to manage the junior varsity at school. And Pit and I decided to organize a team to play in the town's Intermediate League.

We assembled a team made up of our friends, all members of the Y and all seasoned players. We knew their strengths and weaknesses. With Tom McCracken's dad as our coach, we felt we had the talent needed to win the championship of the league.

Pit and I wanted the team to be as professional as possible. Therefore, after our first practice at the Y on a Saturday afternoon, we met upstairs in the conference room. Pit chaired a lengthy business meeting. I took the notes.

Our first item of business was choosing a name for our team. Among others, John Hart suggested we name our team, the Senecas, since that tribe was considered by many historians the most powerful of the Six Nations in the Iroquois League based in New York State. After all nominations were listed on the chalkboard, a secret vote was taken and the name, Senecas, won.

Our second item of business was uniforms. Since we had no sponsors, we knew each player would have to pay for his own. Everyone agreed including me. I agreed to it on faith, not knowing where my money would come from. Then we discussed the uniforms themselves. When all was said and done, the vote favored green and gold for colors. Each uniform would consist of two jerseys, one green with gold trim for home games, the other gold with green trim for away games; green shorts with gold trim; a gold-colored sweatshirt for warming up and green sneakers. Pit volunteered his mom as our official seamstress, hoping she'd agree to sew the team name and the players' numbers on each uniform. When asked, she agreed and did so.

The next item of business was dues. Since we had no other sources of income for our expenses, each player voted to give the team one dollar the first week of practice and twenty-five cents each week after that during the entire season. Bob Ferris and I were elected co-treasurers and were instructed to open a Senecas' savings account at the nearby Oswego City Savings Bank. Bob and I became co-trustees of the account, thus both our signatures were required to withdraw any funds. As one of the treasurers, I was elected to keep the books, and Ed Goodness was elected to be our auditor.

Moving on, we discussed practice sessions. After considering the pros and cons from all player personnel, the team agreed to a regular practice schedule at the Y before league play began and during it to help us maintain our skills. It was further agreed that for each foul shot missed in a game, the player missing it would shoot one hundred foul shots at our next practice. I suppose we were being tough on ourselves, but we knew how important foul shots can be in the outcome of close games.

Since Mr. Loope, the General Secretary of Oswego's YMCA, had agreed to let us use the conference room, Tom McCracken suggested we meet the first Saturday evening of each month for a potluck supper. He figured it would give us the opportunity for some food, fun, fellowship, financial update, future strategy considerations for upcoming games, and anything else of a business nature. His suggestion was heartily approved since all teenagers live to eat, not eat to live.

When league play began, the Senecas were ready. We had practiced faithfully and had three, nonleague games under our belts. We had played town teams in Scriba, Minetto, and Mexico, and we had won two of the three. Both our defensive and offensive play were very strong. Coach McCracken firmly believed that defense was the name of the game.

A starting lineup of Pit at center, Tom and Bob at the two forward positions, and Ed and myself as guards was decided upon during our nonleague games, and it continued into league play. Pit and Tom were both tall, both scrappers, and both had developed high-percentage hook shots. Ed, Bob, and I could handle the ball well and shoot from the outside. Fritz Adelman, Bill Holland, and Hart were very able substitutes.

After seeing 6'7" Dolph Schayes shoot overhead set shots in an NBA game pitting the Syracuse Nationals against the Boston Celtics, I had adopted his method. I combined it with Coach Ziel's "focus on the loop and arch the ball over the loop into the basket," and developed into a high-percentage outside shooter.

Our first league game was a lopsided affair in our favor. Our decision to wear green sneakers continued to pay off on fast breaks. As our ball handler barreled down the court with his head lowered to help him control the bouncing ball, all he needed to see ahead of him were green sneakers, and he knew immediately where to bounce-pass the ball. Thus, our fast break was one way the Senecas racked up many points a game.

As the season progressed, everything we had decided upon at our first meeting came to pass including the potluck supper each month. Thanks to our regular practices, we continued to win league games by wide margins. The only team that beat us was the Methodist Knights and by the narrowest of margins. We also won many of our games against town teams, whose players were men not teenagers.

Whenever any of the Senecas became at all lethargic in a game, Coach McCracken or other players took care of it. For example, Pit often began a game lacking the fierce, competitive drive we needed from him; a tiger-like drive to go after rebounds coming off the rim or backboard at either end of the court and loose balls on the floor. Early in those games, when several players from both teams, including Pit and me, were bunched together in hot and heavy action, I'd deliberately poke him in his ribs or some other part of his body. Thinking an opposing player had done it, Pit's "feathers became ruffled." Another poke or two and Pit became a raging bull, and remained that way throughout the game, and turned in another stellar performance.

By the time the annual Easter tournament was to begin, the Senecas had gelled into a winning team, had finished second behind the Methodist Knights in regular league play, and were favored by many to win the Intermediate Championship. Therefore, I was very disappointed the day I learned that a plaster-of-paris, orthopedic, walking cast would be put on my left leg and foot the day tournament play would begin. When I broke the news to my teammates, I assured them, they could win the championship without me. In fact, I challenged them to "win one for the gimper."

The Senecas advanced easily to the final game. I was in the bleachers when the championship game between the Senecas and the Methodist Knights began. It was a close game throughout with neither team building up any sizable leads. When regulation time ran out, the score was tied, and I was hoarse. Even though both teams kept scoring and the lead kept seesawing, three overtimes were played before the championship was decided.

As final seconds ticked away, the Senecas had a slim lead and held it as the final buzzer sounded. Pandemonium broke out among the victorious Senecas and their fans. Pit ran to the bleachers, climbed between the spectators to where I was standing, and we hugged each other in jubilation.

Later, when the individual awards were announced for our league, Pit made the first all-tourney team and was chosen as the outstanding player. Tom made the first all-tourney team and was given the sportsmanship award. Bill made second all-tourney team and Fritz made third all-tourney team. I had no doubts each deserved the honors bestowed on him.

The role basketball played in my life during my senior year was almost a carbon copy of the season before, except in three ways. First, Goodness, Hart, and Holland left the Senecas and Claude Flack and Bob Schrader were added. Second, I became the manager of the varsity team at school. Third, when several varsity players had been injured during the season, Coach Powers asked me to play on the varsity and relinquish my managerial post. It was a tough decision to make, but the glory associated with playing on the varsity went to my head, and I finally opted for it. I felt sad resigning from the Senecas. However, I attended almost all their remaining games and cheered them on to an undefeated season in league play and a second, and final, Easter Tournament Intermediate Championship.

In the interim between high school and college, I continued playing basketball at the YMCA. I also attended many of the Syracuse Nationals' games. I was not the only member of my family who showed an interest in the Nats. Rose Marie, Marilyn and two of their friends, Gloria Buske and Sharon Allen, did, but for another reason, the physical attraction of certain players.

They formed a quartet, the "Nats' Brats," wrote some original songs about the team and sang at a benefit game between the Nats and local talent in Fulton. Art Deutch, one of the Nats' managers, heard them and invited them to sing at some of the Nats' home games in the Syracuse War Memorial. They accepted without hemming or hawing.

The girls designed their own sweatshirts and made outfits that matched the team's colors. The day they went to Syracuse to order their sweatshirts at Joe Lapchick's Sports Store, the neighbor, who drove them, completed his business, forgot to pick them up at the store, and drove back to Oswego. When he hadn't arrived back at the store by closing time, Sharon called her mom, her mom called the neighbor, then called Sharon back with the bad news. When the girls told Joe their sad tale, he called the police.

The police took the girls to the station, sat them on the counter and had them sing. Then a hat was passed for bus fare and the girls were soon on their way home.

The next day their picture appeared in a Syracuse newspaper with the heading, "Nats' Brats Sing for Bus Fare Home." Mom was mortified, but everyone else thought it was comical.

A week or two later, the Nats' Brats began their singing career. During the half time of the game, a revolving platform was placed in the middle of the court for the quartet to stand on. The house lights were turned off, and different colored spotlights illuminated the platform as the Nats' Brats sang for the enjoyment of the hometown crowd. Their songs were well received, and the girls were given a standing ovation at the conclusion of their program that night and the many other nights that followed.

Here are the words to one of their songs, "We're the Nats' Brats From Oswego," to the tune of "I've Been Working on the Railroad."

We're the Nats' Brats from Oswego, and we ought to know,
That the Nationals are the best team, their playing proves it so.
They're the best team in the whole world, the best in the NBA
If you doubt or don't believe us, just watch our Nationals play.

Watch them fluster their opponents, watch them get the ball,
Watch them as they shoot for baskets, they hardly miss at all.
They can really win this ball game, that's what they're gonna do,
At the end, folks, you can holler, Nats, we're proud of you.

My first year at Providence Bible Institute (PBI), I went out for basketball, and although I was a mere five feet eight inches tall, my outside shooting ability assured me of a position on the starting five. Before the season began officially, our team had several strikes against it. For starters, we practiced one evening a week on a court in a small gym. It was much smaller than regulation. Second, we played our home games on a regulation-size court in a local high school. Thus, we really had no home court advantage. Third, most of the members of our team were much shorter and smaller in build than our opponents. Finally, our coach meant well, but he was a pastor of a church and knew far more about preaching than coaching.

Even though the odds for a winning season were stacked against us, we won several games. However, a win over our arch rival, Gordon College, would have made our season a success. Gordon had beaten the PBI Warriors twice a year for sixteen straight years. Dr. Howard Ferrin, President of PBI, had promised the student body a day off from classes following a win over Gordon.

After Gordon had beaten us 87–75 at home earlier in the season, we were still smarting from that defeat as we prepared to take the court for our second meeting. At the conclusion of our prayer time and last minute instructions, Ray Nickerson, a senior, stood up and challenged us with these words: "This is my eighth and final game against Gordon. I've always dreamed of beating them. Let's go out and win this one for me!" After hearing his stirring words, we all chimed in with victory phrases of our own, left our locker room, burst onto the court amid cheers from our fans and began to warm up, believing in our hearts that we would win. However, we lost 96–51, and Ray's dream died with our defeat.

Several new players joined the Warriors the following season, and Ray Nickerson returned to the team as its coach. Our prospects for a winning season looked promising. Coach Nickerson knew what he was doing and molded us into a team that played well together with no "glory boys" seeking to enhance their own egos.

Our first game against Gordon was in enemy territory. Therefore, the vast majority of the fans present were from Gordon. As we sat in the locker room receiving last minute instructions, Ray challenged us anew to win this game for him.

The game started, and we took an early lead, something we hadn't experienced the previous season against Gordon. As we continued to play them close, we began to believe in our hearts and minds that we could beat them. With the standing-room-only crowd screaming hysterically, the final seconds ticked off, the buzzer sounded, we won by two points, 76–74, and Gordon's dynasty crumbled.

After a time of jubilation, we hit the showers and began dressing. While doing so, we were informed that the official scorer, a Gordon student, had erred, and we did not win the game, even though two other scorers corroborated our winning score. Hearing all this made our blood boil, and we headed home with a question mark on our minds. Did we or didn't we win?

We enjoyed basking in our victory anyway and enjoyed our day off from classes with the rest of the student body. The next day, during our regular chapel service, Dr. Ferrin reported on a phone call he had received from the President of Gordon assuring our team that we had won the game fair and square. A lengthy round of applause mingled with cheers greeted the news. but the incident continued to burn within the souls of the Warriors as the season continued.

It rekindled itself even hotter during the preparation for our second game against Gordon that season. It was a home game, and we thirsted for another victory, one in which the final score could not be questioned.

Like the previous game against Gordon, this one far surpassed all our expectations. As all in attendance cheered, the Warriors were in the process of downing their arch rivals, 68–60. This victory, though not as sweet as the first, sent a message to Gordon that the Warriors would no longer be intimidated by them in any future basketball game.

A few new players and the returning veterans greeted their new coach, Mert Preston, when the first practice began the next season. Like the previous season, our prospects for a winning season looked promising. By the time our first game against Gordon neared, our record was two wins and one loss.

The night of the game, Coach Preston admonished us to do our best, win or lose, and be a credit to both the team and to the Lord at all times. After a prayer, we entered the gym, which was full of cheering fans and warmed up. When the buzzer sounded, calling us to the sideline, Coach gave us a final word of encouragement in our huddle, and the Warriors were ready to do battle. And battle we did!

As the game began, Gordon scored the first five points, but the Warriors fought back and surged ahead 11–6. Then Gordon rang up twelve consecutive points and took a commanding lead. However, by half time, the Warriors had overcome Gordon's lead and headed for the locker room leading 34–33.

Action continued hot and heavy as the second half got underway. I dropped in three straight set shots followed by a hook shot to keep the Warriors close. After Gordon led 46–42, the Warriors started to roll and went on to win 77–64. I scored thirty one points (thanks to Max Ziel and Dolph Schayes), and fans rushed onto the court and carried me off on their shoulders. It was the highlight of my basketball career, my moment of glory!

We finished that season with eight wins and eight losses. More important, we had beaten Gordon soundly. In doing so, we had assured ourselves of a successful season.

During my four years on the Warriors, we beat Gordon four times, and they beat us four; not bad for our teams since the odds were usually stacked against us. Ironically, that arch rivalry ended in the mid-1980s when Barrington College (formerly P.B.I. and Providence-Barrington Bible College) merged with Gordon College, and the Barrington Campus closed.

After graduating, I continued to play basketball at YMCAs, with town teams in local leagues, and wherever else a basket happened to be. As I had with Rupie's secret, I became a disciple for Ziel and Schayes, telling and showing others how to shoot from the outside. Many listened, learned, and carried on the legacy.

Shortly before we were married, Shelley bought me my first pair of ice skates. Like all novices on ice, I fell quite often at first, but my persistence paid off. I soon learned to navigate without falling or ramming into others. Once I had reached this plateau, Shelley and I enjoyed holding hands and skating together.

After we were married in late December, 1957, we occupied an apartment on the Barrington campus of the college. It overlooked a large, oval fountain filled with water and small fish. Since the weather was cold, ice had formed on top.

We soon turned it into an ice-skating rink for two. Music was supplied by records being played on our small record player. Waltz music wafted through an open window and reached our ears below. Thus, we spent many happy, fun-filled evenings on our rink, evenings only newlyweds could fully appreciate.

Swimming had been another of my favorite recreational activities since boyhood. Therefore, the chance to earn fifty dollars a week working afternoons as a lifeguard interested me. At the time, I was teaching in the Somerset, Massachusetts, Junior High School. Ten weeks as a lifeguard at the Somerset Town Beach would be a welcomed change after ten months of teaching and being indoors. And my work schedule would fit in with my graduate school class schedule.

The only snag was my lack of training as a lifeguard, without which I could not be hired. Therefore, I enrolled in a Red Cross Water Safety Instructor's Course in the early spring. At the completion, I would be certified both as a lifeguard and as an instructor qualified to train lifeguards and to teach swimming and diving.

The course lasted several weeks and included both written and demonstrational examinations, and they were difficult. I had to pass all the requirements for lifeguard certification. I had to pass several swimming tests encompassing the various strokes, treading water, and endurance. Finally, I had to pass a diving portion.

The evening of my final written and demonstrational exams, I came home from school early intending to study a bit more before supper. Both Shelley and Mark (age one and a half) greeted me with hugs and kisses. Before going to my study, we shared the news of the day.

When it was her turn, Shelley said, "See this. It's your ceramic figurine from the bathroom into which you discard your used razor blades. While sitting on his toilet training chair, Mark reached over, took it off the window sill and opened the felt bottom. When I came into the bathroom to check on him, he was dropping the razor blades, one at a time, between his legs into the toilet bowl."

"Oh, my gosh!" I exclaimed. "Did he cut himself?"

"Yes, one little nick, but he was lucky, very lucky."

And indeed he had. Double edged razor blades in the hands of a child playing bombardier between his legs and only one nick!

For supper, Shelley fixed me a steak smothered in onions. It was delicious, and I gobbled up every bit. Then I left for my exams with the assurance I would pass both.

Since time was limited, each of us had to swim the endurance part of the swimming test at the same time we swam the required number of lengths of each stroke. And each stroke had to be demonstrated correctly. I had only been in the water a short time, when the onions began to react, giving me the necessary gas to help propel my body through the entire swimming exam. When I finished the exam in record time, everyone wondered how an overweight, twenty-seven-year-old man could do it. I knew the answer but kept mum. After all, I had been swimming since age seven. Why shouldn't I set a record?

A final day of instruction at the ocean and the course ended. I graduated with flying colors and looked forward to my job.

It was early into the swimming season. I climbed down from the lifeguard observation tower, and John climbed up. It was my hour to walk the beach on the Taunton River keeping a watchful eye on the water for any possible swimmers in trouble. I hadn't walked far when a young lad approached me and reported, "A boy was swimming in from the raft. He went under the water and didn't come up."

Immediately the procedures came to mind that had been drilled into my head during my Red Cross course. Remaining calm, I asked the lad to show me where he thought the boy had gone under as we walked quickly down the beach. When he stopped and pointed, I thanked him and started walking into the water searching the bottom with my eyes. When the water reached a certain level around my body, I took a surface dive, saw no one, then took another. I saw him, a blond-headed boy in a prone position on the bottom.

I quickly reached him, brought him to the surface, and began mouth to mouth resuscitation as I carried him to shore. I laid him on the warm sand and continued working, as unobtrusively as possible, to revive him. John phoned for an ambulance.

Soon a circle of onlookers shielded us from other beach goers. But a woman poked her head between two people in the circle, saw what I was doing, and forced her way through. She identified herself as a nurse, felt for a pulse then screamed, "My God! He's dead!" Her loud, penetrating words attracted many others and soon a crowd gathered, but I continued my resuscitation efforts oblivious to everyone but the victim.

Soon after the nurse screamed her fatal diagnosis, a volunteer fireman in the town wedged his way through the crowd, knelt down near me, and identified himself. After my next breath into the boy's lungs, he pushed on the boy's midsection informing me that what he had done was a standard procedure in such emergencies. It really wasn't, but I had no time to argue with him.

His push caused a vomiting action that disgorged stomach contents out of the boy's mouth. I had to stop, use my first two fingers on one hand and quickly wipe vomit off the boy's lips and out of his mouth. Then I returned to my resuscitation procedure making sure air was getting into his lungs by observing the movement of his chest out of the corner of my eye.

After delivering my next breath, the fireman pushed again, and more vomit was disgorged. I had to stop and wipe again, but the man never got the message of his improper procedure. The fireman continued to push after each breath, and I had to stop again and again. However, as unpleasant as it seems, I gave no thought to the vomit not removed as I pressed my open mouth against his to deliver my next life saving breath. How thankful I was that I had practiced this procedure with Shelley during my training and had it down pat.

After what seemed like an eternity, as ambulance arrived, and a mechanical resuscitator took over. The boy was placed on a stretcher, carried to the waiting ambulance and rushed to a hospital. As soon as the excitement was over, I whispered a prayer for the boy's recovery and returned to my post.

As I walked the beach scanning the water, I felt satisfied that I had followed the correct procedures. However, I still felt sad for the young victim. I also wondered who he was and who had brought him to the beach. For no one had come forward during the entire episode claiming to know him. And he was too young to be allowed on the beach by himself.

About an hour later, my boss approached me with a big smile on his face. He reported that the boy had regained consciousness and then congratulated me for a job well done. After hearing the news, I felt terrific and prayed a silent prayer of thanksgiving. Soon after, I returned to my post.

Later that afternoon, my joy was shattered. My boss reappeared and broke the news that the boy had died in the hospital. However, he offered some consolation by informing me that the boy had battled rheumatic fever earlier in his life and had been left with a damaged heart, a heart that couldn't stand such a traumatic shock. Even though the boy had regained consciousness, his heart stopped beating shortly afterwards, and the doctors could not revive him. After hearing all this, I felt sad, but I knew in my heart that I had done my best.

Before my boss left, I mentioned about the lack of someone seeking the boy's whereabouts. After assuring me that he'd look into my concern, he left. When he hadn't reported back by closing time, I left for home with unanswered questions on my mind.

Soon after reporting for work the next afternoon, I got my answers. The boy had come to the private beach adjacent to ours with a relative. Since there was no raft in the water off that beach, he evidently decided to swim out to ours at low tide. From the reports received, he stayed on or near the raft for quite some time. While he was having a good time diving off the raft, swimming near it, and sunbathing on it, the tide changed, and the water began coming in farther and farther putting more and distance between him and dry land. Once the boy decided to swim back to shore, he realized his dilemma and took the shortest route. He headed directly toward our beach, but even then, the distance was too great, and he couldn't make it.

Once I had his name and address, I sent his parents a sympathy card and enclosed a personal note. In time, they responded, thanking me for all I had done for their ten-year-old son. They also mentioned how much their son loved to swim. Since his death was linked to something he loved, they could accept it on a more positive note. And I could, too. But I would never forget seeing him on the bottom of the river, blond hair and all.

One of the favorite pastimes of people living in upstate New York is going to auctions, especially those held at private homes where "everything must be sold" for one reason or another. When Shelley, Mark, Bonnie and I first moved to Oswego in 1967, we attended one such auction and bought many usable items at rock-bottom prices. My favorite purchase was a sturdy, antique oak rocking chair with a leather seat for three dollars and fifty cents.

The next morning, Shelley and I visited a wealthy, elderly lady who lived in a large, well-kept home full of antiques. Early into our conversation, she mentioned that we looked familiar. Presently, she asked if we had been at the auction she and her maid had attended the previous night on route 104. After I answered in the affirmative, she chuckled to herself and had her maid bring to her the two items they had purchased. One was an old, non-electric carpet sweeper. The other was a picnic basket containing a few plastic dishes and the calling cards left by many mice over a period of time. Before I had time to ask myself why a wealthy woman would buy such "junk," she shared the reasons for both purchases.

As she and her maid sat at the auction, mosquitoes began bothering them. At one point, her maid swatted a mosquito that had landed on her head. She used the numbered, auction card given to her earlier for bidding. During the bidding for the sweeper, the auctioneer saw the card move through the air, assumed it was a bid and took it as such. Since no one else bid after that, the sweeper was hers. The picnic basket was bought the same way but by our hostess not her maid. Seeing humor in their "bidding method" and to avoid any negative confrontations at the conclusion of the sale, the ladies paid for their "treasures," and brought them home to discard.

We found her tale amusing but educational as well. When we went to our next auction a few weeks later, we were very careful to keep our cards stationary, unless we were really bidding. At that auction, I paid six dollars for an old pair of wooden skis with bindings and one dollar for a pair of ski poles. Why? I don't know. I had never skied before and had no intention of skiing in the future. I guess the prices were too good to pass up.

Once winter set in and deposited a couple of feet of snow, I decided to try skiing on the hill next to our home. Even though weeds extended above the snow level, I saw no danger in skiing there. However, Bill Schum saw me one evening as he was driving by, and he warned me the next day about the dangers of such folly. But I didn't take his words seriously and continued skiing, enjoying each run.

One afternoon, about quitting time for many at the college, I started down the hill and caught my skis in some weeds. My skis dug in, and I fell forward burying myself in the snow. My bindings failed to release, leaving me in a position that not only hurt, but one in which I could not reach the release on the bindings. Thus, I was trapped and in pain. In desperation, I yelled for help hoping someone, in one of the cars exiting the college across from me, would hear my cries and come to my aid, but no one did. So I bent my body, until I thought it would snap, reached back, and finally managed to release one ski, then the other.

I struggled to my feet, brushed the snow off, picked up my skis and hobbled to my house in pain. Then I got into my car, drove to the hospital, complained of pain in both knees and one foot and had X rays taken. After reading them, the doctor in the emergency room assured me that I had suffered no broken bones, only severe bruises. I believed him, hobbled back to my car, and returned home.

A couple of weeks later after all the pain had ceased, another doctor at the hospital called, said he had looked at my X rays, had spotted a broken bone in my foot, and assumed it had already healed. My admittance of a lack of pain confirmed his assumption. He wished me continued good health and hung up. His last words struck home, therefore, I didn't return to my ski hill.

During my period of healing, Bill had every right to say, "I told you so," but never did. Instead, he waited until I was fit as a fiddle again then came into my classroom and informed me that we were going skiing the following Wednesday night at Song Mountain Ski Area near Tully. He promised to teach me a few of the basics then leave me to practice them on a beginner's slope while he skied elsewhere.

Even though I had a few reservations about skiing, I went and Bill did as he had promised. After an evening of instruction and practice, my fears dissolved. I enjoyed skiing and looked forward to another outing. After a second evening of instruction and practice, both my skills and confidence had increased substantially.

When Bill couldn't go during the day on a Saturday, I went alone. After several practice runs on the lower, beginner's slope, I took the lift to the top of the mountain and skied an easy trail down. It was an exhilarating experience of some length, a run I could handle without undue fear. I spent the rest of my day on this trail enjoying every turn, every bit of scenery and every thrill it afforded me.

During one ride up the mountain on the chair lift, a five-year-old boy accompanied me. Reaching the top, he took off down an advanced trail going lickety-split. I watched him go in envy. However, as I skied the easy trail, I thought of countless skills in other areas that I had mastered and he hadn't, and my envy dissolved. However, our short time together gave me the motivation to leave the beginner's trail behind and proceed to an intermediate one.

For eight Saturdays in a row, I drove the sixty-five miles to Song Mountain and skied until I was dog-tired. Then I crawled into my car and returned home. However, I kept improving and soon found I could run the intermediate trails without difficulty.

Since that winter, I've bought new equipment, ski clothes and accessories. I've skied in the East and in the West, including two of the nineteen ski areas around Lake Tahoe, California/Nevada. Thanks to Bill's instruction and encouragement, I've never gotten seriously injured even though I've taken several spills. But I've seen plenty of other skiers who have. Perhaps Bill's admonition, "Skiing is a great sport, but stay off trails that demand greater skills than you possess," has been the rabbit's foot in my pocket.

That same winter in Oswego, the four of us looked forward to skating on the indoor rink at the college. We went the first evening the rink was open for family skating. As Shelley and I skated together, she suddenly lost her balance and fell, hitting her head on the ice.

Not realizing the seriousness of her fall, I thought she was only pretending when she didn't get up right away. So I nudged her with one skate and admonished, "Come on, Shell, get up. You'll catch cold lying there." But she didn't respond. So I nudged her again and asked her to get up, but she just lay there. Finally, I knelt down, lifted her head and noticed blood on the ice. A quick examination revealed a gash on one side of her head. Immediately, I summoned help and in minutes, she was in an ambulance heading for the hospital. The kids and I followed in my car.

After a doctor treated her wound, X-rayed and examined her, he reported no serious injuries had been sustained. However, he wanted to keep her overnight for observation just in case he had missed something.

Fortunately, he hadn't, and Shelley's injury healed in time with no permanent damage or scar. However, her interest in ice skating suffered a setback, one she never recovered from. Therefore, our ice skating days were few and far between after that. But Mark and Bonnie skated every chance they got, and they still enjoy doing so.

One spring day, shortly after my thirty-fifth birthday, fellow teacher and friend, Bill Schum, hurried into my Campus School classroom. Seeing me sitting at my desk and no students present, he exclaimed in a commanding voice, "Get off your derriere, Furman, and get some golf clubs. We're going golfing next week. I'll let you know what day." With that he turned and hurried out of my room and down the hall.

That's the way Bill is, brief and to the point. But whatever he says, he means. He knew I had never played golf, was completely ignorant of the rules and had no equipment. But his invitation, crude as it was, hit home, and I decided to obey his command and give this game, golf, a chance. What could I lose?

On Saturday, I bought a set of beginner's clubs for under thirty dollars, a golf bag for seven dollars, a dozen balls, some tees and some whiffle golf balls. I procured a cart with books of S & H green stamps. Before the big day arrived, I practiced hitting whiffle balls with my clubs in the backyard. My success doing so gave me a false sense of accomplishment and a feeling that "golf isn't that difficult." Thus, I looked forward to my debut on the fairways.

Wednesday afternoon we drove to Battle Island Golf Course, a favorite among the locals. Before teeing off, it was agreed that Joe, a college student and supposedly excellent golfer, and I would play Bill and Bruce Lester, both "hackers" according to Bill. We also agreed that the losing twosome, after each nine holes, would buy the drinks.

My debut was a disaster! I shot 135, lost six balls, and because my partner had an off day, split the cost with him for all the drinks after both nines. However, an interest in golf had been sown within me and would grow steadily.

The following week, I returned to the scene of my crime and teed off alone hoping to improve a little. After a couple of holes, I caught up with and joined a young woman. She claimed she was a beginner like me, but the way she hit her woods and irons on the fairways, compared to the way I hit mine, made me very suspicious. As we were walking down the eleventh fairway after teeing off, I complimented her for the umpteenth time on how well she performed on the fairways. Then I kidded her about her claim of being a beginner. She insisted she was, then shared the reasons for her apparent skill.

Her coach had instructed her to tee up her ball on the fairways before each shot. According to him, this would make golf more enjoyable to her as a beginner, it would help build her confidence, and it would help her gain certain skills more rapidly. He also instructed her to push the tees she used on the fairways further and further into the ground, as she became more and more proficient in the use of her clubs, until she needed no tees at all. "That's why I play as well as I do, even though I'm a beginner."

Once her secrets were out, I tried everything she told me, and I found her coach had been correct on all counts. Therefore, my skill on the fairways improved dramatically in a rather short period of time, and my enjoyment of the game grew proportionately. I soon became a "golfaholic" and would play until dark on any afternoon I ventured to Battle Island.

During the next eighteen years, golfers, much better than I am, helped me improve my swing, my grip, my chipping and my putting. They also taught me many of the rules. Had I taken a series of lessons at the onset of my interest in golf, I would have learned all this—and more—in a fraction of the time. Thus, my handicap would have been respectable years sooner, I would have lost less money to my brother, Paddy, and my ego would not have been bruised so often. Based on my past experiences, I recommend lessons to any beginning golfer I meet, whatever his or her age. But Jim Murray, writing in *Golf Magazine*, had this to say, "Golf is the most over-taught and least-learned human endeavor. If they taught sex the way they teach golf, the race would have died out years ago." Even so, I still recommend lessons.

Like most golfers, I have a favorite course. Mine is the Jackson Hole Golf and Tennis Club located outside the town of Jackson, Wyoming. Besides the beautiful scenery, provided in part by the majestic Teton Mountain Range, the course is challenging, especially the 579-yard, five-par, second hole. And apart from the beauty and the challenge lies the wildlife.

At any given time, deer, including moose, may wander out of the woods and onto the course, or a bald eagle may light on a tree branch near some golfers. In either case, such events usually disrupt play but are not frowned upon. Instead, they add an enjoyable touch to a round of golf.

During the two seasons I worked in the Grand Teton National Park, I often drove the thirty-eight miles from Colter Bay to this course on my days off. En route, I would have to stop my car now and then, and wait for a herd of buffalo to cross the road, or pause while several stood in the road blocking traffic and taking their sweet time deciding in which direction they wanted to go. On one such early morning, as I slowly drove past several that were standing in the opposite lane, one large buffalo ambled toward my car and rubbed its nose against the window closest to me. Had I my camera, I could have taken an interesting photo to show my family. Had the buffalo a camera, it could have taken one of the startled look on my face.

One of the many reasons I enjoy golf is the sociability aspect. I can go to any golf course alone and join others, not in foursomes, waiting to tee off. This gives me an opportunity to meet new people, some of whom are dressed in clothes similar to those worn by big city pimps. It also allows me to enjoy fresh conversations, hear a few new jokes, laugh if they're funny, console or be consoled on shots that go awry, compliment or be complimented on good shots and/or putts and either give or get helpful pointers on the game.

Of all the odd things people do on golf courses, talking to golf balls is the oddest. Golfers yell at them, plead with them, and curse at them in their efforts to get the balls to do what they want them to do. More pleading takes place on the greens than anywhere else as golfers desperately coax their balls into the cups. After listening to others do this and doing it myself, I no longer laugh at children who talk to their dolls or stuffed animals.

During the winter of 1986, I played my golf at the Riverside Golf Club in Riverside, California. One morning, I teamed up with a man named Pete Leswick and his grandson, Len. During the first three holes, Len swung continually too fast and sliced his ball onto the adjoining fairways. I felt, I could help him correct his problems and make his round of golf more fun. While walking to the next tee, I said nonchalantly, "Gee, Len, you must play a lot of baseball. You grip and swing your clubs as if you have a bat in your hands hitting for the fences. In golf, you need to loosen your grip, slow your swing down and follow through smoothly, once you've made contact with the ball." Len listened, smiled and promised a simple, "I'll try."

Pete must have overheard our conversation. While Len walked to the ball washer on the fourth tee, he came over to me and asked, "Do you know who you're talking to?" I responded, "Yeah, your grandson, Len." Then Pete surprised me, "That's my grandson, Len, alright, but he's Len Dykstra, an outfielder for the New York Mets."

After Pete finished, I'm sure I blushed. My evaluation had been correct. However, I had no idea Len was a professional baseball player, one of the heroes of the recently completed playoffs and World Series. The Len Dykstra who had gotten several key hits, including home runs, in helping the Mets win the world championship. The Len Dykstra who always walked to the batter's box while spitting tobacco and tobacco juice out of his mouth and continued doing so while adjusting his hat, pulling his gloves on tighter and preparing to swing. The Len Dykstra whose book, *Nails*, had recently been published, and the idol of many, young baseball enthusiasts. A baseball hero, and here I was, teaching him how to play better golf. What a treat!

After we teed off and began walking down the fairway, Len verified what Pete had told me. Then he thanked me for my help and concluded with, "You can tell I don't play much golf during the off-seasons."

Pete, Len and I had completed fifteen holes when Len showed us his blistered hands from over-gripping his clubs and decided to call it quits. During our parting words, he promised to continue practicing what I had shown him in golf and to quit chewing tobacco. Since that day, I've often wondered if he did one, both, or neither.

Roller skating, squash and tennis are three other physical activities I've enjoyed over the years, but tennis is the only one of the three I enjoy now.

Whenever I roller-skated at a rink, my rented skates always seemed to go in two different directions no matter how hard I tried to prevent this. Those who went with me always cited my inexperience as the cause, not the skates. I knew better but let them prattle anyway.

I learned to play squash while teaching at the college in Oswego. Bill and Rupie were my worthy opponents on two different days. I had trouble controlling my racket and racked the faces of my playing partner every now and then. Neither of them ever retaliated. Instead, each found other things to do at our scheduled time for a court and stopped coming to play. I really couldn't blame them and eventually gave up the sport.

I began playing tennis at age eighteen and have improved steadily over the years. Until recently, I preferred playing singles. Now I usually play doubles since less running is involved. But playing the net can be deadly.

My main sport today is golf. Walking a golf course and swinging clubs early in the morning is all the exercise I need, as long as I don't lift a fork too often to my mouth.

Chapter XVI
California, Here I Come Again

The day before Christmas, 1963, I was crossing an elevated walkway between two very busy shopping centers in Paramus, New Jersey. Cars streamed in both directions spattering dirty water onto new fallen snow. As I paused and took a long look at the ugliness below, I promised myself, "Next Christmas we'll be living somewhere nicer than this!"

In early January, 1964, I applied for a school administration position through a Christian school placement center. At age thirty and full of administration/supervision courses, I felt I was ready to tackle the "big time" in education. In the blank on the application as to the area of the USA I was interested in, I wrote, "open."

The third week of February the schools in the town where I taught were closed for winter vacation. My family and I left Westwood at 5:00 P.M. on Friday and drove to Boca Raton, Florida, some 1,500 miles south, arriving on Saturday evening. We were to spend five days soaking in the sun, swimming, and relaxing at a Christian conference center known as Bibletown.

While there, I had an interview for a teaching position in a nearby town. At its conclusion, the principal offered me a position teaching sixth grade beginning in September. It was not an administrative position, but my Christmas prophecy was going to come true.

I left the interview feeling great. The school was new, the area was sparsely settled and still quaint, and the weather was perfect most of the year. As I drove back to Bibletown, I whistled a happy tune and praised the Lord. Upon hearing my good news, Shelley rejoiced with me. Mark did, too, even though he had gotten a bad sunburn at the beach during part of the time I was at the interview. The rest of our vacation, we were "riding high" emotionally. Even the thoughts of moving in the heat of summer did not diminish our good feelings.

Bibletown had recently opened a Christian community and was selling lots in Paradise Palms for $3,000. We decided to buy one on time and planned on having a home built by the middle of August. These decisions made us even more excited.

The evening we arrived home, I sorted through the mail and came across a letter from Riverside Christian Day School (RCDS) in Riverside, California. I opened it eagerly and read that the Board of Trustees was very interested in my application for an administrative position. I was asked to read the materials enclosed with the letter. Then, if I were interested, I was asked to fill out the forms enclosed and sent them in.

Talk about a feast or a famine! What should I do? Shelley and I discussed it and decided we should investigate the California position as an alternative to Florida, since it was an administrative position. The paperwork was mailed soon after our discussion, and then we waited.

One evening about a week later, Mr. Steaves, Chairman of the Board, called. During our conversation, he explained that the school couldn't afford to fly me to California for a personal interview. Instead, the Board would like to interview me by phone since there were several phones in the school. I agreed and the interview was scheduled for a Monday in March at 10:00 P.M. my time.

Several days before my scheduled phone interview, I began having pains in my side, so I went to see our family doctor. He suggested that I have a barium sulfate enema and X rays at the local hospital. I agreed. "Fine, I'll set up an appointment and call you in a day or two." Before I left his office, he gave me a strong laxative to take at a certain time the evening before the tests.

He called the next day. To my dismay, the appointment had been scheduled for the Tuesday morning following my Monday evening phone interview. How's that for planning?

The evening of the interview, I took the laxative then sat watching TV until the appointed hour. However, the bathroom call came first and the interview call followed seconds later. Since we had only one phone, and it was mounted on a kitchen wall and not in the bathroom, I did my interview while sitting on a pail in the hallway halfway between the two. I accomplished both task simultaneously.

During the interview, Dr. Johnson asked, "How's the weather there?" When I answered, "Cold and rainy," he mentioned that he had been water skiing that day. Immediately, I had a mental picture of a beautiful river in Riverside and water skiers having loads of fun. Dr. Johnson failed to mention that he had skied on the Colorado River some two hundred miles east of Riverside. But his comment and my mental picture would color my final decision to accept the position if it were offered to me. Both the interview and the laxative drained me by the end of the evening.

My ordeal at the hospital went well. After the enema and X rays, the barium sulfate was drained out. Then air was pumped into my intestines until I thought I would explode. More X rays; then I drove home expelling some of the air en route.

Shelley was a member of a coffee klotsch made up of several young mothers, all of whom attended our church. Once each month, they met in a different home to mend clothes, eat, exchange news, and enjoy some relaxed fellowship. When I returned home, the ladies were there—talking, laughing, and sewing. And there I stood with plenty of air waiting to be released.

Our home was small and our one bathroom was near both the living room and the dining room. For some reason, sound traveled well in that house. Therefore, I had several embarrassing moments in the bathroom as the sounds of escaping air wafted beyond the bathroom door. After the ladies had gone, Shelley confirmed my reasons for being embarrassed. However, she assured me that none of them mentioned it or laughed over it, not even a little bit. I made several trips to the bathroom and expelled a lot of air while they were there, so what Shelley assured me of was hard to believe.

A week later, a letter and contract arrived from RCDS. Even though the salary was $8,000 for twelve months, I signed and became the new Chief Administrator of the school beginning July 1, 1964. We were very excited as we looked ahead to this new adventure. However, Shelley's grandmother Phykitt and her folks, June and Lee Matney, did not share our jubilation.

June 17, 1964, signaled the end of the school year in River Edge. I said my final good-byes to fellow teachers, principal and staff and headed home. That evening, I went to the local trailer rental agency on route 17. After the necessary paperwork was completed, a fourteen foot trailer was hooked up to my 1961, six-cylinder, station wagon. When I arrived back home, I parked the rig in front of my house.

Early the next morning, Shelley, her dad and I began loading the trailer for our trip west. It was a hot, humid day, perfect for the church picnic at a nearby lake, but not for loading a trailer. However, I wanted to get to the school and meet with the current administrative head prior to his leaving on June 30. I felt a few days with him would give me a head start on my new position.

We loaded, we sweated, we loaded, and we sweated all day. Finally late afternoon, everything was in the trailer except Mark's tricycle. Prior to loading, I had my doubts that everything would fit. But using the booklet the trailer company had given me, I added cubic feet to cubic feet, matched pictures and cubic feet of furniture in the booklet to our furniture, calculated again and again, and each time, the total figure eased my doubts but not fully.

We showered, uttered our sad good-byes, took a few photos, and climbed into the wagon. Before driving off, I decided to recheck the hitch. Looking under the wagon, I noticed that the chain on both ends of the hitch had been put over the brake cable and around the rear axle. Recalling a warning sign on the inside of the trailer door, I realized the chains should have gone under the brake cable first, then around the axle. Thus, our trip began with a stop at the local trailer rental. I told the fellow on duty, and his response was, "It's all right the way it's on. If you want it changed, you change it." I believed him and left.

We headed south toward the New Jersey Turnpike. At the entrance, we were turned away by the sign, "High winds ahead. Cars with trailers prohibited." Therefore, we had to take alternate roads to the Pennsylvania Turnpike. We finally reached it and headed west.

With no air conditioning, the heat and humidly were awful, but I needed to continue driving through the night to keep on schedule. Shelley, Mark, and Bonnie slept, though not soundly. The turnpike was two lanes each way, and it was loaded with trucks. Most were tractor trailers moving well over the sixty-five miles per hour speed limit. I was going forty-five to fifty, the speed limit for cars pulling trailers. But we kept moving, uphill and downhill, all night long. Truck after truck sped past, lights glaring, horns honking, and their winds almost pushing us off the road.

By the next morning, we had left the turnpike and were traveling on the few sections of I-70 that were completed and on U.S. Highway 40. At one point in West Virginia, we had to exit I-70 and again pick up route 40. We were driving through a small town when I smelled brake fluid. I put on my brakes, and the pedal went slowly to the floor. No brakes!

Luckily, a garage was up ahead, so I coasted to it, pulled off the road and used my emergency brake to stop. Before getting out, we thanked God that our brakes hadn't failed on the turnpike or on I-70. Considering the hills and the speeding trucks, we could have been involved in a serious accident and even killed.

The garage owner helped me unhook the trailer. Then my wagon was placed on his lift. Once in the air, it was obvious, upon inspection, that one chain had crushed and broken the brake cable allowing the brake fluid to drain out of the entire system. I needed it fixed, whatever the cost, but I worried that I might be overcharged. After all, it was a Sunday, and I had to have it fixed there and then.

The owner replaced the rear brake cable, added brake fluid, "bled" the lines and then inspected the system a final time. Once he finished, we soon had the trailer hitched to the wagon, only this time, the chains were put under the brake cable. Finally, he gave me the broken cable, wrote up the problem on the bill, and then charged me such a fair price, I'll always be grateful to him. Within an hour after stopping, we were on the road again.

Once we were settled in California, I sent a letter and the bill to the main office of the trailer company. They sent me a letter of apology and a check for the full amount of the bill. They also assured me that the garage in Paramus would no longer be allowed to rent their trucks and trailers.

During our first two days of travel, we drove through several large cities plus many small ones. If there were traffic lights at the crest of hills in any city, we hit all of them red. I began to fret that we'd wear out the clutch of our standard shift wagon or burn out the 145 horsepower engine as it labored to pull our loaded-to-the-gills trailer. But the car continued to run smoothly. It was the four of us that often became hot and overheated.

Before leaving New Jersey, we had decided to visit Corky and his family in Clarksville, Arkansas. It wouldn't take us too far out of our way, and a short visit would be a welcome break for all of us. At the time, Corky was teaching at the College of the Ozarks and lived on campus near a large, outdoor swimming pool. So in Springfield, Missouri, we left route 44 and headed south on route 65 into Arkansas.

At the beautiful town of Harrison, we took route 7. It passed through much of the Ozark National Forest and through many small towns. We were in "Ozark Country," and we thoroughly enjoyed the towns, the smell of smoke from lingering early morning fires, the lush greenery and the scenic beauty until "the mountain" loomed ahead.

I'm sure now that it wasn't that high a mountain. But that day, I felt differently. As we slowly drove up switchback after switchback, the water temperature gauge kept moving toward the hot range, and I began to sweat profusely watching it. By the time we reached the top, I was soaked. We pulled off the road, let the engine cool down, had something cool to drink, and enjoyed the scenic beauty in every direction.

We descended the mountain without incident and continued on to

Russellville. We picked up U.S. Highway 64 west to Clarksville and arrived safe and sound and ready for a long swim.

Apart from having to get a flat tire fixed on the trailer, our two days in Clarksville were enjoyable. The heat and humidity were high, but with air conditioning inside and a large pool outside, life was good.

Our trip through the rest of Arkansas, then Oklahoma, Texas, New Mexico, and into Arizona went smoothly. Although the heat was always with us, a constant supply of ice water helped. As we climbed the elevation into Flagstaff, pine trees appeared and the temperature dropped into a more comfortable range. We all felt like settling there, but early the next morning, we began our descent back into the valley, the desert and the heat. At one point, Shelley remarked, "It's like being in a blast furnace." Eventually, the heat made us edgy, and even the ice water didn't help.

That afternoon, we arrived in Needles, California. The temperature was well over 100 degrees. It was Sunday and Christians, like us, did not swim on the Lord's Day. However, I asked a local citizen if there was a place to swim. He mentioned a pool and the Colorado River. We could take our pick. The pool was covered, so we opted for it with assurance in our hearts that a loving God would forgive us in our time of dire need to spend time in a cool, refreshing pool.

By the time we were refreshed and ready to leave Needles in the late evening, the temperature was still ninety-five degrees. We were 225 miles from Riverside and had a desert to cross en route. Shelley and the kids slept while I drove. Around 4:00 A.M., I pulled off the road and slept until almost sunrise.

Early Monday, June 27, we drove down through the Cajon Pass, through San Bernadino and into Riverside. Driving through the pass with the sun coming up was a beautiful sight. The multicolored sky, the mountains, and the flowering bushes along the roadside made a beautiful, "Welcome to Riverside" sign for us weary, unkempt travelers from the East.

Driving south on route 91, we saw the Arlington Avenue exit and took it. A few minutes later, we drove into the entrance to the school and parked in front of the main building. We sat there tingling with excitement as another car drove in. Its occupant was John Weir, one of the Board Members. He was on his way to his office and stopped at the school when he saw the car and trailer. He looked very professional. I looked like a slob, but he looked beyond my appearance and welcomed me and my family to Riverside and the RCDS. We appreciated his welcome.

We bade Mr. Weir good-bye and, following his directions, drove to

Mr. Steaves' home, where we were to stay a few days while looking for our own place. Both Mr. and Mrs. Steaves greeted us warmly upon our arrival at their door. During an enjoyable breakfast, I learned that the resigning head of the school had already left Riverside the middle of June. It was not something I appreciated hearing after our hurried trip. I was also informed that no one had looked for a place for us to live even though I had asked Mr. Steaves in a letter to look around for us.

I was determined not to let this news upset me. After breakfast, Shelley and I left the house to begin looking. We had the Sunday paper's classified section and a Riverside map with us. In a couple of hours, we had looked at several houses. Some of them did not suit us, others were out of our price range. Somehow, we found ourselves on Las Tunas Drive, a street only one block long. We passed a beautiful, custom-built, ranch house with a for sale sign in front. For fun, we stopped and entered the house through an unlocked window in front.

It was a three-bedroom beauty with two full baths, a large kitchen with a breakfast nook, a living room with a fireplace, a dining area, a covered patio and a large, two-car garage containing laundry hookups. It had central air conditioning. Outside, it was fully landscaped with one each of several fruit trees (plum, nectarine, apricot, peach, lemon), rose bushes, a cacti-corner, and other flowers too numerous to mention. A high, cinder block wall offered back and side yard privacy.

We were exiting through the front door when the next door neighbors, on one side, appeared. Al McCully was a dentist in the air force stationed at March Air Force Base. Pat was a cute, spitfire of a woman from Hawaii. They had two girls, Karen and Shannon, about Bon's age. In answer to our questions, the wife informed us that the owners had rented the house previously but did not want to do so again. They were only interested in selling it. We really liked the house, so we jotted down the real estate office number, thanked our new found friends, and left.

We contacted the office and made an appointment to talk to the agent. During our appointment, we learned that the asking price was $27,000. Even though the price was fair, we hadn't sold our New Jersey house nor had we any savings to speak of, so we had little money for a down payment on this or any house. Even though the owners stated that they did not want to rent the house again, I asked the agent to contact them, act enthusiastic and present the following data: I was the new head of RCDS. I could afford $150 a month rent. Since the three bedrooms and the outside trim needed painting, I would paint them. I would sign a one-year lease. The agent laughed and offered no hope but agreed to contact the owners.

That evening, she called us at the Steaves' home. The owners had agreed to our offer and added the following: They would pay for the paint, brushes, and other materials needed. They would pay the water bill. And finally, they would give us the option to buy the house for $24,000 after our lease was up. After hearing the good news, we were ecstatic and couldn't wait to move in.

By Wednesday, the lease was signed and the bedrooms were painted and dry. With help from our new neighbors, the trailer was soon emptied. Thursday morning, Shelley began the task of transforming our new house into our new home. Our prayers and the prayers of others, who were praying for us, were being answered one by one. All four of us were thankful.

The following Sunday, we attended Grace Baptist Church. During the Sunday school hour, Shelley and I attended a large, young-married couples class taught by John Weir. We met several couples, including Garry and Mary Beth McCracken, who would become good friends in the weeks and months ahead. During the church service, Shelley and I were impressed with the choir and vowed to join it if we decided to make this our church home. After the service, we met "Bus" Jellsey. He shook my hand, smiled and commented, "It's so nice to meet you and your daughter" as he smiled at Shelley. She beamed in approval and decided, then and there, to cast her vote for this church. I sealed the decision with mine.

Not many Saturdays later, the McCullys threw us a "Welcome to the Street" party in their back yard. Every family on both sides of the street came with food and drinks. It was a terrific affair, thanks to our caring neighbors. During the evening, Mark and Bonnie met several new playmates.

One of the younger couples we met that night lived three houses down from ours. They had moved from Fair Haven, New York, a small town on Lake Ontario not far from Oswego. We talked a bit that evening and a few other times about back home. One day we noticed, they were having a moving sale. Our chats had made them homesick, and they had decided to move back to Fair Haven. I reminded them about the severe winters in that part of New York State, but it made no difference in their determination.

Since we couldn't change their minds, we bought their bedroom set for Bon, and a few days later, we bade them good-bye as they pulled away from the curb for the last time. We still have the bedroom set, a reminder of them. Every so often, I wonder where they are now and how life is treating them.

We began watering the lawn, trees, ivy, bushes, and flowers faithfully. After a few days, we noticed that something was damaging the bushes, the ivy and some smaller, bushy trees. We also felt crunches under our shoes whenever we walked in the yard after dark. I asked my military neighbor what might be causing this. He came over, lifted ivy, pulled back branches from a few bushes and showed me.

Snails were the culprits, according to Al. They would come out at night, eat to their heart's content, then retreat again into hiding during the daylight hours. He suggested I buy a product that controls snails and gave me the name of one. He further suggested that I water everything in an evening, then put rings of the product around the bases of trees and bushes and along the ground parallel to the ivy.

The next day I bought a large box of the product and that evening I did as I was advised. The next morning, I went into the backyard and saw dead snails everywhere. I called Shelley and the kids to the yard to view the massacre. Then I checked the side and front yards and found thousands more. What power was contained in that box of poison for controlling snails! I was overwhelmed. Seeing the results, I knew I would win the war although raking up the casualties took over an hour.

That evening, I repeated the process again and the following morning, I had more dead snails to rake into piles and discard. In a few days, the problem was controlled and periodic use of the poison assured me of continual victory. I had faced my first problem as a California home occupier and had won.

That year was a good one for fruit trees—too good. For starters, we ate apricots until they were coming out of our ears. We gave many away and dried a great many for future consumption. Even so, many dropped to the ground daily and had to be raked up and deposited into a garbage can. Mark was given the chore of raking them, one he didn't enjoy one iota. I finally learned the reason. As he raked, bees would fly around his head terrorizing him. Luckily, he never got stung.

Since the plum and nectarine trees were loaded with fruit, I had to prop up the lower branches to keep them off the ground. As with the apricots, we tried every way possible to use the fruit in positive ways, but even our neighbors got tired of eating our fruit. The bees certainly overdid themselves pollinating those fruit trees.

Except for a minor problem with termites in the fireplace mantel, we thoroughly enjoyed living in that house.

THE JOB

I put the phone receiver back on its cradle and stood motionless at my office desk. Another parent had just called to complain about the scheduled pick-up time for her two children by one of the school's five buses. I had worked many hours on each route considering such factors as time, distance, and bus capacity. Once I completed a dummy route, I ran it, timed each stop and noted any potential bottlenecks. Once all five had been completed to my satisfaction, bus schedule pick-up cards had been prepared and mailed to all families involved. On Thursday, each driver had been given a copy of his or her route with instructions to run it prior to Monday in his or her own car. The way the routes had been set up and timed, all five buses would arrive within minutes of each other and all before 9:00 A.M.

But now, so many parents had phoned and complained, I knew I'd have to redo two routes completely, make changes in the other three and have them ready for the drivers within thirty-six hours. However, some of the changes would be impossible. For example, two mothers, who lived a few doors apart, both called. One stated emphatically that if the bus couldn't come a half hour earlier than scheduled, she would cancel. The other was just as emphatic and stated that if the bus couldn't come a half hour later than scheduled, she would cancel. Even though the school needed all the bus revenue it could generate, I could please neither parent and lost both passengers.

As I stood there that Friday evening, all the pressures of the summer suddenly boiled over and something within me snapped. I grabbed the stapler off my desk and, in frustration, threw it across the room. It gouged the wall on impact, then fell to the floor. At the same time, I slouched down into my chair, held my head in my hands and asked, "Why me, Lord, why me?"

I had looked forward to my new position at Riverside Christian Day School. Yet, now after two months of long hours and hard work, the problems I still faced were weighing heavily upon me, and the opening of school was a mere sixty hours away.

To begin with, the new, octagon-shaped building, housing five classrooms, bathrooms, cafetorium (combination cafeteria and auditorium) and kitchen were not ready to be occupied since the newly laid, tile floors could not be walked on until Sunday morning. Therefore, all the new furniture was still boxed and stored in the classrooms of the two older wings. Thus, none of the cleaning had been done by our cleaning service, and none of the teachers had been able to get their classrooms ready for school to begin.

I had spent an entire morning in early July with a cabinet maker hired by the contractor. He and I drew up plans for the cabinets in the new classrooms that would incorporate all the suggestions submitted by the teachers before school closed in June. In late August, the cabinets should have been ready for installation. Instead, the cabinet maker had called and confessed that he had lost his copy of the plans and had not built any of the cabinets. He promised to have them done by the end of December if I still had my copy of the plans for him to use. In the meantime, long tables would have to suffice in lieu of the cabinets.

The five buses were not washed nor cleaned inside. The man who usually did this didn't show up as promised, and I couldn't contact him. This meant that I'd have to do it myself, unless I could get volunteers to help.

I finally made a list of what needed to be done, put the stapler back on my desk, and headed for home. I had been at school twelve hours and needed the rest of the evening to recoup myself physically, mentally, and emotionally.

Saturday and Sunday were hectic and exhausting. With the combined efforts of teachers, Parent Teacher Organization (PTO) members, office staff, understanding bus drivers and the cleaning personnel, who cleaned the entire school Sunday night, the school was ready to open Monday morning. And, as scheduled, all five, sparkling-clean buses, filled with excited children, rolled in on time.

As I stood outside the school to greet both parents and students, I couldn't help but notice the large number of very expensive cars that drove into the school's driveway, dropped students off and left again. Being a large, private, Christian school struggling to survive financially, I had assumed most students came from moderate-income, evangelical Christian families, families that were struggling financially to keep their children in such a school environment, thus necessitating the low tuition rates in force. However, the fancy cars and the well-dressed children who emerged from them, told me my assumption was wrong. Therefore, I decided to find out more about the school's clientele.

My findings amazed me. Many of the students came from wealthy homes. Doctors, lawyers, real estate developers, large contractors, owners of large grocery chains, managers of large department stores, and high ranking military officers had children in the school. Albie Pearson, outfielder for the California Angels and the American League Rookie of the Year in 1958, had children in the school.

I then contacted another private, church-related school and learned that the tuition rate for one child was $600 a year, for two children from the same family, $1000 a year, and so forth. Adding this information to what I had already learned about the clientele, I could not understand why the tuition at our school was so low.

Tuition was $250 a year for one child and less for each additional child from the same family. Total tuition for five children from the same family was a mere $500 for an entire school year. It was obvious why the school was struggling financially and why teachers' salaries were so very low.

A beginning teacher at RCDS was paid $1,800 for the school year of ten months. Our highest paid teacher was paid $2,700. At the same time, a beginning teacher with a B.A. degree in the Riverside Public Schools was paid $5,200. How could the Board of Directors expect teachers at RCDS to live on such meager salaries?

At my first board meeting, I presented several facts and figures and strongly suggested that tuition be raised considerably and then offer financial aid to those families that needed it. With the additional income, the teachers' salaries could be raised to a respectable level and other expenses could be met more easily. Sad to say, my suggestions fell on deaf ears. The school continued to limp along financially and the teachers' salaries remained much too low for such dedicated professionals. And I began to question my decision to accept the responsibility of running this school; a decision I would eventually regret.

Once the school year got off the ground, things quieted down somewhat. With Pauline Cree, Della Dyke and Yvonne Miller handling the numerous, routine office matters, I was able to concentrate most of my energies into fulfilling my many administrative duties. However, the one thorn in my flesh was the contractor for the new addition. His stubbornness to accept any of my suggestions was the thorn.

He was a builder, I was an educator. He knew how to build a stage in the cafetorium. I knew it needed to be much larger. However, he blew my suggestion away with, "The school never had any stage before. So this is an improvement even though it's small." He knew how to fasten chalkboards to walls. Considering the heights of first and second graders, who would use them, I knew how high off the floor they should be fastened. He knew how to build storage shelves. I knew the sizes and amounts of the materials, including several sizes of art paper to be stored, and I opted for shelves of various lengths, widths, and heights.

According to the contractor, baffles were not needed in the new bathrooms since children would be using them. I insisted baffles were needed to protect the children's privacy. There were many other disagreements, but I held my ground. In doing so, I won some and lost some including the size of the stage. It remained very small.

Matters came to a head in November. The contractor had installed the main electrical panel for the new building outside the kitchen in a three-sided alcove. Without some kind of door on the fourth side to keep children away from the panel, a dangerous situation existed. After getting nowhere with the contractor, I went to the nearest fire department station and presented my problem to the person in charge. He agreed that a protective door was needed, instructed me to leave a certain number of inches of space at the top and at the bottom and gave me one of their special padlocks to use. I was given one key and the others remained at the station. This would give them easy access to the panel in case of an emergency.

I built the door according to the fire department's specifications and secured it with their lock. Once completed, I breathed a sigh of relief. Another problem solved, or so I thought.

The following Saturday, I was working in my office when the contractor came storming in. Without his saying a word, I knew he was mad as a wet hen and why. I tried calming him down by telling him about my visit to the fire department and the events leading to the locked door at the alcove. But he would not listen and kept insisting that he would lose his license if that door remained. During a heated exchange of words, he threatened to take the door down. I countered his threat with one of my own. I told him, in no uncertain terms, that if he touched the door with any tool, I'd call the police, and I meant it.

With that, he turned, stomped out of my office, went outside and headed for the parking lot. I hoped he had left for good, but in case he hadn't, I stood in the breezeway affording me an unobstructed view of the locked door. Soon he returned and headed that way. I immediately returned to my office and called the police. They arrived before he could carry out his threat. Once everything was said and done, the contractor left, then the police. The door remained intact, so in a way, I had won the battle, but inwardly, I had lost the war.

This incident was the one that broke the proverbial camel's back. I returned to my office, sat down and typed my letter of resignation effective the end of August 1965. In it, I explained, in detail, the reasons for my decision, including the latest one. The next day at church, I gave it to the newly elected Chairman of the Board, Bill Weddle. After the service, he approached me. I could tell he was both surprised and upset. I answered his questions and assured him that I was dead serious about leaving and would not reconsider.

At the next Board meeting, my letter was read and my resignation was accepted with regret. Even so, several Board members asked me to reconsider in the months that lay ahead. I told them I would, but in my heart, I knew my decision would not change.

There was never a dull moment in the months that followed. The long list of goals I had established at the beginning of the school year was slowly being met. I knew something educationally worthwhile had been accomplished each time I checked one off. However, I knew some would not be met by my departure date.

Even though I scheduled each day in advance, I never knew what to expect from one day to the next. When a driver called in sick, I drove his bus route. When our elderly custodian called in sick, I wore his hat. On one such occasion, I found myself ankle deep in water trying to unclog two toilets in one of the boys' restrooms. After succeeding, I was mopping up the water, when a snooty parent saw me. She took me to task verbally for doing so. However, when I offered her the mop, she looked aghast, tripped over her final words and quickly retreated to her car. I laughed to myself and continued. After all, someone had to do it. Why not me? I had plenty of practice in college.

Now and then, parents would drop by my office to chat. One of my favorites was Albie Pearson. He'd amble in, sit on one corner of my desk and enthusiastically begin telling me how much the Lord was blessing him and his family. During our chats, we talked about both spiritual and secular topics. I soon discovered and learned to appreciate his keen sense of humor.

During one of our chats after the baseball season had begun, he invited me to attend some California Angels' games. "Just call me and tell me when you want to go and how many tickets you'll want, and I'll get them for you," he said. I thanked him and promised I would.

One evening, I read that the New York Yankees were coming to play the Angels. Being a Yankee fan since my boyhood, I decided to call Albie for tickets to the game on Friday night. But I did not tell him of my loyalty to the Yankees.

He obliged with four tickets. The seats were along the third base line about four rows back. They were perfect seats for my three friends and me. Albie had several hits in the Angels' victory, so I was not too disappointed that the Yankees had lost. Looking on the positive side, I was the guest of the Angels. I should have been rooting for the entire team not just Albie. My friends were.

The next time the Yankees came to town to play the Angels, Albie again provided me with tickets. Even though I rooted out loud for Albie to get a hit whenever he came to the plate, I was rooting for the Yankees in my heart. Since I only asked for tickets when the Yankees came to town, I often wondered if Albie ever suspected my ulterior motive. If he did, he never mentioned it, never gave even a hint of suspicion.

Early one morning in May, a policeman called me at home to report a burglary at the school. A few minutes later, I walked quickly into the offices. Had I not known otherwise, I would have sworn a cyclone had passed through, leaving behind its telltale destruction. The offices had been ransacked by one or more perpetrators looking for anything of value. A quick check in each office and a well-concealed safe assured me that whoever broke in, most likely, left empty-handed. But the mess left behind would take days to clean up, especially the files in my office.

By the end of June, I had painted everything as promised on the outside of our rented house. Since we could not afford to buy it at the offering price, we sadly moved out, leaving behind all our friendly neighbors but taking with us many happy memories. All our belongings were stored at the school.

Shelley, Mark, and Bonnie had gone to New Jersey to visit Shelley's parents and grandmother. I had moved into the home economics room near the offices and would live there until the end of August. Summer school was in session, and I was as busy as ever. In addition to my administrative duties, I was teaching both creative writing and English, and I was helping with the transportation of students. Thus, living at the school was very convenient.

Late one night, I was awakened by strange voices outside my room. Immediately, I suspected another burglary was in the making, so I quietly dressed in the dark, tiptoed to the door and listened, but the voices had ceased. Garnering up some courage, I quietly opened the door, slithered out, closed the door behind me, and stood motionless against the wall listening for any voices or other noises. Presently, I heard voices coming from a nearby wing on the other side of the school nearest the parking lot.

Figuring the burglars were still looking for the offices, I decided to make my move. Staying under the breezeway and hugging the wall, I slowly moved toward an office door holding my breath, lest I be discovered. I unlocked it with trembling hands, darted inside, relocked it, felt my way to a phone and called the police. Then I groped my way to an office window that gave me a view of the driveway and a section of the parking lot. I opened the window and strained my eyes and ears to see and hear anyone in the darkness outside.

Within minutes, several police cars came tearing into the driveway, fanned out around the school, and illuminated the darkness with headlights and spotlights. I could see some of the officers get out of their cars and, with guns drawn, approach the building. Seeing three black men in the breezeway between the two wings of one rectangular building, the officers yelled, "Freeze!" Immediately, the men responded. They raised their arms above their heads and pleaded, "Don't shoot! Don't shoot!" At this point, I left the office, not realizing how vulnerable I was, and hurried to the scene of the action. I was ecstatic that the burglars had been captured.

I identified myself to the police. It didn't take long for the captured men to identify themselves. They were not burglars at all. They were from the cleaning service and had never been to the school before. Therefore, they had been wandering around the breezeways looking for light switches and the room in which the cleaning supplies and equipment were kept. They had no idea anyone was in any of the buildings. Had they known, they would have asked for assistance.

A few minutes later, the police and I were satisfied that the men were telling the truth. Before the police left, I apologized for any inconvenience I had caused. In return, I was assured that my actions were justified considering the recent burglary at the school.

Once the last police car left, the "burglars" breathed sighs of relief and could now laugh about the incident. They acted out the entire scene, then laughed about it. I laughed too. Then I showed them everything they needed to know. I finally bid them good night and headed back to my room. I was very relieved that everything had turned out the way it had.

Later that day, I phoned the owner of the cleaning service and filled him in on the details of what had happened. Possessing a keen sense of humor, he laughed and laughed. Before ending the call, I urged him in the future to send at least one man out of the two or three, who was familiar with our school. Otherwise, I couldn't guarantee their safety, especially since the school had already been burglarized once. He agreed to do so, then laughed again and hung up.

The remaining days of summer school passed quickly, and before I knew it, I was packing my personal items into a box in preparation for turning my office over to the new head, Susan Nigh. As requested by the Board, I had completed two lists. One contained the accomplishments during my tenure. The other contained several recommendations including higher tuition rates, higher teachers' salaries and set bus routes.

In many ways, I was sad to leave the school, but I would not miss the endless pressures of the job. I was proud of what had been accomplished, yet sad that more hadn't been done. I certainly had done everything I could to make the school a better educational institution. Now it was up to my successor to continue on where I had left off. I wished her the best of luck and the Lord's leading.

Having expressed my final thank yous to the office staff, I walked out the door for the last official time and immediately felt the burdens of the position lifted from my shoulders. Believe me, it felt terrific! Now I could enjoy a brief vacation and look forward to my family returning from New Jersey, the purchase of a home near our church and a new teaching position in nearby Rubidoux. All these thoughts made me whistle a happy tune as I drove out of the school's driveway and headed down Arlington Avenue.

RETURNING TO THE EAST

Mabe Million, a good friend, stopped by after work and helped us load our rental trailer. As we finished cramming the last few boxes in, several friends came by and gave us a farewell party. After it was over, we hugged and kissed everyone good-bye, took a last look at our recently sold house and sadly headed for route 91 north to Barstow. Once there, we'd gas up both vehicles then head east toward Needles. It was late in the evening and soon Mark and Bonnie would be asleep on their beds in the camper. Shelley was driving our station wagon and was following me.

About 2:00 A.M., we stopped in a pull-off area. We were both very tired and needed some rest in the comfort of our bed in the camper. As I lay there, I recalled the happy morning we arrived in Riverside and all that had taken place in our lives during our three years there. It was hard to believe that we were heading back to New Jersey, especially since both

Shelley and I had been so happy to leave it. I only hoped our reasons for going back were as valid as they seemed to be. But only time would tell.

We were on the road again by 8:30. As we were passing through Kingman, Arizona, we stopped for gas and fresh doughnuts. Under normal driving conditions, our truck-camper averaged ten miles per gallon. It averaged much less pulling a fully packed, fourteen-foot trailer. Therefore, the truck needed gas. The gas gauge in the wagon was broken, but I knew the wagon averaged about twenty miles per gallon. After checking how far we'd come from Barstow and knowing both the mileage per gallon and the capacity of the gas tank on the wagon, I informed Shelley that she was good for another two hundred miles. Therefore, I did not fill her tank.

Soon after leaving Kingman, we began climbing and soon came upon road construction on I-40. Both slowed us down. Since Shelley was following me, I began to worry that the wagon might begin to overheat. Therefore, I decided it was foolish to have her follow me and came up with a plan. Since we did not have CB radios to keep in touch, I hopped out of the truck at a construction stop sign and walked back to the wagon. We agreed that she would drive on to Flagstaff and pull off the road soon after passing the "Welcome to Flagstaff" sign. She'd find a shady spot and wait for the kids and me to catch up in the air conditioned truck. Soon after I returned to my truck, traffic began moving. Shelley passed me and was soon out of sight.

It was late morning when I reached Williams. This is one of those towns that has a one-way street east all the way through town and a one-way street west with buildings separating the two. As we drove through town, Bon saw a blue wagon like ours parked on a side street near the intersection and a gas station. She mentioned it to me, but I assured her it couldn't be our wagon since her mom was driving to Flagstaff and would meet us there. So we drove on.

When we arrived at the "Welcome to Flagstaff" sign, we began looking for the wagon but did not see it. I began to wonder where Shelley was as I slowly drove through the length of the town and back again. En route, I stopped at a Chevrolet dealer in case she'd stopped there for a repair, but she hadn't. I headed east again and drove even slower while we scanned the streets, parking lots, gas stations, et cetera. We saw no blue wagon. I finally told the kids, "Your mom probably got tired of waiting for us and has continued on toward New Mexico."

I repeated this statement several times in the next few hours even though I was concerned for her whereabouts. It appeased Mark and Bon but not me. I finally stopped at the Highway Patrol Office in Holbrook, explained the situation and asked for their help and advice. Since there had been no accidents that day involving wagons like ours, the officer said that he would put out an all-points bulletin on both the car and Shelley. Since we were heading east, he instructed me to check at the Highway Patrol Office in Gallup, New Mexico, for any information received in Holbrook and transferred there. We thanked the officer and headed for Gallup. Neither McDonald's nor a Dairy Queen calmed our nerves, especially since it was getting dark.

We arrived in Gallup about ten. By now Bon had finished crying for her mom and both kids were in bed trying to sleep but were just tossing and turning. I stopped at the Highway Patrol Office and checked with the officer on duty. He told me that nothing had come in yet. Then he suggested that we stay in their parking lot in case news came in. If some did, he would awaken me. I agreed to his suggestion, thanked him and returned to the camper. I lay on my bed wondering where Shelley was. Had she been in an accident no one knew about? Had she taken another route by mistake? Had she been abducted? I was very worried, but somehow managed to fall asleep.

At 1:00 A.M., a loud knock on the door of the camper awakened us. The officer told us that Shelley had been found. She was in Williams, Arizona, 222 miles from Gallup and was spending the night in jail. He invited me to the office where a phone call would be arranged. I accepted and soon had Shelley on the line. Here's what she told me.

As she neared Williams, she looked at the odometer. After doing some quick figuring, she realized she had driven over 300 miles since getting gas. Forgetting exactly what I had told her in Kingman, she was sure she was running on fumes and expected to run out of gas at any time. When she reached Williams, she stopped for gas. Checking her purse, she discovered she had no bills, just a little change and none of our gas credit cards. So she parked the wagon on a side street near the intersection facing our route and next to the gas station. While waiting for us to come along, she dozed off. When she awoke, she didn't know if we had passed by yet or not. Eventually, she assumed we had.

At this point in our conversation, I mentioned about Bon seeing the wagon and my shrugging it off as a coincidence since we had agreed to meet in Flagstaff. After all, I told her, there are probably plenty of wagons the same color as ours. Why shouldn't there be a few in Williams?

Since she was sure that she needed gas, she tried to borrow money from a few ministers in town with no success. Then she tried, without success, to sell our lawn mower and some other objects we had put into the wagon when loading. Finally, she went to the police.

The police were sorry, but there was little they could do for her except to try and locate the truck and us. But since it was getting late, they offered her a jail cell to sleep in for the night if she wanted to do so. Without money, hungry and tired, she accepted their offer. A female officer felt sorry for her and bought a sandwich and coffee at a local deli and delivered both to her in her cell. She finally mentioned that her cell was cool and her cot was comfortable. The only drawback was the drunk in a cell a little down from hers who was vomiting now and then and moaning in between.

After hearing her story, I assured her that I would wire some money as soon as the Western Union Office opened. Then the kids and I would backtrack a bit and wait for her to catch up at a picnic area a little west of Gallup. Once I was sure she understood where we'd meet, the phone call ended, the kids and I went back to bed and soon fell asleep relieved that Shelley was safe and sound.

By 7:30, we were up and at the Western Union Office when it opened at 8:00. I wired Shelley twenty dollars, then drove back to the picnic area. After breakfast, we washed up and did the few chores that needed to be done. Then Mark and Bonnie played while I read. It was a cool, sunny morning, perfect for being outside.

Hours later, Shelley drove in. After a joyous reunion, she told us what happened after our phone call.

She slept until 7:30. After washing up, drinking coffee and eating a doughnut at the police station, she thanked the officers and headed for the Western Union Office. It was open, when she arrived, but the operator informed her that his machine was broken, and she would have to go to Flagstaff for her money. Becoming quite frustrated, she explained her plight to him, then he agreed to call the Flagstaff office.

The person in Flagstaff concurred that money had been wired to her, but in order to receive it, she had to tell them the amount. Since we hadn't discussed the amount I would send during our phone conversation, she didn't know and told them so. Following procedures, the operator in Williams immediately informed her that she would not be given the money. While the two operators were still on the phone, she began to cry. At that point the operators must have felt sorry for her and soon ended their phone conversation. After putting the receiver on the phone cradle, the Williams' operator asked to see her license. Once he examined it, he gave her the twenty dollars, and she stopped crying.

Before leaving the picnic area, I checked the mileage log in the wagon. The figures confirmed my suspicions that Shelley had plenty of gas to get her to Flagstaff, and well beyond, without needing any in Williams. Besides the figures, she could have easily checked the tank itself. The tank was located on the passenger's side near the rear. Had she removed the gas cap, she could have stuck the broomstick she had in the wagon into the tank and discovered she had plenty of gas. Either way, I felt the entire incident could and should have been avoided.

Before leaving the picnic area, I made sure she had money and gas credit cards. When our caravan headed east, she followed me. We continued on through New Mexico, the Texas panhandle and into Oklahoma.

Since it was so hot in Oklahoma, we decided to try again. We agreed that when she reached the entrance to Clinton, Oklahoma, she would pull off the road at the first shady spot and wait for us to catch up. Once we both understood the plan, she took off and was soon out of sight.

Eventually I came upon a large billboard containing the words, "Welcome to Clinton, Oklahoma!" in large letters and some other words informing everyone passing by that Jane Anne Jayroe from Laverne, Oklahoma, was Miss America 1967. The huge sign was there in broad daylight, but not Shelley in our blue wagon. I asked the kids, "How could she miss this sign? It's a billboard!" Neither had an answer.

As I had done in Flagstaff, I decided to drive through Clinton hoping to find her parked in a shady spot. It was a town like Williams, a one-way street east, one west and buildings between the two. I drove slowly through, and we saw no wagon. I was about to turn around when Mark thought he saw something blue farther down the road. Instead of turning, I continued and, sure enough, there she was a mile east of Clinton. Her excuse, "I didn't see the sign."

I was already a bit angry before hearing her words. After hearing them I was very angry. How could she have missed such a large sign? A small one, maybe, but not a billboard! From there until we almost reached New Stanton, Pennsylvania, she followed me.

It was Sunday near suppertime. We were climbing a hill on I-70. I saw a billboard extolling the hot chicken dinners at the Howard Johnson's Restaurant ahead at the next exit. A hot meal would hit the spot, so Mark, Bon and I agreed we'd stop. About a half mile from the exit, for a reason unknown to me, Shelley pulled out and passed us. Gone were the delicious, hot chicken dinners we were going to enjoy at "Ho Jo's." By the time I caught up with her, we were almost to the Pennsylvania Turnpike. I don't recall her reason for passing us, however, I do recall eating canned stew for supper in silence.

It was dark, traffic was heavy as usual, and we were all very tired when I pulled off the turnpike and into a safe place to sleep. I made the mistake of stopping near the crest of a steep hill. Soon after we went to bed, we could hear truckers shifting and gunning their engines to make it up the hill. The almost constant noises made sleeping difficult. At one point, while waiting for sleep to come, I recalled our trip west and what might have happened, had we lost our brakes descending such a steep hill as the one close by. At least this night, we were safe from possible harm. This realization didn't cause me to fall asleep any sooner, but it did comfort me.

The next day, we arrived in Westwood. It was hot and humid. The mosquitoes were hungry for our blood and attacked viciously. However, our relatives were happy to see us, and we were happy to see them. Thus, we took the good with the bad and reached for a cool drink, glad that our trip was over and that we had arrived safe and sound.

In the years since, I've told this true story of our trip from California to New Jersey many times, and people have enjoyed it. However, Shelley still swears that at the gas station in Kingman, I said, "You're good for 200 miles," and not, "You're good for another 200 miles." We'll never agree on exactly what I said. However, what excuse can she give for missing the "Welcome to Clinton, Oklahoma" billboard? None.

Chapter XVII
Our Truck/Camper: A Status Symbol

We hadn't lived in California very long before we realized one status symbol was to have two vehicles in one's driveway: a car and a pickup with a camper on it. A few years before we arrived, Californians, by the hundreds, would hook their trailers to their cars and their boats to their trailers and head for the lakes, the ocean, the Colorado River or some other place for recreational purposes. Eventually, the law was changed stopping the car-trailer-boat convoys. Thus, the age of campers on pickups was born; another California first.

In the fall 1965, I "pushed Shelley out the door," and into substitute teaching. It was my hope that she could earn enough money for a down payment on a truck-camper by the next spring. After all, we were now Californians and half our driveway was empty. Since she'd had no teacher training in college, subbing proved difficult for her, but she stuck to it.

By May, we had our new, heavy-duty, three-quarter ton pickup, and a ten and a half foot, cab-over camper on it. The truck had been a demo, thus, it was loaded with options. However, it had coil springs necessitating my having half-leaf springs installed in the rear to control swaying. I replaced the two windows between the truck cab and the camper with a leather boot. The boot would allow cool air from the air conditioner to enter the camper, and it would allow the kids to pass from the truck into the camper and vice versa.

The camper had all the luxuries of home. It could sleep four comfortably. It had a gas stove with an oven. It had a double sink. We could carry our own water supply in a holding tank, or we could hook up to water lines at camping areas. We even had a toilet. It consisted of a pail inside a box with a toilet seat on top. It recessed out of the way when not in use.

Even though the camper was not large, it suited our needs. There was a place for everything within reason. Mark and Bon enjoyed being on the bed in the camper, that extended over the cab, whenever we traveled. They could play games, look out the windows at the scenery, sleep, or raise Cain.

However, the latter was a no-no, and a few times it led to disciplinary action by me.

As anyone knows who has a camper on a truck, camping is easy in such a rig. You get to a camping area, pull into your assigned space, turn on the bottled gas, hook up the water, if there is a hookup, and that's it. You're soon ready to enjoy the great outdoors. We did, for over two hundred days, during the two and a half years we owned the rig.

After a couple of spring weekend trips to beautiful La Jolla and the southern California coast, we decided to travel ten weeks during the summer. In the middle of June, we left our lawn, flowers, shrubs, and trees in the hands of a high school boy to care for and headed north toward Oregon, Washington and Canada.

The first leg of our trip took us north on route 395 and into the high desert. It was very hot, so the air conditioner was on. As we drove toward Lone Pine, the gas needle was going down faster than the mileage traveled indicated it should. I knew the gas tank held twenty-one gallons, and it was full when we left Riverside. I also knew from our weekend trips that the truck averaged ten miles per gallon. Knowing these facts, I assumed the fuel gauge was not functioning correctly. As we approached Lone Pine, the needle read zero. When I finally filled the tank, it took 20.8 gallons. I had not realized we were climbing most of the time from Riverside to Lone Pine cutting down on the miles per gallon.

After gassing up and doing everything else travelers do at gas stations, I asked the attendant to point out Mt. Whitney (the highest mountain in the conterminous United States at 14,491 feet). Instead of pointing to the mountain, he pointed to an iron pipe mounted somewhat horizontally on another pipe that was vertically fastened to the ground. I walked over, looked through the pipe in the direction of the mountains and saw Mt. Whitney. The owner of the station had used great ingenuity when he put those pipes up. Now, tourists, like us, could see the particular mountain without bothering him or anyone working at the station. The last time I went through Lone Pine in 1989, the pipes were still there ready for use.

Fifteen hundred miles and three states later, we entered Canada and continued driving north until we met the Trans-Canadian Highway and headed east. We camped one night in Banff National Park. Since summer had just begun, it stayed light until well after 11:00 P.M.. Therefore, while other campers played catch nearby, we pulled our curtains shut and, much to their chagrin, put our two to bed.

When we reached Regina, Saskatchewan, we stopped at the Royal

Canadian Mounted Police Training Center and Museum. We were taken on a very interesting tour. While there, Bonnie became sick and had to return to the camper. When the three of us arrived back, ready to move on, she was asleep on her bed. Instead of riding in the truck with Shelley and me, Mark climbed onto the bed in the camper over the cab for a nap.

Late that afternoon it began to pour. We were several miles west of Brandon, Manitoba. Suddenly Shelley and I felt a swoosh of air followed by screams from Bonnie. I quickly pulled off the road and stopped.

Entering the camper, we saw what had happened. For no apparent reason, the long, safety-glass window in the front of the camper over the bed had blown in and disintegrated into hundreds of small, square pieces. Mark was covered with them. He was sleeping at the time and his head was turned away from the window. He escaped without injury, not even the slightest cut.

As I sized up the situation, I murmured to myself, "Why me, Lord? This shouldn't be happening to me. To someone else, maybe, but not me." But it had, so I had to think fast and act quickly.

I instructed Shelley and Mark to hold the seat cushions from the eating area benches over the blown out window while I continued on to Brandon for repairs. As they held the cushions tightly against the opening, Bon began to vomit, and I gladly returned to the truck cab. Shelley alternately called, "Good girl, " to three year old Bonnie as she held a plastic bowl under her chin. Then Shelley encouraged Mark who announced that his hands felt "ugly."

I arrived in Brandon and found most stores closed since we had entered a different time zone. It was six o'clock, my watch showed five. There were no glass repair shops open and Winnepeg, Manitoba was 135 miles farther east. Panic time! Bon was sick. Rain was pouring down. Our window was out, and I was 135 miles from Winnepeg. My fortitude was certainly being tested.

While at a gas station filling up, I mentioned my problem to the attendant. He listened courteously then responded. He knew a man in Brandon who had a business, next to his home, in which he used thin sheets of wood and other materials. Perhaps he could cut a piece of some material he had on hand to fit the space until we could get to Winnepeg. I copied down the directions to his home, thanked the attendant and left.

I found the man at home and explained my problem. Yes, he had thin, waterproof materials that would work. Within an hour, he had installed a temporary, opaque "window" that didn't leak. His fee was nominal, for which I was grateful.

The rain continued, Bon remained sick, the cushions were soaked, and the camper smelled. Otherwise, everything was fine. We made it through the night and early the next morning, we headed for Winnipeg.

I called my insurance agent from Winnipeg. Then I found a repair shop and had a window made from a sheet of clear plexiglass. I knew it would be safer than a window made of safety glass. And it proved to be so.

The remainder of our trip to New Jersey was uneventful. However, once there, everything changed. Campers on trucks were almost unheard of in the East. Therefore, when we arrived in ours, heads turned in our direction. Every place we went, crowds gathered. We enjoyed showing the inside of our home-away-from-home to many, many gawkers as far east as Provincetown, Massachusetts.

Our trip back to California in August was going well until we were passing through a town in Colorado. It was morning, and I stopped for gas. Shelley and Bonnie headed for the ladies' bathroom. Shelley was carrying the toilet pail, Bon a few toiletries. Mark and I used the men's bathroom, filled the tank, checked the oil, cleaned the windshield and got back into the cab. After waiting several minutes, we heard the camper door open. Thus, we figured Bon and Shelley had returned, so I left the station.

Several minutes later, I called through the boot and asked Shelley for a cup of coffee. No answer. I called again and still received no answer. I looked at Mark, he looked at me. Both our expressions asked the same question. Did we really hear the camper door open? Our question was soon answered. We only thought, we heard the door open and close.

I quickly slowed down, turned around and headed back to town. As we approached the station, there they stood, stonefaced, on the corner, with Shelley still holding the pail while pedestrians walked by. Once they were inside the camper, I headed west again. For some reason, no one said anything for several minutes. I finally broke the silence and asked for a cup of coffee and received it.

We spent a couple of days in beautiful Rocky Mountain National Park. The morning we left, we headed south on route 34. Not far from Granby, we were following a station wagon pulling a trailer. Near the crest of the hill, the driver of the wagon slowed down and stopped for a moment. He then turned left and crossed the northbound lanes in order to enter a picnic area. The area was rather full, therefore, he was having trouble getting both his wagon and trailer off the road.

Before he succeeded, a new Chevrolet came barreling over the crest of the hill heading north. Brakes were applied in a desperate attempt to stop, but the attempt proved futile. The car ricocheted off the left rear side of the wagon and rammed the attached trailer with such force that it almost sent the trailer crashing over a nearby embankment.

As soon as the car came to a halt, I parked my truck, jumped out and ran to the car to offer assistance. I expected to see badly injured occupants and braced for the worst. As I opened the door on the driver's side, a frightened, older couple were unfastening their seat belts and audibly thanking God for his mercy to them. Neither appeared to be physically hurt, not even a scratch. But they were shaking. I stayed with them until police arrived, then wished them well and left. Even though their new car was totalled and their long-awaited vacation ruined, they were alive and well.

As we continued on our way, I noticed Shelley wearing her seat belt, something she had done very infrequently prior to our seeing this accident. She got the message.

We arrived home in late August. It was dark when we pulled into our driveway. We headed for the front door and suddenly froze in our tracks. We could hear voices inside. Immediately several unpleasant thoughts raced through my mind. We slowly backtracked as far as the sidewalk and stood without saying much for several minutes. Finally, I whispered what I planned to do and ordered Shelley, Mark, and Bonnie to stay where they were.

Being the brave soul that I am, I decided to sneak back to the darkened house and listen to the voices. I did so but couldn't hear them very well. So I slowly crept around one side toward the master bedroom. The voices grew louder and louder, and I became angrier and angrier as I realized our bedroom was possibly being used for a party or even an orgy. Arriving, I slowly stood up and peered through the window expecting the worst. All I saw was a TV set on, and the voices were coming from it.

Even though I was relieved, I still had unanswered questions on my mind. Who turned the TV on? And when? Was the person still inside? If so, where was he now? Could there be more than one?

After slowly circling the house and hearing no other voices, I decided to enter, baseball bat in hand. No one was there. But not all my questions had, as yet, been answered. I checked the TV settings, and then I had my answers. Somehow, we had left the TV set on the automatic "on" switch.

The first night in June after we left, the TV came on and had been on twenty-four hours a day all summer.

As I turned the set off, I asked Shelley, "How long do you think this set will continue working before something burns out?" It was a rhetorical question that needed no answer at the time. However, the answer came in 1984 when I had to replace a tube. Since then, the set has been working fine, a tribute to RCA.

During our fist year in California, we visited the cities of Tijuana and Ensenada, Mexico, a few times. However, now that we had our rig, we decided to travel south of the border during my Christmas vacation. We chose the seaside city of Mazatlan as our final destination. It lies 750 miles south of the border, the climate is tropical, and the ocean is perfect for swimming and surfing. We left Riverside anticipating a grand and glorious time.

Our first overnight stop was in Nogalas, Arizona, to visit some missionary friends, the Courteols. Julian was the head of a small Bible school for Mexican Christians in Nogalas, Mexico and had a real love for the Mexican people. Our visit, though short, was enjoyable.

Before retiring for the night, Julian gave us a few good tips about traveling in Mexico, tips I found to be very valuable. First of all, he advised us to leave early in the morning and cross the border, thus avoiding the customary long lines of cars waiting to cross. Second, in Mexico, he strongly urged us to buy Mexican automobile insurance as soon as an office had opened. Third, he warned us not to drink any of the water, not even a mouthful. However, with a smile on his face, he encouraged us to carry Kaopectate in case any of us forgot and drank some water. Finally, he cautioned us to watch for signs along the two-lane road we'd be traveling that said, "Puente Angosto," meaning narrow bridge.

Seeing my furrowed brow, he quickly explained the last tip. Whenever we saw such a sign, we were to be prepared to stop at the narrow bridge ahead. In Mexico, when two vehicles are approaching a narrow bridge, day or night, from opposite directions, the driver who flashes his high-beam headlights first, has the right of way on the bridge. He stressed the importance of obeying this custom. I thanked Julian for his words of advice and went to bed.

It was still dark when we drove up to the border crossing and stopped. The guard asked us a couple of questions then allowed us to proceed. Julian had been correct, there were no lines. I was pleased that we entered Mexico so quickly.

There were many narrow bridges to cross as we traveled south. Therefore, we were glad Julian had enlightened us. It was obvious, that two cars could not safely pass on any of the narrow bridges we passed over prior to daylight and our breakfast stop.

While Shelley prepared breakfast, I checked the truck and camper. I noticed our water tank inside the camper was leaking. I could only guess that the low temperature in Nogalas had indirectly caused the leak. I deduced that the surface water froze, expanded, and cracked the metal seam of the tank. Thus, there was only one thing we could do. We filled every available container with water, then dumped the rest on the ground. We had saved enough for drinking and cooking if we didn't waste too much. Mexican water would be suitable for bathing.

As we drove the 750 miles to Mazatlan, we saw many new and different sights. We saw dead horses and dead cattle along the roadside, victims of the open range policy. We saw families living in abandoned railroad boxcars even though most Mexican families lived in adobe houses. We saw stacks of wooden racks, filled with empty soda bottles, outside most of the adobe houses. I assumed that even the Mexicans couldn't drink the water or, perhaps, there was no water nearby. We saw young girls and women sweeping the dirt in their grassless front yards, smoothing it out with their primitive brooms. Grass or no grass, they were keeping their yards neat.

As we traveled, we noticed a tremendous number of trucks with Mexican plates. Most of them were full of people, not only in the cabs but in the truck beds as well. Any Mexican buses that we passed were crammed full of passengers. Thus, narrow bridges presented real life and death problems for any driver ignorant of the "rule of narrow bridges" that Julian had taught us.

Whenever we stopped in a town for gas and food, children would soon appear from every direction and just stand and look at our beautiful rig. Now and then, a few were brave enough to touch the smooth, shiny camper. As they did so, I wondered what thoughts were going through their minds. I knew, in my mind, that our camper's interior was prettier and had more conveniences then most of their homes. With our limited knowledge of Spanish, we could not readily talk to them. However, the cookies we handed out, and the smiles we received back said it all.

We crossed the Tropic of Cancer and arrived in Mazatlan the day before Christmas. We rented a space in a trailer park outside of the city and near the ocean. The owner really packed them in, so we were very close to a large trailer from Texas on one side and a large motor home on the other. A stalk of bananas hung outside the trailer slowly ripening.

As Christmas Eve approached, tourists decorated small palm trees and bushes with colored lights, Christmas balls, tinsel and icicles. That evening we sat in our camper eating canned ravioli and listening to the Christmas section of Handel's *Messiah* oratorio. We could smell a turkey roasting in the oven of the trailer and could see Christmas lights through our windows. It was a perfect Christmas Eve, so we decided to open our gifts and not wait for Christmas morning.

We spent most of Christmas day at the beach relaxing on the warm sand, surfing and swimming in the ocean and riding rented horses. Peddlers tried to sell us silver jewelry at rock-bottom prices, but we were too dumb to buy any. And we were constantly asked to buy small boxes of Chiclets by the children, who combed the beaches regularly. It was fun, fun, fun, all day in this tropical paradise.

In the late afternoon, the owner of the trailer park had a piñata party for all the children. At one point, Mark narrowly missed getting bashed in the head by a blindfolded youngster swinging at the piñata with a club. Mark was trying to grab some of the candy that was falling out of the partially broken piñata. All of the children had a turn with the club and each managed to grab plenty of candy once the piñata was opened spewing its contents on the ground.

We decided to go out for dinner that night and mentioned our plan to the man in the trailer next to us. He suggested a restaurant in Mazatlan he and his wife both enjoyed. Then he further suggested that we order a particular meal, one he raved over as being delicious.

We took his advice, found the restaurant, ordered his suggestion without looking at the menu, and waited. When our food came, it was small portions of chicken covered with a spicy sauce and some vegetables. As we ate, I looked around and saw people eating large, delicious-looking steaks with all the trimmings. However, being from the United States, I assumed the steak dinners were much more expensive than our "delicacy" and continued eating.

After paying our bill, I decided, just for kicks, to look at a menu and see what a steak dinner cost. To my utter amazement, it cost less than the meal I had. How could this be? Chicken more expensive than steak? I inquired about this and learned that chickens were scarce in Mexico and cattle were plentiful. Thus, chicken was a delicacy and more expensive. I felt badly that we had eaten chicken when we could have feasted on juicy steaks at a cheaper price. And to top it off, our chicken dinners gave us terrible indigestion. I decided, that night, not to listen to such advice again unless I knew in advance what I was ordering. Even then, I would look at a menu first and see what other options were open to me.

The next morning I rode the rickety, crowded bus to Mazatlan while Shelley, Mark and Bonnie enjoyed the beach. I found a section of the city that was not meant for tourists but was where many of the local citizens shopped. After roaming slowly through several small shops, I noticed the lack of paper bags being used after sales were made. The shop owners or employees wrapped most items in newspaper including live chickens and the pairs of sandals I brought for the kids. Sandals purchased only after I had practiced the art of dickering over prices masterfully. Having seen other shoppers do it, I assumed it was another Mexican custom, one I found enjoyable.

When it was time for lunch, I stopped at a small, outdoor stand. I ordered a beef burrito and a milkshake made with canned milk, fresh strawberries, and papaya. The total cost was two pesos, the equivalent of sixteen cents in U.S. money. Both items were delicious!

After I finished, I put my glass back on the counter. The kindly gentleman, who ran this business, smiled and took the glass. He turned, swished it around in a tub of cold water, and set it back on the counter ready for his next customer. To my surprise and relief, I didn't get sick.

After arriving back at our camper, I discovered that we needed a block of ice for our refrigerator. I bought one from the peddler who came by daily. The ice was made from dirty water, and I could see pieces of straw in it. As I looked in amazement, my thoughts went back to my boyhood and the blocks of ice Mom bought for our iceboxes. We often ate small bits of that ice, but this ice was not meant for human consumption. It was strictly for cooling things off.

I also bought milk. It came in sealed, heavy-duty plastic bags, another first for me. I opened one bag, poured a glass and drank it. It was cool, fresh and delicious. I smiled to myself and said, "Cows are cows the world around no matter how their milk is packaged." Once opened, the bag could not be stored easily, so I poured the rest of the milk into another container before putting it into the refrigerator.

The same day, someone caught a huge marlin and had it cleaned. Then pieces were offered to whomever wanted them. I accepted the offer, and we enjoyed delicious, fresh fish for supper, a welcome respite from the canned fare we had been eating so many previous nights.

One evening Shelley took her birth control pill and washed it down with a swallow of water from the sink's faucet. It had slipped her mind that the faucet was connected to the water supply in the park and not our holding tank. Within a half hour she became very sick. Montezuma's revenge attached her in all its fury. She spent the next thirty-six hours padding back and forth to the women's restrooms. In between she stayed in bed. After the first twenty-four hours, I knew we'd have to cancel our remaining days in the park and head for home. Shelley was in no condition to stay any longer.

The morning we were leaving, a car, towing a large, damaged trailer, pulled into a vacant spot across the narrow dirt road from ours. A group of gawkers, including me, gathered around the owners and asked what caused the damage. With tears in his eyes, the man told them. He and his wife were driving south, and a truck was heading north. Both vehicles arrived at a narrow bridge at the same time. Unknown to him and his wife, the driver of the truck had established his right of way by flashing his headlights. They saw the lights but didn't know what they meant. Both vehicles entered the bridge, and confirmed the law of physics that states, "Two object cannot occupy the same space at the same time." Once on the bridge, in his effort to get out of the truck's way, he rammed his trailer into the bridge's railing and tore off most of the right side.

As I listened to his story, I felt sorry for the couple. They had both recently retired and were now looking forward to their golden years. Our words of encouragement did little to cheer them up. However, their countenances changed when the park owner appeared and informed the couple that someone in Mazatlan could fix their trailer as good as new. This good news cushioned the sadness we all felt over their loss.

Heading north, we stopped to make breakfast just a sort distance beyond the Tropic of Cancer. We pulled off the road in an area surrounded by dense vegetation and no visible signs of life. While we ate, we left the camper door open to enjoy the fresh air. At one point, I looked out and saw a young woman standing there. She was holding a young boy clad in a shirt and nothing else. She stood there looking at our world without speaking. She had so little, we had so much. She was poor, we were rich. Shortly before we left, she turned, walked back into the woods and disappeared.

As we drove through town after town, I noticed two things. First, at the entrance to each town, a large fountain and a large "Welcome to . . ." sign in Spanish had been erected. Secondly, the main street through each town was paved, but all the other streets were not. They were made of dirt and were rutty.

In one of the cities we passed through, I needed to cash a traveler's check. I pulled up and stopped next to a taxicab. I rolled down my window and looked toward the cabbie. When our eyes met, I asked in a rather loud voice, *Pecunia?* He responded with a puzzled expression, so I repeated, *Pecunia, pecunia?* His facial expression was the same only this time he muttered, *No comprendo, señor.* I was about to ask again when Shelley yelled to me from her bed in the camper, "Dave, *pecunia* is the Latin word for money. You want a *banco.*"

Swallowing my embarrassment, I turned a third time toward the cabbie and said, "*Banco?*" Immediately, he grinned, responded, "*Si,*" motioned me to follow and drove off. I did so and soon drove up in front of a bank. He waved as he continued down the street. I cashed my check, left the bank and noticed a bakery across the street.

Everyone likes fresh, baked goods and I'm no exception. I entered the bakery, spent a few seconds enjoying all the delicious aromas, then asked one of its employees, in my "best" Spanish, about purchasing some items. She smiled, most likely at my poor use of Spanish, and pointed toward one section of the bakery. I ambled over and noticed many items for sale. Each kind was in a large basket. She handed me a basket with instructions to wait on myself. I reached down and picked out some rolls from one basket, a loaf of bread from another and some cookies from a third. After paying, my items were bagged and I headed back to the truck. As I walked, I thought how different this bakery was from those in America, and the prices were much lower.

It was dark on the evening of our second day of driving when we reached Guaymas. Shelley was still sick. I parked on a bridge in the city, made supper and afterwards enjoyed a cool stroll. Eventually the kids and I joined Shelley for some peaceful sleep. Sometime during the night, I heard a slight noise outside the camper but ignored it. I was too sleepy to get excited over a slight noise

Early the next morning, I stepped out of the camper and noticed the cap was missing from the water pipe used to fill our holding tank. It was identical to a gas cap, so I assumed someone had taken it for use on their vehicle. I knew now what was happening when I heard the slight noise. I put tape over the end of the pipe until I could replace the cap.

Repair completed, I walked to a market for some eggs and milk. Before returning, I bought and ate what I assumed was a soft ice cream cone, but, in reality, it was ice milk. It was a mistake I would regret.

After breakfast, I drove to a beach on the Gulf of California for a time of relaxation and swimming. Soon after arriving, the ice milk attacked. I needed a bathroom in a hurry, yet there was none anywhere in sight. I was about to explode when I discovered a small, abandoned, one-room building near the beach. It became my bathroom over a period of hours. After several doses of Kaopectate and many visits to my bathroom, I felt better and knew I would live.

Before leaving the beach, I decided to take a swim with Mark and Bonnie. As I was about to come out of the water, I noticed a man walking on the sand and coming toward me. As he neared the water's edge, he stopped, took off his shirt and dropped his pants revealing his bathing suit and two artificial legs. He sat on the sand and removed his pants, shoes, socks, and legs. Then he worked his way into the warm water for a swim. The kids and I tried not to stare, but I was transfixed by this man's courage to enjoy life even with a physical handicap. Before I left the water, we shared a bit of conversation and a few laughs. He was from Walnut Creek, California, and was in the medical profession.

Once we had dried off and dressed, we piled into the truck and headed for Nogalas and the Courteols. They again welcomed us with open arms. This time we appreciated being there even more than the last. Having just spent several days living in our camper, we enjoyed their warm, cozy home full of fragrant smells and Christmas decorations. It was a little taste of heaven for all of us, especially Shelley who was still sick.

The next morning we thanked our friends and headed for home. We arrived safely. We were thankful for all the good times we had enjoyed and would cherish the memories for several years. But we were glad to be home. We found Mexico to be a wonderful place for a vacation. However, Shelley and I both learned one important lesson: Don't consume their water in any form!

As long as we lived in California, we used our rig very often. However, once we moved to Oswego in the late summer of 1967, the lack of time and decent weather curtailed its use. After returning from a Christmas vacation to Florida, I rented a barn, a few miles from our home, to store the rig. Each Saturday, I'd drive to the barn and run the engine and air conditioner for several minutes. I vented the exhaust to the outside with sections of pipe once used to drain water from gutters. I carried out this ritual for six months.

For six weeks in the summer of 1968, I lived in the camper while attending summer school at the State University of New York at Buffalo. I parked it near the men's gym, so I could shower and shave there. I liked this setup. It was safe, quiet at night, near all the facilities, and free. On weekends, I took pleasurable jaunts here and there but came home to roost Sunday evenings.

Even though we took two trips that summer, one to Fergus Falls, Minnesota, and the other through some of the New England states, we realized we were not using the rig enough to keep it, and I hated the thought of storing it again for six months. Therefore, in late August, we cleaned the inside of the camper and washed and waxed the outside of the entire rig. Then I parked it near the highway with a "For Sale" sign attached to the inside of the windshield. During the next three weeks, several people stopped and looked at it, but no one made us an offer to buy it. I decided we were destined to keep it, and I took the sign off.

September 21 was Bon's seventh birthday. I was directing some outdoor games at her party when an older couple stopped and asked if I wanted to sell the rig. They were retired and planning to travel to the southwest that winter. After they inspected both the truck and the camper thoroughly, I took them for a ride. They sat in the truck cab going and in the camper coming. It was just what they wanted and offered to buy it at the price I had previously written on the "For Sale" sign.

We decided to sell it, and a few days later, all the paperwork was completed. As the elderly man climbed into the cab to drive it home, we all stood on the lawn with tears in our eyes. We felt like we were parting with a member of our family. During our period of ownership, we had stored up countless happy memories and a few unhappy ones. As the truck disappeared from sight, all that we had now were those memories.

Chapter XVIII
Vas Valves: A Noble Medical Project

By the ripe old age of thirty-eight, I had read a few articles about vasectomies. I had learned that a vasectomy is the cutting and tying of the tubes (vasa deferentia) that carry sperm from the testicles. Since I had a son and daughter and a wife who planned on not having any more children, I seriously considered having a vasectomy. After all, I had to "keep up with the Joneses," at least with Mr. Jones. So I began checking around for a doctor who did this "simple surgical procedure," as one article described it.

During my checking, I did further reading that enlightened me. I learned that the male's testicles or testes consist of a complicated system of tubes in which millions of sperm are produced and stored. A tube called the vas deferens carries sperm from each testicle to a tube called the urethra. A whitish fluid, called semen, is produced by the prostate gland and the seminal vesicles and is mixed and stored with the sperm in the vas deferens. The semen, which contains the sperm, is released through the urethra. The urethra runs through the penis. Thus, a vasectomy simply shuts off the sperm supply to the semen and makes a male sterile. However, few vasectomies are reversible: once sterile, always sterile.

I called a few doctors and one referred me to Dr. Joseph Davis in New York City. I contacted his office and was invited to come and see him. He and a colleague wanted to talk to me about a medical project that the two of them were involved in related to vasectomies. I accepted his invitation and an appointment was made for the following week.

Soon after I met Dr. Davis and Louis Bucalo, they got right into the "meat and potatoes" of why I was there. I heard again that many men, who've had vasectomies, and others, interested in getting vasectomies, would later express a desire to have the procedure reversed. Such reversals are usually not successful. Thus, once sterile, always sterile. Recalling my reading, I smiled to myself and continued listening. The two were looking for twenty men to participate in their project funded by the government.

After hearing all that they had to say, I signed on as one of the twenty. The rest of this chapter deals with their project and my participation in it.

On November 11, 1971, I reported as scheduled to a hospital in New York City. Phase one of the project was to begin. I was admitted then taken to an operating room where Dr. Davis showed me a set of tiny valves.

The valves were made of almost pure gold, an element completely safe for use in the human body. Since they were gold and a minimum number of sets had been made, each set was very costly. Mr. Bucalo had developed them. They were similar to T-valves used in regular plumbing jobs. They could be opened allowing a liquid to flow through them or closed stopping such a flow.

As phase one began, I was given a local anesthetic in my scrotum. Then a tiny slit was made in the left side of my scrotum. The vas deferens was snipped in two. A valve, in the open position, was inserted into the two tube parts reconnecting one part with the other. A second valve was then inserted into the vas deferens on the right side of my scrotum. Finally, both slits were sewn shut and the procedure was completed.

As I drove back to Ossining, some thirty-five miles away, I felt a bit groggy and has some discomfort in my scrotum. As the anesthetic wore off, the discomfort increased making it more difficult to concentrate on driving. By the time I reached home, my head was clear, but the pain persisted.

At the time, I was teaching at the King's College in Briarcliff Manor, New York. I shared an office with Barbara Baker and Marian Lehmer. We were professors in the elementary education department. Since my pain lasted a few days, I walked slower than usual and sat down very slowly. I'm sure these two, plus other faculty and students who saw me walk or sit, assumed I was suffering with a case of hemorrhoids. Being an evangelical Christian college, I'm sure no one had the nerve to ask me, and I never told anyone the real reason for my actions.

Now that the valves were in place, phase one would last several months. It sought to determine if sperm would travel through the open valves and, if they did, how many and how active would they be. Therefore, ten specimens of my semen had to be procured over a twenty-day period, put into small bottles, stored in my refrigerator, and taken to a laboratory near New York City. Once examined, I was informed that active amounts of sperm were evident in the specimens. Thereafter, I had to deliver a fresh specimen every so often as scheduled. As time went on, the sperm count continued to increase, and the sperm were very active. Phase one was succeeding very well and continued to do so.

When phase two began, I was opened again and the valves were turned off. Again I suffered discomfort for a few days and sensed more suspicions from colleagues and students, but they mentioned nothing about it, and neither did I. I just laughed to myself, now and then, and thought, *Wouldn't they be surprised if they knew?*

More specimens of semen were examined to determine if I would become sterile. I did and then the next question was asked. Would I remain sterile over a period of months or would the sperm find some way to swim past the valves? Phase two extended into the summer of 1972. I was going to Europe in late June for a fifty-six day history seminar through ten countries. I would be traveling with twenty-three others. A few days before leaving, I mailed a semen specimen to the laboratory from upstate New York. A few days later, I received a phone call from the lab.

The technician informed me that a trace of sperm was in the semen specimen. Perhaps a valve had shifted in one of the vas tubes allowing sperm to swim between the inner tube wall and the outer valve surface. I asked how many sperm were in the trace. His nonchalant reply was, "Oh, ten million or so, but they're very lethargic."

His reply raised my blood pressure a few points, and I quickly asked him how many sperm would be in a normal ejaculation of a young, healthy male. His reply, "Oh, as high as 400 million." Hearing this, I thought, "My gosh! That many and it takes only one, uniting with a fertile egg in a female, to produce an offspring. And sperm, using their long tails, are powerful swimmers. No wonder there are so many unwanted pregnancies." The technician's last words were, "Don't be alarmed, just take precautions. Have a great trip! See you in the fall." I took his advice and enjoyed my trip.

When it was time for phase three to begin, I drove back to the hospital, was reopened and the valves were turned on again. This was the crucial phase in the project. Would sperm once again pass through the valves, or would tissue growth prevent them from doing so?

On my way home, I began to feel more discomfort than before, and it lasted longer. This increase, and my reactions to it, led me to believe that any at the college who saw me walk or sit were sure I had hemorrhoids, but still no one even hinted at it. They'd look, frown, and finally express a facial expression that summed up their feelings, "You poor man. You ought to have an operation. Preparation H doesn't seem to be doing you much good." However, once the pain ceased, and I returned to normal in my walking and sitting patterns, looks of pity faded.

Slowly the sperm count in the specimens increased as did the vitality of the sperm. As time went by, the count rose higher and higher signaling the success of phase three. Everyone in the project was elated with the results.

Finally, on November 30, 1973, I was opened for the fourth and final time. The valves were removed, and I was given a vasectomy by Dr. Davis. However, an intern "closed me up." As I drove back to the college, I experienced more discomfort than I had the three previous times.

It didn't take long before the discomfort became pain and my scrotum began to swell up like a cow's udder. As the swelling continued, I realized why cows always look so sad, especially pregnant ones. Infection set in and I was in agony. Dr. Davis prescribed some medication, but it didn't help much.

At the college, I once again became the object for pity—only this time more so. I walked very slowly without smiling. I sat down very, very cautiously even though I had an extra cushion on my chair. Many times I wanted to yell, "No, I don't have hemorrhoids! At this point, my scrotum is badly infected. If you want to know why, make an appointment to see me, and I'll tell you. Now stop staring and whispering among yourselves!"

My scrotum remained swollen and very sore into December. Even so, we drove to Florida to celebrate Christmas with my in-laws. All that sitting with my swollen scrotum pressed between my legs almost killed me. But I survived, and we finally arrived in the warm, sunny south and looked forward to our visit. After a day, watching me shuffle along and sit gingerly, my mother-in-law also diagnosed my condition as hemorrhoids and suggested to Shelley that I have surgery and get rid of them. Shelley didn't tell her the real reason for my movements. She simply agreed that I should look into an operation. After that, the subject was dropped, and I continued to suffer in silence.

My scrotum remained swollen and sore into January. However, it slowly returned to normal size and the pain ceased. I'm sure my colleagues and the students were as relieved as I was.

For all practical purposes, the project was a success. A solution to the problem of vasectomy reversal had been found. I, along with nineteen others, had shown it would work.

Soon after our project ended, another began at the University of Miami's Department of Urology. I heard through the grapevine that Mr. Bucalo was interested in developing valves using magnetic minerals. Such valves could be turned on and off with a magnetic force from outside the scrotum. Recalling the pain I had suffered, I murmured to myself, "Now that's a great idea!"

Not long ago Dr. Davis answered a letter I had written to him. In it, he reported that the project has not progressed because of problems with the interface between the gold valve and the vas deferens. He also mentioned that there was an attempt to use a magnetic material, but it was not successful. Therefore, a simple solution to vasectomy reversal remains unsolved. I thought it had been found and have the scars to prove it.

Chapter XIX
Europe: A Dream Come True

I settled into my seat, dog-tired, after being awake over thirty-six hours without a wink of sleep. My head kept spinning as thoughts raced to and fro, each one screaming for my attention. After meeting Dick Harding and Cathy Fransson, the passengers flanking me, I excused myself, put my seat back, closed my eyes, and waited for the air sickness pills I had taken earlier, to lull me to sleep. But sleep did not come, only visual reminders of the past week at LeTourneau Christian Camp: my working with Jack Seabrook, Tom Olson, Sr., and others putting the long, three-sided dock in Canandaigua Lake section by section; taking a day to level it; then the storms, packing winds and rain the likes of which I'd never experienced before, battering the dock and breaking it apart like kindling and scattering sections hither and yon; lassoing salvageable pieces and reining them in before the huge waves carried them away; brooks becoming raging rivers spewing tons of water into the lake raising its level over five feet in three storm-filled days; the flooded workshop as a result; the flooded, closed Rochester airport necessitating my long, overnight bus ride to Boston, and on and on.

But now the evening I had been waiting for had arrived. It was June 24, 1972, and I was on my way to Europe for fifty-six exciting days. Exciting because I was finally going to see and explore so many places I had read about and taught to my upper elementary school classes for ten years. My dreams were finally going to become real, and I licked my lips in anticipation of what lay ahead.

Since Europe is full of history, the Gordon College European Seminar was the perfect way to experience the sights and sounds of ten countries with ample time for each. Since I added Greece and Yugoslavia to the Seminar's basic itinerary, I was a member of the Baker Team and would travel with twenty-one other participants under the leadership of Diane Black and her aide, Richard Foster. All this for $700 plus my $300 spending money.

The more I thought about my trip, the more excited I became, and soon I was wide awake and raring to go. As the KLM plane taxied toward its takeoff runway, I sat up and looked out the window nearest me. I wanted to see what Boston looked like from the air. As the plane left the runway and climbed into the clear, evening sky, I was not disappointed.

After a tasty dinner, I again put my seat back, and this time I fell asleep in seconds. Before I knew it, I was being awakened by Dick. We were about to land in Amsterdam. I should have been excited, but I was not. I was still groggy from being so sound asleep. However, I prepared for landing and looked out the window as we approached the runway and bumped down. From the air, Europe looked no different from America, but all that would change in a matter of hours.

I soon had my one, twenty-seven-inch suitcase in hand and headed with everyone else to a currency exchange window. I needed to cash a few traveler's checks and buy some Dutch guilders. As I waited patiently for my turn, I glanced at a clock and noticed it was 7:00 A.M. Doing some quick calculations, I figured I had slept about five hours on the plane. Thus, I had a good excuse for my frequent yawns as I waited. Business completed, I left the terminal with some of my new friends and entered a bus that would carry us to the beginning of an adventure few people experience in their lifetime.

As I had prepared for this trip, I established two major goals for myself. First, I was determined to see Europe through my own eyes as the Baker Team explored each city, town and village listed on our itinerary. Second, I wanted to go beyond the historical landmarks: the museums, churches, palaces, the ancient ruins, and all else that makes Europe an historical mecca. I wanted to explore the out-of-the-way places in each area we visited. I longed to mingle with the common folks, to experience the unordinary, to smell and taste new foods and drink new drinks. I was hungry and thirsty to try all of Europe and absorb as much of it as possible into my body and soul. And Amsterdam was my first feast.

The bus eventually arrived at a small hotel where several of us were to stay for the next five days. Five of us males, including Larry and his alarm clock, were assigned to one room containing five, single beds in a space meant for two to three. I didn't mind the close quarters, since they gave me a chance to get to know the other four fellows. What I did mind was the lack of adequate bathroom facilities and the lack of enough hot water to service the number of guests in the hotel. And, worst of all, I didn't like

Larry's alarm clock going off at 5:30 every morning because he was an early riser.

During our five days there, we visited many historical places including Rembrandt's house, Amsterdam Historical Museum, Oude Kerk (Old Church), Nieuwe Kerk (New Church), Rijksmuseum, Dam Palace and the Anne Frank House made famous by the *Diary of Anne Frank*. As a group, we also enjoyed a scenic ride on the canals, a visit to the diamond cutting district and two lectures at a local university providing us with more knowledge of Holland's history.

One day we took a trip to the Zuider Zee in the northern part of Holland. This trip provided ample opportunities for us to take photos of windmills and other interesting sights native to Holland. On the way back, we stopped in small towns, spoke with children and adults, window shopped and walked down streets lined with Dutch homes. We tried some baked goods that looked delicious but were too bland for our sugar-encrusted taste buds. Several bought souvenirs. We drank in as much of their culture as time permitted before returning to Amsterdam.

On the lighter side, Dick and I spent hours each evening walking and exploring unknown territory. We were anxious to see where our feet would take us and what oddities we'd spy along the way. During one such walk, we saw an American college student sitting on a sidewalk, strumming his guitar and singing, hoping passersby would stop, listen, enjoy, and toss a guilder or two into his opened guitar case. His feet were wrapped in thick, blood-stained bandages, mute evidence that he had sold his shoes for money and was now suffering physically for doing so. We listened a few minutes to his melodic tales of woe, felt sorry for him in his condition and dropped a few coins into his "bank" before moving on.

He was not the only destitute American we passed on our walks. There were hundreds of others who had come to Europe expecting to survive on a few dollars a day. However, they soon found out that the demand for both cheap sleeping and eating places far outnumbered the supply, and this remained the same in every country we visited. For the lucky ones, money was telegraphed to them by their parents. But for the majority, their dreams of spending a happy, fun-filled vacation traveling around Europe soon turned into nightmares as they faced a shrinking supply of money. After seeing a few young people in such dire conditions, I was very thankful, I had chosen the Seminar as my mode of travel through Europe.

During another walk, we bought french fries. They were served in paper cones with a large plop of mayonnaise on top instead of catsup. After eating a few dipped in mayo, I found myself enjoying them and thinking if Canadians can enjoy vinegar with their french fries, why can't the Dutch enjoy mayonnaise? After all the interim years since my trip, whenever the threat of cholesterol is overshadowed by my raging appetite for something tasty, I often revert back to french fries dipped in mayonnaise.

As we continued walking, we began to pass one sex shop after another. Looking at the various displays in the windows, I was utterly amazed at all the sex paraphernalia one could purchase to enhance and satisfy one's sexual fantasies. A little farther on, we realized we had entered a red light district when we saw, not only red lights aglow outside many doors, but pretty young women standing outside the doors, silently advertising their wares.

Since I tend to be inquisitive, I stopped and asked one girl a few questions. Yes, prostitution was legal. Yes, each girl had periodic examinations required by law. No, she had no qualms about her chosen profession since she was providing a service men could chose or ignore. In answer to my question regarding the cost, she replied, "Twenty-five guilders ($7.50 U.S.) for ten minutes." Then I asked, "What if a man doesn't finish in ten minutes?" Hearing my question, she looked me straight in the eye and, with just a hint of a smile, answered, "Don't worry, he'll finish." With that I thanked her. Then we continued strolling through the district looking casually at each girl as any person might do when window shopping.

My final evening in Amsterdam, I strolled to the waterfront and soon came upon the Harbor Towers Building. I noticed that the Captain's Table Restaurant was on top. It offered any patron an unobstructed view of the city. Therefore, I decided to dine there and took the elevator.

Entering the restaurant, I requested a table near the windows and was soon seated. Before scanning the menu, I looked out over the city and spent several minutes pinpointing structures I had visited and other familiar landmarks.

When I finally looked at the menu, I noticed that most of it was printed in Dutch. Therefore, I took the easy way out and ordered the Captain's Special. I assumed the entree would be some kind of fish. When my meal was served, I was surprised to see chicken. I chuckled to myself as I murmured under my breath, "Here I am in the Captain's Table Restaurant atop the Harbor Towers Building eating the Captain's Special and it's chicken!"

It was then I began to realize what surprises a language barrier could hold in store for me, even in Holland where the majority of people speak

English as well as Dutch. The surprise in this case was minor since I like chicken as much as fish. However, I began to wonder what other surprises lay in store as the language barrier continued throughout Europe. I decided the best thing for me to do was "roll with the punches" and consider my trip an adventure into the unknown.

The next morning, Baker Team headed for Brussels, Belgium with a stop at the medieval city of Bruges en route. While walking about the ancient buildings in Bruges, I stopped at a public restroom building, entered the men's side, stepped in front of a urinal and began using it. Before I had finished, a cleaning woman entered and began her tasks seemingly oblivious of the men there. I thought, "How odd," but I soon learned this was acceptable behavior on her part. She had cleaning to do and was going to do it, men or no men. Even though this scene was repeated several times during my travels, I never got used to it and became a bit embarrassed each time.

Our accommodations in Brussels were at a crowded youth hostel. We males shared our barrack-type bedroom with a group of tired, American teenagers on an extended bicycle tour. After being awakened at 5:30 A.M. by Larry's alarm going off, several angry members of their group suggested that everyone put some money in a pot, buy the clock and smash it to smithereens. Good as the idea was, it was not implemented, much to my disappointment.

After touring the large market square amidst several beautiful, ornate, gilded buildings and a few other tourist attractions, I struck out on my own. I soon found myself staring at some weird looking meat dishes on display in a specialty meat market window. Curiosity got the best of me, so I entered and spoke a few words of greeting in English. Much to my delight, the man behind the counter answered back in broken English allowing us to have a conversation. I soon learned that his market sold only those parts of an animal not normally sold in meat markets—thus the specialty sign. In answer to one of my questions, he began pointing to each item naming it as he went. I was surprised that anyone would spend good money for such items to eat; items I had never tasted in my life.

Seeing my negative facial expressions as he pointed and spoke, the man must have wanted to change my opinion about his store. For once he had finished, he offered me a sample from three different meat dishes, each one in a different sauce. One consisted of cubed pieces of cattle brain in a white, spicy sauce that tasted pretty good to me, and I told him so. Upon hearing this, he smiled, then took a paper cup, filled it with the same delicacy and handed it and a wooden spoon to me free of charge. I thanked him, turned and left.

As I continued walking, I ate a little now and then, and soon realized I could not consume all of it as the spicy sauce was giving me indigestion. Instead of throwing the rest away, I decided to take it back to the youth hostel and let others sample it. When I arrived, it was suppertime and most of the Baker Team members had already eaten. Nevertheless, I sat down at one table of females and offered each a sample but did not tell them what they were sampling.

After everyone had tried it and had given me positive feedback, I revealed the truth. Immediately their facial expressions changed and a few headed for the nearest bathroom. I had eaten enough to know that one small spoonful shouldn't make any of them sick, so I enjoyed my little practical joke. However, if any of them did become sick, I was verbally prepared to fight for my exoneration. None did.

During our whirlwind tour of Paris, Diane's words rang true, "So much to see and enjoy; so little time." Before I could catch my breath, we were leaving Paris and heading for the medieval town of Vezelay, once the crossroad for the Crusaders. As I sat in one of the three minibuses assigned to our team, I had time to relax and reflect on my three days in "gay Paree." I promised myself that I would return someday and bring with me the attire demanded for entrance into the famous Moulin Rouge. I would not be turned away a second time.

After a tour of an impressive eighteenth-century palace at Versailles, we continued on toward Vezelay. En route, Diane informed us that we would be staying at a youth hostel, run by an order of Catholic brothers, and we should not expect much in the way of supper. Therefore, once we had arrived and were settled in, I headed for the dining room at the appointed hour with her words still ringing in my ears. Arriving, I noticed bottles of wine and baskets of bread on each sparsely set table.

After everyone had been seated and a blessing offered, large serving bowls of steaming hot soup were placed on the tables. I'm sure we all figured this was it, so we enjoyed ample amounts of the delicious soup, hunks of fresh bread and wine. But we were proven wrong when serving bowls filled with tossed salad appeared. Eagerly we wiped our soup bowls clean with pieces of bread and filled them with salad. As we enjoyed more bread and wine with our salad, we figured this definitely had to be the last course. However, we were wrong again.

Smiles of surprise and applause greeted our hosts as they entered the dining room with bowls of hot creamed peas and potatoes. After cleaning our bowls again, we enjoyed the tasty third course. Finally, we were all on the brink of gluttony when the final course graced our tables, bowls of vanilla pudding. Much to everyone's delight, Diane had been wrong, but with such full stomachs, how could we not forgive her?

After our banquet ended, everyone pitched in and helped with the cleanup and dishes. As we worked, we talked, we laughed and we sang. We started with the only chorus we knew in French, *Alouette*. The brothers sang with us, so we repeated it six times and sang more robustly each time. Then we sang several in English as the brothers clapped in time to the music and smiled approvingly. By the time the last pot had been dried, and the last chorus sung, we realized anew that music is, indeed, the universal language.

Our work completed, Dick and I strolled around this ancient, historical, hilltop town. As I looked off in different directions, I could imagine Crusaders coming and going centuries before when Vezelay was a large, thriving community bustling with activity. Now it was nothing more than a sleepy little town in France. Before returning to our quarters, we entered the age-old Catholic church and examined carefully all the relics it contained. We were impressed.

When we five fellows finally got ready for bed, we knew Larry's alarm clock would not be going off at 5:30 the next morning. Since I caught him napping our last afternoon in Paris, nothing he said now would convince any of us that he should be an early riser unless he woke up on his own. Therefore, we all looked forward to a good night's sleep, and we were not awakened until the reveille gong sounded at 7:30.

From Vezelay, we drove through the countryside to Geneva, Switzerland. During an interesting tour the next morning, the Baker Team gathered at the foot of John Calvin's statue in Reformation Park. As they sat on the grass, relaxing, I presented my paper dealing with Calvin's views on education. It proved to be a thrilling experience for me, and it remained so even after one team member shook my hand vigorously and remarked, "I don't care what the others said about your paper, I thought it was terrific!" As soon as my facial expression changed to a more somber one, he smiled broadly and said gleefully, "I gotcha."

Our next destination was Lauterbrunnen, a lovely village at the foot of the Jungfrau in the Bernese Alps, for some mountain climbing and relaxation. The afternoon we arrived, I took a long, leisurely walk while drinking in the beauty of the surrounding landscape. Eventually, I sat down upon a bench next to an older man. I greeted him in English, and when he responded, I realized he was from America. We began chatting, telling each other where we'd been and what we'd seen. Finally, I exclaimed, "Isn't this scenery gorgeous?"

"It's all right," he answered. "Ever been to Colorado?"

"Yes, but why do you ask?"

"There are over fifty-three mountains in Colorado over 14,000 feet high. There are none in Switzerland."

I confessed that I didn't know such information, but still it couldn't detract from the scenic beauty at the moment. A few minutes later, this proud, loyal Coloradan challenged me to check his facts as he rose and left. Eventually, I did. He was correct. But what's a thousand feet, or so, when it comes to high, snow-capped mountains? Especially in a country as pretty and majestic as Switzerland.

I enjoyed three glorious days of excitement. I hiked to the beautiful, quaint, carefree resort town of Murren. I hiked to Trummelback Falls and watched the falls cascade with tremendous force more than 1,000 feet through a series of tunnels and hollows in the cliff wall. I rode the cog railway to the top of the Jungfraujoch. While there, I skied, rode a dog sled and toured the ice castle.

I felt sad leaving Lauterbrunnen behind as we headed for Italy. To get there, we had to cross the Susten and Saint Gotthard Passes. As we neared the top of one, a blinding snowstorm greeted us. During a rest stop, we enjoyed an unexpected snowball fight on July 11.

Our first night in Italy, we camped in an area that became so windy, I was sure our tents would not only blow down but blow away. Miraculously, they didn't. It was at this campground that I began to wish I had brought bars of soap and a roll of toilet tissue with me since the restrooms had neither. Unknown to me at the time, we'd face a similar situation several more times during our eleven days of camping.

After a short stay in Florence, the cameo capital of the world, we drove over the Apennines to the seven hills of Rome. On one of our tours, we wandered through the Forum and Colosseum on the trail of the Caesars. Another tour centered on Christian Rome following paths of early Christians from the catacombs to great medieval churches.

During my free time, I walked to other historical buildings, churches and fountains soaking in as much history as possible. During my first walk, I took my life in my hands whenever I crossed a street without a traffic light. From this experience, I surmised that drivers in Rome keep one hand on their high-pitched, deafening, car horns and one on their steering wheels as they roar about the city. Early into my second walk, I was having trouble crossing the street. An Italian who spoke English noticed me and gave me some advice. He instructed me to step off the curb, look away from the oncoming traffic and begin walking. "Then," he continued, "the traffic will stop for you. Otherwise, you'll never get across."

Taking his advice, I finally got up enough courage to try it. Scary as it sounds, it worked. However, a few drivers, now and then, peeled rubber in their screeching attempts to stop on time. On those occasions, had I not been looking the other way, I'm sure I would have had a heart attack.

Sunday in Rome promised to be a scorcher. Since no team activities were planned, I decided to take a train to Ostia, an ancient harbor city seventeen miles downstream from Rome, look around, then take another train to a beach on the Tyrrhenian Sea Coast three miles from Ostia. I knew the coast would be cooler, and a swim would be invigorating. In my mind, it would be a perfect way to spend a hot day, so I threw what I needed into a paper bag and headed for the train station.

When I arrived, I checked the schedules and once I knew what trains I needed to take, I approached the ticket window. Using the marked places on my schedule and some data on a piece of paper, I soon had tickets for going and coming. After boarding the correct train, I sat next to a young woman who spoke some English. During our conversation, she had reason to suspect that I was sold two round trips. After examining my tickets, her suspicions were confirmed. Noting this, she laughed then warned me about unscrupulous Italians who love to take advantage of tourists. Then she encouraged me to return to the ticket window upon my return and demand a refund.

My day went as planned, and when I alit from the train back in Rome, I went directly to the ticket window. The same agent was there and acted as if he didn't understand as I stood there, with the extra set of tickets in hand, trying to explain his error. Frustrated, I turned to leave. An American, who spoke Italian, sensed my predicament and spoke to me. After I explained what had happened, he took the tickets, went to the same window, spoke loudly and forcefully to the agent and soon returned with my full refund.

After thanking him, I turned to leave. As I did so, he warned me, "Ya gotta watch these Italians. Some of them are bad apples." And he was right. After two such warnings, I was more cautious and enjoyed the rest of my days in Italy without being taken in by any more "bad apples."

Early the next morning, Baker Team headed for Brindisi, an old port on the Adriatic Sea for citizens of ancient Rome embarking for Greece, and the current port for tourists, like us, also embarking for Greece. We were to take an overnight ferry, with sleeping accommodations, to the port at Patras, then continue on to Athens in our minibuses. Our trip across Italy was tiring but very scenic. We passed lush green vineyards, olive groves, gardens on hillsides, rich-looking villas, towns of all sizes and countless numbers of people going about their daily tasks. At this time of the year, Italy was a lush green boot. When we arrived in Brindisi, we were given free time to roam about but warned to be back at the dock on time or miss the ferry.

Dick and I spent our time exploring as much of this ancient port city as possible, then we stopped for supper. Soon after eating an Italian dish that I can't even pronounce, let alone spell, I was in desperate need of a bathroom. However, as I had already realized early in my trip, public bathrooms were not very plentiful in European countries and doubly so in Italy. In agony, I finally convinced a clerk in a grocery store to let me use the one there.

Following his directions, I soon discovered it tucked away in one corner of the storeroom. Had I not seen it for myself, I would not have believed it. Had I not needed one so badly, I would not have used it. The toilet consisted of two foot prints and a hole within a concrete square surrounded by a two-inch-high, concrete skirting. I quickly stepped on the footprints, dropped my pants and underwear, squatted over the hole and went. When I finished, I looked for some toilet tissue but saw none. I panicked then remembered I had some napkins in my pants' pocket. Carefully, I fished them out and used each one very frugally. When I was ready to leave, I exited the bathroom door then turned, took a final look in disbelief and exclaimed to myself, "God bless America!"

After a full day of activities in Athens, the hub of the ancient classical world, I was bushed, so I turned in early. My four roommates were still out, allowing me the peace and quiet I longed for. As I lay on my bed in the darkened room, I mentally reviewed the day. Our tour to the hilltop ruins of the Acropolis, dominated by the Parthenon temple, was as exciting as I had anticipated. In my years of teaching, I had seen many pictures of the Parthenon in books. But none could compare to standing there and gazing in awe at this massive structure.

As I gazed, I reflected on knowledge I had gained about the Parthenon over the years. It was an idealized spiritual self-portrait of a people whose confidence in the Athenian gods, Athenian moral values and Athenian mercantile success was at a peak. And there I stood, in the twentieth century, being reminded of the glory that was Greece centuries before.

I'm sure Ictinus, the architect of the Parthenon, jumped for joy when the last line had been drawn and the last calculation made on his plans for the ultimate temple, a gift to Athena, the goddess of war and wisdom, from men who willingly submitted to her. Nine years later (447–438 B.C.) this sculptural entity, set on a hill to be viewed from the outside by all Athenians, was completed. I'm sure Ictinus did not realize, he had drawn plans for a temple to Athena that would stand for centuries allowing me to view it with the same awe as he probably had.

The next sound I heard was from the lips of a Greek cleaning woman awakening us, as she walked past our beds and drew the window drapes flooding our room with sunlight. We lay there in our shorts, but our near nakedness didn't seem to faze her one bit. As she turned away from the window and walked past us again, she bade each of a "Good morning" in English and left.

As soon as we were ready, we left the YMCA and walked the short distance to the YWCA where breakfast was waiting. As I sat drinking a final cup of coffee, I noticed a familiar face in the crowd but couldn't place it. "Where have I seen him before?" I asked myself several times but I could not answer it. The last mouthful swallowed, I got up to leave then made the connection. He was the chap in Rome who interceded for me at the train station and got my money back. I immediately walked over to his table, reminded him who I was, then chatted a bit about our travels since that Sunday in Rome. I came away thinking, *It's a small world.*

After breakfast, the Baker Team took an all day trip to Corinth, where in A.D. 52 the Apostle Paul arrived and labored a year and a half as a tent maker and preacher of the Gospel of Christ. It was in Corinth that Paul wrote the Epistle to the Romans and started the Christian Church that was destined to cause him great concern and heartache. As I walked along the streets, many of the colored symbols, denoting what kind of shops were within, were still evident on the ancient structures. From Corinth, we traveled to Mycenae to see the ruins of the palace of Agamemnon.

Once we arrived back in Athens, Dick and I headed for a section of the city frequented by the less affluent citizens and a few tourists. Early on, we realized street signs in Greek would be little help in finding our way back to the YMCA, so we memorized guideposts along our route. Eventually, we came upon a sidewalk cafe and for a few drachmas each, we enjoyed our fill of souvlakia washed down with ample amounts of soda.

Friday morning, I cashed in my leftover Swiss francs and Italian lira for drachmas. While at the bank, I cashed two traveler's checks but did not receive forty dollars in drachmas for my forty dollars in checks. I had taken Karl Malden's advice and didn't "leave home without them." However, when I paid the per check fee to buy them, I was not informed that another fee would be charged, in most European countries, for cashing them. Since there was nothing I could do, I did what I had done in the other countries. I took the drachmas, thanked the teller and left.

That afternoon, Baker Team drove the forty-three miles along a dramatic cliffside road to Sounion, one of the country's major tourist attractions. Sounion, a cape at Attica's southern tip, offers a stunning view of the Aegean Sea from the fifth century B.C. temple of Poseidon. As we sat in the heat listening to Diane's talk on the temple, the sea kept beckoning us to "Come, swim, cool off in my beautiful, clear, blue water." Whether Diane read our minds or not, at the conclusion of her talk, she suggested we take a swim. Cheers and applause greeted her words, and soon we were in the water carrying on like a bunch of happy, energetic children.

Saturday and Sunday, except for a Sunday morning visit to the Areopagus where Paul preached on Mars Hill, we were free to do as we pleased. Some bought loaves of bread, fresh fruit, and wine before boarding a ferry to one of the nearby Greek islands and a beach, where they'd camp overnight before returning on Sunday. However, I chose to stay in Athens and visit the museums and other historical sites I had not seen.

By Saturday evening I was beat, but I dragged myself to the Odeon of Herodes Atticus (outdoor amphitheater) and enjoyed Bach's *Mass in B Minor* presented by a German orchestra and chorus. Even though I couldn't understand the words, the music lifted my spirit to heights I hadn't experienced before. After the performance ended, I felt terrific and walked the streets for two hours humming as I did so. That night I realized that music is not only the universal language, it is also the universal tonic for tired bodies.

Late Sunday evening, Dick and I walked the switchback trail to the top of the Hill of Lycabettus from which we could look across the city and see the Acropolis lit up in all its glory. As we were walking back down in the dark, we passed a cafe on the side of the hill and decided to dine there. After being seated at a small table from which we could see the lighted Acropolis, we ordered plates of food, containing several items common to

Greece, and a bottle of wine. As we ate, we were glad that only a single, dim light from the candle on our table was present. Since each item was foreign to our taste buds, neither of us wanted to see what we were eating. However, I must admit, I enjoyed the entire meal, and, even though some items were spicy, I did not get indigestion.

Early the next morning, we left Athens and headed for Olympus and the beginning of ten continuous nights of camping in Greece, Yugoslavia, and Austria. But I was prepared. I had plenty of toilet tissue and two bars of soap tucked inside my suitcase.

Our campground near Thessalonica was adjacent to a beach on the Aegean Sea. Both were overcrowded with vacationers. Therefore, our tents were pitched in a area no one else wanted. I understood why soon after climbing into my sleeping bag the first night. My body was no match for the rough, sharp lumps and bumps below me, thus I tossed and turned most of the night. How I wished, I had brought an air mattress with me. It was on the "What to Bring" list, but I figured I could sleep eleven nights on the ground without too much difficulty. This campground proved me wrong.

Even though I awoke tired from my restless night of sleep, I rode an old, beat-up bus to Thessalonica and spent most of the day enjoying the Byzantine art and architecture including nine major churches. Even though the temperature and humidity got into the 90s, I kept walking and sweating, looking and sweating, resting and sweating.

Eventually, I came to streets where the Apostle Paul walked during the winter of 49–50 A.D. I strolled down each one, seeing all I could see and, for fun, imagining I was the Apostle Paul. As I strolled, I recited every verse I could think of from the Epistle to the Thessalonians written by Paul shortly after his departure from the church he founded there. As I recited, I sweated, but I enjoyed my little game just the same.

Once I had sweated all I could stand, I boarded a large ferry and soon arrived back at the beach and the campground. As I walked across the sand, I noticed several nude children building sand castles, women with the tops of their one-piece swimsuits down, others wearing only the bottom piece of their bikinis, and members of both sexes wearing suits so skimpy, I'd be embarrassed wearing one. Whoever started the rumor that Californians are the beginners of fads and weird styles should have checked Europe out first. I finally reached my tent, put my modest swimsuit on and cooled off in the refreshing sea.

A few hours after leaving Thessalonica the next day, we arrived at the guarded border of Yugoslavia. If I ever felt like a foreigner seeking to enter a strange country, it was here. Our passports were scrutinized very thoroughly, finally stamped and handed back. We were allowed to change American money for Yugoslavian dinars and told, in no uncertain terms, that no dinars could be taken out of the country once we were ready to leave. With that information drilled into our heads, we were allowed to proceed.

Our first stop was a campground near Skopje. As soon as our tents were pitched, we headed into Skopje, one of the oldest cities in Yugoslavia and the capital of Macedonia. In the nine years since a violent earthquake virtually destroyed the entire town along with 1,000 of its citizens, the tremendous spirit of the Yugoslav people had conquered the destruction and made the city one of the most popular tourist spots in the entire country.

Dick and I were enjoying the walking tour outlined in our guide book when we entered old Skopje. Seeing a cooperage nearby, we watched barrels being made. The coopers were using the same process that had been used since the Turkish era of the fourteenth and fifteenth centuries. Once we had seen enough, we left and continued our stroll.

As we were passing several small shops, we looked through the windows of each and paused at one that caught our attention. Two young men were seated at a small table drinking what looked like dishwater out of mugs. Curiosity got the best of us, so we entered and walked over to the counter. Once I had the counterman's attention, I used pantomime to tell him, I would like a sample of what the men were drinking. He understood immediately, smiled, poured a little into two glasses and handed them to us. I drank mine, and it was delicious. It tasted like apple juice and lemonade mixed together in just the right proportions. I licked my lips and rubbed my stomach, the only way I knew to tell the counterman I liked it.

Evidently, the men at the table had watched the entire scene. For as soon as I rubbed my stomach, they arose, came to the counter, bought two large mugs of the drink, turned and, with smiles on their peasant faces, handed them to us. Before we could attempt to thank them, they turned and left. We sat at a table and slowly drank this cool, tasty, refreshing drink and practiced saying the name, so we could enjoy it often during our stay in Yugoslavia. The only thing that bothered me was its color. A mixture of apple juice and lemonade would not look like dishwater, but its delicious taste overshadowed its color.

When we returned to the campground, we heard music in the distance. Curious, several of us walked in the direction from which it came. We soon found the source, a nightclub with a dimly lit, large patio containing tables, chairs and a dance floor. Once we had occupied two tables and had bought some nonalcoholic drinks, we headed for the dance floor. Even though the music was not familiar, we could dance to its rhythm. Soon our inhibitions disappeared, freeing us to wiggle and jiggle in time to the music, much to the delight of several other customers watching our every move.

Soon men in uniform began to appear. Presently, some of them asked our girls to dance using gestures instead of words. Soon the dance floor was alive with couples, who shared a common desire to have fun, even though a language barrier prevented them from conversation. Once again, music was the universal language, and no spoken words were really necessary.

The fun continued until a loud whistle penetrated the dance music. Immediately, all the soldiers left the dance floor, returned to their tables, grabbed their hats, ran to the low wall surrounding the patio, leaped over it and disappeared into trees, bushes, and the darkness beyond. The questions we had about their speedy exit were soon answered. Minutes later, a high ranking army officer entered and began questioning one of the waiters. Putting two and two together, we soon surmised that the soldiers should not have been there. The whistle from a lookout had saved their necks. However, I was glad they had come and danced with our girls. What better detente could there be than that?

The next day, we drove to Belgrade, the capital, for a look at Tito's "national socialism." During our seven and a half hours on the two-lane highway, my hair turned a little whiter. After several close calls, by drivers passing us at the worst of times, I was beginning to believe that driver's licenses were not required of citizens in this country. Then we began coming upon several accidents involving cars, buses, and gypsy wagons. In some cases, the vehicles involved had passed us only minutes before. After seeing several of these, I was convinced that licenses were definitely not required. On the other hand, this two-lane road was a major highway linking several major cities. A four-lane expressway was desperately needed to carry the volume of traffic safely. Since one didn't exist, the number of close calls and accidents continued turning my hair whiter with each passing mile.

The history of Beograd, the city's Yugoslavian name, goes back into the Stone Age when the site was earliest inhabited. The Greeks, Celts, and Romans were all here and used its unique river location to the best advantage. Thus, there were many relics of the city's past to visit plus many historical landmarks including the Frescos Museum, the Mosque of Barjak, and others.

As Dick and I trudged from one place to another, I was amazed at the number of parks we passed. Some were small, others large, but all were well kept and very popular with people of all ages. Every so often, we stopped and rested on one of the park benches and enjoyed the peace and beauty only a park can offer. We also enjoyed mugs of "dishwater" frequently. Since it had no effect on our senses, we deduced it was nonalcoholic.

Soon after Dick and I went our separate ways, I bought some picture postcards, prepared them for mailing and headed for the large, central post office. When my turn came, I showed the clerk my cards and the initials, USA, under each address. She sold me the required stamps, which I licked and placed on the cards. Then I handed them back to her. She took them, cancelled each with a hand stamp, turned and tossed them into a bushel basket on the floor behind her. "Great!" I groaned to myself as I turned to leave. "Those postcards will never reach the recipients." But I misjudged their postal system. Each card was delivered at its destination within a reasonable length of time.

That evening I had supper in one of the many cafes Dick and I had passed earlier while on our walking tour. After eating and enjoying my Yugoslavian food, I passed an ice-cream parlor and stopped in. For one dinar (eight cents), I could buy a scoop of ice cream about the size of a golf ball. I bought three scoops, each one a different flavor. A taste of each convinced me it was the creamiest, most delicious ice cream I had ever eaten.

Several times that evening, as I strolled around the huge Republic Square, I met others from Baker Team. Each time I walked with them to the ice-cream parlor and bought another cone containing three different flavors. When I returned the sixth and final time with new customers, the employees treated me like a long-established customer and gave me my final three scoops free. When I thought about the number of customers I had brought them that evening, I felt I deserved a free cone and accepted it graciously. I thanked them the only way I knew with a slight bow and smile. From the expressions on their faces, I knew they understood.

Leaving Belgrade, we faced another six hours of travel on the same two-lane road. Even though we faced the same dangers as before, our drivers kept their cool and reacted quickly, when necessary, to assure our safe arrival in Zagreb, the capital of the Republic of Croatia. As in our two previous cities, there was much to see both ancient and modern. Its delightful location on the Sava River to the south and mountains of Zagreb to the north has made it a popular Yugoslavian city for tourists.

It was in the Gallery of Modern Art that I saw a painting by a Yugoslav artist that remains as vivid in my mind today as the day I saw it. It was a painting of a boy sitting on the snow in a graveyard and leaning against his mother's tombstone. The boy is dead, having succumbed to the bitter winter elements while sitting on his mother's grave too broken-hearted to leave. The painting was done so realistically, it captivated my imagination to the point where I could almost feel the bitter cold that caused the untimely death of the boy. Of the hundreds of paintings I looked at during my trip, this one stands out in my mind. Why? I don't know. Perhaps it was the sadness I felt while looking at it.

As I continued my walking tour, I met a Yugoslavian fellow in a park who spoke English. Delighted, we began to chat. Since I couldn't remember the name of the "dishwater" drink, I described it hoping he could tell me its ingredients. After hearing my apple juice-lemonade theory, he laughed heartedly then asked, "Do you really want to know what it's made of?" When I responded in the affirmative, he informed me. "It's simply sugar, flour, and water mixed together in the correct proportions and fermented until the taste is achieved." I was both amazed and disappointed—amazed that those three, simple ingredients could produce such a delicious drink but disappointed that it was not as nutritious as I had imagined. As least I knew now why it looked like dishwater.

Having been enlightened, I lost my appetite for the drink. Even though I knew it would still taste the same, the thought of drinking a fermented mixture of water, sugar, and flour turned me off. And not even the sight of children, teenagers and adults drinking large mugs of it on a hot afternoon could change my mind.

Once we crossed the border and entered Austria, I breathed a sigh of relief. We had driven the length of Yugoslavia and had escaped unscathed. Otherwise, I had enjoyed Yugoslavia for many reasons, and I left with many happy memories I still cherish today.

Our final three nights of camping were in a campground just outside the town of Villach, Austria, in a valley surrounded by beautiful scenery. Everyone on Baker Team needed this period of rest and relaxation and took full advantage of it. Swimming in the lake bordering our campground, hiking through fields of flowers, climbing a switchback trail to a scenic lookout point high above the valley floor, and exploring several of the unique shops in town were good therapy. When we left on our six-hour drive to Salzburg, we were ready to tackle the final eighteen days of our trip before flying back to Boston.

Having seen the movie, "The Sound of Music" several times, I was anxious to visit this famous musical center of Austria. Therefore, when we arrived, I eagerly set out on a walk that would take me past several of the places shown in "The Sound of Music" as well as the house where Wolfgang Amadeus Mozart was born and spent the first several years of his short life. Time ran out before I finished, so I resumed my tour the following day.

Salzburg is located near the German border. It's built on both banks of the Salzach River with the Alps in the background. I could see why Hitler chose this area for his retreat in the Bavarian Alps. I could also understand why the musical Von Trapp family ("The Sound of Music") hated to leave Salzburg prior to World War II and eventually resettled in one of the most picturesque mountain areas in Vermont. I'm sure it reminded them of their former homeland.

The birthplace of Mozart is now a museum. Therefore, I was able to see mementos of the composer's youth including his violin, spinet, and musical manuscripts. Mozart was a musical genius. And here I was, standing in his birthplace and home for many years, looking at items he handled and used so long ago. It sent goose bumps up my spine. I'm sure my time there was one reason I enjoyed the movie, "Amadeus," years later.

The icing on the cake came that night when several of us attended a festival of folk dances. It was part of the annual Musical and Drama Festival going on at the time. The few schillings we paid to enjoy such a wonderful evening were well worth it. The lilt of the folk music, the rhythmic movement of the dancers, their colorful costumes, and the expressions of joy on their faces once again reminded me that music is the universal language that knows no bounds.

I would have been content spending the rest of my trip in Salzburg enjoying the festival activities, but I still had places to see and dreams to dream. Early the next morning, we headed for Koblenz, West Germany, a fortress town at the confluence of the Moselle and Rhine Rivers. Koblenz was devastated during World War II but has since been rebuilt. We were to join another seminar team at Koblenz and board a ship for a week-long trip on part of the 820 mile, "romantic" Rhine River. Each day, we'd stop at an historic city or town for sightseeing and talks by members of our team and the team joining us.

As we drove across the rest of Austria and much of West Germany, the scenery was absolutely breathtaking. As we passed through Munich, flags and signs reminded us that the summer Olympic games would soon begin. And unknown to us at the time, these games would be scarred by a terrorist attack on the Israeli athletes.

Everyone was in high spirits from all we had seen, when we arrived at the Dachau Concentration Camp. It was a sobering experience to see the evidence of man's inhumanity to man through the photos in the main building and the physical evidence on the grounds. I walked from building to building reverently, as I sensed that I was walking on hallowed ground, When we left and reboarded our vehicles, I sat silently for a long time, debating within myself why a personal, loving, all-powerful God would allow such brutality to rack his chosen people. An answer was not revealed to me then or since. Thus I'm still searching for one.

We arrived in Koblenz that evening and stashed our belongings on the boat. Before we sailed the next day, I exchanged my remaining schillings for German marks, took a walking tour of Koblenz, and ended it at the Fortress of Ehrenbreitstein, long considered a veritable Gibraltar. Since it stands on a precipitous rock several hundred feet above the Rhine, I took a chair lift to reach it. From the top, I had an excellent view of the meandering Moselle River and its union with the Rhine.

If someone was to ask me to describe, in one word, the scenery on the portions of the Rhine we navigated, I would answer, "Castles." These huge, ancient, stone structures, built on hilltops high above the river, had an ominous look about them. I'm sure if stones could talk, those used to build each castle, would have eerie tales to tell of bygone days. Days when heads were chopped off boatmen and placed in iron, see-through baskets and hung outside the castles. They served as reminders to those sailing the river, that tolls must be paid as required or they faced similar fines. Even though the baskets were no longer used, they still hung outside the castles in full view of boatmen as stark reminders of days gone by.

After a full day heading upstream on the Rhine, we docked at Bingen, a modest but very scenic town, ideal for exploring castles and long walks through the vineyards. During my stroll through the town, I stopped at an outdoor stand and bought some German food for supper.

As I stood at the counter eating, the owner, an older man with a limp, spoke English and began talking to me. During the course of our conversation, be began reminiscing about World War II and how great the Japanese soldiers were. Strange words from a former German soldier who had fought in the war. As he spoke, I soon realized that he was obsessed with his praise for the Japanese soldiers yet virtually had none for his own.

I continued my walk with his words still ringing in my ears. Suddenly, two questions popped into my mind, "Did he ever shoot any of the American soldiers fighting in Germany? If so, did he wound or kill any?" Finally, a third question fought its way to the forefront of my mind, "Did he shoot at any of my uncles including Richard, who died from his wounds?" Stark questions, indeed, but ones I could never learn the answers to, so I soon pushed them out of my mind.

Besides toilet tissue and soap, I discovered, on this leg of our journey, that ice was not always readily available in Europe. That evening I needed some ice to help me combat a migraine headache in its early stages. Therefore, I went to the kitchen of a large hotel near our boat and asked for some ice or ice cubes. At first, the head of the kitchen was reluctant to part with any, telling me their supply was limited. Finally, my persistence paid off, and he gave me six small cubes from a tray in the refrigerator. After thanking the man, I mentioned the value of having an ice-making machine in such a large hotel. He looked at me in such a way that I knew he had never heard of such a machine, and his words soon confirmed it.

We remained at Bingen another day. Since my headache was gone, I hiked along the River to Rheinsteinburg and explored one of the few completely furnished castles on the Rhine. Then I caught a ferry and crossed to the village of Assmannshausen and walked around. From there I took a chair lift to the top of a ridge and walked along a path to the Niederwald Monument. The view from the monument, which commemorates Bismarck's success in unifying Germany in 1870, was excellent in all directions.

From the monument, I continued walking along the ridge away from Assmannshausen and rode another chair lift descending to the quaint village of Rudesheim, famous for its wine harvest festivals. While there, I visited the 900 year old Bromserburg Castle. It has a collection of 1,400 valuable drinking vessels and glasses dating back to Roman times. Before catching a ferry back to Bingen, I sampled several wines and came to the conclusion that I would never be a wine connoisseur.

When we left the following morning, the captain turned our boat around, headed downstream, eventually passed Koblenz and tied up at Remagen, one of the oldest towns on the Rhine. Remagen was originally a Celtic settlement. It is known to Americans as the site of a memorable breakthrough of the German Rhine Defenses in World War II.

As American forces advanced towards the bridge at Remagen in March 1945, explosives were detonated by a German engineering officer in an attempt to blow the bridge apart and stall the American advancement. After the detonation, the bridge, though damaged, did not collapse; thus it allowed the American forces to cross, opening the way to the Ruhr and into the interior of Germany. However, not long after the crossing, the bridge did collapse. As we sat looking at its remains, I imagined what took place there and the frustration the German officer must have felt after the detonation, seeing the bridge shake on its foundations and remain crossable.

Our next port of call was Bonn, a thriving city and the capital of the West German Republic. There was much to see, both ancient and modern, including the house where Beethoven was born in 1770 and lived until he was five. Like Mozart, Beethoven's birthplace is now a museum. For one mark, I entered and enjoyed seeing many mementos of his past while listening to some of his music in the background.

When we finally pulled away from the dock in Bonn, I was weary of sight-seeing and my feet were burning from so much use. Therefore, the trip from Bonn to Cologne was a welcome respite.

Cologne stands at the crossroads of western Europe, thus it is a large, bustling, thriving city. During World War II, 42,000 tons of bombs were dropped on Cologne and heavy shell fire in 1945 by American forces did a tremendous amount of damage. Since the war, there has been a great deal of new building giving it a modern appearance, although some of the old, historic structures still exist.

One is the 512-foot high cathedral that dominates the skyline. In the eyes of the German people, it is the most magnificent church in the world, and I could see why. The cathedral suffered a number of direct hits in the war, but the structure, though badly damaged in its interior, held together. As I gazed at this architectural masterpiece, I could see the scars left behind from bullets hitting it, mute evidence of the battle, that preceded my visit, several years before.

When our visit to Cologne came to an end, we sadly left our boat, boarded a train and headed for Ostend, Belgium, where we'd catch a ferry and cross the English Channel to Dover. As our train rumbled across the remainder of West Germany, the tiny country of Luxembourg and on to Ostend, I had time to relax, enjoy the scenery, and reflect on what I had seen, heard, experienced, and eaten in West Germany. I would think of the former German soldier who said, that without a doubt, the Japanese soldiers were the best.

Crossing the English Channel from Ostend to Dover was a "piece of cake"; a far cry from what I had expected. Once we landed in Dover, I could read and comprehend any sign, any menu, in fact, anything in print. Even though I was in England and not American, being able to read and comprehend the written word made me feel as if I were home. However, the impeccable English accent brought me back to reality.

Baker Team arrived in London that Saturday evening. After checking in at the YMCA, I walked around the neighborhood, had a bite to eat, and turned in early.

The next morning I attended a formal church service at Westminster Abbey. Afterwards, I visited the Cloisters. Then I walked along the Thames River for exercise, had a bite of lunch and, when Big Ben struck one, joined the other members of Baker Team.

Our first stop was John Wesley's Chapel, home, and burial ground. While we sat in the pews of the chapel, a team member gave a delightful talk on Wesley, the man and his ministry. She concluded by having us sing one of Wesley's hymns.

Our next stop was the famous Hyde Park to hear orators speak out on various topics dear to their hearts. Most stood on wooden boxes to be seen. The size of their audiences varied from a few to a great many. Religion and politics seemed to be the favorite topics of the day. One older man, recently born again, was preaching the Gospel so dynamically, even the Reverend Billy Graham would have stopped and listened, had he been there.

That evening after supper, I watched some British programs on television. The programs were different from those aired in America, nevertheless, I enjoyed them. I enjoyed, even more, the absence of commercials every few minutes.

After a good night's sleep and a hearty English breakfast, I was "rarin'" to go. A stop at a bank for some English pounds, and I was ready to begin a walking and bus tour of London. My first stop was the church of All Hallows-Barking-by-the-Tower. This church of medieval origin was gutted during World War II and has been rebuilt in an interesting blend of old and new. I was interested in the origin of its name but couldn't find it. If I were a member, I'd make a motion to have it changed at the church's next congregational meeting.

After visiting the Billingsgate Fish Market and picking up an odor on my clothes that several cats thought worthy to follow, I proceeded to a Christopher Wren church with a well-kept ornate interior. With a few cats still following me, I continued walking to the monument to the Great Fire of 1666, which destroyed the original Saint Paul's Cathedral. By now the cats were gone as well as the fish odor on my clothes. Thus, I stopped at Saint Paul's Cathedral upon arrival and entered.

Though built during the Renaissance and sporting a massive dome, Saint Paul's conforms to the basic medieval cathedral plan. The view from the dome was worth the climb up the stairs, and the Whispering Gallery proved to be true. I leaned my head near the wall and whispered. My words carried to the ears of another person half way around the large gallery. Then he whispered back, and I heard his words clear as a bell.

Leaving Saint Paul's, I continued on and eventually completed the first part of my tour. I stopped for some fish and chips at a sidewalk cafe and some rest for my weary feet.

Once I had both, I struck out again and visited more of the popular tourist attractions including the Houses of Parliament, Tower of London and Crown Jewels, and the impressive Changing of the Guards at Whitehall.

At Whitehall, there was a bright yellow, circular line on the stone surface and signs warning all spectators to stay behind the line. As I waited patiently for the ceremony to begin, I wondered why it was necessary to have such a line and warning. Unknown to me at the time, I would soon have my answer.

When the new guards rode in on their horses, they remained mounted and formed an arc; the heads of their horses facing the other guards' horses and their rear ends facing the spectators. The horses were on the inside of the yellow line. Once the ceremony began, the crowd of spectators pressed closer and closer to the line in an attempt to see better and take souvenir photos. At the worst possible time, first one then another of the female horses began to relieve themselves. Urine was sprayed on several spectators in the front row who were either over the line or standing on it. Even though the ceremony continued in its serious vein, I had to laugh and was now content to be standing in row three.

The next day I visited the British Museum and discovered a long line of people waiting to enter once the doors opened at ten o'clock. I soon learned that a special exhibition of the Treasures of Tutankhamen was on display. By the time the doors opened, the line had reached the cut off point between those who would definitely get to enter an hour before the museum closed, and those who wouldn't. Lucky for me, I was inside by 11:00 but did not wait to see King Tut's treasures that were taken from his tomb in Egypt. Instead I took in many of the other exhibits including the "Seven Wonders of London."

The Elgin Marbles are one of the seven. They are the remains of sculptures that adorned the Parthenon at Athens.

The Rosetta Stone is another. It is an inscribed slab of black basalt rock found at Rosetta in the eastern delta of the Nile River in 1799. The Rosetta Stone is unique, not for beauty, but for the fact that its discovery revealed to the world Egyptian history of six thousand years ago. The Stone proved to be the key that unlocked the riddle of ancient Egyptian writing, a riddle that took British scholars twenty years to solve.

The third, the so-called, Book of the Dead, represents the scriptures of Egypt. It is a collection of advice, funeral texts, and directions for the soul's journey after the death of the body.

Fourth is The Codex Alexandrinus, one of the three earliest manuscripts of the Old and New Testaments.

Fifth is The Magna Carta, the most jealously guarded and priceless treasure in the British Museum. It embodies in human law, for the first time in history, the principle of personal liberty and the rights of man.

The sixth is the wonderful Assyrian Creation Tablets that tell the Babylonian story of the creation and the flood. Their date is about 2,000 years before Christ. According to the Tablet of Creation, man was brought into existence so that the gods might have worshippers.

The last is the Portland Vase, probably the most valuable piece of human craftsmanship in existence. A funeral urn, probably of the first century A.D., it is known also as the Barberini vase. The vase can be imitated but not copied. The brittle nature of the material, which might break at any moment in the hands of an artist, makes the work one of almost superhuman difficulty, yet every line of every fixture on the vase is perfect.

The next day, Baker Team traveled to Canterbury, fifty-six miles from London. Canterbury is an historic cathedral city. In the cathedral, destination of Chaucer's pilgrims, Thomas Becket was murdered in 1170. Here, too, is the splendid tomb of Edward the Black Prince. Near the end of our tour in the cathedral, an acappella choir, from an American university, presented a delightful concert.

As I sat listening to the sacred music, my thoughts drifted back to my three years in the acappella choir at Providence-Barrington Bible College (formerly Providence Bible Institute). Warren Adams, our director, made singing in the choir a joyful experience even during the rehearsals. We presented concerts in churches, in schools, at military bases and at the White House in Washington, D.C. Thus, I could easily identify with members of this choir, who expressed on their faces what they were feeling inside their souls as they sang each anthem, hymn arrangement or gospel song.

By the time we left London the following Saturday morning, I was exhausted from six days of go, go, go, and do, do, do. Therefore, I enjoyed our relaxing two and a half hour drive to Dover and found myself humming selections from the musical, "Godspell," which I had attended the evening before.

The ferry pulled away from the dock on time and headed for Ostend almost four hours away. To lessen my chances of getting seasick, I had eaten a light breakfast, void of any liquids, and taken a seasickness prevention pill before the ferry sailed. Therefore I settled into a chaise lounge to enjoy the warm sun and take a catnap now and then.

However, the rough channel soon changed my plans. I became seasick and made several trips to the men's bathroom. I was not alone. Many, many others suffered the same fate. After I had given up everything in my stomach, I felt a little better and eventually managed to nap a little on my lounge. Having experienced such a terrible trip from Dover to Ostend, I was very thankful the trip from Ostend to Dover had been so pleasant.

When the ferry docked at Ostend, I cheered for joy and embarked as quickly as possible. Given free time, I strolled through several nearby streets; enjoyed the cool, channel breezes; ate two dry, bland rolls and regained my health. When I finally boarded our coach, I was ready for our five-hour drive to Amsterdam, our overnight stay there and our morning flight to Boston.

Once we arrived in Amsterdam, I took a final walk, ate some french fries with mayonnaise and said a final good-bye to this interesting city. Then I returned to my hotel and went to bed, letting some of my cherished memories lull me to sleep.

After an uneventful trip across the Atlantic Ocean, we neared Boston. Before landing, I said my sad farewells to all my friends. Once we arrived at the terminal, I left the plane quickly, walked into the terminal and headed for the nearest drinking fountain. Finding one, I took a long drink of ice-cold water, something I could not do throughout Europe. Finishing, I raised my head and turned to leave. There, in line, were several others from the seminar longing for the same treat. "Only in America!" I proclaimed loudly as I walked away and headed for the baggage area, and from there, to my flight to Rochester.

I arrived in Rochester on time and soon had my suitcase in hand. As I headed toward the terminal exit, I saw the Seabrooks, my ride back to LeTourneau Christian Camp and my car. Evidently, they did not recognize me with my beard—one I began growing in Europe after getting weary of shaving with cold water. They walked past me, and I had to yell and identify myself. I had to admit my two-tone beard would fool anyone. It was gray on the sides of my face and red under my nose and around my mouth. Once they recognized me, they laughed at my beard and welcomed me home. However, their young daughter, Sharon, still didn't recognize me and stayed as far away from me as possible.

As we drove to camp, I could only begin to tell Jack and Shirley about my trip. It had been a tremendous experience for me, and I felt I had accomplished my initial goals and more. Therefore, I'm sure my mouth "ranneth over."

Chapter XX
Tent Camping: Wet, Wild, Wonderful

By the time spring of 1973 came along, Shelley and I felt ready to tackle camping the way it is supposed to be done: in a tent. I had a dream that Mark (fourteen) and Bonnie (eleven) were both old enough to enjoy the adventures, the thrills, and the joys of camping as a family; not in the luxury of a camper on a truck, a trailer or a motorhome, but in a tent complete with cots, sleeping bags and pee can.

One Saturday, armed with an article on what to look for in a good tent, I went shopping. I finally bought a 10' x 10' box-shaped tent with a 7' x 10' awning. My choice fulfilled all the requirements in the article. I also bought a large plastic cloth to put on the ground under the tent to protect the tent's floor, a three-burner Coleman stove, a Coleman lantern, and some gallons of fuel. With books of S & H green stamps, I procured another sleeping bag, so we'd have four. We had other gear at home including four used, army cots given to us by Jack Seabrook.

The following Saturday, we decided to put the tent up in the backyard and spray water on it, as directed in the instructions, to seal it. We spread the tent out on the grass, emptied the pole bag, and soon discovered several poles missing. At that point, I thanked the Lord that we weren't in the middle of nowhere. I returned to the store and was given a new, complete set.

After returning home, we completed the job. Once the tent was erected, a little inspection assured us that we had a good, sturdy, roomy tent. Working as a team, we took it down then repeated the complete procedure again, each person doing his or her assigned jobs in the correct order. By late afternoon, we felt competent in this aspect of camping.

June rolled around and school finally ended. We were eager to hit the road for the summer. Our planned itinerary would take us to the northwest, then south along the Pacific Coast, back east via southern routes to Tennessee and the Great Smoky Mountains National Park, and finally northeast to New Jersey and home. Along the way, we planned to spend time in several national parks and monuments as well as visit relatives and friends in several states.

I took the middle seat out of our 1968 VW bus. Two small dressers, facing toward the rear of the bus, were put behind the front seats and tied in place. Each of us had two drawers for clothes and personal items. The final two held our camera, film, games, playing cards, plus other odds and ends. The rest of the gear was stored behind the rear seat and in the area between the dressers and the rear seat. The gear included the tent, cots, sleeping bags, lantern, cooking utensils, dishes, five gallon water jug, Coleman fuel, stove, axe, crosscut saw, large ice chest, one gallon jug, two one-quart thermos bottles, clothes line and tools. For recreation, we took a baseball bat (also for protection at night), gloves, ball, four frisbees and fishing gear. Since there had been lines at gas stations in early 1973, we took five gallons of gas, just in case we needed it. Finally, we took an ample amount of canned and packaged foods. Believe it or not, there was still room for the four of us to sit comfortably.

The day we were to leave, each of us took a guess as to the total number of miles we'd travel. The highest was in the 7,000 mile range. All four guesses were recorded in the bus's log book. By the end of our trip, we had traveled over 10,000 miles.

We began our trip on I-80 west through New Jersey and part of Pennsylvania. We stopped at a campground near DuBois. A motor overhaul had been done on our bus just prior to our trip. This necessitated an oil change after driving 400 miles. There was a VW dealer in DuBois, so we camped near there.

We arrived in the late afternoon. However, the ritual of choosing just the right campsite took some time. It was a ritual we would repeat again and again that summer much to the frustration of Bonnie. We finally opted for a spot with grass near the water spigot and not too far from the outhouses.

The tent was erected like clockwork (practice makes perfect) and soon everything was in place. After a hearty supper, chores were completed. Then a game of catch, followed by some fun with the frisbees, drained our pent-up energy. We built a campfire, sat around it, roasted marshmallows, gazed at the stars, sang a few songs and swatted many blood-starved mosquitoes. In the eyes of Shelley, Mark and me, we were really living. In Bonnie's eyes, she was enduring.

Once our fire had died out, we got ready and went to bed. Each in his own sleeping bag, each on his own cot, and all knowing in which corner the can and toilet tissue were placed. The bat was under my cot.

After saying our good nights like the Waltons, there was silence in the tent and outside for about ten minutes. Then we all heard what sounded like something ripping. Soon we heard it again, then a third time and a fourth. Before long, our suspicions were confirmed. The canvas on Mark's cot was ripping badly. After one examination with a flashlight, I knew his cot was doomed, but he stayed on it, facing what was to come, like a captain on the deck of a sinking ship. Before long, the end came, and Mark ended up sleeping on the tent's floor.

During the night, my cot also began to rip, and it, too, "died" the following night. It finally dawned on me that the canvas had rotted from being stored in a hot attic for many years. Now I knew why Jack had seemed so pleased when I accepted his offer. His smile had said it all. And his hearty laugh, some months later, when I told him of our experience, underscored his pleasure in getting rid of four of the cots.

A few days later, I bought two new cots in St. Paul, Minnesota. I should have bought four as the other two "died" during the summer. Instead of replacing them when it happened, Mark and Bonnie opted for the tent floor.

The next morning, I left early for DuBois to have the bus serviced. It was raining. Upon leaving the tent, I noticed evidence that raccoons had been around during the night. We had left a partial bag of candy kisses on our picnic table. Only the wrappers remained. Besides this, all the garbage can lids had been removed and the contents examined. The culprits had left a mess on the ground around each can.

I drove to DuBois and had a nice, hot breakfast since the garage wasn't open. I felt guilty eating it. I knew my family would be eating cold cereal, buns, and milk on a rainy, cool morning in a cold tent. But I managed to finish every bite and drink three cups of hot, fresh coffee. Hunger and thirst won out over my feelings of guilt. I'm sure the principle of "survival of the fittest" had something to do with it.

The bus wasn't ready until noon. This delay plus the rain meant another night in our campsite. This would put us a day behind our schedule, but there was little I could do about it. Instead of fretting, I stopped in a grocery store, bought some fresh vegetables, meat, and bakery products and headed "home."

Upon my arrival, Shelley broke some bad news. The tent had a leak at one corner near the bottom. It was allowing water to enter. At that moment, I suddenly missed our truck and camper, but I didn't express my feelings. A close examination revealed the area that was leaking. Shelley got some strong thread and soon had the torn seam repaired.

By late afternoon, the rain had stopped, and we were able to cook a hot meal and enjoy the outdoors again. Several hours in the cold tent playing the game "Aggravation," had Shelley, Mark and Bonnie a bit stir crazy. Therefore, after supper and chores, they were delighted to play catch, toss the frisbees and look for dry firewood for our evening campfire. However, the latter was the least delightful.

Tossing the frisbees that night was the beginning of our summer-long practice sessions to master tossing them. We practiced until we could keep all four going at the same time, as we stood in a square about ten feet from each other. We enjoyed gales of laughter learning this, but we slowly became very good at it. Eventually, we showed off in many campgrounds around the country not only that summer but in the next two as well.

Early the next morning, I awoke to bright sunshine. I got up, quickly dressed and then, in my nicest, loud voice, exclaimed, "Good morning! Welcome to Happy Valley Ranch. Everybody up!" You can guess the results: dirty looks, moans and groans, and remarks under their breaths. But my persistence paid off and, within an hour, we were on the road again heading for a friend's home in Sturgis, Michigan.

Apart from the rain, I was beginning to enjoy tent camping and prayed for little rain the rest of the summer. My prayers were answered. We did not experience another rainy day or night of camping until late August in Tennessee.

It would be impossible to describe most of our days of camping over a three-year period. However, some of our experiences are worth relating, especially for any who think camping in a tent is all peaches and cream.

Once a campsite is chosen, the main task is putting up the tent. This sounds easy, and it is if you have an area of ground into which your tent's plastic stakes can be pounded. However, during our years of tent camping, we found that people with trailers and motorhomes occupied most, if not all, of the campsites best suited for tents and left those least suited. They occupied the grassiest, flattest and most shaded sites, and those with the best fireplaces and picnic tables, and those closest to water supplies and bathrooms. Yet, in countless cases, the fireplaces and picnic tables were seldom used and the bathrooms seldom visited since most of these vehicles were self-contained. Therefore, we often had to pitch our tent on rocky, hard, uneven, grassless ground with no shade and no trees to shield our tent from winds.

En route to Glacier National Park, we stopped at a campground in Great Falls, Montana. Our tent was pitched on the last row of campsites adjacent to some open fields. There was a trailer on each side. The bathrooms were some distance away. It was a beautiful, hot afternoon. Therefore, after we set up camp and secured everything carefully, we left to go swimming in the local pool, have supper at McDonald's and visit Sulphur Springs and Great Falls, both popular tourist attractions.

We arrived back after dark and stopped at the bathrooms before going to our tent. While there, a sudden gale came out of nowhere, blew for about five minutes, then disappeared. I became concerned that the tent would blow down, since we hadn't used any extra ropes on the strategic poles. We always did this for extra security, whenever we camped in a windy area. But here, the wind was not a factor, when we pitched the tent.

When our bus's headlights lit up our campsite, our hearts sank. Our tent lay in a heap. After parking, we jumped out of the bus and ran to the tent. The poles were bent at the top and some of the stakes were pulled out of the ground. To our campsite's left stood four male adults by their trailer. One reported, "We watched it during the wind storm hoping it would remain standing. It did for quite a while, then a sudden strong gust toppled it over." Had each held a strategic pole, instead of just watching, the tent would have remained upright. But what could I say to them for not doing so? I finally remarked, "Camping has its good and bad points."

Since it was dark and the poles were bent, we quickly loaded everything into the bus and left. I was still upset and needed to calm down, so I drove fifty-one miles to Fairfield and rented a motel. After breakfast the next morning, we straightened the mess in the bus and then continued toward Glacier National Park. While driving, I thought about how I might unbend the tops of the poles so we could pitch our tent in Glacier. An idea came to me that I hoped would work.

Arriving at the park, we visited two beautiful areas on the eastern side: East Glacier and Many Glacier. Then we drove over the Going to the Sun Highway to Lake McDonald and the Apgar Campground. By the time we arrived at Apgar, we had seen enough natural beauty to last a lifetime. Eventually, this park would become my favorite in many ways.

Once we had been assigned a campsite and had unloaded our gear, I was ready to try my idea for repairing the poles. I lit one burner of our stove, put the bent end of one pole into the fire for several seconds and turned the pole in my hands. Once I took the pole out of the fire, I tried straightening it with a pair of pliers, and it worked. Finally, I dipped the hot part of the pole into cold water and, presto, it was as good as new. I repeated the process until all the poles were straightened. Soon our tent was erected and the chores completed. As a reward, we rented a motorboat and took a casual ride on beautiful Lake McDonald, feasting on the beauty surrounding us.

Several days later, after a marvelous time in Glacier, we were passing through Spokane, Washington, and decided to camp in their city-owned campground. While checking in, I read a large sign that stated, "No refunds!" We proceeded to the campsite area. Like so many previous campgrounds, all the good sites for tents were taken by trailers and motor-homes.

We finally picked a site that wasn't too rocky. As we began to erect our tent, I soon ran into a snare. I could not drive our plastic tent stakes into the ground. So we tried a second site then a third, but the problem remained. Our plastic stakes just bent. I finally realized we needed steel stakes to pitch a tent in any of the open campsites, but we had none.

Hot, sweaty, frustrated, and angry, we put everything back into the bus and drove back to the registration building. In less than thirty seconds, my facial expressions and words had convinced the person, who checked us in, to refund our money with no arguments. By the time I had calmed down physically and emotionally, we had driven 109 miles to Moses Lake.

The only campground there was by a small lake. A strong wind greeted our arrival. One look at the campsites told us there was little to shield us from the wind. We weighed our options and decided to stay. After registering, we picked a site near the main bathroom building. We would use the building as a windbreaker for our tent, plus we'd use additional ropes on each strategic pole. It proved to be a good choice, wind or no wind, and we enjoyed our stay. When we finally broke camp and left, we headed for Mt. Rainier National Park.

Like all our national parks, Mt. Rainier is beautiful and interesting. The round visitor's center is second to none. It offers spectacular views, valuable information, interesting displays and delicious food. There are also campgrounds in the park and sections, within them, are only for tents.

After spending ample time at the visitor's center, we drove to one of the campgrounds and chose a perfect campsite on the outer edge of one loop. We leisurely set up our tent, completed other chores, and made supper. Toward evening, Mark wanted to chop some kindling for a campfire, so he crossed the narrow, dirt road, went to the campsite opposite ours and borrowed a hatchet from its occupant. Before returning it, I suggested he invite the woman over for smores (graham crackers with pieces of chocolate and roasted marshmallows between them) once it got dark and our fire was going. He did, and she accepted.

We lit our fire about 9:30 and soon after, Judy appeared. For the next hour or so we enjoyed the fire, our fellowship, and some smores. Being a seasoned camper, Judy had many interesting tales and bits of information to share. One that especially interested me was something she mentioned about bears in this park. She warned us not to leave any food out on our table or elsewhere including any in our ice chest. She emphasized that all food and our ice chest should be locked in our bus at night. She warned us that bears were able to open ice chests to get the food inside, thus the reason for locking it in our bus. After hearing what she had to say, we agreed it was good advice.

After an enjoyable evening, she thanked us and walked the few steps across the road, past her truck and back to her site. Within seconds, she came running back screaming, "There's a bear in my campsite! There's a bear in my campsite!" Realizing the potential danger a black bear can be, I grabbed our flashlight, and all of us walked quietly to the edge of her campsite. Shining the light, we saw a large, black bear about ten feet away. It was next to her picnic table, upon which sat her ice chest.

The bear was standing on its hind legs with one front paw resting on Judy's opened ice chest, while the other paw held the meat it was eating. Responding to my light, it turned, and its eyes reflected in the beam. Seeing the light, it grunted and continued eating. I sent Mark to find a ranger. Then, as I kept the light on the bear, I ordered in a commanding voice, "Shoo, Shoo! Get out of here! Scat!" What resulted from my orders? Absolutely nothing. The bear continued eating and looking in our direction. We held our ground, it held its. No one moved for several minutes, while the bear ate all the food it wanted from the ice chest.

Before Mark and a ranger arrived, the bear finished eating, then picked up a large box of raisins, turned, ambled down into the bushes and disappeared into the inner part of the loop, where many others occupied campsites. We never heard whether or not the bear visited any of the other campsites within our loop. All we knew was what had happened to Judy. It was ironic in a way. She had warned us about storing our food and ice chest in our bus. Yet, she had left hers on the table. She hadn't "practiced what she preached." All of us learned a lesson that night even though, in ways, it was a humorous experience. Imagine me telling a bear to shoo and scat as if it would. Having been raised on Walt Disney movies, I guess in my heart, I expected it to obey my simple commands.

This was not the first bear we saw during our camping trips west. We saw several during our first trip to Yellowstone National Park, most at a safe distance. However, one day, we were driving south on a road in the park and passed another VW bus. Only this one was parked to the right off the road. I turned and asked Shelley, "Did I see what I think I saw?" She responded, "I believe so." Then I declared, "If I don't get a picture of what I saw, no one will believe me," I turned the bus around and drove back to where the other bus was parked. I pulled off the road and parked my bus opposite the front of the other one, about ten feet away. I left the engine running with the emergency brake on. With camera in hand, I opened my door, hopped out, and walked to within six feet of the other bus, took my picture, retraced my steps, reentered our bus, and headed south once again.

What did I take a picture of? A man, by himself in the other bus, was sitting in the driver's seat. His entire body was turned towards the open, front passenger's door. He was taking pictures of a large, black bear facing him. The bear was sitting on the ground between the open door on its right and the rest of the bus on its left. I could not believe anyone could be so stupid. One quick move and the bear could have entered the bus. There was no way the photographer could have prevented it from doing so. Nor could the man have quickly driven away, since his bus engine was turned off. "Unbelievable," I exclaimed as I drove away, "Simply unbelievable."

We were only a mile or two down the road, when a ranger's car flew past us, lights flashing. Where he was going or why was only speculation on our part. But my guess was, he was heading for the VW bus.

While in Yellowstone, we were camped at Fishing Bridge. There was a trail that ran from our campground, along Yellowstone Lake, through some high grass and along a river to the bridge, and the area where the general store, cafeteria, and gas station were located.

One afternoon, the four of us were on the trail heading to the store. As we rounded a bend, we thought we heard someone yell something, but we couldn't tell what it was. So we kept walking. Soon another yell then another. The third time we heard, "Turn around! Backtrack! Don't come any farther. Moose on trail!" Stopping in our tracks, we looked toward the bridge still some distance ahead. We saw a ranger on the bridge and assumed he was the one calling to us.

Then we looked up the trail and saw a large, adult, female moose off the left side of the trail and, to our surprise and joy, a baby moose off the right side. Immediately, we knew why the ranger was calling to us. Had we continued walking the trail and gotten between the mother and her young, the mother would have attacked us fearing for the safety of her baby. And we were no match for that moose. We quickly backtracked and took an alternate trail to the store. Thanks to that ranger, we avoided what could have been a tragic accident. Instead, we continued to enjoy Yellowstone and finally left taking many, happy memories with us.

During our four trips to Glacier National Park, the threat of bears, being near or on the hiking trails, was always present. Whenever we were on a trail, we had bells to ring, or we sang, or we made lots of noise If bears were close by, they would hear us coming and get out of our way. At least that was the theory the rangers had expressed in writing and had posted at each trailhead, and it was also expressed orally at the evening, campground meetings. It worked, for we often saw bear tracks on the trails, and often they were quite fresh. We did see our share of bears but always at safe distances.

A final contact Shelley and I had with bears happened during a trip to Jasper, Alberta Province, Canada. We were traveling in a station wagon and sleeping in it as well. One night, we parked in a boat trailer parking lot across a dirt road from a lake. We were a few miles outside Jasper.

Prior to leaving on this trip, we taped mosquito netting over the windows behind the two front seats. This allowed us to open those windows at night for fresh air without being eaten alive by the giant mosquitoes that inhabit the cool, northern areas of the USA and Canada during the summers. With such an arrangement, we always slept soundly.

I was the first to wake up in the early morning. When I did, I raised my head, turned, looked over the front seat and through the windshield. Staring back at me was a black bear. It was standing on its hind legs and resting its front legs on the hood. I quickly uttered, "Shell, wake up! There's a bear looking at us, and he's licking his lips." I spoke too loudly. My voice startled the bear, and it quickly retreated into some bushes nearby. "Darn," I said, "That would have made a great photo to show friends back home!"

Later that day, we were on a loop hiking trail in some woods near Jasper. We had only walked a short distance, when we spotted a bear on the trail ahead. Its nearness told us to backtrack and take another trail. The new one ran parallel to the first but up a hill. We began ascending the hill, and as we neared the halfway point, we noticed the same bear working its way up the side of the hill toward us. Basing our assumptions on nothing concrete, we figured it wouldn't attack. Therefore, we continued up the hill and soon left the bear behind. I don't know what we would have done, had the bear followed us. Before completing our hike, we saw several more bears but all at safe distances. Considering how dangerous bears can be at times, we considered ourselves fortunate to have seen so many on this hike and that none showed any interest in bagging a human trophy.

True tent campers like us must learn to put up with two basic parts of nature: insects and weather. As everyone knows, there's not much humans can do about weather. But insects can be controlled, providing insect sprays are available. Mosquitoes and flies are the two main insects tent campers must deal with. Usually, we could control them, but there were a few times when they had the upper hand.

Since mosquitoes thrive in cooler climates, we were attacked unmercifully by them in Kootenay National Park, Canada, while we were putting up our tent. And our repellent did little to keep them off us. By the time we had finished and had the chores completed, we all had countless, large bites on our bodies, and we spent much of the evening scratching them.

Later, on that same trip, we were camped near Sicamous, British Columbia, Canada. Late in the afternoon, we drove to Lake Mara to bathe, since there were only outhouses at our campground. We arrived at the lake, bathing suits on and soap in hand. Bon hopped out of the bus and yelled, "Last one in is a rotten egg!" Spurred on by her words, we tore across the sand and into the water, where we froze in our tracks. The lake was freezing cold! We quickly retreated to shore and, in time, could feel our feet and lower legs again.

As we stood there, we knew we had a choice to make. We could either stay dirty and sweaty or try to get used to the water a little at a time. We all opted for the lake. Slowly, we inched our way farther and farther from the shore. As we did so, we put water then soap on our faces, necks, arms, chests, backs, stomachs and thighs. When we were about twenty feet from the shore and well lathered up, a horde of bloodthirsty mosquitoes suddenly appeared out of nowhere and headed straight for us. Two terrible choices immediately confronted us. We could either dive into the ice-cold water, or we could stay where we were and get eaten alive. A few bites made up our minds.

We dove into the water and stayed under only long enough to rinse the soap off. Surfacing in pain, we waded quickly to shore, ran to the bus, hopped in, and quickly closed the doors and windows. As we sat there shivering and itching, we dried off. Even though we itched a long time, we were clean again and could snuggle up to one another. But what a price we paid!

Another time, we were camped outside El Paso, Texas. Ciudad Juarez, Mexico, was nearby, so we spent a hot afternoon there enjoying what all tourist enjoy in such a city. Before returning, we bought four T-bone steaks for $2.80 U.S. money.

That evening, after a swim in the pool at our campground, we set the table, prepared a salad and a hot vegetable and sliced some fresh bread. When all this was finished, Shelley began frying the steaks. We really enjoyed the aroma, and so did a legion of flies.

They planned their attack perfectly. As soon as Shelley put the first steak on Bon's plate, the flies zeroed in on it and attacked like a squadron of World War II dive bombers. Bon tried to shoo them away with her hands and succeeded for a few seconds. She quickly cut a bite of meat and was about to stick her fork into it, when the flies returned and some landed on her meat. Her timing was perfect, much to her dismay. Her fork came down and she speared—simultaneously—the bite of meat and a large fly that had landed on the meat, as skillfully as any medieval swordsman. Her disgusted yell could be heard a mile away.

We soon realized that we were fighting a losing battle. However, being true campers, we ate with one hand and shooed flies away with the other. Since the lighting was not the best, I'm not sure whether or not any of us ate any flies with our meat. Whether we did or didn't, the steak was delicious.

At times, where you pitch your tent is important. At a campground near Memphis, Tennessee, we were assigned a campsite in an overflow area since the regular campsite area was full. The site was grassy, shaded by a tree and had a sturdy, picnic table. We set up camp, ate supper, swam in a small lake in which small fish bit our legs, enjoyed an amusement park nearby, and finally went to bed thoroughly exhausted.

Before daylight, I was awakened by noises outside our tent. I asked myself, "Who could be out there at this hour and why?" I looked out a tent window but saw nothing. The overflow area had no lights. So I clutched my bat and lay there listening. I dozed off but was soon awakened by more rustling noises. Someone or something was moving about in the grass near our tent. Again, I peered out but saw nothing.

As I lay there with my bat ready for action, I fell back asleep. Presently, we were all awakened by noises, and by something making contact with our tent on two sides. Bonnie thought we were goners for sure. I slid off my cot, bat in hand, and crawled to the nearest window and noticed that it was just beginning to get light. I carefully peeked out expecting the worst.

What I saw made me laugh. Horses were grazing near our tent. Unknown to us at the time of registration, the overflow area and the horses' grazing area were one and the same. Had I known this before the noises began, I would not have lost any sleep over them. Since I hadn't, I was a bit upset, yet relieved knowing horses were out there, not thugs or skunks or some other pests.

On another occasion, we were in Vermont and sought a campsite late one afternoon. Choices were few at a campground we entered. The one we finally chose lay several feet below a dirt road. A sloped, dirt driveway led to it. There were no trees, but bushes lined the site on two sides.

After looking the site over, we pitched our tent below the driveway to the right of the actual campsite spot. There was more grass and fewer rocky patches. One side of the tent faced the driveway, the front faced the regular campsite spot and the other side and rear bordered the bushes. We used our extra ropes to strengthen the stability of the tent including extra ropes on the awning poles. We wanted to be prepared for adverse weather if it came.

The afternoon of our second day there, a storm struck. High wind and a deluge of rain befell the campground. A few minutes into the storm, we realized our tent was in danger. Wind and rain were buffeting it and muddy water was pouring down the driveway toward the side of the tent facing it. I went out and put large rocks on the tent stakes to keep them in the ground. Also, I quickly dug a trench along the side of the tent threatened by the muddy water. It diverted the water away from the tent and toward the bushes. We were still in trouble as the wind and rain increased.

We finally did what we had to do. Everyone left the tent and entered the storm. Bonnie and Shelley each held one corner of the awning and the supporting pole. Mark and I each held one corner of the rear of the tent by holding the supporting pole and canvas. Since our arms were raised, water poured into our shirt sleeves, over our armpits, down our sides, and disappeared somewhere in our underwear. We were fortunate that there was no lightning and that it was a warm, summer day.

The storm lasted about forty-five minutes. Then the sun came out. We checked for damage in our soaked clothes and shriveled, prune-like bodies. Out tent and its contents were okay. Other campers were not so lucky, especially those who were away at the time. Many of their tents had blown over or were badly flooded, if windows had been left open, or both. Looking at the uprooted tents, my thoughts returned to the night in Great

Falls, Montana, when ours blew over. I could empathize with the unfortunate campers here.

We learned a final lesson early in our tent camping days. During the peak camping seasons, it was important to arrive at a campground early on Friday and stay there until Sunday morning. Otherwise, we found no campsites available and ended up sleeping in our bus.

During one of our camping trips west, we visited San Francisco on a Friday. We had come from Oregon and northern California and were heading south along the coast toward Los Angeles. We figured a few hours in San Francisco would give us the opportunity to visit Fisherman's Wharf, descend Lombard Street, climb to the top of Coit Tower and enjoy the views from there, and ride a cable car. However, I knew that we needed to leave the city before the afternoon rush hour began, so we could get to a camping area near Santa Cruz before it was full.

We were on schedule, when we boarded a cable car at Fisherman's Wharf for a ride to the end of the line. What a thrill! People packed in like sardines; the conductor, worming his way through, collecting fares; some passengers hanging off the sides while grasping hand holds; the slow climb up the steep hills and the ride down as the brakeman strained every muscle to keep the car under control. I could see why a ride on a cable car was such a popular tourist attraction.

At the end of the line in the center of the city's shopping area, we hopped off and entered the long line of people waiting for a return cable car. We inched our way forward as car after car left filled with fellow tourists. Finally we were ready to board the next car when Mark, age fifteen, asked if he could board the following one, so he could hang off the side. We agreed and left him behind.

The return trip was just as delightful as the first. We soon arrived back at Fisherman's Wharf, our original starting point, and disembarked. We stood there waiting for Mark to appear on the next cable car. When the next two arrived and Mark wasn't on either, we began to wonder where he was.

We finally spoke to a conductor. He informed us that only every other car, returning to the Fisherman's Wharf area from downtown, came to this station. The others went to a different station a few blocks away. Hearing this, I panicked. Where was Mark? Still downtown? Or a few blocks away at the other station? With such crowds of tourists everywhere, how could we ever find him?

After quickly weighing the options open to us, we walked to our bus and drove to the other area in the hope that he'd be there. But he wasn't. So we drove back to the original station figuring maybe he had walked to it from the alternate one. But he was not there. I asked myself, "Did we pass him as he was walking from one station to the other? Was he still downtown? If neither of these was the case, where could he be?"

By now, forty-five minutes had passed, and it was getting close to the rush hour. We were standing outside the van at the original station wondering what to do next. Soon we saw another cable car descending the final hill before the station. Shelley thought she saw Mark hanging off its side with his "Wall Drug" inscribed hat firmly in place. As the car drew nearer, we realized it was Mark.

When Mark saw us, he waved his hat in triumph. Once the car rattled into the station and stopped, Mark hopped off and hurried toward us with a broad smile on his face. In answer to my question of where he had been so long, he replied that he had been downtown trying to get on a cable car that he could hang off the side of. It seemed other tourists kept beating him to the hand holds, and he didn't want to sit on a seat. So he waited and tried, waited and tried until he was successful. When he finally arrived back and told his tale, I was upset with him for taking so long, but relieved that he had finally rejoined us unscathed.

By the time we worked our way through the tourists, the cars, the bikes and the buses and entered a freeway, we were caught in the rush hour. However, we didn't rush, we crawled mile after mile, stopping, starting, stopping, starting, ad infinitum. By the time we reached the first camping area near Santa Cruz, it was full. It was the same story at all the others along the coast north of Big Sur.

It was after dark by the time we reached Big Sur, and still we had no prospects of getting a campsite. But it was too late, anyway, since we couldn't pitch our tent in the dark. To add to our misery, we were all tired and hungry. And I was frustrated. I finally stopped at a small store and bought some milk, bread and bologna for our supper.

While we ate, I broke the bad news. We would have to sleep in our bus each in his or her seat, There was no room to lie down. My news was not well received, but it was the only choice we had. It was a restless night for everyone. However, this experience plus another similar to it taught us to get to a campground early on Friday and stay there until Sunday. Once we learned this, we never had to sleep in our bus again. Thank the Lord for that.

During our three summers of tent camping, we traveled all over the

United States and from the eastern end of Canada to the western. We enjoyed national parks, national monuments and countless historical sights in both countries. But most of all, we enjoyed what each section, in each country, had to offer in customs and traditions. We enjoyed the people, too. We found that most were like us, simple human beings, made in God's image and desiring only the best for their lives.

Chapter XXI
Tragedy then Assurance: They're with Jesus

The phone rang once then twice. Shelley, only half awake, reached over and picked up the receiver. A few seconds later, she arose, walked to our bedroom door and called Bonnie to answer the phone. Once Bon was on the line, Shelley placed the receiver back on the cradle, sat down on the bed, turned to me and remarked, "That was Betty Grieve, and she was crying. It sounded like Rob was in the background crying, too. I wonder what's wrong?"

It wasn't long before Bonnie knocked on our door and entered. She was white as a ghost. From the look on her face, I knew something was terribly wrong. As Shelley and I sat up in bed, Bon murmured, "Last night Eric Borloz, Tommy Carroll, Mark and Brian Hayhurst, and Maria Van-Beers went to be with the Lord." And then she began to cry.

That's how we received the news of this terrible tragedy on Sunday morning, November 11, 1978. The three of us were stunned. How could this be? Why, I had sat next to Brian during choir rehearsal only Thursday evening. And Mark had recently presented a talk and showed slides of his summer missionary trip. Now they, along with the other three, were dead? I could not fathom such a tragedy and had trouble believing it.

The evening before, Bonnie had baby-sat for Mrs. Horn. Ordinarily, she would have gone to the weekly Bible study with several close friends including these five. Brian and Mark would have picked her up as they usually did. However, since she had turned Mrs. Horn down the few previous times she called, Bon decided to sit.

We left for church at our usual time expecting to sing in the choir as usual. Arriving, it was obvious who knew and who didn't. Tears flowed freely from those who knew. As the news spread from person to person, family to family, shock, disbelief and grief permeated the air, and people became silent or cried softly. Even though the choir sat in the choir loft, the choir number, "How Lovely Is Thy Dwelling Place," was cancelled. Bon sat with some friends in the rear of the sanctuary.

The service began. Pastor Fred Beveridge, slowly and prayerfully, reconfirmed what we already knew. Five of the young people from our church had been killed the night before in an accident involving the Hayhursts' VW bus and a 1973 Ford Econoline van. The two brothers in the other vehicle had also been killed. At that point, details were sketchy.

As the service continued, I sat in the choir loft and scanned the congregation. I noticed that the parents of all five teens were present. I thought to myself, "What a testimony to their Christian faith."

When the service ended, people filed out silently. Each was grieving for the victims and even more so for the families of the victims. Clearly, our church family was hurting.

Putting together bits and pieces of information from this person and that, I finally completed the puzzle. After the Bible study, most of the teens went to an ice-cream parlor in Hillsdale for some food, fun, and fellowship. Afterwards, Brian offered to take Maria and Beth Robertson to their homes in Saddle River and Upper Saddle River, towns not far from Westwood. Brian, Mark, Maria, Beth, Tommy and Henry Ver Der Werf piled into the bus. However, at the last minute, Henry decided not to go, since his parents were expecting him home early. Eric, who was in Betty Grieve's car, got out and hopped into the bus. He told the others his parents wouldn't mind if he was a little late getting home. Finally, Bob Grieve wanted to go also, but his sister insisted that he shouldn't. After some words between the two, he got into his sister's car sulking. Had Bonnie been there, she definitely would have been in the bus. Surely fate had intervened on her behalf.

As the bus left the parking lot, the scene was set, and the cast assembled for the tragedy that would soon unfold. Based on my previous joy rides, when taking teenagers home, the cast probably sang Christian choruses, swapped clean jokes, laughed a lot, and enjoyed the fellowship. They soon arrived at Beth's home, but her parents were not there. So they drove around the area awhile then returned and dropped her off. The remaining five then headed north on East Saddle River Road at thirty-five miles per hour toward Maria's home and their final destiny.

At the same time, two brothers were speeding south in their larger van. Both had been drinking. At a section of the narrow road that's raised and curves slightly to the right, the driver of the Ford, going approximately 100 m.p.h., passed a car driven by John McNally and carrying three other teens. Before the driver of the Ford could get back into his own lane, his van smashed into the VW bus. The impact meshed the two vehicles together and sent all seven of its occupants into eternity.

The first car on the scene was the passed one. One of its occupants, hysterical and in shock, managed to walk to a nearby house and called the police. Once on the scene, police and ambulance personnel cut the two vehicles away from the bodies and transported them from the scene. During the extraction process, the parents were notified. I thank God, Shelley and I were not two of them. Through the entire ordeal, Bonnie was sleeping safely in her bed. I often wonder how Shelley and I would have reacted had Bonnie been in the bus. Would our faith have given us the strength to endure such a loss without blaming God? Thankfully, we did not have to answer that question.

"THEY'RE WITH JESUS!" was the headline Monday afternoon. It leaped off the front page of the *Record*, Bergen County's largest newspaper. The headline was a quote attributed to Donald Hayhurst, who made the statement upon hearing of his sons' deaths and the death of the others. However, it was also the belief of the other parents. The report following the headline confirmed what I had already pieced together. But it went into greater detail as to how the parents were being sustained by their faith in Christ and His healing power. At first, it seemed that these five teenagers had died senselessly. Then I realized their deaths were not in vain. Thousands of people were reading and hearing the same message evangelist Billy Graham preaches, "Ye must be born again!" In a sense, the five gave their lives that others might hear the Gospel.

The wake for all five was scheduled for Tuesday evening. At first I didn't want to go. I had attended many wakes in my life, but this one would be different. What could I say to members of four families, who were grieving over the loss of loved ones? I tried to rehearse what I might say, but the words stuck in my throat. Every thought I had seemed empty compared to what I was feeling. Words just didn't do justice to the situation at hand. So I went not knowing what to say or how to say it.

The wake for the four boys was held in one funeral parlor. Maria's was in another nearby. Shelley and I went to the boys' first. The large room, containing the four closed caskets, was bathed in flowers, and the combined scent was heavenly. When we arrived, the room was already crowded with mourners of all ages. Some were talking quietly, some were crying softly and some were praying. Others were hugging and several were sitting quietly with their thoughts.

I went through the receiving line and spoke to family member after family member: mothers, fathers, sisters, brothers, grandparents, and others. Many smiled, some even laughed at our short conversations. Somehow, I believed, each could sense how I felt inside, even though I could not adequately express it. All of them were my friends. And friends often have a sense of knowing what each other is thinking or feeling without the necessity of spoken words. I sincerely hoped this was true on this occasion.

Maria's wake was similar but on a smaller scale. I don't recall what I said to her mom and dad. I do recall hugging both. As Leo Buscaglia has written, "Arms were made for hugging."

Wednesday was a beautiful, sunny, fall day. The funeral was scheduled for the afternoon. We arrived early and took seats on the center aisle near the front of the sanctuary. The five caskets, surrounded by countless flower arrangements, were in place. The main sanctuary filled up quickly even though extra chairs had been set up everywhere possible.

By the time the service was to begin, the church was packed. The sanctuary, vestibule and fellowship hall were full. The remainder of the 900 people, who came and could not be seated, stood in the rear of the sanctuary. News crews from major television networks were in the broadcasting room ready to tape the service.

At the appointed hour, the youth choir entered and took its place in the choir loft behind the pulpit. Then the ministers entered and the service was underway. It was magnificent! One of triumph over death! The choir sang, Bonnie spoke on behalf of the teenage youth group, and the congregation sang. Several of the parents, whose teenagers were in the caskets, rose to their feet and gave testimonies to the Lord's goodness in this, the hardest test of their faith.

Pastor Beveridge knew all five very well. Thus, he talked about each both seriously and humorously. Pastor Beveridge recognized that each was a fairly normal teenager with certain idiosyncrasies and shared a few associated with each teenager. He also stressed that each was a born-again Christian and ready to meet the Lord at the appointed hour the previous Saturday night.

After the Pastor's message was completed, the congregation was instructed to sing the hymn, "What a Friend We Have in Jesus." Near the end of verse one, Mrs. Hayhurst stood, walked to the platform, ascended it and walked over to the pulpit. A hush fell over the congregation. Below her were the caskets containing her sons, Brian and Mark. She reached out, took the microphone and sang verse two to the hushed audience.

> Have we trials and temptations?
> Is there trouble anywhere?
> We should never be discouraged,
> Take it to the Lord in prayer.
> Can we find a friend so faithful?
> Who will all our sorrows share?
> Jesus knows our every weakness,
> Take it to the Lord in prayer.

When she finished, everyone stood spellbound and no one moved for several seconds. Finally, the silence was broken as people, all over the sanctuary, began wiping the tears that were streaming down their checks. But the impact of her singing lingered on.

When the service ended, people filed out quietly and headed for their cars. The final burial site was eight miles away in Paramus. As the procession began to the cemetery, we became part of it. At every intersection along the entire route, an officer of the law was present, allowing the entire procession to pass as one continuous unit.

Arriving at the burial site, I noticed four, freshly dug graves, side by side, ready for the final interment. The fifth was nearby in a family plot. A large crowd gathered around the open graves and soon the short service was completed. Shelley and I placed a single flower on each casket, whispered a final farewell to each teen, turned and walked slowly to our car.

The funeral for the brothers in the Ford was Wednesday evening at a church in Spring Valley, New York. As a Christian testimony to the brothers' family, the parents of our five attended. After the service, our parents expressed words of sympathy and hope to the parents and other family members of the dead young men. Had Bonnie been taken from us in this accident, I wonder if I would have gone to that funeral and expressed such sentiments. I was thankful that it was another question I did not have to answer.

It's been over twelve years now since that fateful night. Even though the five are gone, they are not forgotten. I often think of them and their families and wonder if the healing process has been completed in each family member. I trust that it has. And if it hasn't, I pray that it soon will be.

In 1983, a book entitled, *His Five Smooth Stones*, was written by Herm Weiskopf (Publisher: Fleming H. Revell, Old Tappan, New Jersey). Its title was taken from part of a verse in the Bible: I Samuel 17:40. The book allows memories of the five, born-again teenagers to live on.

Chapter XXII
There's More to Jobs Than Money

One day I sat down and made a list of all the paying jobs, both full time and part time, I've had during my working years. Counting all of my jobs while attending Providence-Barrington Bible College as one and all of my Mulcahey jobs as one, my list totaled forty-two. Then I classified them into four groups: four church related, twelve professional, thirteen blue collar and thirteen service related. At any given time, I had one to three jobs. Usually one was full time and the others part-time. One reason I've had so many is due to the fact that I've moved at least twenty times, not to keep one step ahead of the law, but for legitimate reasons.

Lest you, the reader, think I plan on writing about all those not mentioned elsewhere in this book, let me share a story with you that will ease your fears. A commencement speaker, at a seminary graduation, chose to speak on four points. Each one stood for a different letter in his alma mater, Yale. So he began and spoke twenty minutes on Youthful, twenty on Ambition, twenty on Life and twenty on Eternal. After the ceremony had concluded, everyone in the audience left except one graduate, who remained seated with his head bowed in prayer. The speaker, seeing him, went to him. After the graduate concluded his prayer, the speaker asked, "Son, did my address touch your heart that much?" The graduate responded, "No, sir. I was just thanking the Lord you didn't graduate from the Massachusetts Institute of Technology."

Part of the summer after graduating from high school, I worked at a frozen food processing plant. During my short time there, spinach was the only crop processed. The processing began outside. Spinach was pitchforked off the back of farm trucks or from piles on the ground onto a conveyor belt that carried it into the plant.

Once inside, conveyor belts carried the spinach past inspectors, who sorted it; through a blanching tank that partially cooked it; through a cold water tank and past more inspectors. Then it was conveyed upstairs where machines chopped it; placed the correct number of ounces into small, frozen food boxes; sealed the boxes and placed wrappers around them.

The boxes were conveyed to the ground floor; placed on large, metal trays; and the trays were placed on shelves in large freezers. Once the contents of the boxes on each tray were frozen solid, the boxes were placed in cartons. The cartons were sealed and conveyed to a large, frozen food locker, where they remained until loaded into refrigerated trucks for delivery.

The work was sporadic. As long as trucks loaded with spinach arrived, the processing continued around the clock. And employees worked twelve-hour shifts.

During my brief period of employment, I worked at three stations. One was pitching tons of spinach onto the moving conveyor belt. My second station was temporary. The conveyor belt that carried spinach through the cold water tank broke. Thus, I spent several hours, using the same arm motions one would use to propel a canoe, moving spinach through water the length of the tank with a paddle. I was glad it was only temporary. I could not have paddled twelve hours a day for any number of days. As it was, I'm sure I paddled the equivalent of fifty miles or more. After I left this station, my arms and shoulders ached for several days.

A third station, dealing with quality control, was inside the locker. Every ten minutes I donned a heavy parka; entered the locker; took a thermometer, designed with a tubular extension; stuck it into the side of a carton coming off the conveyor belt, and recorded the time on the carton near the thermometer. Then I checked the temperature reading on the thermometer that had been stuck into a carton four hours before and recorded the reading on a chart attached to a clipboard. A temperature of thirty-two degrees below zero was expected. After completing these two simple tasks, I exited from the bitter cold locker, took my parka off, wiped my fogged-up glasses, and waited until it was time to reenter. This was the perfect station on hot, humid days, and I enjoyed it.

Twice I reported for work at 7:00 A.M. and discovered the plant had shut down during the night for lack of spinach. On one of those mornings, when the plant started up again, a dead rat, drowned after falling into one of the water tanks, lay among some spinach being conveyed past the second group of female inspectors. Instead of jumping onto their chairs and letting out bloodcurdling screams, one inspector calmly grabbed its tail, flung the rat over her shoulder onto the floor behind her and returned to work. I was awed by her behavior and told her so. She smiled and informed me that such occurrences were not uncommon.

"But what about the germs from the rat?"

She chuckled a little then assured me that spinach, frozen to -32° F, would be free of living germs. But if the cold didn't kill all of them, the boiling water, used in the cooking process, would. After our short conversation, I changed my mind and decided to continue eating spinach after all.

My sophomore year of college, I lived on the miracle-dollar Barrington campus. It was so named after the successful sealed bid of $331,001 by the Trustees of the college was one dollar higher than the sealed bid submitted by a second interested party.

I held two jobs during the cold months, not out of desire, but out of need. I still had a large portion of my college bill to pay plus some other expenses. I was working from 4:00 to 7:00 every morning of the week in the boiler room on campus. Yet, when a local restaurant needed a dishwasher from five to midnight six days a week, I took it.

Two jobs, a full schedule of classes, studying, acappella choir rehearsals and concerts, varsity basketball practice and games left little time for sleeping and virtually none for any kind of social life. There were times when I felt like a walking zombie, and times when I fell asleep in class or in chapel. But my financial needs motivated me to continue working both jobs.

Now and then in the afternoon, I'd take a nap, and my three roommates were most cooperative in keeping their voices down and their radios off. That's not to say, however, that they didn't enjoy an occasional prank with me being the goat.

One such prank occurred on an afternoon after chicken pot pies had been served at lunch. Roommate, Don Forbes, worked in the food service department and collected all the small, foil pans which he later brought to our room. While I was sleeping on my back, he and Victor Anderson (another roommate) covered my body with pans. When I rolled over, most fell to the floor en masse. I woke with a start and a sudden outburst, "What was that?"

At that moment, Don and Vic enjoyed their little prank. However, I, only half awake, looked at the mess on the floor then at them and muttered, "Clean it up." After speaking, I returned to my pillow and the rest of my forty winks. When my alarm went off, both the pans and my roommates were gone.

There's not much that can be written about washing dishes in a restaurant. However, this one had a radar range in its kitchen. It was the forerunner of modern day microwave ovens. I had never seen a radar range before and was fascinated by its ability to turn cold food into hot food in seconds without overheating the plate the food was on. And I was even more fascinated by some of the ways the chefs used this machine.

Whenever a customer ordered rare roast beef, a chef would slice pieces off a well-done roast. He'd put the pieces on a plate, pour beet juice on the meat, put the plate in the oven, set the timer and push the "on" button. In a few seconds, he'd remove the contents and put the hot meat on a clean plate. The meat would now look like rare roast beef and taste like it as well. The first time I saw this done, I was skeptical, but after eating a piece, transformed this way, I became a believer.

One night, after a very busy seven hours of work at the restaurant, I returned to my dorm. As I walked down the wide hallway toward our room, I could hear a pin drop. Arriving, I looked through the glass portion of the door at darkness, grabbed the doorknob, turned it and pushed expecting the door to open. Instead, it began to fall inward. In panic, I quickly reached out with both hands to grab the door trying desperately to prevent it from crashing to the floor and breaking the glass portion into a million pieces. But I failed, and the door continued its downward plunge until it landed, not on the oak floor, but on several pillows and a mattress placed there earlier.

Once my heart was out of my throat, I entered the room, flicked on the light switch and nothing happened. The bulb was missing. Resigned to my fate, I undressed in the dark, wound my alarm clock and crawled under the covers on my bed half expecting a snake or some other creature to greet me. However, none did.

As I lay there, the silence was soon broken by a snicker here and another there as Don, Vic and Morris Burke tried hard to enjoy the complete success of their prank without laughing out loud, causing my verbal wrath to befall them. However, I enjoyed their ingenuity and the prank that resulted from it. But I never divulged my feelings to any of the three.

My last two years at Providence-Barrington Bible College (PBBC) were spent on the Providence campus. It was located on a hill behind the capitol building in a poorer section of the city. This campus was a far cry from the elegant Barrington campus home only to each year's sophomore class. Several one to three story, antiquated, wooden houses of all sizes served as dorms, classrooms, music studios, snack bar, bookstore, post office, infirmary and radio station. A large, antiquated building housed the administrative offices, library, student lounges and more classrooms. Winn Hall, the only brick building on campus, was built next to a casket company and housed the dining facilities, a combination chapel/auditorium and two more classrooms. A maze of sidewalks, dirt parking lots and a macadam play area rounded out the campus.

The motto of the college, "It's the spirit that counts," soon found its way into the innermost being of each student arriving on campus as freshmen. Otherwise, many would have left soon after seeing the campus for the first time or seeing their rooms in the dorms. As it was, the motto helped students look beyond the drab physical facilities and enjoy a learning environment and friendships not found in secular colleges.

Meals were served family style, and the food was plain. After the inspirational, music-filled, two-hour chapel each Tuesday morning, lunch usually consisted of corn soup, hard rolls, a cottage cheese/peach salad and eskimo pies. Most college students today would balk at such a meal, but students at that time and place enjoyed it.

A chance to fellowship through the conversations around the tables more than made up for the lack of lean cuisine. If the food served at any meal didn't suit one's fancy, peanut butter and bread were always plentiful. During meals in which leathery roast beef, tongue or coffee jello were served, I often filled up on bread and peanut butter myself. Students, at times, humorously referred to the college as the Peanut Butter Bible College.

I held several part-time jobs during those two years. I cleaned Boone Street Dorm where I lived for seventy-five cents an hour, cleaned the dining room floor for a dollar an hour, bussed meals in the dining hall for $135 per semester, cleaned several houses for one dollar an hour and did a great deal of gardening and landscaping on the grounds of an Englishman's home for one dollar an hour. These jobs helped pay my college bill and other expenses. They could be sandwiched in between classes, choir, basketball, studying and some social life. However, I had to maintain a strict time schedule, much to the dismay of my dates, who saw me checking my watch much too often. Unknown to my dates, I usually had to clean the dorm or dining hall after returning them to their dorms. Thus, while they slept soundly, I was busy earning my keep.

Boone Street Dorm was an old structure on the edge of the campus. The stairs creaked, the windows rattled, the plumbing moaned and groaned, and the radiators let everyone know whenever hot water or steam was surging through them. In addition to the stairways, a fire escape was provided on each of the three floors. It consisted of a thick length of rope, one end of which was securely tied to a hall radiator near a window. In case of fire, if stairways were inaccessible, the ropes, knotted at two foot intervals, were to be used and students were to lower themselves to safety. Needless to say, during fire drills, only stairs were used, never the ropes.

Was the dorm safe? Not being a building inspector, I wouldn't know. However, after returning from one vacation, I noticed that the rear outer hall at the third floor level had buckled outward enough for me to slip my hand between the wall and the door casing that had been attached to it at that spot. After reporting this, an inspection was made, and the dorm remained open.

As old and decrepit as it was, the dorm was home to several male students, and I kept it clean. These two factors instilled within each occupant a loyalty to their dorm and a kinship with each other, both unsurpassed in any other dorm on campus. Its occupants were proud to say, "I live in Boone Street Dorm." Why? I never figured out. I do know it was the dorm most visited during the annual open house, when female students could tour male dorms and vice versa. Apart from this one day, dorms were off limits to those of the opposite sex.

Pranks were also part of living in Boone Street. A fellow named Bill was the main culprit. Dropping balloons filled with water from third-story windows onto unsuspecting passersby and rolling empty, galvanized trash cans down stairways during study hours were two of his favorites.

One evening, everyone in the dorm decided to get even with Bill and devised the ultimate prank. After Bill went to sleep around eleven o'clock, his roommate's signal put the prank into operation. Since Bill arose at 5:30 to be at work in the kitchen by 6:00, every clock and every watch in the dorm were set ahead to 5:20 allowing ten minutes for the wheels to be set in motion.

When Bill's alarm went off at "5:30," he woke up, dragged himself out of bed and remarked to his roommate, who was also getting up, how tired he still felt. As he headed for the washroom facilities, he passed fellows he'd normally pass in the morning and everyone greeted him as they normally did. When he hit the showers, men, who normally would be there, were there. When he went to the washroom to shave, it was the same story. Thus, Bill showered, shaved, dressed and headed for the kitchen in the darkness as he normally did that time of year.

As soon as he left the dorm, all time pieces were reset to the correct time, and everyone went back to bed and fell "asleep." As I lay in bed, I wondered what the final outcome would be.

When Bill reached the kitchen door and found it locked, he located the night watchman and asked him for a key. When the watchman questioned Bill's need for one and told him the time, Bill didn't know what to think. Shortly thereafter, he began to suspect a prank and headed back to the dorm.

When he arrived, he found the entire dorm "asleep." Entering his room, everything appeared normal including his "sleeping" roommate. Bill aroused his roommate, who "woke up," yawned and growled at Bill for "awakening him." His roommate played his part perfectly, leaving Bill to wonder if he were losing his mind. Bill finally crawled into bed and eventually fell asleep.

When Bill's alarm sounded at 5:30, he arose, the same scene was repeated, and everyone acted completely ignorant, when questioned by Bill. After receiving no positive feedback from anyone, Bill became very nervous and expressed his fear, that he was losing his mind, to his roommate. Yet his roommate didn't reveal the truth about the prank. Bill left the dorm on time and headed for the kitchen talking to himself.

During breakfast, the dorm captain sent one of the hostesses to the kitchen with a message for Bill. Soon he entered the dining room. Once there, all the men in the dorm rose to their feet, faced in his direction, and in unison asked him, "How did you like our prank?" Then each fellow laughed in victory. At that moment, I'm not sure if Bill was more embarrassed or more relieved. But I know for sure he was both. For each dorm member, it was a delicious moment. One I still smile about whenever I recall the prank and Bill's beet-red face as he stood in the dining hall that morning.

The summer after graduating from college, I enrolled in a six-week, summer school, graduate program at Framingham State College in Massachusetts. I attended classes mornings, cashiered part time in an A & P and worked full time on the graveyard shift as an orderly in a local hospital. It was a grueling schedule, especially the thirty-two hours without sleep beginning on Friday morning and ending Saturday afternoon. But, if I was going to meet my financial obligations and have money left over to pay for Shelley's engagement ring, I knew I had to work both jobs.

The A & P was very busy. Each cashier had a bagger to keep the lines moving. Unlike most cashiers today, the ones then used to bet on who could take in the most money in the same amount of time. Since I was new to the job, I stayed out of the betting. However, I was amazed at the speed and accuracy at which the cashiers checked out orders.

Before assuming my orderly position, I completed several hours of intensive training. It was given to me by an instructor in the school of nursing affiliated with the hospital. Therefore, my duties ranged from assisting nurses and doctors to completing various tasks alone.

Shortly after beginning my employment, I was trained to run the telephone switchboard, so I could relieve the night operator for an hour each night. During this hour, I had time to study, read or write letters unless an emergency arose. Then I often had to call in hospital personnel and/or family members of patients. I preferred the quiet hours.

I enjoyed my work even though certain events saddened me. One day a young, married woman, with small children, died of cancer. For several nights, prior to her death, I tried to comfort her with Scripture. A staunch atheist, she would hear none of it. Yet, in her final hours of life, she kept crying out for God, pleading for His presence to be made known, for His help and healing power. She was only semi-conscious during those final hours. Therefore, there was little I could do for her except pray silently that a loving God heard her pleas.

Another patient, not informed of his lung cancer, was admitted. At first, his labored breathing, with wheezing, was like that of an asthmatic. Each day his condition deteriorated a little more.

One night, still unaware of his cancer, he slowly spoke to me as he gasped for each breath. "My brother had asthma. He had a medication that would clear it up. I don't understand why the doctors or nurses don't give me something for mine." I couldn't give him the answer he was searching for and tried desperately to change the subject, but he kept coming back to it.

Several times, during the last night that doctors expected him to live, I sat in a chair next to his bed, As he slept, I smelled his flowers, read his magazines and ate some of his chocolates. The few times he woke up, I held his hand, spoke words of assurance, quoted verses of Scripture and prayed. He died shortly before my shift ended.

One night an older woman was admitted. She was suffering from second and third degree burns over her entire body. Her body looked like it had been put on a spit and roasted over an open fire. She had been smoking in bed and had fallen asleep. Her cigarette ignited her bed linen.

Even though the fire was extinguished shortly after firemen arrived, it left her on the edge of death. Whenever she regained consciousness, she must have felt excruciating pain for she pleaded with God to let her die. And He soon obliged.

After my shift ended one morning, I stopped by the children's ward to cheer up a little girl who had been hit by a drunk driver several weeks before. She had escaped death by the narrowest of margins. Except for her face, her entire body was in plaster of paris casts. After our few minutes of conversation and laughter, I left not sure who cheered up who. After my initial visit, I often returned to visit her and other children in the ward.

One was a young boy suffering from terminal leukemia. On my first visit, he proudly showed me an autographed baseball from the Boston Red Sox and an autographed picture and note from comedian Red Skelton. Knowing Mr. Skelton had a son with terminal leukemia, I was touched by the contents of his note. It was a sad morning for me, when I arrived at the children's ward and learned of the boy's death the previous day.

On another night, I was called to the emergency room. When I arrived, I saw a doctor and a nurse working feverishly over the body of a man. The nurse quickly handed me the man's pants and instructed me to check the pockets for some identification. Upon taking them from her, I realized immediately that diarrhea was wide spread on the pants. However, I checked one pocket after another until I found some ID. Then I got rid of the pants and washed my hands twice.

While waiting for new instructions, I learned that the man had spent the day at a clambake and was on his way home. He was hit by a car while crossing a road after exiting from a bus. The man's guardian angel must have been with him, for his injuries were not serious. But I'm sure he had lots of pain.

Once he was placed in a clean bed, I was assigned to care for him in a limited capacity and soon discovered why. The man promptly soiled himself, his night shirt and the bed linen. The stench was terrible, but I endured it and soon had everything back to normal. Then he discharged more diarrhea, and I had to repeat the cleaning and changing procedures again. When this occurred the third time, I asked, "Lord, why me?" But I received no answer. After four such occurrences, I was ready to quit my job. However, when it was time to relieve the switchboard operator, I was allowed to leave and thanked the Lord all the way to the switchboard.

July and August passed quickly. After working my final night at the hospital, I jumped into my car and headed for the camp in Pennsylvania where Shelley worked as a counselor. As I drove, I thought about the summer and what I had accomplished. I had done well in graduate school. I had met all my financial obligations, including the engagement ring, and had money left over. I had been hired as a teacher in Somerset, Massachusetts. I had rented a place to live in Barrington, Rhode Island. It was halfway between Somerset and the Providence campus of the college where Shelley was a senior. On the lighter side, I had increased my speed considerably as a cashier but declined invitations to bet. I knew I was not as fast as two or three of the other cashiers.

Then I thought about my two months as an orderly. I had experienced joy and sorrow. I had laughed with patients and cried with others. Some patients, upon seeing my white shirt and black bow tie, called me doctor and asked me medical questions I could not answer. I had cared for patients with a wide range of illnesses. Some got well, others didn't. Thus, I had to deal with death from newborn infants to the aged. I had worked with nurses, who really showed an interest in the patients, and others, who didn't. I had learned to run a switchboard. And I found time to study, when things were quiet.

Finally, after taking everything into consideration, I wished I had pursued my eighth-grade ambition to become a doctor. I should have taken Henry David Thoreau's advice more seriously, "If one advances confidently in the direction of his dreams, and endeavors to live the life which he has imagined, he will meet with a success unexpected in common hours." Who knows, I might have made it, even though I had neither the high I.Q. nor the money necessary for medical school.

I'm sure most, if not all, teachers remember more about their first year of teaching than any others. And I'm no exception. As a faculty member in the Somerset Junior-Senior High School, I taught thirty-eight seventh graders. My class represented a wide range of I.Q's; a wide range of reading, language arts and math proficiencies and a wide range of socio-economic backgrounds. Had it not been for my help-along teacher, Don Griffith, I doubt that I would have lasted the year. He and I swapped our classes twice a day. I taught language arts and geography to his, he taught math and science to mine. Beyond this, he taught me the ropes about many things, especially discipline.

In those days, corporal punishment was legal in Massachusetts. Even though it was seldom used, students knew the law existed. Therefore, most students behaved themselves. They did not want to feel the "board of education" on their behinds. However, for those who didn't behave, Don had his methods of disciplining them, and I learned from him.

Whenever Don had reached the end of his rope with a student, usually male, he'd take him into the hallway. Since he needed a witness, he'd invite me to join him. We'd leave both classroom doors open. Once in the hallway, Don made sure the student stood with his back near a row of lockers. Then Don would start chewing the student out. Every so often, he'd feign a punch, and the student would quickly veer back and hit his head on the lockers. Don's words and the noises from the head hitting the lockers wafted into both classrooms and turned potential trouble makers into pussycats. Even though Don and I never laid a hand on any students, his methods worked. Thus, we controlled our large classes and were able to spend most of our time teaching, not disciplining.

There were no special education classes for students who would have benefitted from them. There were no workbooks, no ready-made tests or ditto masters. Even so, Principal Francis Kilgrew made it very clear to all the teachers that every student in every class was to be taught. No student was to be seated in the rear of any classroom and ignored. I still remember his words, "Discipline within the boundaries of the law, but make sure you teach every one of your students. That is your job!" And for doing so, I made a yearly salary of $3500 and netted $2832. It was paid over twelve months at $236 a month.

As a novice in the profession, I made my share of mistakes but learned from them. For example, I dished out an hour of detention to any student who used the excuse, "I forgot and left my homework at home." I stopped doing this after I inadvertently left my keys at home one morning and couldn't unlock my desk or my closet. The morning this happened, several students thought I should spend an hour in detention, and I did, the next time it was my turn to supervise those there.

During our Christmas vacation, Shelley and I were married on December 27 in Westwood, New Jersey. Our wedding was audio taped. One afternoon, soon after returning to school, I played the tape for both classes. Near the end of the tape, my class gathered around the tape recorder to hear the traditional kiss between the bride and groom. As they strained to hear, Mr. Kilgrew walked in to observe. I turned red with embarrassment, but the students didn't budge until they heard the kiss. Satisfied, they returned to their desks.

Once Mr. Kilgrew knew why they were gathered around the tape recorder, he smiled in approval and sat quietly until I was ready to begin my next lesson. Then he observed in earnest several minutes, left a written evaluation and left. After he was gone, I breathed a sigh of relief.

If someone were to ask me, "What so you remember most about your first year of teaching?" I'd have to answer, "Certain students." Lenny Cowen was one of ten children. He often brought his breakfast to school, peeled it inside his desk and popped an orange section into his mouth whenever my back was turned. When I suspected him of doing this, I checked his desk one day after school. I found plenty of orange peels. However, I never confronted him about this. Therefore, he continued to enjoy an orange most days, and I continued to enjoy the aroma.

Richard Tinsley was as interested in the local high school's sports as I. During the year, I gave him sixty-eight one-hour detentions. Most were attributed to his stubbornness in many areas. Yet, two years later, when I left Somerset, he began sending me newspaper clippings that covered all of the high school's sports. He continued sending them until he graduated from high school and entered the armed forces.

There was tall, lanky Norman. I was not aware that he needed a heart operation until the day we returned from Thanksgiving vacation. That morning, I remarked to the class, "Well, I bet you all enjoyed a great Thanksgiving dinner, turkey and all the trimmings." Norman spoke and stated, "Not me. I had bread and water." When I pressed for the reason why, he informed me that his family's income was small and as much money as possible was being saved for his operation.

That evening I called his mother, and she confirmed what her son had said. However, she assured me that they did not always eat bread and water, especially on holidays. It just happened that their food ran out before her next paycheck was given to her. And without a father around to help support the family, finances were tight. Some years later, Norman had a successful operation.

There was Eugene. He had epilepsy, and I didn't know it. One day during a class track meet, he had a grand mal fit and almost scared me to death. Had I known more about epilepsy and Eugene's secret, I would have handled the situation much more effectively.

There was Patty Alfónso who won a banana split from me after rattling off, in order, the forty-five prepositions she had learned several months earlier. And Mary, who did her homework every night except Thursdays. When questioned about this, she looked me square in the eye and answered, "Thursday night is my library night and NOTHING stops me from going to the library and getting five new books to read!" What could I say? She was an excellent reader and an all-around terrific student. To top it off, the town library ordered many books on the basis of what Mary requested, since she had virtually read every book in the library except reference books.

In June I asked the students to evaluate the year and make two lists: one, what they liked about seventh grade, and two, what they disliked. Homework overwhelmingly topped their lists of dislikes.

The following year, I gave less homework, but it still ranked number one on the disliked lists at the end of the year. Each year for several years, I continued to give less and less homework, yet each year it continued to be number one. Over those same years, I found that if I prepared more thoroughly and used every minute of class time constructively, the majority of my students needed little homework. Yet their academic results were higher and were verified on their achievements tests.

In September, 1958, I began my second year of teaching in Somerset. I had agreed to direct the junior high school chorus and oversee the intramural basketball program later in the year. Therefore, my salary jumped more than the normal one step increment to $4100. However, with a baby on the way, I still needed my two part-time jobs to make ends meet.

As the weeks ticked off, Shelley's delivery date drew nearer and nearer. Shortly after midnight on November 14 her labor pains began. I drove to the hospital, and she was admitted. Her doctor encouraged me to go back home and get some sleep. He promised to call me once Shelley delivered. I took his advice.

Later that morning, I went to school anticipating a call from her doctor at any time. Early that afternoon, I was called to the office. Excited, I told my class, "This is it!" then quickly headed that way. As I walked, I kept asking myself, "Is it a boy or girl?" Arriving, I picked up the phone to find out. However, Shelley answered my "Hello," and told me her labor pains had stopped, and she was being discharged. Therefore, would I pick her up after I finished teaching.

Once she was in the car, I headed to a grocery store. On the way, Shelley informed me that my insurance would not cover her one day stay in the hospital. Therefore, we'd have to pay the bill once it came.

That evening after supper, we sat down to watch TV. Around ten o'clock, her water bag broke. We quickly headed back to the hospital ten miles away. After admitting her, I was again encouraged to return home. Since husbands were not allowed to stay with their wives during labor and childbirth, I took the doctor's advice. I returned home, told our landlady to expect a call, watched a little TV, and went to bed. Around 2:00 A.M., the phone rang in Mrs. Cole's bedroom. It awakened both of us, and she answered it. Soon she came banging on my bedroom door. Barely awake, I raised my head off the pillow and grunted, "What?" She yelled back, "Your wife has given you a son!" I responded, "That's nice," then put my head back on the pillow and fell back asleep.

When I awoke the next time, I hopped out of bed and quickly prepared to go to the hospital. En route, I bought flowers. I was eager to visit Shelley and see my son, Mark, for the first time, a royal treat indeed. My visit with both was a once in a lifetime experience until a few years later when Bonnie was born.

Not long after Shelley returned home with our bundle of joy, the hospital bill arrived. Not knowing what to expect, I nervously opened the envelope. We were billed for one full day. And the cost? Sixteen dollars.

The same month I began teaching in Somerset, I became choir director at the Hebron Baptist Church in Seekonk and pastor of the Old Hornbine Church in Rehoboth. The choir was typical for a church its size. I had two basses, two tenors (one male and Shelley), a few altos and too many sopranos. Every member was faithful and rarely missed a rehearsal or Sunday morning.

The first Wednesday night rehearsal after Shelley and I returned as a married couple, the choir rehearsed in a different room than normal due to a party in Fellowship Hall. After the rehearsal, the choir joined the large circle of party goers for some food, fun, and fellowship. Once Shelley and I were seated, we were chosen to be "it" for the next game. We were blindfolded then given the end of a rope and instructed to pull on it. Obeying the instruction, we pulled and pulled until we heard, "Stop!" We stopped and waited for the next instruction.

"Remove your blindfolds!"

We did as ordered. There was a large box attached to the other end of the rope, and the box was full of wedding gifts. As everyone smiled and clapped, we realized the party was for us, and we hadn't suspected a thing.

Apart from the gifts, the party had an added significance. I had only been the choir director for four months. Yet I now knew that we had been accepted as friends and not merely as servants in their church. This meant a great deal to both Shelley and me.

The Old Hornbine Church had been established in 1753 and the original church building was still in use. An early nineteenth century pulpit Bible, pews for slaves, a potbellied stove in the sanctuary and an old pump organ all bore witness to the church's longevity. Had I not known otherwise, I would have added the organist to the aforementioned list.

My first Sunday afternoon the congregation consisted of a heavyset older woman and her overweight middle-aged daughter, who came in their model-T Ford; a small, frail-looking woman originally from England and the elderly organist who pumped away and sang along with me as I provided the special music.

As the service progressed, the number of wasps that were flying around my head kept increasing. I'm sure in their own way, they were trying to decide whether or not to attack me. Several buzzed around my head, and I had to duck. But none scored a direct hit on any part of my body much to my relief and that of my congregation.

In a effort to increase attendance, I printed one hundred fliers and put them into local, rural mailboxes, called on several nearby families and had a friend paint a large sign for the outside of the church. It proclaimed, "Bible Centered Preaching for Christ Centered Living." The sign began to attract others to our weekly afternoon service. On Easter Sunday, twenty-three attended.

Even though I was paid only five dollars a week, the offerings would not cover my salary plus the other expenses of the church. This situation had existed for many, many years. Therefore, in order to maintain the church, two successful money-making clambakes had been held each year for almost one hundred years and were still being held. Of course, those who organized and ran the clambakes had changed through the years, but the menu hadn't.

People came from miles around making each clambake a festive affair. However, a clambake wouldn't be a clambake without beer, so it was served. However, I'm sure the thought of drinking beer on holy ground preyed on the minds of most beer drinkers. Thus, most followed the Bible's teaching and drank in moderation.

After teaching three years in Somerset, I resigned, and we moved to New Jersey. We took with us many happy memories and left behind many dear friends. In the years that followed, I taught full time in several other places. In each, certain students so impressed me that I still carry a fondness in my heart for them.

In Paramus, New Jersey, I taught Linda Sexton, a tall, gangly sixth grader. While under my tutelage, she began baton twirling lessons. I encouraged her to stick to it and become the best twirler possible. By her junior year in high school at age seventeen, she had won more than one hundred medals and trophies, had been selected Miss New Jersey Majorette and had been selected to co-captain the Philadelphia Eagles (professional football team) Twirling Team. I like to think my encouragement, years before, had something to do with her success.

In River Edge, New Jersey, Patty James entered my life as a sixth grader. Her personality, sense of humor, self-motivation, thirst for knowledge, and creativity made teaching her an absolute joy. She was one of a kind.

A second student was Mary Ann Spahn, a pretty, dark-haired girl of average intelligence, who could flash her gentle, sweet smile at times when another, in her situation, couldn't. Mary Ann had a severe physical problem that indirectly affected her school work. She had been born with a spastic colon and had difficulty controlling her bowels. Medication didn't help and a special diet helped only a little. Therefore, she lived under the constant threat of needing a bathroom and not having one near. Her attendance at school was not as good as I would have liked. However, her younger brother often came to my classroom and whispered into my ear that his sister had had an accident while walking to school and had returned home. On those days, she came in late or not at all.

Figuratively speaking, my heart bled for her, but there was little I could do except seat her next to the door and give her permission to head for the girls' bathroom whenever the need arose. There were a few times in school that year, when her bowels moved faster than her feet. On those occasions, she went to the nurse who assisted in the clean-up process. Depending on the outcome, she either returned to class or was sent home. Either way, her self-esteem suffered another damaging blow.

I'm sure her most humiliating experience as a sixth grader occurred one day in June, when all sixth graders in the district went to the junior high school for a day of orientation. Mary Ann was sitting in the second row of the packed bleachers in the gym listening to one of the speakers. Without sufficient warning, she suddenly needed a bathroom and made a frantic effort to leave the gym but failed.

I shall never forget the look on her face as she quickly walked past me at the end of the bleachers. It was one of complete humiliation and devastation; one that pleaded, "Let me crawl into a hole and pull the dirt in after me!" And all I could do was walk with her to the office after she came out of the bathroom, and wait with her until a taxi arrived to take her home. Before she entered the taxi, I gave her a quick hug and whispered, "I love you," into her ear. Immediately a smile crossed her face. Seeing it, I knew she would overcome another in a series of embarrassing situations.

In 1977, thirteen years later, I was back in New Jersey and living in Westwood. While reading the *Bergen Record*, an obituary caught my attention. Mary Ann, age twenty-six, had died September 17. Saddened by her death, I went to her funeral. Afterwards, I spent a few minutes talking to and consoling her parents and brother.

From our conversation, I learned that Mary Ann had had an operation to correct an ulcerated colon. Once the doctors opened her up, they discovered cancer in the colon and outside the abdominal wall. Therefore, a colostomy was performed. During the night following the operation, she suffered hepatic (liver) failure and quietly passed away in her sleep. In a way, her death was a blessing.

Twelve years after Mary Ann's death, I've written this as a eulogy in her honor. I sincerely hope I've done her justice.

During the four years I taught in New Jersey, I also served as Youth Director in a large, Reformed church; drove buses part-time and worked three summers as a senior counselor at Knight's Day Camp, owned and directed by Maurice Sternberg.

Maurice is a genius at putting sound camping theory into practice and maintaining a balance between small group activities and those encompassing the entire camp population of five hundred or more. The camp was always a beehive of wholesome, enjoyable activity, and I thoroughly enjoyed working there.

One summer, I was in charge of fifteen boys, all about six years, eight months old. A junior counselor assisted. I had the boys for either four or eight weeks. Near the end of each boy's camping experience, I had to write a letter of evaluation for his parents, expressing both positive and negative comments. However, after any negative comment, I usually added a sentence or two expressing any improvement I had noticed in the boy's behavior.

That summer, I had the son of a psychiatrist for eight weeks. The boy was large for his age, strong, very competitive and a bully. The other boys, in my group, often cringed in fear after being bullied. As hard as I tried, I could not help the boy change his behavior to any acceptable degree.

After reading my final fifteen letters, Maurice came to me. He was concerned over the one to the bully's parents. In Maurice's mind, there were too many negative comments without corresponding positive ones denoting improvements. I had taken great pains writing that particular letter, so I held my ground and told Maurice that I had seen little or no improvement in the negative areas. Therefore, I could not lie and write positive comments just to please his parents. Against what he considered his better judgment, he allowed the letter to remain as written. But he predicted I could kiss any tip from the boy's parents good-bye, once they read it.

Most parents were very appreciative of the way the counselors handled their children. Therefore they tipped an average of twenty dollars per child at the end of eight weeks. Thus I stood to lose that amount.

The afternoon of the parents' final visit, I handed out my letters and stood rather nervously near the psychiatrist. He opened the envelope, took out the "kiss of death," read it then smiled ever so slightly. He turned to me and expressed his opinion of its contents, "You sure have my kid pegged to a T." Then he reached into his pocket, took out some bills, handed me twenty dollars, thanked me for "putting up with my son for eight weeks," and shook my hand. I thanked him for his generous tip and returned to my group. I was smiling from ear to ear, and I felt terrific inside. Once again, truth had triumphed, and I was a little wealthier because of it.

The summer after my third season at Knight's Day Camp, we moved to California. I became the Administrative Head of the Riverside Christian Day School. When I left that position, I returned to teaching in Rubidoux, California. As in all my previous teaching positions, certain students stood out.

One was Suzie Sheets, a student in one of my two sections of language arts/social studies core. She had a thing about insects, so much so, that at times I wondered if she hadn't developed from a species of beautiful butterflies. A round-robin story that she and five classmates wrote, entitled, "The Traveling Termites," is a literary gem. I often read it to my college classes and at creative writing workshops in the years that followed. At each reading, it invoked gales of laughter from the audience. I still have it stashed away ready to use again.

From Rubidoux, I took a position in the Campus School in Oswego, New York. One student I'll never forget was Nancy Nitardy. She was the most competitive student I ever had.

Early in the year, I realized that several children, including Nancy, were very weak in their number facts and multiplication tables. Therefore, I instituted a variety of different activities to correct the situation. Now and then, I played math games with the class and rewarded a correct answer with a Lifesaver candy.

At first, Nancy never received a reward. However, she faced her math deficiencies head on and worked like a beaver to overcome them. Her thrill of victory slowly replaced her agony of defeat. In a few weeks, she began smiling victoriously after giving each of her correct answers and piling up reward upon reward.

Nancy was on the girls' swimming team at the YWCA. After each meet, she'd bring her ribbons, mostly first place, to school and display them on our <u>Achievements</u> bulletin board for a period of time. I always complimented her on such victories and encouraged her with such statements as, "Keep it up, Nancy. Someday you'll swim in the Olympics." Well, she kept it up and almost made the Olympic Swimming Team a few years later.

Another student in the Campus School was "Peanut" Laurent, a short, spunky girl, who, I'm sure, has been a tremendous asset in the ERA movement since its inception. She lived in the country and had several brothers to contend with.

One morning, a class of college students, majoring in elementary education, was in my classroom to observe a science lesson on the lever, one of the six simple machines my fifth graders were studying. Unhappy with the simplicity of most science kits, I brought a square cinder block, filled with concrete in the center; an eight foot long, two by eight inch board and a triangular block of wood for a fulcrum from home. I stored the wood in my office and the cinder block in the back of the room.

At the point in my lesson when I needed the cinder block, I asked for a strong volunteer. Several in the class pointed to one particular boy as the strongest, so I chose him. With his chest puffed out, he proudly went to fetch the block but could barely lift it let alone carry it to me. Embarrassed and deflated, he returned to his seat. Immediately, several hands shot up again, including Peanut's.

In fun, I hemmed and hawed over my second choice continually stressing how strong the person had to be. Finally, I chose Peanut, much to the disgust of the male "doubting Thomases" and the glee of the girls. Smiling, she bounded out of her seat and, with all eyes focused on her, walked to the cinder block. She bent down, grabbed it firmly with both hands, and lifted it to her mid-section with a grunt. As everyone looked on in disbelief, she carried it to the front of the room and placed it at my feet. Pandemonium broke loose and increased when she turned, faced everyone in the room, raised her arms as a weight lifter would, flexed her muscles, and smiled.

June 21, 1971, finally arrived. I was exhausted mentally and very overweight physically after a very busy year at The King's College. Now I looked forward to a relaxing eight weeks at the Hesses' home in Norfolk. I needed time to rejuvenate my mind, body, and soul.

A few days after arriving, I became restless and decided to find a job of a physical nature, so I could lose weight. I read the newspaper employment ads, then drove to the city hall and made out an application for employment cutting grass in the Forest Lawn Cemetery on Granby Street. Once my application had been read by the head of the cemetery division in the Parks Department, he frowned, looked at me, and remarked, "According to your application, you'll only be here a little over seven weeks."

"I know, but I can cut a lot of grass in seven weeks."

My comment brought a smile to his face. "I'm sure you can," he said. "You're hired." With that he paged his secretary and I was soon processed. I left with a card telling me to report to work the following Monday at 8:00 A.M.

My first day on the job almost killed me! The weather was hot and humid. There was little shade to escape the sun's rays. The required dress: long pants, work shirt, heavy work shoes and socks only added to my sweaty discomfort. The walking pace expected, while pushing a large rotary mower, was fast. There were two ten-minute breaks and a thirty-minute lunch hour. Finally, my favorite beverage, hot coffee, was not palatable. Only cold water and soda were.

I dragged myself home at 4:30. Rose Marie said I looked like a walking corpse, but I ached too much to be that lucky. I ate a little supper, lay in a tub of warm water for an hour, then fell into bed more tired than I had ever been in my life. Yet I was not sorry I had taken this job. After all, I was working outside, which I enjoyed, and I knew I would lose a great deal of weight.

The next few days were carbon copies of the first, but each was a little less tiring. Within a week my body had adjusted quite well to the weather conditions and the pace. I also found I could once again enjoy a cup of hot coffee at break times and at lunch. As I hoped, I was shedding pound after pound. To top it off, I could cut as much grass as anyone on the crew even though I chewed up countless artificial flowers, hidden among the tall grass, in the process.

Once I had adjusted to the job, I spent more time during breaks and lunch times talking to the other employees. I soon realized they were not saints even though we worked in a cemetery considered by many to be hallowed ground. I'll always remember two, Charlie and Gus.

Charlie was in his twenties. He was a simple-minded, happy-go-lucky person who enjoyed the simple life that he led. Charlie would bet on anything. One payday two fellows bet Charlie ten dollars that he couldn't eat an entire super grinder and drink a quart of soda during the thirty-minute lunch hour. Charlie won the bet, but lost the food and drink within an hour after returning to work. The last time I saw him that day, he was slowly walking toward his car.

Gus was an older man with a gray beard. He always did his share of work. One day during lunch, he mentioned that he had spent twelve years of his life in a mental institution. Over the next several days, I noticed nothing in Gus's behavior or in what he said during our conversations that suggested he had any current mental problems. Then one morning he came to work sporting a black beard. He had dyed the gray with shoe polish. From then on I had my doubts.

My last two weeks I was assigned to trim grass from around the bases of tombstones, headstones, and monuments. Some I could do with an edger, others I had to kneel and pull the grass out with my hands. This job afforded me the opportunity to read the inscriptions on each stone. Many dated back to the Civil War, giving me an historical glimpse of this terrible war that often pitted brother against brother, father against son, and family against family.

On the less serious side, after reading hundreds of inscriptions, I agreed with the statistic that most husbands really do pass away before their wives.

One day I trimmed around the tombstone of a husband and wife. What I read surprised me. The husband had died on my birthdate (April 7), and his wife had died on Shelley's birthdate (October 26). As I continued working, I wondered what the odds were for something like that to have happened.

Another day I trimmed around the tombstone of George Dewey Hay (1895–1968). He was a Memphis, Tennessee, newspaperman turned radio announcer, who carried his love of country music to radio, first in Chicago and then Nashville, Tennessee. Hay originated the Grand Ole Opry and was its master of ceremonies for nearly thirty years. He was instrumental in furthering the careers of hundreds of performers.

Hay called himself "The Solemn Old Judge." If he was solemn, it was only in the face of those who sought to change or corrupt the purity of the barn dance ballads he sought to preserve.

Hay was elected to the Country Music Hall of Fame in 1966.

I also edged around the tombstone of Joe. H. Weatherly (1922–1964). The inscription on his stone states, "The Riverside Raceway Clown Prince of Racing. NASCAR Grand National Champion driver 1962–1963." His stone is in the shape of the former Riverside (California) International Raceway.

By the time I completed my final day of work, I had lost thirty pounds and was rejuvenated in body, mind and soul. I left behind many good friends, but took with me some happy memories and a desire to explore other long-established cemeteries.

Since then I've explored many. The Mount Moriah Cemetery is located in Deadwood, South Dakota, an old town in the Black Hills. The graves of Wild Bill Hickok and Calamity Jane, notable figures of the frontier days, are there.

Dodge City, Kansas, was a route point of the Santa Fe Trail. Famous lawmen such as Bat Masterson and Wyatt Earp maintained a precarious order, and a noose still decorates the "hangman's tree" where a form of justice was meted out. Boot Hill Cemetery is still a popular tourist attraction.

One can gain a glimpse of the once prosperous silver and gold mining town of Virginia City, Nevada, by spending time in its cemetery. Tourists flock to this town rich in history and now advertised as the world's liveliest ghost town. In 1862 Samuel L. Clemens worked as a reporter on the *Territorial Enterprise*, Nevada's first newspaper, and used for the first time the pen name, Mark Twain.

Shelley cut an article out of the May 3, 1987, edition of the *New York Times* newspaper and sent it to me. Its title: "A Trans-Atlantic Voyage Aboard the Ill-fated *Hindenburg*." I was both surprised and pleased that it had been written by Karl R. Zimmermann, Sr., a former employer of mine who lives in Oradell, New Jersey.

As I read it, my thoughts drifted back to 1981 and 1982 when I worked nights in his home as a nurse's aide. I had often sat by his bed and listened as he aptly described, now and then, his thirty-five trips across the Atlantic by ocean liner and once in the *Hindenburg* zeppelin. It was his trip in the airship that interested me the most.

According to his oral description, there were two decks. The larger upper deck contained a lounge, dining room and twenty-five staterooms. The fifty-four passengers, who each paid the one-way $400.00 fare, could relax in the lounge, look out the slanted windows at the scenery below and enjoy fresh air coming through any open windows. Even though all the furnishings, including the piano, were made of aluminum, the sofas and easy chairs were comfortable.

One long table ran the length of the dining room surrounded by comfortable chairs. While eating, the passengers could look out many windows as well as enjoy cool breezes wafting through open windows.

The staterooms reminded Mr. Zimmermann of railroad bedrooms although the staterooms were slightly larger. Each contained upper and lower berths, a small desk, a sink for washing, but no toilet. Since he never mentioned a dresser being in a stateroom, I'm assuming drawers were built into the closet or luggage storage space.

The lower deck contained showers, toilets, bar, and a smoking room. It was reached via an elaborately decorated staircase.

The duralumin floors were covered with thick carpeting. As he walked about the decks, he noticed the floors gave way slightly and his feet sank in. According to him, this took some getting used to.

The tour of the airship was the high point of his entire trip. Entering the ship's huge shell, he noticed immediately that the bags containing the volatile hydrogen gas did not fill the entire hull as he assumed they would but only a small section at the top.

At one point he had to cross a narrow catwalk suspended over open air and ocean. Being a large man, he did not cherish the thought of crossing but did so, determined to finish the tour. However, he gripped the handrails until his knuckles turned white. His reward was a visit to the control car and an introduction to Commander Ernst Lehmann and Captain Pruss. During his time there, Mr. Zimmermann was delighted to learn how the *Hindenburg* was maneuvered and see a demonstration of it.

Upon learning the *Hindenburg* had caught fire and crashed on May 6, 1937, approximately nine months after his trip, he turned on a radio in his home and sat listening to broadcast after broadcast as the horror of the accident was reported. What he heard made him cry. Many passengers and a crew he knew personally had perished.

Barely a thousand passengers experienced what Mr. Zimmermann did: a trans-Atlantic crossing by zeppelin. After hearing him tell me of his trip, I knew others would be as interested as I. Therefore, I had often encouraged him to write about it, as well as other experiences in his illustrious life. But he always rebuffed me with such comments as, "I'm a C.P.A. (certified public accountant). My son (Karl, Jr.) is the writer in this family."

What he said was true. His son had written and published several books on trains, including *The California Zephyr*, and innumerable articles also related to trains. He still writes. However, I was elated that Karl, Sr., had finally penned this article, since he, not his son, had taken the trip. And it is his name on one of the passenger lists that appears in a book he owns on the *Hindenburg*.

Now that he's written and published this article, perhaps he'll write others. Even though he's in his eighties and confined to his bed most of the time due to a degenerative nerve disorder, his mind is as sharp as a new razor. He could write interesting articles on a myriad of topics, including his thirty-five crossings of the Atlantic by ocean liner; his memories of Germany, garnered as a boy and young adult while visiting his grandparents; his seventy plus years as a New York Yankees baseball fan that began "when programs and a big bag of peanuts both cost a nickel."

He could write about his early college years at Pennsylvania University, when he decided to become a CPA instead of a lawyer, because, in his words, "Lawyers lie too much and I do not lie." Many experiences, related to his chosen profession, would make interesting reading.

He could write about his tenure in the U.S. Navy during World War II. And after the war, he played an important role in the disbursement of funds under the Marshall Plan in Europe; funds that were not mismanaged or wasted.

If these topics are not enough, I'm sure he could write about many others including his beloved parents; how he met his wife, Catherine; the opera, and most recently, the elation he felt, and why, when the Berlin Wall was opened on November 9, 1989.

For eight and a half months in 1988, I worked the graveyard shift as a cashier in a "den of iniquity" according to a few evangelical friends and one distant relative. Actually it was a large gambling casino in the beautiful Lake Tahoe, Nevada, area.

Early in my orientation and training, my basic job description was explained orally, "Your job is to give people money (cash checks, sell rolls of coins, etc.) so they can give it back to us." Rather cut and dry, to say the least, but that's basically what I did, and most customers obliged and gave it back, I hoped, enjoying themselves as they did so.

One night, when customers were few and far between, a long-time employee in the cashiering department punched a name into a computer terminal and invited me to, "Look at this one." What I saw on the screen boggled my mind. The woman who had the account I was looking at, had cashed over $23,000,000 in personal checks during her many visits to this casino. On her final visit, she bounced $49,000 in markers. Since then, she's gone to the great casino in the sky. However, her memory and unpaid debt are forever stored in the computer; a reminder to all cashiers, past, present and future, that not all gamblers play for "peanuts."

Chapter XXIII
Driving Limousines in New York City

En route to California in 1985, I stopped to visit Corky, a professor at the School of the Ozarks in Point Lookout, Missouri. While we were having coffee in the cafeteria, a group of students stopped by our table. Corky introduced them to me and me to them. He mentioned I had been a teacher, a school administrator and a college professor. This information didn't seem to impress the students at all. Then he mentioned my years as an executive chauffeur in New York City and immediately their ears perked up, their facial expressions changed to awe, and they all sat down and began asking me the questions I'd been asked many times before. What famous people had I driven? Is it difficult driving in New York City? Had I ever driven so and so? And others. At that point, I realized my claim to fame centered not in my years as an educator, but as a chauffeur in and around the "Big Apple."

In September 1978, I began taking courses at a junior college. I was studying to be a nurse. I needed a job weekends, so I answered an ad in the local newspaper. I soon found myself working for a limousine service based at the main corporate airport for New York City in Teterboro, New Jersey. The owner had a fleet of about twenty Cadillac limousines plus a few less fancy vehicles. My starting pay was $2.25 an hour plus tips and no benefits. My attire was black suit, shoes, socks, tie, hat and top coat. A white dress shirt rounded it out. Even my umbrella was black. I certainly matched the black limos.

Working part-time weekends was not very lucrative. Usually I would have a wedding in Lodi, Hoboken, or some other town near Teterboro. Sometimes it would be a one-limo job, at times two and occasionally three or more. The normal tip was ten dollars. Most of our jobs were for blue collar families, living in small houses or in apartments. After driving for several, I found there were two things that amazed me about weddings. One was the attendance. Only a few people attended the ceremonies, yet many attended the reception. A second thing centered on the photographers. The time they used to take pictures, far exceeded the length of the ceremonies and the travel time in the limos combined. I drove many weddings, but one, in particular, stands out in my mind.

It was a wedding in October. The ceremony was over, and we were heading for a park near the Hudson River, where pictures were to be taken. I was behind the lead car, carrying the bridesmaids and ushers. All of a sudden, I saw smoke coming from under the lead car. I quickly grabbed my phone and called the other driver. Without hesitating, he pulled over to the curb, cut the engine and got out. He then assisted the bride and maid of honor out of one door while the groom and best man exited from the other. I pulled in behind him and parked.

The other driver and I looked underneath the limo to determine the problem if we could, but we saw nothing suspicious. So the driver restarted the engine, and we checked again and found nothing askew. We concluded that the limo was safe to ride in, but its occupants did not, and they let us know it in no uncertain terms. Therefore Dominic called the office and another limo was dispatched to our location. While we waited, I could sense anger building up inside the groom, who was well over six feet tall and very muscular.

Once the replacement limo arrived, we loaded up and continued to the park. By the time we reached it, the sun was quite low in the west, casting long shadows where the pictures were to be taken. Now the entire wedding party plus the photographer were upset, and I couldn't blame them. But there was nothing I could do about it.

The photographer was done in record time and soon everyone was back in the limos, heading for the reception at a country club in Rockleigh, New Jersey. As I drove, I could hear quietly spoken gripes and groans emanating from the passengers behind me. But I didn't say anything. Instead I put the radio on and tuned in to a station playing relaxing, soothing music for my sake and theirs.

It was dark when we reached the reception. I was sure all the guests were there eating, drinking, and wondering where the wedding party was. Our passengers got out, and not one said a pleasant word to either of us drivers. And no tips were given. But, at that point, neither of us expected one.

We reentered our limos and were about to head back to base, when the owner called me on the phone. He informed me that the wedding party had exceeded their prepaid time limit and owed for an additional hour. Therefore I was to collect the money owed from the groom. After the message was received, I sat there talking to myself then got out and walked to the other car. Considering what caused the excess amount of time in the first place, we could not believe the owner was asking for additional money. I finally told Dominic, "I'd better go in, see the groom and get this over with."

I entered the front door, found the reception and eventually the groom. Recalling how big he was and how angry when he left the limo, I used all the tact I had, relaying the message given to me by the owner. After hearing what I had to say, if he could have spewed fire and smoke like a dragon, he would have burned the place down. However, with guests present, he constrained himself physically. But verbally, he spewed his anger out at me in a low tone of voice, and finished by saying he would not pay the additional money and would call the police if I didn't leave immediately.

I retreated quickly to my limo and relayed the message to the owner. After hearing it, I expected him to forget the issue and bring me back to base. But he didn't. Instead he ordered, "Go back in there and tell him that if he doesn't pay the additional money, I'll call the police!" At that point, there was nothing I could say that would make him change the order, so I didn't try.

I went back inside, a five foot eight inch David, with no slingshot, to face a six foot three inch angry, muscular Goliath. I took as much time as I could to find him. He was nowhere in sight, so I headed for the men's restroom to wash my sweaty brow. As I walked in, he was coming out, but he didn't notice me. I didn't feel this was the time or place to deliver my boss's ultimatum, so I was safe for the moment.

While washing my brow, the best man walked in. Since he appeared calm and was much shorter and less muscular, I decided to discuss the problem with him. He listened attentively, then he invited me to go with him to see the groom. In fear and trepidation, I agreed and followed him to where the groom was sitting. The best man whispered something into the groom's ear, then it was my turn to speak.

I mouthed my little piece, as nicely as I could, then waited for the explosion. It came but not as powerfully as I had expected. I don't recall what he said. However, I do recall the way he looked, spoke, reached into his pocket, pulled some money out, and slammed the amount due into my hand. After thanking him, I casually mentioned the tip due under the contract he had signed. He swore a bit, handed me five dollars, then cried, "Get the hell out of here!" I took his advice and left. Once outside, I offered to split the tip with Dominic, but he refused saying, "You keep it. You earned it."

While driving back to base, I reviewed what had happened. I realized that driving limousines was not always going to be pleasant or profitable. And it wasn't. The following story is another example.

It was a cold, rainy, Sunday afternoon in January 1979. It was the day before my final exam in Nursing I. I was studying in the chauffeur's lounge, waiting to be sent out on a trip. The phone finally rang. I was given my instructions and, with notebook under my arm, walked to my limo. I stopped for gas and headed for a home in Upper Saddle River. By now it was late afternoon and getting dark. As I drove, the rain continued to pour down, making driving difficult.

I reached my destination on time, parked my limo and made a quick dash to the house. Once inside, I met my passenger, Jacque, a college age boy from France, who spoke only a few words of English. He had been visiting his girlfriend, Beth, and was now returning home. My job was to chauffeur him to John F. Kennedy Airport in time for his 8:00 P.M. flight.

We left Beth in tears as we headed for our destination. Even with the rain, the darkness, and the heavy Sunday evening traffic, we had plenty of time, barring no unforeseen circumstances. I was ahead of schedule as I crossed the Whitestone Bridge, connecting the Bronx and Queens, and continued south on the Whitestone Parkway. *Ten miles to go*, I thought to myself, *Then back to base and home again, home again, home again, Dave.*

However, I was quickly brought back to reality by the glowing alternator light on the dash, signaling me that something was wrong. I quickly called base, left the parkway and drove to Kissena Blvd., hoping to find an open service station, where any needed repairs could be made. As I did this, I silently prayed that only a fan belt had broken; a part easily replaced. Thus, I did not panic but took this problem in stride. There were several stations on Kissena, but none of them was open. Not wanting to damage the engine, I pulled into a closed station, got out, raised the hood and, with flashlight in hand, confirmed my earlier diagnosis. The alternator belt had broken.

Relief replaced my apprehension as I slammed the hood shut and hopped back into the limo and out of the rain. "No sweat," I said to myself, "Find an open station and get a new belt. A piece of cake." However, I could not find an open station nearby, so I called base again. I was instructed to park the limo then call in my location. Once this was done, I was to get a taxi for my passenger. Finally, I was to stay with the limo until a tow truck arrived from New Jersey. As a postscript, I was instructed not to collect the fifty-five dollar fee which meant no tip for me.

I parked at a closed Texaco station at the intersection of Kissena Blvd. and an avenue, then called in my location. Next I turned toward my passenger. The question mark on his face told me he didn't know what was going on, and I couldn't tell him. I had little money in my wallet, so I had to get some from him, but how? Using a crude sign language, a pad, a pen and my flashlight to see with, I finally got the message across.

His face lit up with a smile. He reached into his pocket, pulled out a one hundred dollar bill and handed it to me. "Oh, no, not a hundred!" I moaned to myself. "I'll never be able to cash that!" However, I soon discovered that he had no other U.S. currency, so I clutched the bill in my hand and left the limo. I left my friend sitting on the back seat still wondering what was happening.

Black topcoat or no black topcoat, I was getting very wet, as I hurried down the boulevard, looking for a phone and a place to cash the bill. What luck! I soon came upon an open cafeteria, entered it, wiped my face and glasses and approached the counter. I quickly explained my problem to the counterman. He said he was sorry, but he was not allowed, under any circumstances, to cash a bill that large. However, he directed me to another man standing across the room. I quickly walked over to him and repeated my tale of woe. After listening patiently, he muttered, "Wait a minute. I'll be right back." He turned, walked to the rear of the cafeteria and soon returned with the manager. After listening to my plight, the manager agreed to cash the bill and also offered to call a taxi for me. After cashing the bill, I told him I was parked at the Mobil station down the boulevard. He called a taxi company and relayed this information. I thanked him, turned and saw the time. It was seven o'clock.

Back through the downpour, I trudged. When I reached the limo, I realized I had given the taxi company wrong information. We were at a Texaco station. The Mobil one was across the avenue. "What a stupid mistake!" I moaned to myself. "Now I'll have to stand over there and wait for the taxi." After giving the money to Jacque, I walked to the other station. I did what I could to shield myself from the rain, but it wasn't much.

The minutes ticked away and by 7:20 no taxi had arrived. I began to panic. In desperation, I hurried to the intersection and waited. Each time a car stopped for a red light on the avenue, I knocked on the passenger's window. I had hopes of getting a ride to the airport for my French friend. Dressed in black, rain pouring down, a dark night, and here I stood, knocking on car windows expecting people to open them. What a hopeless fool I was. Finally, one woman rolled her window down about an inch. I quickly told her my problem and offered the driver ten dollars to take Jacque to JFK. Once the light turned green, the car drove off, leaving me standing there soaked and discouraged.

By 7:30, I abandoned this plan and ran back to the cafeteria. The manager called the taxi company again, gave it the correct location of the limo, said something in another language and hung up. Then he turned to me, smiled, and assured me that a taxi was on the way. I thanked him and headed back to the limo. By now I was shaking, partly from being wet and cold, and partly from fear that my passenger would miss his plane.

At 7:40 a beat-up taxi drove in. The driver rolled his window down and looked in my direction. I got out and walked a few steps to his taxi. He sat there, dry as a bone, a Whopper in one hand and a milk shake between his legs, completely oblivious to the time. I quickly transferred Jacque's luggage, told the driver his ten dollar flat fee plus a two dollar tip would be paid by his passenger out of a twenty dollar bill and warned him not to "bleed" this unsuspecting Frenchman for more.

Once this was completed, I quickly climbed into the back seat of the limo and quickly made Jacque understand the cost of the fare, and the change due from a twenty dollar bill. As he left the limo, he shook my hand and placed some money into it. I quickly put the money into my pocket, thanked him, and hustled him into the taxi. Before the driver left, I warned him again about "bleeding" his passenger. He smiled, nodded his head and drove off into the night.

As I climbed back into the limo, I opted for the back seat, where I could stretch out and wait for the tow truck. Whether or not Jacque would make his flight was now out of my hands. I had done my best. Now it was up to the taxi driver. I pulled out the money given me. It was fifteen dollars. At least the day was not a total loss financially.

I sat there soaked to the skin, cold, hungry, and unable to see my nursing notes well enough to study. However, I figured the tow truck would soon arrive, and I'd be home in time to study. I figured wrong. I sat over two hours waiting. It finally arrived at 10:15.

During the ride back to base, the driver apologized for being so late. He mentioned that it had been a very busy night. The weather had caused a lot of accidents. Consequently, he had several calls to answer before coming to tow me home.

I arrived home after midnight. I shed my wet clothes, took a hot shower and went to bed without studying. I needed the sleep and decided to take my chances on the exam. The exam was difficult, but I earned an A-, for which I was thankful.

The following Sunday, I was sent to the same home to chauffeur Beth's father to Teterboro Airport. During the ride, what had happened the week before came up. I explained the details, and my passenger found much humor in my tale. Once I finished, and he stopped laughing, he told me the following.

Jacque arrived at JFK at 8:05 and figured he had missed his flight. But fate was on his side. The scheduled takeoff had been changed. Therefore, he finally left at ten o'clock. While waiting to leave, he phoned Beth and told her what had happened based on his limited knowledge. He also mentioned not being charged the fifty-five dollars but only the twelve dollar taxi fare. After hearing all this, I realized everything had turned out all right and that Jacque had made it home safe and sound.

When I decided not to continue my studies in January 1979, I began driving limousines full time. I stayed with the same company and worked anywhere from sixty to ninety-five hours a week. Since my hourly wage was still $2.25 an hour, tips were the lifeblood of my earnings. Since most of the companies that used our service had contracts with it, the normal 15% tip was added to the charge tickets.

As glamorous as it may seem, driving limousines in and around New York City is not all that it is cracked up to be. There are many pitfalls.

The weather is one. According to several sources I checked, the New York City area averages 42.7 inches of precipitation a year. Most of it is rain. This precipitation is spread over twelve months. Thus, there is no dry season similar to Seattle, Washington.

Spring and fall are the two best seasons for chauffeurs weatherwise, although they are far from ideal. There's a lot of rain, but temperatures are generally moderate and can be tolerated while wearing the basic black uniforms. However, once a chauffeur gets wet from any form of precipitation, he usually stays wet the entire time he's on duty.

Summers are beastly! They're hot and very humid. Anyone who lives in the East knows what they're like. Whenever you're outdoors, you feel as if you have a wet bath towel wrapped around you. Since black absorbs heat, it's even worse in a black suit.

Most limousines are air conditioned. However, due to the high summer temperatures and the slow movement of traffic, air conditioners must often be turned off to keep the limos from overheating. While waiting for passengers, chauffeurs cannot sit in idling limos with air conditioners on for even a few minutes without the dangers of overheating. Therefore, they usually stand outside their limos. If they're in the shade, that's a plus. However, the humidity is everywhere, shade or not, and chauffeurs can't escape it.

Winters are cold, damp, and often windy. Precipitation includes ice, sleet, and snow. Driving becomes difficult and dangerous. Ice often forms on windshields, blocking one's vision.

Again, limos can't be idled endlessly to keep drivers warm, while waiting for their customers to return. Therefore, the limos are started periodically to heat the interiors up then shut off again. Drivers fluctuate from being warm to being cold over and over again.

New York City has about 6,000 miles of streets to plow when it snows. Many are very narrow, making driving treacherous on them. Plows often bury cars on both sides of these narrow streets when plowing. Then the car owners shovel it back into the streets when digging out their cars. It's a no-win situation.

A second pitfall chauffeurs face is parking and standing while waiting for their customers. This is especially true in the borough of Manhattan. Traffic officers, known as brownies because of their brown uniforms, often hassle drivers. They make drivers circle blocks again and again instead of allowing them to stand in front of the buildings from which their customers will eventually exit. Much of the time, traffic is so heavy, it takes up to half an hour to circle a block once. Often, while I was circling a block, my customers would come out, expecting me to be there. When I wasn't, they'd hail a taxi and leave. I'd continue to circle, because I'd assume their meeting was running longer than expected. At times, it would be two to three hours before the dispatcher would contact me and send me to another job or bring me back to base.

Third, traffic in Manhattan is as bad as movies such as "Only in America," and "Crocodile Dundee," show it to be. Except for late at night, it crawls. During the Christmas season, it crawls much slower than normal, at a snail's pace.

During the transit strike in 1980, the entire island of Manhattan came close to gridlock many times. It was scary. It often took me as long as forty-five minutes to drive one block, east or west, in midtown Manhattan. At times, customers would exit from my limo and walk the remaining blocks to their appointments. They knew they could walk faster than I could drive. On other occasions, customers would walk several blocks to meet my limo, since I couldn't drive to them in a reasonable length of time.

One day, after the strike had ended, I was driving customers to an appointment in lower Manhattan. I was moving east on Liberty Street at about 12:15, when traffic slowed to a crawl. I didn't know why for several minutes. Then I found out. A truck had parked illegally on the right side of the street. On the left side, several cars and a truck were parked legally. The truck was parked parallel to the other truck. There wasn't enough room between the two trucks to drive between them. Therefore all the vehicles ahead of mine had to climb the curb on their right, drive down the wide sidewalk past the truck and then back into the street.

When it was nearly my turn, I noticed there was ample room for the legally parked truck to back up, allowing vehicles to pass between the trucks. Since the driver was leaning against his truck, I rolled my window down and asked if he'd please move his truck back several feet, so traffic could pass between the two trucks. He looked at his watch then at me and snarled, "It's now 12:25. My lunch hour ends at one o'clock. I ain't moving this truck till then." So I, too, climbed the curb, drove down the sidewalk past the illegally parked truck then dropped back onto the street and continued to my destination.

Pedestrians are a fourth pitfall. They're everywhere like ants. They hurry and scurry often oblivious to the signals and traffic. Many hate to yield the right of way to any vehicles—especially limousines. More than once, while I was crossing an intersection in the Times Square area, minority teenagers, boom boxes on their shoulders, spit in my face through the open window on my side, as I slowly passed them standing on the curb. Thank God, they weren't chewing tobacco.

A fifth pitfall are the taxi drivers. They deserve to be in a class by themselves. Not only for their poor grooming habits or the way they dress, but for the way they drive. Most insist on always having the right of way and rarely give it to another driver. They usually drive as if they're at a racetrack. They weave in and out, cut cars off, slow suddenly, speed up and change lanes without proper signaling, all the while honking their horns and yelling obscenities to other drivers and pedestrians. They thrive on refusing to take fares that are only going short distances. They know all the longest routes to get from anywhere in one part of New York City to anywhere in another part. A "direct route" is not in their vocabulary. An example follows.

Early one morning, I picked up a customer at a hotel on Fifty-fifth Street. He was going to JFK Airport. As soon as he entered the limo, he instructed me, "Driver, be sure you go by way of the Triborough Bridge."

When I asked his reason for this request, he enlightened me. The day before, he had taken a taxi from JFK to the hotel, and the driver had come via the Triborough Bridge. When the driver dropped him off, he said, "Be sure you tell the taxi driver tomorrow that you want to return to JFK by way of the Triborough Bridge."

Upon hearing this, I explained to him that it was a set fare, from his hotel to JFK, and not a meter fare as in the taxicabs. Then I took out my New York City map. I showed him where we were, where JFK is, and where the Triborough Bridge is. I then showed him my proposed route through the Queens Midtown Tunnel at Thirty-fourth Street and the expressways beyond. One look changed his mind. I had him at his terminal in twenty minutes. He gave me an extra tip for being honest and for setting him straight.

Finally, taxi drivers never pull over to the curb when picking up or discharging passengers. This is true even when there is plenty of room at the curb. Drivers simply stop in a traffic lane and make all the drivers behind them wait while passengers pay their fares and get out or new passengers enter.

Taxi drivers live in a world all their own. I've never seen one, but I'm sure there's a manual, that New York taxicab drivers operate by, entitled "Fifty Ways to Make Life Miserable for Non-Taxicab Drivers and Pedestrians." As a chauffeur, I experienced all fifty many times.

A sixth pitfall centers on thieves who can strip a car in minutes. Therefore, most chauffeurs are instructed to stay close to their limos at night and keep an eye on them. Thus, eating places are chosen carefully. The ideal ones are those that have well-lighted parking areas and tables near the windows, where drivers can sit and keep an eye on their limos while eating. Luckily, I found a few such places, or I would have starved.

A seventh pitfall involves the prostitutes who roam the streets looking for business. Many nights, while I was waiting for customers who were eating in fancy restaurants or attending Broadway productions, prostitutes, dressed fit to kill, walked by and offered their services to me. My usual answer was, "No thanks. I'm on a job." One night, in response to my answer, a lovely, well-dressed prostitute remarked, "That's okay. We can do it in the back of your limo." I politely declined, but it was a wee bit tempting. She was really cute.

An eighth pitfall centers on the biological need to go to the bathroom when nature calls. As a chauffeur, it was often not possible to do this. Bathrooms were not that readily available. When nature called, I had four options. I could hold it in. I could use a jar that I kept in my limo. I could drive to a place where I could safely park and leave the limo unattended. Finally, I could take a chance and leave the limo where it was parked, run to the nearest building, find a bathroom, and hope I'd be back before the limo was ticketed. I used all four at various times. However, the fourth option cost me twenty-five dollars one morning.

It was 8:05 A.M. I was on Second Avenue heading for the Waldorf-Astoria on Park Avenue. I noticed that my favorite bagel luncheonette was coming up on my left. I needed to go to the bathroom, and I needed something to eat. Even through it was illegal to park on this avenue after 8:00 A.M., I pulled up in front of the luncheonette and parked. I jumped out, ran into the luncheonette, ordered two cinnamon-raisin bagels to go, ran down a few stairs to the bathroom, used it, ran back up the stairs, put forty cents on the counter, grabbed my bagels and ran out the door to my limo. I was gone no more than three minutes. Yet a brownie had just finished writing a ticket and was putting it under the windshield wiper on the driver's side.

In response to my plea for mercy, the officer expressed his sorrow and insisted there was nothing he could do, since the ticket had already been written. He also mentioned that if my flashers had been on, he would have assumed that I would be back shortly and would not have ticketed the limo. That mistake cost me twenty-five dollars. Now that it's in the past, I sometimes joke about my two $12.70 bagels.

I had learned an important lesson. From that day on, whenever I found myself in similar circumstances, I left the flashers on, and I put a sign on the dash of the driver's side. It stated, "Driver gone to the bathroom. Be right back. Please do NOT ticket. Thanks." And no officer did.

All limousine drivers agree that it's virtually impossible to drive in and around New York City for any length of time and not get one or more traffic and/or parking tickets. Since the company I drove for made each chauffeur pay for any tickets received, I tried very hard not to get any. After paying the first one for illegal parking on Second Avenue, I tried even harder. But I received others. Some I deserved, others I didn't.

One afternoon, I was sent to the city to chauffeur five executives from the same company in Cincinnati, Ohio, back to their plane at Teterboro Airport. Their meeting ran longer than expected, so we were late heading back. As we approached the heavy, stop and go traffic leading to the Lincoln Tunnel, one executive asked me to try and make it back to their plane by

5:30. If I did, their pilot wouldn't have to file a new flight plan. I responded, "I'll try."

I finally inched my way to the entrance of the middle tube of the tunnel and began crawling through it behind the slow moving lane of cars, trucks, and buses. Traffic in the opposite lane was coming into New York City with no delays. We were in the tunnel only a short time, when I noticed traffic in the opposite lane had ceased. I glanced at my watch and saw that it was 5:05. Then I looked up and saw that the red lights in the opposite lane had changed to green. I knew then that both lanes were now outbound lanes. However, with a double yellow line in the tunnel, I knew I should not change lanes, and I stayed where I was. About halfway through, three cars in front of me changed lanes, and I did too. All four cars picked up speed, and soon the exit came into view. I knew, then, that we'd make it to the airport on time with no sweat.

As soon as the cars hit daylight, a traffic officer was there and motioned to all four drivers to pull to the left off the roadway. As I did so, I wondered how he knew we had changed lanes. The question no sooner entered my mind when I looked in my rear view mirror and saw a yellow and blue police car exit the tunnel in our lane with traffic behind it. Then I knew. Whenever such a lane direction change is made in the tunnel, the first car through is a police car for safety. I knew all four of us drivers were caught red-handed. As I waited for my ticket to be written, the five executives said nothing to me. They just talked quietly among themselves.

Several minutes later, we were able to continue on our way. My effort had been in vain, and I had the ticket to prove it. Finally, one man asked me how much the fine would be. I answered, "Twenty five dollars." At that moment, I thought maybe each of the five would kick in $5.00 toward it, since I was trying to get them to their plane on time. None did, and I paid the fine out of my wages.

After this episode, I made the following resolution. Whenever anyone would ask me to do anything that could or would cause me to break the law while driving, I'd say to the person, "I'll be glad to, if you'll lend me your driver's license before I begin. Then, if I get pulled over, I can give your license to the police officer." It worked. I never received another ticket with passengers in my limousine.

One afternoon, I was inching my way across Forty-second Street to a pick up on Park Avenue. I was in no hurry, so I wasn't fussing and fuming over the heavier than usual traffic. After what seemed like an eternity, I neared Fifth Avenue. Another green light, and I'd cross one of the busiest intersections in Manhattan. The light changed, and I slowly started through the intersection behind the cars in front of me. More than halfway through, I had to stop abruptly. A truck, alongside the curb ahead, suddenly pulled into our lane of traffic. By the time traffic began to crawl again, I was still in the intersection. The light changed to red, and my long limo was blocking two lanes of southbound traffic on Fifth Avenue.

I knew it was illegal to make a right turn onto Fifth Avenue during this time period, yet I realized my predicament. I made a quick decision, turned the wheel sharply and headed south on Fifth Avenue. I knew I could turn on Fortieth Street and continue to my destination.

A policeman was standing on the corner. He saw what I did and must have known why. Yet he ran to his car, jumped in and overtook me before I reached Park Avenue. I pled my case, as he wrote my ticket. My words fell on deaf ears. All he kept saying was, "This is only a summons, not a conviction." At that point, I was sorry I had made the turn. Had I stayed on Forty-second Street and waited until I could move again, I would have received no ticket. But many drivers would have been very angry and would have vented their wrath verbally. However, I would have saved twenty-five dollars.

I could have taken a day off from work to appear in court, and I might have won. However, the Christmas rush was in full swing, and I couldn't afford to. I would lose too many trips, the day I'd spend in court. So I paid the fine, but Mr. Niceguy was through being nice.

In the long run, I was fortunate. I met chauffeurs who paid hundreds of dollars each year for traffic and parking tickets. As one chauffeur explained to me, "It's part of the job, and there's little you can do about it." He was correct, but it's an expensive part.

New York City is a mecca for tourists. There are a few cities like it anywhere in the world. Imagine seeing camels walking up Sixth Avenue early on a December morning and wondering where they came from, only to find out later, that they're part of the live Nativity scene at the spectacular Radio City Music Hall Christmas program. Imagine seeing an older woman on a street corner entertaining passersby with a large snake, her pet, wrapped around her body. And, for only a little money anyone can have it wrapped around his or hers, while a camera clicks and another hard-to-believe photograph is taken for viewers back home.

Imagine a bundled up, homeless man, in the bitter cold of a winter's night, sitting on a sidewalk grate. He's kept warm by the heat coming through the grate. As you watch, unnoticed by him, he drinks his beer.

Every so often, he carefully opens his pants, urinates through the grate, closes his pants and continues drinking.

These are just a few of the oddities I saw while driving limousines. Thousands more occur everyday. They're all part of the life in this teeming city of millions. It's a city that never sleeps. It offers excitement twenty-four hours a day.

On occasion, I would be assigned to show tourists the highlights of the city, especially the borough of Manhattan. Prior to doing this the first time, I made a list of places that I assumed tourists would enjoy seeing. Included were Central Park, Lincoln Center, Carnegie Hall, Madison Square Garden, Empire State Building, World Trade Center, Statue of Liberty, New York Stock Exchange, United Nations, Rockefeller Center (especially during the Christmas season), and a few of the hundred museums. Once tourists were comfortably seated in my limo, I'd hand them my list to read. A bit later, I'd ask if there were others they'd like to add. Almost without exception, there were five: Harlem, Forty-second Street and Times Square, the Bowery and Chinatown. Finally, a trip to the "Big Apple" wouldn't be complete without taking a ride on its famous, crime-infested, graffiti-scarred subway system. Thus, it was also added.

One day in August, I took a couple on the "grand tour." Besides all the items on my list, including their additions, we saw a purse snatcher run in front of my car followed by three policemen trying to catch him. We saw a Toyota commercial being filmed during the days when red, five gallon gas cans were an integral part of such ads. And we saw a demonstration outside the Irish Embassy by IRA supporters. At the end of the long day, I asked the couple, what they enjoyed seeing the most. Without hesitation, they agreed on the purse snatcher, the commercial being shot, and the demonstration. Not even their ride on the subway could top these three.

Who said tourists to the "Big Apple" lack culture? I must confess, not all of them do. One time, I took three women to the Metropolitan Museum of Art. They spent about thirty minutes inside before returning to the limo. According to what they told me, they would have stayed longer, but they were not allowed to take photographs. And what good are cameras if they can't be used on a vacation at will? I smiled to myself, as I continued their tour.

One evening in 1981, I was reading a well-known weekly magazine. A list of the one hundred highest paid executives appeared in it. The top salary was 1.4 million and the lowest fell somewhere in the 500–600 thousand dollar range. I noticed that the executive at the top of the list was one I had chauffeured many times. So I took a pen, read down the list and put a check mark next to each executive's name whom I had chauffeured many times. When I finished, I counted forty check marks.

Then I looked again at each name, placed it with a face and recalled all I could about the person. When I had completed this process forty times, one fact stood out beyond all the others. Only one had ever given me a cash tip out of his pocket. All of them had signed the charge tickets, billing their companies for the costs, and a few had even put in a twenty percent tip instead of the normal fifteen percent. But only one had ever reached into his pocket and had given me his own money in addition to the tip on the charge ticket. That one was W. H. Krome George, Chief Executive Officer of ALCOA.

I recalled meeting his company plane many times in the late afternoon, driving him to the Links Club for a dinner meeting and waiting for him. Often, when he'd come out, he'd get in the front passenger's seat and remark, "I don't feel like riding back there. I'll sit up here, so we can talk."

And talk we did. He'd often mention the pleasure he found working in his wood shop at home; the therapy of working with his hands after working with his mind on his job. He used this time to get rid of the stress built up each day as CEO of ALCOA. I learned a great deal about ALCOA, in particular, and the aluminum industry, in general, during our chats.

Every time he'd exit from my limo at the airport, he'd thank me and sign the charge ticket. Then he'd dig down into his pocket and hand me ten or twenty dollars before boarding his plane. I always appreciated his generosity and told him so.

I was not unhappy with the fifteen or twenty percent tips automatically charged to the various companies, whose personnel I chauffeured. It was the fact that an additional cash tip by an individual always made me feel that my service was appreciated by him personally. And an extra ten or twenty dollars here and there certainly helped my financial situation at home.

There were certain customers who always gave cash instead of a tip on the charge ticket. Edward DeBartolo, Sr., was one. His normal cash tip was fifty dollars for a partial or full day of chauffeuring. However, one evening, he and his wife had dinner at the home of friends in Connecticut. We arrived back at the Westchester County Airport at 10:50. Before boarding his plane, Mr. DeBartolo apologized for keeping me out so late on a job and handed me a hundred dollar bill. In my line of work, 10:50 was not late. But, being the kind of person he is, he showed his appreciation through his words and tip. And I appreciated both.

There were individuals who always gave cash in addition to the tip on the charge ticket. Golfer Arnold Palmer and country singer Kenny Rogers are two examples.

Whenever Kenny Rogers would come to New York City, he'd reserve two or three limousines to handle his party. Once his plane had landed at Teterboro Airport, and the limos were ready to leave for the city, he'd greet each driver, introduce himself, hand each driver a fifty dollar bill and instruct each to put a twenty-five percent tip on the charge ticket for each day the limos were used by him or members of his party during their stay in the "Big Apple." I found both Kenny and his wife, Marianne (Marianne Gordon was a regular on the TV program, "Hee-Haw") to be likeable, caring, fun-loving, and down-to-earth people; the type anyone would enjoy having as next door neighbors.

I've often been asked what my biggest tips were. Two come to mind.

One weekend, I had a Saudi Arabian prince, his U.S.-based aide/bodyguard and three of the aide's friends. I met them Saturday afternoon at LaGuardia Airport and drove them to the Waldorf-Astoria Hotel. When I arrived, I drove into the covered entrance, known as the tunnel, where passengers with luggage were discharged. As I was unloading their luggage, the aide mentioned that he would like me to stand by in this area, so the limo would be readily available when needed.

I quickly explained that no cars, including limos, were allowed to park or stand in this area due to the heavy volume of traffic coming and going. Then I pointed to a fellow not far from where we were standing. "See that fellow over there? He's in charge, and he's very strict about the rules here." I no sooner got those words out of my mouth when the aide walked over to the man, spoke to him as he pointed my way, handed him some money, returned to me and reported, "I've just arranged to have you stand by, as much as you need to, this evening and tomorrow."

With that he turned and entered the hotel. I pulled forward away from the doors, parked my limo, got out and leaned against it. As my eyes met those of the man in charge, he winked at me in approval. Whoever said, "Money talks," was certainly correct.

That evening, I drove the aide's friends to a Broadway theater, waited, and then drove them back to the hotel. From there, I headed back to base and home.

Sunday morning I took the aide's friends sight-seeing. In the afternoon, I took them to another Broadway theater to see "Sweeney Todd." After dropping them off, I headed for a McDonald's not far away.

It being Sunday, I was able to park my limo just down the street from my destination but right in front of an illegal, three-card monte scam. As I was returning to my car with an ice-cream cone in hand, I stopped to watch the two hustlers strip people of their money. A third kept both eyes open, constantly watching for any policemen who might be walking or driving their way.

As I watched the black teenager do his thing with the three cards, I was sure I could pick out the black card from the two red ones once he stopped shuffling them on his wooden box table top. And I did, in my mind, three times in a row while other suckers lost money. Finally, I was the only sucker left. They baited the hook, and I bit.

With complete confidence that I could win, I took a twenty-dollar bill out of my wallet and threw it down onto the table. The dealer shuffled the cards. I kept my eyes glued to all three as he did so. When he finished, I greedily reached down and flipped over my winning black card only to discover a red card staring at me. How could this be?

Though my confidence was shaken a little, I told myself that I still could win, so I plunked down another twenty. The cards were shuffled again under my watchful eyes. The shuffling completed, I reached down, knowing for sure which card was the black one. With a smirk of triumph on my face, I flipped it over. There, to my horror, was another red card. The dealer, wearing a broad smile, quickly snatched my twenty dollars and prodded me to try again.

At that point, anyone in his right mind would have licked his wounds and walked away, but not me. I wanted my money back plus some of theirs. I walked to my limo, opened the trunk, reached into my secret hiding place and took a fifty dollar bill out of the five hundred dollar advance given me by the aide toward the rental cost of the limo.

I quickly retraced my steps and when it was my turn again, I placed the entire fifty on the table. Seeing the fifty, the dealer's eyes sparkled and his white teeth glistened through another broad smile. Then the smile left his face, as he concentrated on flinging the three cards back and forth, back and forth until the shuffle was completed. The entire time, I watched intently. When he stopped, I knew I had pulled out a much needed victory. I wanted to shout, "Hallelujah" as I reached down and flipped over my winner. Aghast, I saw another red card! The dealer's reaction was pure joy as he stuffed my fifty dollars into his pants pocket. My reaction was pure bewilderment and defeat.

Suddenly, the full realization of what I had done hit me like a ton of bricks. Smile gone, confidence destroyed, humiliated beyond belief and soundly defeated, I turned and walked slowly back to my limo. I got in and just sat there thinking. I asked myself, "How could I have been so stupid?" I had heard many times about the three-card monte scam, had seen many people lose money in it, and should have known better. Now ninety dollars poorer and very upset with myself, I drove back to the theater to wait for my passengers. I only hoped my tip would be a big one, since I owed my boss fifty dollars.

Once my passengers were safely back at the Waldorf, I stood by and waited for my next trip. At seven o'clock, the prince and his aide came out, entered the limo and instructed me to drive them to JFK Airport. Once we arrived, I waited until the prince boarded a 747 and his aide returned to the limo. I drove the aide back to the Waldorf, then carried both him and his luggage to another hotel nearby. By now, it was close to ten o'clock, and I was standing in the lobby of the new hotel waiting for new instructions.

Instead of giving me any, he asked me how much the bill was at that point. After some quick calculations, I answered, "Four hundred, seventy-five dollars." He quickly laid his briefcase on a counter near where we were standing, unlocked and opened it. I immediately saw two pistols. The aide must have seen the surprised look on my face for he uttered, "Yes, they're both loaded and ready for use. After all, I have two jobs in one. I'm the aide to the prince, and I'm also his bodyguard whenever he comes to America. Don't worry, Dave, I won't shoot you." With that he laughed, reached in, took out some cash, closed the briefcase, and locked it.

Then he turned to me and told me to keep the remaining twenty-five dollars of the advance. Then he handed me an additional $300, thanked me for a job well done, bade me good-bye, turned and briskly walked towards the elevators. I quickly caught up to him, thanked him sincerely, then left the hotel walking on air! And who, in the same situation, wouldn't have?

One evening at home, I received a phone call from John Nagle, a pilot friend of mine. Before moving to a new job in Houston, Texas, he and his wife had lived in New Jersey. Laura had taught second grade in the same school as Shelley. Now John was a pilot for a Texas oil man and business was booming. John called me to tell me that he was flying into Teterboro

Airport on the following Tuesday afternoon with four passengers including his boss, Milton Jones. He told me that he had already called the limousine service I worked for, and requested me to chauffeur his party. Knowing the generosity of his boss, John assured me that I would be tipped well if I performed well. I thanked him and waited for Tuesday to arrive. Now and then, I wondered just how good a tipper his boss would be. I'm not a greedy person at heart, but what John had said caused me to contemplate this.

Late Tuesday afternoon, I was given the assignment. I met the plane as it taxied to a stop, greeted John who then introduced me to his four passengers. The two men were true Texans right down to their fancy boots and accents. I'm sure the two women were true Texans also, but I couldn't tell by the way they were dressed: no hats, no boots, just expensive clothes on two pretty Texas belles. But their Texas accents and mannerisms soon gave them away.

From the very beginning, I enjoyed being their chauffeur. Therefore, I put my "best foot forward." It was 2:00 A.M. Wednesday when I finally dropped them off at their hotel. Mr. Jones mentioned that he needed the limo at 9:30 that morning. Then he thanked me, handed me a hundred dollar bill and insisted I add the normal fifteen percent to his charge ticket. I thanked him, bade them all good night, and headed for New Jersey. I was a little richer but very tired, and I knew the night would be a short one.

That morning I was at their hotel on time and stayed with them until 2:00 P.M. Mr. Jones handed me another hundred dollar bill and gave me the afternoon off. However, I was to be at their hotel at 7:45 that evening. John had been correct. His boss did tip well, very, very well.

That night, after a Broadway play and lengthy dinner at the 21 Club, I returned my friends to their hotel. Once again I was given a hundred dollar bill, thanked, and told to add fifteen percent to the charge ticket. With Christmas coming on, these hundred dollar bills would mean a Merry, MERRY Christmas!

Thursday morning I took the four of them to Wall Street and later to the New York Stock Exchange. While they were at the Exchange, I made a luncheon reservation at historical Fraunces Tavern in lower Manhattan. After a busy morning in the business world, the four thoroughly enjoyed lunch in the same place that George Washington bade farewell to the officers in the Continental Army after the Revolutionary War ended.

Their visit to the "Big Apple" ended with lunch. I soon had them back at their plane. Before boarding, each thanked me, and Mr. Jones pressed another hundred dollar bill into my palm with a final reminder to add the normal fifteen percent to the charge ticket. I was overwhelmed by his generosity and told him so. He listened attentively then smiled and declared, "Dave, you earned it." With that he boarded his plane. Before taxiing away from the terminal, John opened a side window in the cockpit and yelled, "I'll let you know when we'll be coming again." I waved as he closed the window and turned the plane toward the runway. With the four hundred dollars in bills and the ninety-three dollars on the charge tickets, I knew in my heart that it would be a very Merry, Merry, Merry Christmas. And it was!

Mr. Jones did fly in quite often after that, but his stays were usually shorter. On occasion, I would meet his plane and drive him to a meeting in New York City. As he'd exit from the limo, he'd ask, "Dave, do you mind checking my bag in at my hotel?" I'd answer, "Of course not." Then he'd reach into his pocket, pull out his clip of money, peel off a hundred dollar bill, hand it to me and say, "Thanks a lot. I appreciate it." To this day, I'm sure he doesn't know just how much I appreciated his generosity. Back then I was glad he was doing so well in the oil business, and I hope he still is today.

As a chauffeur, I had a great many wait and return assignments similar to the ones mentioned in the preceding pages. Some lasted a few hours, some all day and others several days. My job was to have my limo ready for use at any given time. At times, I waited several hours without moving the limo at all. At other times, I'd be busy driving my passengers here and there all day. It was while I was waiting outside various hotels and restaurants that I met such celebrities as John Ritter, Dinah Shore, Lawrence Welk, Henry Cabot Lodge, John Forsythe, Imelda Marcos, Ed McMahon, Andy Williams, Walter Cronkite, Ted Kennedy and Jacob Javits.

Some of my wait and return assignments afforded me many interesting and humorous memories. One morning I was sent to the Regency Hotel on Park Avenue to pick up an executive I had never driven before. I was to chauffeur him around for several hours, then return him to his company's plane at Teterboro. I arrived at the Regency quite early and parked alongside the curb. I could see the entrance to the hotel clearly, so I moved to the front passenger's seat and began to read a morning paper. Even though my party was not due for another half hour, I'd look up every so often to see who might be going in or coming out of the hotel.

At one point, a bearded man dressed in weird clothes came out. He raised his arm, signaled, and soon a maroon limo pulled up and he got in.

As it drove away, I thought to myself, *Probably a member of some rock group in town*. Then I went back to my reading.

When I looked up again, I saw three men about to walk past my limo. I recognized the one in the middle as former President Richard Nixon. I immediately recalled what Rose Marie had expressed to me some months before. "Buddy, if you ever meet President Nixon, get his autograph for me. I'll frame it and hang it in my kitchen." Thus, I threw open the door and jumped out.

All three were startled. Then the two men, flanking Nixon, quickly reached inside their suitcoats. Unknown to me at the moment, they were Secret Service Agents assigned to protect Mr. Nixon. I soon realized they were reaching for their guns, thinking I was a threat to Mr. Nixon's life. However, they quickly sized up the situation and didn't draw.

Mr. Nixon stopped, and I introduced myself. We shook hands, chatted a few minutes, and then I asked him for his autograph for Rose Marie. He gladly agreed. I gave him paper, pen and her name, and he began writing, "To Rose Marie Hess . . . " I don't recall the rest of what he wrote, but when she received it from me, she framed it and proudly hung it in her kitchen.

After I thanked him, we chatted a little more then shook hands and said our good-byes. He continued on his way as I stood there watching him walk up Park Avenue. Seeing him go, I recalled both the good and bad events in his administration.

It was now time to meet my party, and I noticed a well-dressed man standing in front of the hotel. I walked down to where he was standing, introduced myself, told him who I was looking for, and asked if he was the person. He politely answered that he wasn't. Thus, I walked back to my limo, leaned against the passenger's side and waited for someone else to emerge from the hotel.

As I did so, another limo driver, parked two cars behind mine, walked up and started talking to me. Soon he asked if I had seen Sylvester Stallone come out of the Regency about a half hour before. I responded that I hadn't. Then he questioned me, "Didn't you see the guy with a beard come out and get into the maroon limo?" I answered with a question of my own, "Was that Stallone? I thought he was a member of a rock band." The other driver laughed then informed me that Stallone was in New York City filming one of his movies; a movie I've seen twice since that day.

We then chatted about my visit with Mr. Nixon and the autograph he wrote for my sister. He had seen me jump out of my car and was sure the

Secret Service agents were going to shoot me. Why he laughed after he said that, I'll never know.

He finally asked what I was talking to Erik Estrada about in front of the Regency. I assured him that I had not talked to Estrada, but he insisted I had. Then it dawned on me. Estrada was the man I approached about being my party. However, I hadn't recognized him, and he hadn't given me his name during our brief conversation. I remarked to the other driver, "So that was Erik Estrada, the star of the TV program, CHiPs, and I didn't even recognize him. How about that! I wonder if he felt insulted?"

At that point, another man came out of the hotel. Since I had to check and see if this man was my passenger, I ended our conversation and headed toward the hotel entrance. The man was my party, and soon we were on our way to his first appointment. As I drove, I murmured to myself, "So far it's been an interesting day."

On another wait and return, I was assigned to chauffeur the Chief Executive Officer (CEO) of a large motel-hotel chain and his wife for three days. During that time, he had several important business meetings to attend but was not on time for any of them. It was not my fault. The limo would be waiting for him, and I would allow plenty of time to get him where he needed to be. But he'd already be late by the time he would come out of his hotel and climb into the limo. Even at night, when he and his wife went out on the town, they would be late getting to the theater, a restaurant or wherever else they might be going.

On more than one occasion, I asked myself, "How can this man be CEO of this chain of motels-hotels and never be on time for any of his meetings?" They were both charming people, and I enjoyed my three days with them. But punctual they were not.

A few months later, I was reading a news magazine. An interesting article caught my eye. It contained a list of people in the U.S. who owned great amounts of stock in the various companies with which they were associated. I read down the list, past the Gettys, Hiltons and others, until my eyes fell upon the name of this CEO. What I noticed amazed me. The previous year, this CEO owned $117,000,000 worth of his company's stock, and his dividend that year was $11,000,000. The question I had asked months before had been answered. I suppose, if I had that amount of dividend income in one year, I wouldn't be too concerned about punctuality at meetings either.

Quite often, wives of executives accompany their husbands to New York City. While their husbands tend to business affairs, the wives shop, eat, explore a museum, or do whatever suits their fancies. As a chauffeur, I would often spend the day taking them to well-known stores. On occasion, I would be asked if I knew of places in the vast garment district that sold top quality clothes at discounted prices. I did and would take women, who asked, there. One such outlet was on Twenty-sixth Street near Seventh Avenue. Once there, most women would shop to their heart's content.

One day I was leaning against my limo waiting for two women when two men, pushing a rack of beautiful, full length, imitation fur coats, came out of a nearby factory building and headed for a parked truck. As they passed near me, I exclaimed, "My wife would sure like one of those coats!" Without any hesitation, one of the men shot back, "Twenty bucks and it's yours." I'm sure he was serious, but I declined the offer. It would be stealing, and I knew both would probably lose their jobs if caught. But what a bargain it would have been—a Christmas present par excellence!

The ladies eventually returned, huffing and puffing, full shopping bags in each hand. They were ecstatic at their good fortune. As I put their treasures into the trunk, I saw one woman's sales slip sticking out of one bag. It was for over $1800. I gulped in amazement.

On another occasion, I took two different women there and was sitting in my limo listening to some music. Soon after they entered the store, a short Jewish man came out, hurried over to my window and rapped on it. As soon as I opened it, he asked, "Did you bring customers to my store?" I responded with a "Yes." Immediately he reached into his pants pocket, took out some bills, handed me ten dollars and exclaimed, "You take care of me, I take care of you!" I thanked him. As he turned and began to walk back to his store, he suddenly returned to my window and asked, "Did the man in the car in front of you bring customers to my store?" I answered, "I don't know, but he probably did." With that, he turned and quickly walked to the other car. I saw the driver's window go down and money pass from the store owner to the driver. Then he turned and hurried back into his store.

Almost immediately, the large, black man got out of his pink Cadillac and sauntered back to my car. He asked, "Do you know why that man gave me this ten dollar bill?" I told him, and when I finished, he began to laugh heartily. Finally, he remarked, "I didn't bring him any customers. I just parked here so my wife could walk to the corner and buy two shishkebabs from the vendor there." After his explanation, I also laughed. But that's the way life is in the "Big Apple." One hand always feeds the other, right or wrong.

Soon the ladies returned empty handed. The prices were still too high for them. However, I didn't feel guilty about taking the ten dollars. Instead, I recalled all the other women I had taken there, including the one who spent over $1,800.

That evening, I took these same two shoppers and their husbands to the 21 Club on Fifty-second Street for dinner. Later, on the way back to the airport, I overheard one of the women ask her husband, "How much was it, honey?" His nonchalant reply, "Oh, four hundred dollars." To this she responded, "Gee, maybe I shouldn't have had those raspberries on my ice cream for five dollars."

After hearing this conversation, I smiled to myself and recalled an important lesson. It's not how much money one has, it's how much one enjoys the money. I had certainly enjoyed my $3.50 dinner that evening, paid for with part of my ten dollar gift. But did she enjoy those raspberries?

"Of all the celebrities you chauffeured, who was your favorite and why?" These two questions have been asked more than any others by those who learned of my chauffeuring days in New York City. The answer is easy: former football great, O. J. Simpson or, to many, "The Juice."

I recall clearly the afternoon of the day I was assigned to be his chauffeur for a week. I was sitting in the chauffeur's lounge, waiting for my next assignment, when I was called to the office by Peter, the young dispatcher. He gave me the assignment with excitement in his voice. Once his instructions were completed, he begged me to get O.J.'s autograph for him. Since Peter was a football fanatic, I knew he coveted my assignment, so I promised him I would. I left the office and headed for New York.

As I drove, I recalled O.J.'s great career as a running back for the University of Southern California in the 1960s. I recalled his years in the National Football League, including the season he ran for over 2,000 yards; a record still unsurpassed. I recalled the Sunday I watched TV and saw him, a member of the Buffalo Bills, run as hard as ever in a blinding snowstorm, seeking to score yet another touchdown for his team. I recalled his short-lived career with the San Francisco Forty Niners and his retirement caused by physical disabilities. I knew that someday he would be inducted into the Football Hall of Fame and, since that day, he has. Other thoughts went through my mind as well. The accidental death of one of his children, his divorce, his TV commercials for a rental car company, and his roles in various TV programs and movies were some of them.

By the time I reached his hotel and stood outside his room ready to knock on his door, I was as excited to meet this idol of millions as Peter was for his autograph. I rapped and waited. Presently the door opened and there stood O.J., a mere mortal, half awake, unshaven and bare chested. He smiled. I smiled. We introduced ourselves, and soon we were chatting like old friends in the comfort of his room.

After a few minutes, I felt O.J. was a special person and my friend, so I asked him a personal question: "Do you miss playing football?" He pondered my question for a few seconds, smiled and answered, "Dave, if you were a running back in the NFL, and every time you carried the ball, you knew at least 750 to 1,000 pounds of muscle wanted to pounce on you and, in some cases, tear your head off, would you miss it?" I immediately answered, "Not one bit." O.J. finally admitted he missed the glory but not the weekly practices, the soreness after each game, and the other negatives. But now that his playing career was over, he looked forward to what the future held for him.

The first time he left his hotel and walked to my limo, I began to realize just how special he was. An older man passed him, turned around and quickly retraced his steps. He asked O.J., "Aren't you The Juice?" O.J. smiled, admitted he was and shook the man's extended hand. They chatted a bit. Then O.J. wrote something on a piece of paper, signed it, handed it to the man, shook his hand again and entered the limo. I knew we were on a time schedule, yet O.J. took time with this stranger.

This was to be his pattern again and again. He never snubbed anyone who recognized him, even though he would arrive a bit late, now and then, for an appointment. Eventually I asked O.J. about this. He said, "Dave, people have given me my success, and they can take it away. I owe them a great deal."

I spent parts of several days chauffeuring O.J.'s girlfriend (now his wife) and model, Nicole Brown, to modeling agencies around Manhattan. Since each agency provided clothes for her to wear during her photo session, she'd come out of the hotel each morning wearing jogging shorts, a blouse, and jogging shoes. Whenever I'd drop her off near an agency, she'd jog to the entrance of the building. All the nearby men, young and old, would stop, watch her jog until she entered the building and then smile broadly to each other or to themselves. She was a real cutie, and they all recognized this.

The week was flying by, and soon Friday evening arrived. O.J., Nicole, and another couple were going to relax and enjoy a night on the town. After a late dinner, I drove them to the Mistique, a disco on First Avenue.

As I stood outside my limo enjoying the cool night air, an old, black man came down the sidewalk. As he slowly approached, I could see he was a real down and outer in need of a bath, a shave, and clean, untattered clothes. He came over to me and, with breath that reeked of alcohol, asked, "What big shot do you have tonight?" When I answered, "O.J. Simpson," he got excited and inquired when O.J. would be back. I confessed I didn't know.

We began to chat, and soon Bill was telling me his life story. Since I had no place to go, I listened and enjoyed what he had to share. I realized life had been good to him at times, even though it wasn't good now.

Just as Bill was ready to move on, O.J. and his party came along. Bill's eyes lit up and his wide, toothless smile appeared as I said, "O.J., I'd like you to meet a new friend of mine. O.J., this is Bill. Bill, meet O.J. Simpson." Without any hesitation, O.J. took Bill's hand in his and shook it heartily. He then politely introduced Nicole and the other couple.

While the other three entered the limo, O.J. stood there talking and laughing with Bill as if they'd known each other for years,. When their conversation ended, they shook hands again then Bill turned and walked away as O.J. entered the limo. I pulled away from the curb and beeped my horn as we slowly passed Bill. He turned and waved, a broad smile on his face. We all waved back. Once again, O.J. had given a small part of himself to another human being.

We headed for the Xenon Disco on Forty-third Street. When I reached Fifth Avenue, I headed south and soon stopped for a red light. Our windows were open and O.J. was clearly visible, since he was sitting on the jump seat, behind me, next to a window. A young black woman, sitting in the passenger's seat in the car to the left of ours, looked our way, and suddenly her eyes opened wide in excitement. She turned to her companion and exclaimed loudly, as she pointed, "I think that's O.J. Simpson. I think that's O.J. Simpson!! Look over there! Isn't that him?"

The light changed, and we proceeded to the next red light. The same car stopped next to ours, and the excited woman looked our way and asked me, "Is that O.J. Simpson?" I nodded, "Yes." Then she became more excited, as only certain women can do.

The light changed to green, and I continued down the avenue. By now everyone in the limo was enjoying the occasion, especially O.J. He leaned over and whispered into my ear, "Dave, if we meet that car again, ask the young lady if she'd like my autograph." I said that I would.

At another red light, we met again. I quickly yelled to the woman, "At the next red light, I'll pull closer to your car. Have some paper and a pen ready, and O.J. will give you his autograph if you'd like it."

"He will? He will?" she shouted. "I'll have it ready. Oh! Oh! O.J.'s autograph!"

A few blocks later at another red light, I pulled close. She handed pen and paper over to me. After swapping a few words with her, he began to write. The light changed to green then back to red, and O.J. kept writing. Neither car moved, and, miraculously, no one behind either car honked. Finally O.J. finished, handed the paper to me, and I passed it to her. She read it quickly, screamed excitedly, blew him a kiss and drove away.

We continued on to the Xenon. About 3:30, two men, walking by, stopped and one asked, "Who ya drivin, pal?" When I answered "O.J. Simpson," they didn't believe me, so I showed them the charge ticket that O.J. had already signed. "When's he comin' out?" was their next question. When I responded, "I don't know," they decided to hang around for a while. In the course of our conversation, I learned that they were truckers and had to be at a terminal in New Jersey by 5:30 to begin their run.

When five o'clock rolled around and O.J. still hadn't appeared, they gave me a message for him and left. They allowed themselves just enough time to get to the terminal on time. When O.J. and his party came out at 5:15, I was sorry these two fans had missed him. However, I delivered their message to O.J., and he smiled in appreciation.

Sunday morning I drove O.J. and Nicole to the airport. En route, O.J. complied to my request for Peter and wrote more than his autograph. After reading it, I knew Peter would be ecstatic.

At the airport, he and Nicole thanked me, and O.J. slipped an envelope into my hand. After our parting good-byes, both turned and walked into the terminal. I returned to my limo and opened the envelope. Inside was a hundred dollar bill and a note which read:

To my friend, Dave,
Thanks,
O.J. Simpson.

Almost from the very first time I met him, I knew O.J. was a special person. He had shown me it was true in many ways and at many times all week. And now I knew he was also my friend.

One morning in early May 1979, Joe, Nick, and I were sitting in the chauffeur's lounge waiting to be sent out on our next jobs. During our conversation, Joe mentioned something about the approaching prom season. Soon he and Nick were having a great time recalling some of the past proms assigned to them. Being a new chauffeur, I was all ears and enjoyed the humorous and not so humorous stories they shared. Nick's favorite expression was, "You wouldn't believe . . . " and then he'd go on to tell a preposterous tale about drinking, drugs, and/or females, that happened on a prom he'd driven. Some you wouldn't believe, unless you knew him as well as I did.

Neither one enjoyed working proms for various reasons. Since the owner gave special rates to prom-going young people, the tips were about half the normal amount. Second, most prom assignments lasted all night. Finally, a driver never knew what to expect from the young people: what they'd do or how they'd act—good, bad, or somewhere in between.

The basic rules, established by the owner, allowed almost anything. However, if any physical damage was done to the limo, an additional charge was levied. For example, if someone vomited inside the limo, a forty dollar charge was levied. It was as simple as that. Get drunk, use drugs, have sex, but don't damage the limo or else!

Based on the number of limos I saw while doing my first prom, I realized how important a part they played each spring. From a safety standpoint, I'm sure many lives of drunk and high teenagers have been saved, simply because they were being driven and not driving themselves. The monetary price was small since a limo could easily transport three couples. And at the reduced rate, it was a real bargain. I'm sure many parents gladly paid for the limos to put their minds at ease.

As a chauffeur, I had my share of proms each spring. I soon found that most of what Joe and Nick had kidded about was true. Some young people drank, some smoked marijuana, but, apart from holding hands and an occasional kiss, no sex ever took place, and no one ever vomited. But all couples laughed, talked, sang, and thoroughly enjoyed themselves.

Whenever my boss decided to send me on a prom assignment, he never told me in advance. The news usually reached me over my radio as I was returning to base at the end of a long day on the road. "Head over to Jersey City and call me from a pay phone when you get there." Such a message almost always meant a prom. And the call back to base on a pay phone confirmed it.

After working all day, I did not look forward to working all night on a prom assignment. After I'd arrive back at base early the next morning, I'd catch an hour or two of sleep on a short sofa in the chauffeur's lounge. Then I'd get up, wash, shave, put on clean underwear, socks, and white shirt. Once ready for work, I'd soon be on the road again and would grab a bite to eat as soon as I was able.

Of all the proms I drove, one stands out in my mind. It was a hot, humid, June evening. I was sent to Jersey City. The address led me to a large project of high-rise buildings. Try as I might, I could not find the correct one.

I slowly circled the project twice and was about to circle it again, when I saw two, tall, good looking, black teenagers walking toward the street. They were dressed in suits and carrying corsage boxes. I quickly pulled over to the curb and waited for them to reach me. I soon discovered they were half my party.

Once they were in the limo, I asked, "Where to, gentlemen?" One responded, "Driver, you have to climb the curb here and drive on the wide sidewalks to get to our dates. There are no streets in the project, and our girls live in buildings near the center."

As crazy as it sounds, I did as requested and followed his directions. "Turn left at the garbage cans, turn right after the small playground, another right after the next building . . . " I soon found myself in the middle of the project and also in the middle of hundreds of black and Hispanic tenants from very young to very old. The young were playing various games, while the teenagers and adults were standing around talking, laughing and enjoying the relief from their hot apartments.

No one seemed to mind the presence of my limo as I drove up, stopped, got out and opened a rear door, so one fellow could fetch his date. As I stood there, countless eyes were looking my way. I thought to myself, *I wonder what Abe Lincoln would think and say if he were here?* As I continued to wait, a little girl stood near the limo. Presently, she reached out and touched it. Immediately her mother slapped her hand and scolded, "Don't put your greasy hand on that clean car!" The girl wanted to cry but didn't. I felt sorry for her, but no one else came near the limo. The one slap warned everyone away.

After what seemed like an eternity, the fellow and his pretty date appeared. Once they were seated in the limo, I headed for the next stop. Another wait and then both couples were ready to enjoy their senior prom with all its glitter and glamour.

I carefully drove out of the project, off the curb and into the street. Soon I arrived at the prom location. It was not at their high school, like mine had been. Instead, it was a dinner dance at a large, fancy restaurant that catered only to private functions such as proms and wedding receptions. After depositing my two Prince Charmings and their dates at the entrance to their ball, I left, got something to eat and returned. I parked my limo near several others, chatted with other drivers, listened to my radio, catnapped and waited for the hours to pass. They did but very slowly.

Around 1:00 A.M., couples began leaving and soon mine were in the limo. To them, the night was young. Following their instructions, I headed for Manhattan. They wanted to party at one of the discos. I knew this was the standard operating procedure for most prom couples in and around New York City, so I headed that way.

After arriving in Manhattan, I was directed to several discos. At each, the two males got out, entered the disco, returned shortly, and reentered the limo. My suspicions were soon confirmed as I pieced together what I heard from their whispering. The discos were too expensive.

I was then directed to an old-time dance hall. Once the fellows returned, I heard more whispering. The gist of what was said impressed me. If they went dancing, they would not have enough money left to pay me my full tip.

After more whispering, one fellow instructed me to drive around Central Park and anywhere else I cared to, until it was time to return to Jersey City. Hearing this new instruction, I knew my tip was assured, and that made me feel good. However, their decision to assure it, made me feel even better.

I did as requested. Shortly after entering Central Park, their talking and laughing ceased. Like most teenagers, I figured, they were "making out." I looked in the rear view mirror to see if my suspicion was correct. It wasn't. All four were sitting there, heads on the backs of their seats, sound asleep. I smiled to myself and kept driving.

In the wee hours of the morning, I headed back to Jersey City and their project. When I climbed the curb, all four woke up, and one gave me directions. Before dropping anyone off, they all thanked me and gave me my full tip. In return, I thanked them for my tip, congratulated them for being such nice, young people and wished them well in the future.

As I drove back to base and the sofa that awaited me, I had a warm, happy feeling. The events of that prom have remained in my memory for a long time.

Chapter XXIV
Working and Playing in the Grand Teton National Park

I stood in the parking lot of my motel in Jackson, Wyoming, gazing at the snow-covered mountains. It was the middle of May 1982. My heart beat with excitement as I anticipated the four and a half months of work that lay ahead in the Grand Teton National Park.

As I gazed, I recalled the first time my family and I visited the Tetons. Most mountain ranges prepare travelers, like us, with their foothills. The Tetons seem to have none. Instead the forty mile-long range soars suddenly and full blown above a broad valley. Below, the Snake River curls past sparkling lakes and sun-splashed meadows. That first visit was a short one, but others followed.

Now, after months of anticipation, I was here, finally here, looking forward to my job as a boat wrangler at Colter Bay Marina near the north end of the park on Jackson Lake. During previous visits, I had stood near the tackle shop at the marina and had looked out over Colter Bay, filled with boats of all sizes, Jackson Lake beyond and then the snow-patched Tetons, dominated by 12,605 foot Mt. Moran in my line of vision. It is one of the most beautiful scenes in the world, and now I was to enjoy it for several months. How lucky could I be?

Tomorrow I would drive to Jackson Lake Lodge, check in, and then continue on to Colter Bay, my new home away from home. I felt like a child again, anticipating the excitement of what was to come, and the expected joys it would offer.

Early the next day, I checked in then drove to Colter Bay. There were piles of snow everywhere and few paths, even to the dorms, thanks to late snowstorms. However, I managed to carry my belongings in without falling, and soon my half of room B-7 in North Dorm was organized. I had a place for everything and everything was in its place. I only hoped my roommate would be as neat.

Early the next morning, I was sitting in a chair, bent over, tying my shoe laces. When I straightened up and looked across the room to the two, full-length, side by side windows, an adult moose looked back at me. He stood sideways, framing the windows, with his head turned looking in. I sat motionless and groaned internally. Had my camera not been in my car, I could have taken a photograph of man and beast staring each other down. As it was, I could only sit there and watch the moose rub its nose against one window pane and then lick it. Finally, the moose turned, ambled down a path near the parking lot and disappeared into the woods. I'd seen moose before but never one so close. If only I'd had my camera. What lousy luck!

I learned later that moose are plentiful in the Grand Teton National Park. I saw many of them that summer, some even near the marina. However, one unhappy visitor to the park wrote to the head of the company I worked for and complained, "My family and I came to the GTNP expecting to see at least one moose. We didn't see any. I think you ought to import more moose, so tourists like us won't be disappointed."

When I arrived at the marina for my first day of work, I was surprised at what I saw. Instead of a bay filled with water, I saw little water and the floating docks covered with several inches of ice. I asked myself, "How can there be so little water in the bay, when the Tetons are covered with snow and the runoff from them fills the lakes and bays and feeds the rivers in the park?" My question was soon answered. I was informed that a huge amount of runoff was yet to come. Therefore, park officials had opened Jackson Lake Dam allowing the lake level to remain especially low until the anticipated runoff could fill the lake and bays without putting undue stress on the dam itself. However, with so much runoff yet to come, the lake would remain low and Colter Bay would eventually lose all its water until the crisis passed sometime in June.

Once the crisis passed, the dam would be partly closed, the lake would be filled to a safe level, and Colter Bay would gradually return to its peak summer depth of roughly fourteen feet. In the interim, the marina would open on a limited basis the end of May. Therefore, there was plenty of work to do, and few people to do it.

Later that morning, Dick Rightmer, the marina manager, handed me an aluminum, straight-edge shovel and asked me to clear the docks of the ice and snow. I soon found the task virtually impossible using such a shovel. I needed a steel, sharp, long-handled ice chopper or a steel spade to do the job easier, but neither was available. So I hacked away the best I could, making slow, but sure, progress. It was tiring work, but I kept at it all morning and into the afternoon.

Around 2:30, I took a break and walked to the tackle shop for a cup of coffee. I was sitting on a bench outside with Dick, and Harold May, the boat mechanic, when along came another dock worker. Doug had returned for a second season, and this was his first day on the job. Why he was reporting for work at 2:45 instead of 8:00 A.M. was beyond me.

I finished my coffee and returned to the dock I was working on before my break. I assumed Dick would send Doug to help me, but for the next hour and a half, the three of them sat there talking and having a good time. While they did so, I continued chopping at the concrete-hard ice, breaking off piece after piece and pushing it into the shallow water.

From this early experience, I began to learn that Doug, and some others like him in their early twenties, were goof-offs and would do next to nothing on the job. In fact, at a later time, Doug asked me, "Why do you work so hard? You're only supposed to do as little as possible, draw your pay and have fun." My answer to him was, "Doug, I believe in giving my employer an honest day's work for an honest day's pay." For the entire season, both of us stuck to our work ethics.

There were others at the marina that had mine and worked hard, and there were some that followed Doug's and did very little. The thing that bothered me the most was the fact that Dick and Ray Sullivan, the assistant manager, knew, yet did nothing about it. None of the goof-offs were reprimanded in any way or fired. Two of the worst were Tammy, who had a hangover most of the time, and Dom, who would sneak onto one of the tour boats, whenever he had early morning duty on the docks, and sleep, while others did his share of work, cleaning canoes and rowboats and doing other duties.

By the end of that first day, all three docks were free of ice and snow. I dragged my weary body back to my room and, after a long shower and supper, went to bed exhausted.

The next morning, Ken McCormick, a twenty-two year old, reported for work at the marina. Since Doug had been sent to the grocery store to stock shelves, Ken and I became a two-man team following Dick's orders. Our first task was to repair several minnow traps then load them and bread, for bait, into a rowboat. We then positioned the baited traps in the shallow water around the bay.

After we finished, we reported back to Dick. He handed each of us a pair of long wading boots and a pitchfork. We were to wade through the water around the docks, gather lakeweed, put it on the docks, then later use a wheelbarrow to move the piles up the steep dock ramps and dump them along the road parallel to the bay. From there, it would eventually be loaded onto a truck and carted away.

While putting on the boots, I found mine to be much too small, causing pain, while Ken's were much too large, giving him trouble walking and keeping his balance in the water. However, since our shoe sizes were the same, swapping boots would not solve anything. We informed Dick about our problem with the boots. But did he care? Not on your life. His only concern was getting the tremendous amount of lakeweed away from the docks and out of the bay, while the water level was so low. Neither Ken's nor my comfort interested him in the least.

All morning we sloshed around in the water, carrying pitchfork after pitchfork of lakeweed to the nearest dock and depositing it there. Slowly, we built up sizable piles.

About a half hour before lunch, we left the water, stuck the pitchforks into a pile of weed, shed our boots and climbed into our rowboat. We returned to each minnow trap and emptied its contents into a five-gallon pail partly full of water. Once emptied, we added new bread to each trap and lowered it back into the water. Once we were back on shore, we put twelve to thirteen minnows into a small, plastic bag. Once all the minnows were bagged, we placed the bags into the freezer at the rear of the tackle shop.

After lunch, more lakeweed was pitched onto the docks and later taken to the road in wheelbarrows. In the late afternoon, the minnow procedure was repeated. That first day we bagged about 1,200 minnows.

For several days, this routine continued, alternating between the lakeweed and minnow jobs. Then one morning, we headed for the traps. Our pail was ready to receive the catch. The first trap was empty, but we took it in stride and headed for the second. However, the second trap was also empty, as was the third. As we headed for the fourth, both of us aired reasons for this but did not conclude anything. To our chagrin, none of the twenty traps contained a single minnow. As we rowed back to shore, we saw a few dead trout in the water but thought nothing strange about this.

Once back at the shop, we met Harold and told him the bad news. Harold replied that he wasn't surprised. With the water level in the bay and in the channel connecting the bay to the lake dropping lower and lower, the minnows knew it was time to leave the bay and head for the lake or face certain death. The dead fish waited too long to escape and paid the ultimate price. Harold finally assured us that minnows would return later in the summer.

By now a good supply of frozen minnows was ready for avid fishermen seeking such bait. Since live minnows cannot be used by fishermen in Wyoming, frozen minnows are readily bought, quickly thawed, and then used to catch some of the biggest trout caught anywhere in the United States.

Once the minnows left, our main task was limited to the lakeweed removal, a job both Ken and I disliked. As the days came and went, the piles along the road grew higher and higher, longer and longer. There were tons of it there and still more in the bay. We often asked ourselves, would we ever change jobs?

Two days after the minnows left, Ken and I arrived for work and discovered an empty car parked several yards into the bay. Mud and water were covering its lower part. Its position, in relation to the boat launching ramp, led us to speculate that its driver had mistaken the ramp for a road and had driven into the bay. But why he had continued forward until his car sank into the mud and stalled, was a mystery to both of us.

With our boots on, we approached the car and noticed a GTLC employee sticker on the windshield. I repeated its number several times out loud, then we headed back to shore. After giving the number to Dick, one phone call and the owner was identified. He was a young male dishwasher at Colter Bay. Once he was reached, he was ordered to the marina.

When he arrived, he told his sad tale. He was new to Colter Bay and had driven down the ramp by mistake. Since he could not back his car out, he had no choice but to leave it there. After listening patiently, Dick gave the owner until 5:00 P.M. to have the car towed out of the bay or else. By the designated hour, it was gone. That evening, upon returning to the dorm area, I saw the car being washed by its owner. I stopped to chat a few minutes. I learned then that the fellow had been drunk the night before and didn't know where he was driving until it was too late to stop and back out. He laughed as he spoke, and I laughed as I listened.

As the Memorial Day weekend approached, we were finally taken off the lakeweed detail. Canoes and rowboats had to be moved from their winter storage building to the bay and cleaned. Three larger boats, used for guided fishing trips, and the two, fifty-passenger, tour boats had to be cleaned, washed, and waxed. A myriad of other jobs also needed to be done, but with no water in the bay, the official opening of the marina would not be on the traditional Memorial Day weekend but sometime in June.

Therefore, the marina crew remained at a minimum. The rest had been reassigned to other jobs around Colter Bay Village until the marina would be in full operation.

Friday morning, May 28, I woke up and peered out the window. To my surprise, about two inches of fresh snow covered the landscape. "Great," I complained to myself. "Just what we need, more snow." After getting ready for work, I grabbed my camera and joined Dee Lehman and Nancy Perry. We headed for the cafeteria, stopping, now and then, so I could take a picture.

After a hearty breakfast, I walked to the marina. The sun was peeking through the clouds. Its rays, on the new fallen snow, added to the beauty of the morning. I stopped and took another picture here and another there.

At the marina, I peered out over the lake toward the mountains. Through the pass, on each side of Mt. Moran, dark storm clouds were heading toward the marina. "Would this new storm bring more snow?" My question was answered before lunchtime rolled around. The storm arrived and snow began to fall. Work was stopped for lunch then canceled. The snow continued all afternoon and into the night.

Saturday morning dawned clear and sunny. Thick snow lay everywhere. The scenery was so breathtaking, I took picture after picture in an effort to capture, forever, the beauty all around Colter Bay Village.

Arriving at the marina, I took a few more pictures then put my camera away and began to work. I began shoveling the docks off, pausing every now and then to look at the blue, blue lake and sky, the green trees coated with snow and the snow-covered mountains. I realized, anew, how very lucky I was to be working in such a picturesque setting. This realization brought a song to my lips and a lift to my spirit. I was truly grateful to be here, whatever job I was given.

By Memorial Day, most of the snow at our level had melted, but the mountains remained completely white. Work at the marina continued slowly but surely. The tackle shop opened for business and the marina, itself, opened on a very small scale. It didn't take long for avid fishermen to discover how great the fishing was. Whether from shore or from boats, anglers were catching large trout. Thus, the tackle shop did a brisk business, from the day it opened, selling, among other items, many bags of minnows.

One customer was a young lady named Judy, a fellow employee. Since she worked at Jenny Lake Lodge near Jenny and Leigh Lakes, she enjoyed fishing there. The Lodge was still closed but being readied for opening day by its small staff.

She decided to try her luck one more time before the hustle and bustle began in her area of the park. On a Sunday morning, with gear in hand and knapsack on her back, she gingerly walked to secluded Leigh Lake, meeting no one along the trail. Arriving, she quickly baited her hook and began fishing, hoping to catch a few trout for a staff cookout that evening.

A few minutes passed, when the stillness was broken by twigs being stepped on. "Someone else coming to fish," Judy thought. "I'll enjoy the company." She turned around to greet the newcomer and froze in horror. A huge, black bear was heading her way. She remained motionless, hoping the bear hadn't seen or smelled her. She knew it would be futile to run, so she stood there, pondering what to do if the bear came her way.

Suddenly, the bear reared up on its hind legs and headed her way. As Judy later related it, "I knew I was a goner for sure. There was no way I could escape. So I decided to slowly reach down, pick up my knapsack and throw it in the direction of the advancing bear. I hoped it would distract my potential attacker long enough for me to run behind the nearest tree, bend down and kiss my derriere goodbye. For I knew I was going to die."

As these thoughts raced through her mind, the bear kept coming to within ten feet of her. Then, for no apparent reason, it dropped down on all four paws, turned and ambled back into the woods. Judy didn't stick around to see if it would return.

One evening early in June, I was reading an interesting article on the Teton Mountain Range. The word, Teton, in French means breast. Some of the higher peaks look like breasts including the highest at 13,770 feet. Thus, the Frenchman who named the range, named the highest the Grand Teton (The Grand Breast).

A couple of mornings later while working on the main dock, I saw a married couple I knew walk into the tackle shop. I presumed they were going to buy bait and go fishing. Soon after they entered, I heard sounds of laughter. My curiosity aroused, I decided it was time for a coffee break. I stopped what I was doing, walked up the ramp and into the shop. What I saw made me laugh. His wife, whose breasts were the size of two eggs fried, was wearing a T-shirt that stated, "Not all Tetons are Grand!"

As more and more staff arrived, the four employee dorms were becoming alive with activity. The lower level of North Dorm was for males, the upper for females. Since I was one of the first employees to arrive, I made an attempt to meet and welcome each new fellow who moved into the dorm.

One was Roger Yost, soon to be known to me as "Crazy Roger." He was a farm boy from Ohio, tall, lean, strong, and adventurous. He had a terrific sense of humor and laughed at all my jokes, good or bad. He was not afraid of work, a quality I appreciated in him. His main fault, if it can be called that, centered on girls. He was girl crazy and tried to put the make on any pretty girl he met. He considered himself a twenty-two-year-old stud. We soon became good friends and enjoyed daily bull sessions.

During our early conversations, he'd say, "Dusty and I did this . . . " or "Dusty and I did that . . . " I hadn't met Dusty as yet and wondered who he was and in what dorm he was living. I knew there was no one with that name living in North. Finally, I asked Roger when he was going to introduce me to Dusty. He laughed then informed me that Dusty was his car, an old, Plymouth *Duster*. Hearing Roger extol the virtues of Dusty made me recall my first car with nostalgia, only I hadn't give mine a name.

Roger disappeared his first two days off from his job as a busboy in the coffee shop. I had no idea where he and Dusty had gone, or why, and no one else in the dorm did either. When I saw him again, he was all smiles and wearing a new polo shirt. The message, in large letters, on the front proclaimed, "NO GUTS, NO GLORY!" The one on the back, "Why ski a mountain when you can ski a skillet?" Having read his shirt, I knew now where Roger had been, and he confirmed it, filling in all the details.

High up on Mt. Moran there's a large glacier shaped like a skillet (frying pan). The "handle" extends far up the mountain from the large round basin. It was no secret that skiers often crossed Jackson Lake by boat and spent many hours scaling the mountain with loaded backpacks, sleeping bags, ski boots, poles and skis. Why? Simply to experience the thrill of a ten-minute ski run down the handle and across the basin of the skillet. Then the remainder of the two-day adventure was spent descending the mountain, recrossing the lake and returning to civilization.

Roger had heard about this two-day trip and managed to go on one. I enjoyed hearing him tell of his adventure, especially the skiing part. According to Roger, he was having a great run, enjoying the thrill of it and the beauty of Jackson Lake far below. All of a sudden, a large boulder, moving faster than he, rumbled past, knocking his right ski pole onto the air. Roger immediately realized how close death had been; a mere yard to the right, and he would have been a goner. Shaking, he stopped to rest, enjoy the scenery, regain his composure and go to the bathroom, a normal result of sudden fear. Several minutes later, he continued the run and arrived safely at the bottom of the skillet, rejoining the others already there.

As he finished his tale, I looked again at his original shirt, his tribute to himself. However, I could sense the fear he had experienced, and I knew he would never ski the skillet again, and he didn't.

* * *

Day after day in June, the hot sun continued to melt the snow on the mountains, and the clear, icy-cold water rushed down to the streams, rivers and lakes below. Jackson Lake Dam remained open through the first half of June. Then it was partially closed, allowing the lake and all the connecting bays to fill. As the official opening of Colter Bay Marina neared, the entire staff was finally brought together for orientation and training.

Nancy Perry, a cute blonde, was raised in Charleston, South Carolina. She had attended both a private, girls' high school and college. She had had the normal, fancy, coming-out party and possessed all the trappings of a true southern belle. However, the Nancy I knew and grew fond of had no southern accent, unless someone said, "Nancy, talk southern." Then she'd continue her conversation in a true southern manner for a short time and then laugh heartily. Nancy could swear with the best of them, had a tremendous sense of humor, loved jokes, enjoyed adventurous outings and had a laugh I'll never forget. She enjoyed cigarettes and beer and mentioned to me on one occasion, "You know, Dave, I'd kill for beer." She loved parties and would be the first one to arrive and the last to leave. She was not only a true life-of-the-party person, she was a good worker and fun to work with.

Tom Moulton was one of the fishing guides. He was raised in the West and was taught early in life to hunt and fish. He was a simple mountain man who enjoyed hearing and telling jokes whenever the time was right. In my estimation, he was the most successful guide. He seemed to know where the fish would be in the vast depths of Jackson Lake. Most of the fishermen he took out caught their limit. Once back at the marina, Tom would clean the fish at a rapid pace, knowing exactly where to make each cut.

Dave Feezer was a real thorn in my flesh. He was also a fishing guide but enjoyed drinking beer, flirting with girls, and bothering me more than his job. He was also raised in the West and had eaten many buffalo steaks in his lifetime. In the fall, he worked as a hunting guide and had many humorous tales to tell of experiences he had had while guiding hunters from big cities on excursions into the wilderness. Once, when a bird flew over my head, and its droppings landed on me, Dave remarked to the whole world, "It's a good thing cows don't fly!"

There were many others on the staff, but these three, plus Ken, were the most unique.

Boat wranglers, like myself, had a large number of duties to perform. Some were simple, others involved specific training. All were necessary for the smooth and safe operation of the marina. As the training wound down, and the bay filled up, the marina finally opened officially, catering to the whims of thousands of vacationers.

Like all marinas, Colter Bay was a continual beehive of activity from early morning until late in the evening. There were canoes, rowboats, and motorboats to rent. The guided fishing boats were coming and going. The two tour boats, filled with happy vacationers, made several trips each day. Those who rented buoys for their boats, relied on us dock workers for ferry service to and from their boats. And there were always plenty of people who came to the marina to sit and enjoy the beauty.

Canoes were rented by a wide range of people, from novices to experts. Therefore, it was not uncommon to see novices tip over or beach canoes soon after leaving the dock, especially on days when wind was a factor. One calm day, two young women in their twenties, both very overweight and with shapes like pears, rented a canoe. I tried to change their minds and rent them a motorboat, but to no avail.

After I put their pocketbooks, cameras, and cans of soda into the canoe, they got in. They listened to my instructions rather impatiently and were "biting at the bit," so to speak. I finally untied the mooring rope from the dock cleat, gave the canoe a little shove away from the dock and watched. Almost immediately the canoe began to sway as the women began their journey across the bay. Less then twenty feet from the dock, they lost their equilibrium, and the canoe tipped over, sending its contents and screaming passengers into the cold water. I wanted to laugh but contained myself until the women were safely on shore, their belongings fished out of the water and the canoe righted and returned to the dock. Then, seeing the humor in what had just happened, the women broke into gales of laughter. Several wranglers and tourists, who had seen the entire incident, joined them.

Much of the time Jackson Lake is as smooth as glass. Other times light winds cause ripples. However, there are times when sudden storms come through the mountain passes and move across the lake with ferocious intensity. In minutes, such storms turn the calm lake into one with large waves. Together, the winds and waves spell danger to all boaters, especially those in canoes, rowboats, motorboats, and sailboats. Therefore, those who rent small vessels are instructed not to cross the lake. They are also instructed to stay within a safe distance of the lake's shoreline. Both instructions plus a few others, are very necessary for their well-being.

Late one beautiful, calm, Sunday afternoon, early in the season, the marina was extremely busy. All the rentals, plus many other boats of various sizes, were on the lake. Around 5:30, I walked the short distance to the employee's cafeteria, filled my tray and took a seat near the windows. I was almost finished eating, when a sudden windstorm came out of nowhere. I sat there a few minutes and watched as pine tree after pine tree was blown over, many landing on cabins nestled among them.

I hurried back to the marina, and the scene that greeted my eyes amazed me. Instead of beaching their rentals along the lake's shoreline, and waiting out the storm (as instructed prior to leaving the dock), most sought the safety of the bay. This caused a massive traffic jam in the long, narrow channel that connected the bay to the lake. Several canoes had capsized in the channel, and their occupants now stood on the adjacent banks. I'm sure they were cold but glad to be alive. Several rowboats and many motorboats had been beached near to and along the channel banks. However, in their haste to reach land, most of the operators of the motorboats had forgotten to tilt the small motors out of the water before beaching the boats. Therefore, I assumed damage had been done to some, if not all, the propellers and other lower parts.

A few people in canoes were too far out in the lake when the storm hit. They were saved from drowning by occupants of larger boats that just happened to be in the right spots at the right times.

Within a half hour, the storm abated and the lake calmed down. Luckily no one had been seriously injured, and no one had drowned. However, many had lost possessions. It took the boat wranglers until sunset to retrieve all the rentals that had been beached or had capsized. By closing time, things were back to normal.

During July and August, other windstorms followed. After one such storm in the late afternoon, one of the motorboats finally arrived back at the dock. Two very scared and very drunk fishermen were in it. They had ventured across the lake and were fishing, drinking, and having a great time when the storm struck. Instead of going to the nearest shore and waiting the storm out, they foolishly headed for the marina.

As they were crossing the wave-tossed lake, the fear of drowning gripped them. To calm their fears, they kept passing a bottle of booze back and forth until it was emptied. Somehow, they were able to overcome the strong wind and the large waves lashing their boat and make it back to the dock. As they sat there, catching their breath, the wind died down, and the storm abated.

Thirty minutes later, they felt calm and composed enough to leave the boat. However, in their alcoholic condition, stepping from the boat onto the dock was a bit unnerving for both. Thus, they were given helping hands by the wranglers on duty. They were physically unable to carry their fishing gear and ice chest to their car, and they paid two of us ten dollars each to do so. The last time I saw them, they were walking slowly and unsteadily up the path toward their car. I only hoped they would sleep it off before driving back to their cabin.

A similar storm and a similar situation occurred several days later. Only this time it was getting dark when the small motorboat arrived back at the dock. A family of five was in it, including two small children and a tiny baby. One look told me that the wife and children were scared to death. But not the husband.

He was all smiles and in a state of jubilation over his catch of trout. Perhaps he had been scared, while crossing the storm-tossed lake, and hadn't let his family know it. But he showed no signs of fear now, only joy at his catch.

As I lifted the two children out of the boat, I could feel their small bodies shaking, so I whispered words of assurance into their ears and kissed each on the cheek. Holding their small hands in mine, I walked with them across the dock, up the ramp and into the tackle shop. Their parents and baby sister soon joined them. Before leaving the shop, both children gave me a hug and a kiss.

As I walked back to the dock, I wondered how this traumatic experience would affect the children in the years to come. Would they grow up with a fear of participating in water activities? Would they dread going out on bodies of water in boats? I could ask myself such questions, but I would never learn the answers. I could only hope that this one incident would not leave a lasting scar on either of them.

One evening one of the larger boats, used for guided fishing trips, was anchored off Elk Island. It had been used to transport food and supplies to the island for a steak fry. Now it was empty. A sudden storm came up, and soon large waves began to lash the boat. The combined efforts of the wind and waves caused the boat to roll upside down. When it was discovered, it was floating with just the bottom showing a tiny bit above the surface of the water. Shortly after the storm abated, it was towed back to the marina.

After two days of deliberations, a plan was set in action, and it was righted. Surprisingly both the large and small outboard motors had remained intact throughout the ordeal. Once it was righted, Harold faced the monumental task of tearing down, cleaning and reassembling both motors before permanent damage would result. The task of caring for the boat was left in the hands of the wranglers.

Not all days were calm and serene, and not all storms were sudden. There were days when a light breeze blew, and there were days when storms occurred but with ample warning. However, unless the winds were strong and the lake especially rough, business went on as usual.

On calm days we had our share of motorboat renters who didn't listen well enough to our instructions and often wound up banging into other motorboats, ramming the dock, running ashore, or a combination of the three. We had the most difficulty teaching people who spoke little or no English how to operate our small seven and a half or nine horsepower motors, and explaining the "rules of the road" in the bay and on the lake. On days when wind was a factor, our problems were compounded and often chaos resulted.

Since the winds generally came from the west, boats would be blown toward the shoreline of the marina and not away from it. Canoes and motorboats were often victims of the wind as they pulled away from the dock. Inexperience and sudden fright by the operators often sent the vessels pell-mell toward shore, when the operators really wanted to go in the opposite direction. Some succeeded in reversing their direction and happily headed out toward the channel and the lake beyond. Others, not so lucky, found themselves on shore with bewildered looks on their faces but eager to try again. However, after their first failure, they listened very attentively to the repeated instructions. Most succeeded in their second attempt to conquer the rigors of boating on Jackson Lake. A few never did, and I felt sorry for them.

Inexperienced boat operators were not the only victims of the wind. One windy day, one of our tour boat pilots approached the dock from the right side. His intent was to park the empty boat parallel to the end of the dock and tie up there until his next trip. As he came nearer and nearer, I told Nancy and Tammy, "I'm going to stand far away from that section of dock, just in case Ben goofs." The words no sooner left my mouth, when Ben misjudged the force of the wind and his location. The nose of the boat hit the floating dock; slid up on it; sent the stairs, used when boarding passengers, flying; and finally stopped. The surprised and shocked look on his face was worth a thousand words. I will never forget it. After a quick examination of the boat for damage, none was found. Therefore, the pilot reversed his engines and slowly left the partly submerged section of dock. His second attempt to park the boat was successful.

Once the red-faced pilot exited both the boat and the dock, we enjoyed the humor in the accident and couldn't wait to tell other employees what had happened. I'm sure everyone thought it was funny except Ben. Perhaps his goof was the reason he returned the following year as a security officer and not as a tour boat pilot. However, this is only speculation on my part.

All summer, fishermen of every age invaded the lake. Some sought relaxation and a few fish each day for eating. Others sought large fish, hoping to have their names immortalized by the size of one large, record-breaking trout.

Late one afternoon I was returning to the marina after eating supper. As the main dock came into view, I looked toward it. From the lack of activity, I knew something was wrong, but what? As my eyes moved to the end of the dock, I saw someone lying there, and a wrangler performing CPR while others looked on. I ran to the dock to assist. When I reached the victim, I stopped and was stunned. Jack, another of our tour boat pilots, lay there. His wife was standing nearby, and Nancy was comforting her.

Soon a man hurried down the ramp and walked quickly to the end of the dock. He identified himself as a doctor. He bent down, examined Jack's vital signs, and pronounced him dead. Jack was quickly covered with a blanket until he could be legally moved off the dock.

I went over to his wife to console her and said, "You have my deepest sympathy. Jack was a good man and a good friend. I'm going to miss him." She looked at me, tears streaming down her face, and uttered a comment that I was not prepared for. I'm sure she noticed the shocked look on my face as she turned and walked away. I never found out whether her words were uttered out of anger at Jack for dying so suddenly, or if she really felt that way.

I learned later what had happened the day Jack died. Even though Jack and his wife knew it was against the rules to cross the lake in one of our motorboats, they did so to relax and fish in Jack's favorite spot. While they finished, the boat drifted slowly into an area containing a lot of lakeweed. When they decided it was time to head for home, Jack attempted to start the motor. He pulled on the starting cord several times with no success. He then remarked to his wife that he needed to clean the lakeweed away from the propeller in order to start the motor.

He leaned over the motor and stayed in that position. When he didn't respond verbally to his wife's question a minute or so later, she knew something was wrong. She managed to pull him into the boat and away from the motor. Then she tried to start it but couldn't. A quick examination of Jack's vital signs sent chills up her spine. She knew her husband was in serious trouble.

In a fit of panic, she grabbed an orange life jacket, stood up in the boat, waved the jacket and cried for help, praying that someone on a larger boat would see and/or hear and respond. One soon did and came to her aid. Jack was tall and heavyset and could not be lifted from the motorboat into the larger rescue boat. Therefore, the motorboat had to be towed back to the dock. This took additional valuable minutes. En route, Jack's wife performed CPR on him as well as she could. After arriving at the dock, approximately forty-five minutes after Jack's attack, wranglers took over. But it was too late, Jack was gone.

Ironically Jack had experienced chest pains on and off the preceding few days before his final attack. He not only mentioned this to his wife, who suggested he see a doctor, he mentioned it to others, including me. He was sure it was nothing serious, only indigestion from the food he was eating in the employee's cafeteria. How wrong he had been!

About a week later, the coroner from Jackson came out to spend an afternoon in his boat on the lake. While I gassed his boat, our conversation turned to Jack's death. The coroner informed me that the autopsy showed Jack had suffered several small heart attacks prior to his fatal one. As the coroner put it, "If Jack had gone to a doctor when the pains first began, he most likely would be alive today." I don't know if his wife was ever given this piece of information, but I was determined not to do so, and I never did.

Among the serious fishermen who kept boats moored in Colter Bay, there was one couple more serious than any of the others. They had fancy equipment on their boat, which they used to track schools of fish. When fishing, they used steel line, so large fish wouldn't have a chance to escape once hooked.

Late one afternoon, he pulled their boat up to the end of the main dock and secured two ropes, fore and aft, to the cleats. I stopped cleaning the blood-spattered motorboat I was sitting in, and headed toward their boat. I had to inform them that a tour boat was due any minute and needed to dock where they were.

A few steps into my short walk, I saw the man bend down and then straighten up again. In his hands was a large trout weighing twenty to twenty-five pounds. Without showing any joyous emotions, he tossed the fish onto the dock. I thought to myself, "How odd! Any other fisherman would be dancing a jig over such a catch. Yet he showed no emotion at all."

As I neared his boat, I exclaimed excitedly, "That's some fish! Did you catch it?" He replied, he had, yet he still showed no jubilant emotions. Then, before I could say anything else, he asked me to help him a minute on the boat. I obliged and hopped aboard.

I saw his wife standing nearby, smiling from ear to ear. At her feet lay the largest mackinaw trout I had ever seen. No one had to tell me that she had caught it. Her husband's lack of joyous emotions and hers, bubbling over, told me. Together, we lifted the fish onto the dock and laid it next to his. Even though his was large, hers dwarfed it. After they thanked me for the help, I delivered my message then returned to the motorboat and continued washing the blood off the inside. This bloody mess was made by fishermen gutting their fish inside the boat, while still on the lake.

By the time I was finished, the two fish and the couple were gone. Their boat was tied to their assigned buoy. The next day I heard the news. The trout caught by the woman measured forty-nine inches in length and weighed forty-nine pounds. It was the largest mackinaw trout ever caught in Wyoming. The woman had succeeded in getting her name in the record books, her picture with her catch in the newspaper and on television, and her feat was mentioned on several radio stations. However, no one ever mentioned that it had been caught on steel line; the poor fish never had a chance once it had been hooked. I'm sure it was stuffed and hung over the fireplace in their home. Or maybe it wasn't, since the man of the house didn't catch it. After all, his wife was not a woman of the eighties and that might have made all the difference in the world as to what eventually happened to her record-setting fish. For all I know, he might have cleaned, filleted, fried and served it to several friends at a backyard picnic. Not being a man of the eighties myself, I wouldn't have blamed him if he had.

According to Glenn, the senior tour boat pilot, the most important jobs for the wranglers were to assist people boarding a tour boat, prior to departure; being on the end of the dock when a tour boat returned, ready to catch the mooring lines and quickly secure them to the dock cleats; then assisting passengers off the boat. Few employees at the marina agreed with Glenn's priorities, but rather than face his temper outbursts and verbal abuse, the wranglers agreed to his demands and did as ordered.

Early one morning, I was on duty, assisting people who were boarding for the Elk Island Breakfast Cruise. Near the end of the line were three half-awake female employees whom I knew. As they boarded, I did my best to change their, "What are we doing here this early in the morning when we could still be in our comfortable beds," expressions—but to no avail. With Glenn at the helm, the boat departed, and I began cleaning canoes, rowboats, and motorboats. Every now and then, I'd look around, breathe deeply, and enjoy the start of another perfect day at Colter Bay. My cleaning chores were interrupted several times by early risers. They were eager to rent canoes and paddle across the mirror-smooth bay and into the tranquil lake, hoping to see some wildlife on shore, as they glided silently through the water, cameras ready for action.

A few minutes before nine, I saw the tour boat in the bay. It was moving toward the dock, weaving its way past several boats moored to buoys. It soon arrived alongside the dock and the stern mooring line was thrown to me. I quickly grabbed it, looped it once around a cleat and tugged on it in order to bring the stern closer to the dock before securing the line to the cleat. To my surprise, as I tugged, the line slipped off the cleat. I lost my balance and did a less-than-perfect dive into the cold, clear water.

Surfacing quickly, I climbed back onto the dock near the stern of the boat, hat still on my head, glasses still on my nose. People on the boat, who had seen what happened, were laughing—including my three half-awake friends. One came near and declared in a rather loud voice, "Gee Dave, you didn't have to go to that extreme to make us smile!" Her comment made me laugh. I realized the joke was on me, and I took it in stride.

I put the stairs in place, and the passengers began to disembark. Some, who were told what happened but did not see it, asked me to do it again, so they could take pictures. Others just snickered, while many laughed heartily. As I stood there, dripping wet, I saw the humor in my accident and maintained my composure.

As soon as possible, I hurried off the dock, trails of laughter behind me, and was granted permission to go to my room. Once there, I emptied my wallet and spread its wet contents on my bed to dry. Then I changed clothes and shoes and hung the wet ones up to dry. When I returned to the dock, I discovered instant fame had befallen me and would last for several days. I took it in stride but made sure another reason for fame would not occur, at least not at the marina.

Elk Island, a wilderness area in Jackson Lake, is a good distance by boat from Colter Bay. It was here that the hungry passengers on the daily breakfast cruises and the twice-weekly steak-fry cruises stopped to eat. Being a wilderness area, no permanent structures could be erected. Therefore, everything, except the two outhouses, had to be taken out each spring from the mainland and returned each fall.

Dana DeWitt was in charge of the Elk Island activities, plus he was the chief cook. Each morning a different wrangler would be assigned the Elk Island duty. This was also true for the evening steak fries. At 5:30 A.M., Dana and the wrangler would meet at the main Colter Bay kitchen, assemble everything needed, load it onto an old truck, drive the short distance to the marina, carry everything down the ramp to the dock and load it into an aluminum boat with a twenty-five horsepower motor attached.

Once loaded, the boat moved as silently as possible across the bay, through the channel, and into the lake. The throttle was then opened, and a fast trip was made to the dock at the island. Here everything was unloaded and carted or carried to the "kitchen and dining room." Then preparations were begun in earnest.

When the hungry vacationers arrived, delicious aromas filled their nostrils. Coffee was brewing over a campfire in blackened, old western, antique coffeepots. Dana's specially prepared home-fried potatoes, lake trout, and scrambled eggs were all cooking in large pans on a makeshift gas stove.

A table nearby was laden with trays, cups, silverware, napkins, pitchers of cold orange juice, tea bags, packages of cocoa, and trays of sweet rolls. Picnic tables were ready to be used. Red and white checkered tablecloths covered them. Containers of condiments were on each. Benches flanked each table on both sides. Dana ran a high-class operation.

Once the food was almost ready, Dana would gather everyone around the campfire, welcome them, introduce his helper and give a few instructions. This completed, people would line up and make their way past the table containing the trays, cups, et cetera. Then they would pass the gas stove and be given a plate of hot food. Once served, they would proceed to a table to eat and enjoy the beautiful, scenic mountains, the wild flowers, and other gifts of nature.

As each guest opened the aluminum foil containing a whole, cleaned trout with head intact, there were always mixed reactions. The majority took this in stride and heartedly ate the eatable portion of the trout. Others took one look, made faces, uttered various negative remarks, and refused to eat theirs. They gladly gave them to others who enjoyed such fare.

The wrangler would serve the famous Elk Island coffee. Many found it as strong as expected. Others didn't. But everyone drank plenty. Hot water for tea and cocoa was also served. While doing so, the wrangler would chat informally with the guests.

Once the initial serving was done, Dana and the wrangler would answer questions, offer tidbits of information and enjoy the chitchat. Second helpings were then offered, and the hot drinks continued to flow as long as guests wanted them.

As people finished eating, they would mill around taking pictures, walk closer to the wild flowers or wild birds, and just enjoy themselves, in general, until it was time to leave. Almost everyone was very appreciative and expressed it verbally at some point. A great many took pictures of Dana and the wrangler, as well, to remind them of their time on Elk Island.

Once the boat pulled away from the dock, Dana and the wrangler would eat their breakfast, clean up, load everything that needed to go back to the kitchen into the boat and head for home. Once they arrived, everything was lugged up the ramp, trucked back to the kitchen, and unloaded. The wrangler would then return to the marina, and Dana would begin food preparations for the next meal on the island.

The twice-weekly steak-fry cruises were basically the same except for the number of people, the time and the menu. Fifty to one hundred guests could be accommodated. Two boats were needed to carry everything, including several large bags of ice, to Elk Island. And preparations took longer.

The menu included a large salad bar. It was set up in a canoe that spanned two tables, and the ice kept everything cool, crisp, and fresh. Steaks, cooked to order, specially prepared home-fries, corn on the cob, hot homemade bread, apple pie, coffee, tea, and punch rounded out the menu. It was a delicious meal. The cold food was always cold, and the hot food was always hot.

The steaks were all about the same size and thickness. Shortly before the meal was to begin, Dana would cover the large grill with steaks. As they cooked, he would poke them with two fingers on one hand. He could tell, using this method, to what degree each steak was done. Thus, steaks, rare, medium, well, and everything in between, were served with the utmost accuracy.

Both the breakfast and the steak-fry cruises were delightful experiences and very popular with tourists and with employees. At times, however, weather became a thorn in the flesh to everyone, both the workers and the guests. Elk Island lies much closer to Mt. Moran than Colter Bay, and it lies right in the path of storms that come through the passes on either side of Mt. Moran. Windy conditions and rainstorms could turn a delightful dining experience at Elk Island into a nightmare in a matter of minutes. Since there was no real shelter from the weather in such adverse conditions, people would take cover wherever they could find it, under the branches of trees or under the picnic tables.

As the rain poured down, the food, drinks, and guests were at the mercy of the elements. Food floated on plates, drinks were diluted and everyone was drenched from head to toe. If the storm passed over quickly, the meal could be saved, fresh drinks could be poured and guests could dry themselves by the campfire, since it seldom went out. In the end, people could still enjoy themselves. However, if the opposite occurred, the entire experience would be a nightmare. This was especially true for those who had no sense of adventure and/or couldn't see any humor in such an outing. After all, Mother Nature controls the weather and is most unkind at times.

One evening a heavy rainstorm struck just as everyone was beginning to eat. About a quarter to a half mile on either side of the guests, the sun was shining brightly. Yet, over our area, the rain poured down and turned a pleasant dining experience into a disaster. It poured through the entire meal, ruining clothes, food, drinks, and appetites. No more than five minutes after the soaked, unhappy, and still hungry guests had left, the rain stopped and the sun appeared.

Breathing sighs of relief, Dana and I sat by the fire drying out, eating a leisurely meal, and almost feeling guilty while doing so. Then we began the tedious task of cleaning up and transporting everything back to the mainland. The bags of garbage were especially full. However, I was sure the stomachs of the guests, who had been there, weren't.

As I worked, I thought to myself, *If only the Park Service would let us put up a large, canvas canopy over the tables, the weather would have a somewhat less negative effect during such storms.* However, I knew, without a doubt, this would never come to pass. Elk Island was a wilderness area and that's the way it would stay. And to this day, it has.

When not working, employees found relaxation and enjoyment in a number of ways. For those who enjoyed the more physical pleasures, there were several. Hiking the many scenic trails in the park, mountain climbing, swimming in the cold lake or heated pool, biking, playing horseshoes, basketball or softball, and horseback riding were available. On days off, a round of golf could be enjoyed at a course near Jackson.

One favorite outing for both males and females was to a hot spring. It was reached by hiking through muddy areas after parking some distance from the spring. These outings were usually begun in the evenings. Beer, wine and munchies were taken as were bathing suits, towels, and flashlights. However, nude bathing was more common than not, as the participants alternated between the hot spring and a cold stream nearby.

Less physical activities included Ping-Pong, played on a table that had seen better days; matching wits with friends while playing one of the many box games, none of which had all its parts; watching the one, snowy channel on the TV; writing cards and letters extolling the beauty of the park; doing one's laundry; cleaning one's room; relaxing on one's bed and listening to music coming from the room next door or down the hall; and the most popular one, sitting outside around two adjoining picnic tables "shooting the breeze" while guzzling cold cans of soda or beer.

The less than creative recreation director scheduled various activities for some evenings. Included were Ping-Pong tournaments, bingo nights, weekly, full-length movies, dances and parties. On bingo nights, a quarter might win you three or four dollars depending on how many bingo fanatics showed up. The movies were shown on a projector too small for the recreation hall. Thus, seeing and/or hearing them was often impossible. But, as the recreation director growled at me on more than one occasion, "What do you want for fifty cents?" How this twenty-one-year-old female managed to graduate from a reputable four-year college with a major in physical education/recreation was beyond my comprehension and still is.

The first gala affair was a Halloween costume dance in the recreation hall. I borrowed parts of several different staff uniforms from friends, coordinated them with parts from mine and went as a "jackass of all trades." Soon after arriving and looking around at others, I realized mine was not the most creative, or the most original, and would never win a prize. Even so, a few fellow employees paid me compliments.

As more and more employees arrived, I was very surprised to see several macho-type males dressed as women. I asked myself, "Had they done so because women's clothes were readily available for costumes; because they enjoyed wearing women's clothes and were playing out a fantasy; or both?"

As I continued to look around the hall, my eyes fell on a knockout, in this case, someone sensationally attractive. This person had beautiful hair, styled to perfection; a face with just the right amount of makeup to accentuate each delicate feature, and a slender, well-endowed body. A beautiful red dress, red high heels, and just the right amount of jewelry, enhanced the natural features of this goddess of love and beauty.

Determined to meet this gorgeous stranger, I casually sauntered across the hall, rehearsing my introductory compliments to myself. When I arrived and stood face to face with this beauty, Gomer Pyle's famous words, "Surprise! Surprise!" suddenly exploded in my mind. For there stood my friend, Ken, smiling and asking how I liked his costume. Two female friends had transformed him from a fellow lakeweed gatherer into this creature of beauty, and he was enjoying every minute of it, high heels and all. It being a costume party, I should have suspected someone like Ken would be there.

I was still getting over the shock and disappointment of this encounter, when two more female employees arrived. These two came as babies. They wore white towels for diapers, skimpy white blouses and white socks. They had painted freckles on their cheeks and noses. Their hair was styled baby-like with colored bows, and each carried a large lollipop. One glance and I could tell they were not meant to be twins since one was far more physically endowed than the other. Jokingly, I murmured to someone standing next to me at the time, "Now there are two babies whose diapers I wouldn't mind changing!"

The dance music was provided by a stereo system turned up so loud people in China could have heard it. My pleas for turning it down either fell on deaf ears, or the disc jockey couldn't hear what I was yelling into his ear. At any rate, the loud music evidently wafted to the Superintendent of the Park's home some distance away. He was trying to sleep and didn't appreciate it. So he sent two park police to the hall in an effort to have the volume of the music lowered. They delivered the superintendent's message and left. The volume was lowered some but not enough as far as those trying to sleep within a half mile radius were concerned.

Eventually a second message arrived, and the police stayed this time until the volume was lowered considerably. However, this was the beginning of the end of our dances. During a second dance, a couple of weeks later, the Park Superintendent again was unable to sleep due to the loud music. Therefore, he sent park police to the hall and shut us down for good.

A few parties were held after that but without dancing, they were rather boring. However, at these parties, everyone could easily hear the conversations that were taking place. Even so, I missed the enjoyment of dancing, as did many others. But I didn't miss the loud music.

Smaller and more intimate get-togethers often took place in the dorm rooms. The number of people ranged from two, often a male and a female making mad, passionate love, sending moans and groans wafting throughout the hallway, to more people than one room could comfortably hold.

Two fellows, who shared a room at one end of the hall in my dorm, seemed to have more get-togethers then anyone else. One evening I was passing by the open door to their room and was invited in for a drink. I accepted and joined the circle of those already there. Most of them were friends of mine, including Ken.

A couple of drinks sprinkled with conversation later, the door was shut. Then someone took out two, funny-looking cigarettes, lit one, took a deep puff and passed it to the person on his right. This person did the same and the next and the next. It didn't take me long to realize the cigarette was a reefer (a marijuana cigarette), and it would soon be passed to me. I could either take a puff or pass it directly to the next person.

Having never tried marijuana or any illegal drug and being curious, I opted to take a puff when my turn came. Following the instructions given to me, I puffed, inhaled the smoke deeply and didn't exhale for several seconds. When I did exhale, very little smoke came out. Another round, another puff, a couple more rounds and a couple more puffs on a second reefer, and suddenly I became very tired. I thanked my hosts, walked down the hall to my room, lay down on my bed and fell asleep in seconds.

The next day at work, I asked Ken about my sudden tiredness the evening before. He informed me it was a result of my smoking marijuana for the first time. "Big deal!" I thought. "What's so great about marijuana if it puts you to sleep?"

About a week later, I was invited back to the "den" for more fellowship, drinks and marijuana smoking. This time, as I entered the room, I saw a plant growing in a pot on the floor near a dresser. A lamp cast a purplish light onto the plant. Being naive, I remarked, "That's a nice looking tomato plant." Once the laughter died down, my ignorance of botany decreased a tiny bit as I learned about and observed a healthy marijuana plant growing nicely in that room.

As the evening progressed, I became very tired. Therefore, I excused myself, walked to my room and fell asleep. Marijuana was sure curing any insomnia I had.

Two weeks later, I was passing another room on the way to mine and was invited in. I accepted, entered the room, sat down, joined in the conversation and waited for drinks to flow, but none did. After a short time passed, the door was closed. Seeing this, I thought to myself, "Here we go again." One fellow then produced a funny looking gadget, he called a bong, and a bag of marijuana.

I soon learned that a bong is a large, weird-looking pipe used for smoking marijuana. The results are far more powerful than smoking reefers. The pipe was loaded, the marijuana lit, and the first drag was taken, inhaled, and held deep inside the lungs for as long as possible by the bong's owner. The supplier's turn came next as the process was repeated. Then the bong and marijuana continued around the room until it arrived where I was sitting.

I quickly recalled my two previous marijuana parties, and how tired I became. Therefore I decided to give this drug one last chance to thrill me. Besides, it was free, so I had nothing to lose and everything to gain, or so I thought. I took the bong, waited until the marijuana was in place and lit. Then I took a deep drag, held it as long as I could and finally exhaled. Nothing happened to my senses.

The bong made three more trips around the room, and each time I joined the others. After four bongs, I didn't know what the others were experiencing, but I felt no euphoria at all. I was sure I was holding it in my lungs long enough, so I began to wonder if I was immune to its effects.

Eventually there was only enough marijuana left for one final bong, and I was chosen unanimously to enjoy it. I accepted. Once the marijuana was lit, I took an even bigger drag than the four previous times. I inhaled it deep into my lungs, held my breath as long as possible, and finally exhaled. Very little smoke came out. I put the bong down and began chatting with the others. This time I did not become tired and wondered why. Maybe Ken's information was valid. This was my third marijuana party, and now I didn't even feel tired. Why anybody would spend thirty dollars for a quarter ounce of this drug was beyond me.

Suddenly, without any warning whatsoever, I felt myself leaving my physical body, or so it seemed. As I looked around the room, everyone was still talking and laughing, but I was not one of them. I was in another realm. I was sure they were talking and laughing about me, so I asked a few questions such as, "Why are you laughing at me?" As soon as I asked a question, I couldn't remember what I had asked. And when someone answered, I immediately forgot what he answered. I could not concentrate on anything for more then a few seconds. Thus, when someone asked me a question, I'd answer him and then immediately ask, "Did I give you a correct answer? I can't remember what I just said." Everyone assured me that I had, and then they'd laugh some more, putting doubts in my mind.

As all this was taking place, I kept looking across the room to the door, wondering if I could walk to it and down the hall to my room. My mind kept telling me I couldn't, so I didn't try for several minutes. I sat there feeling completely helpless and confused. My mind was spinning a mile a minute yet focusing on nothing. I had been drunk a few times in my life, but I had never experienced anything to match what was happening at this moment. I was scared to death, having no control over my mind or body.

I finally managed to overcome my fear and rose to my feet. I walked slowly and unsteadily across the room and down the hallway, zigzagging back and forth, like a true drunk, banging into both walls. As I opened the door and entered my room, Jim looked up from his newspaper and began asking questions. I glanced at my roommate and sensed a wee bit of concern for my well-being. Most of his questions were forgotten before I could even attempt to answer them. I couldn't remember what I did say, however, before I flopped on my bed and uttered something about wanting to sleep.

Another fellow from the party soon entered the room and informed Jim of what had happened. When he finished, Jim, a former drug user and alcoholic, began to laugh in amazement that his roommate, Mr. Straight and Narrow, would ever use marijuana. Thus, he became determined to keep me awake and make fun of my condition. Smiling broadly, he encouraged me, in an exuberant voice, to, "Go with the flow! Live it up! Enjoy it while you've got it!" His words fell on almost deaf ears. All I wanted was some sleep, an escape from the effects of those five bongs. Eventually sleep did come, and Jim's party ended.

Two hours later I woke up. My head was pounding, but my mind and body were one again. I was, as they say, coming down from my high. I rolled over, went back to sleep, and woke up the next morning feeling much better. However, the events of the previous night were still fresh in my mind. I vowed then and there to abstain from further use of marijuana and any other illegal drug. I had played with fire and got burned. I'd have to be crazy to play again.

As one warm, beautiful, summer day melted into another, the marina continued to be a beehive of activity. However, as the second half of August slipped by and September took over, there were signs that fall was approaching. Every day became a bit shorter and each night a little cooler.

The water level in the bay continued to drop and the floating docks continued their unnoticeable, yet, gradual descent. Slowly the ramps became steeper and steeper. Some old-timers, who had boats in the bay, could "smell fall in the air," and a few even made preparations to take their boats out. One old codger remarked to me, " 'T'aint never too early to begin thinkin' 'bout winter once September gets here." However, I didn't want summer to end, so I tried to ignore the signs and continued to enjoy each summer day to its fullest.

Labor Day was very busy. Droves of locals and tourists descended on the marina, seeking one final, relaxed respite from the rigors of the real world, to which they would soon have to return. Far into the evening celebrations continued on many larger boats. Then gradually the noise died down, and the familiar sounds of waves lapping at the moored boats and bells tinkling could be heard. It was the end of a great day; the icing on the cake of a great summer.

The next day reminded me of the morning in May, when Ken and I found the empty minnow traps. Only this day, it was people, not minnows that were lacking. It was another sure sign that fall was around the corner, signaling the end of a shortened marina season.

As the days continued to come and go, and nights became longer and colder, nature left calling cards here and there. Heavy frost coated ramps and docks. Heavy dew on the small motors made them more difficult to start. The insides of the aluminum canoes and boats became slippery. And water pipes broke here and there as the cold froze the water in the pipes and expansion took place cracking the pipes. Such signs were omens that the first snowfall was imminent.

Realizing that staff would soon begin to leave, Ray decided it was time to have the annual Marina Minnow-Beer Initiation Ceremony at the John Colter Bar. The date and time soon arrived. At 8:00 P.M. sharp on a Tuesday evening, everyone had assembled and was sitting in a rather large circle.

Ray rose to his feet and welcomed everyone. Then he explained the ceremony and made sure everyone had a beer. He became the first to partake in the ritual. Still standing, he uncovered a pail, reached in, took a squirming minnow out of the water, dropped it into his beer, put the mug to his lips and drank the contents. Reactions to what he did were mixed from those in the circle and from others outside the circle who had come to the bar to drink, talk, and relax. The ritual continued as the first person to Ray's right took a minnow, dropped it into her beer, and, with a look of horror on her face, drank it down trying not to gag.

I was sitting halfway around the circle sipping a seven and seven. I hate beer, and everyone there knew it, so I assumed the ritual would pass me by. Slowly the pail moved closer and closer to me, past Tammy, Ken, Nancy, and others. Like it or not, each partook. Then the pail was placed at my feet.

Before I could offer my excuse, the bartender placed a glass of water on the table next to me. Ray had thought of everything. As everyone watched, I did what I had to do to save face. I reached down, grabbed a minnow and dropped it into the water in the glass. It swam furiously around enjoying its new home. As I reached over and picked up my glass, everyone became silent. I raised the glass to my lips and drank it down trying not to think of its contents. I received a few congratulatory smiles as I put the glass on the table. I breathed a sigh of relief, passed the pail to the next person and returned to my seven and seven for comfort.

The pail finally arrived back at Ray's feet. There was an ample number of minnows still swimming around enjoying life. I'm sure everyone, including me, assumed the ritual was over, until Ray stood. He challenged us anew, then reached into the pail, grabbed two minnows, dropped both into his glass of beer, and downed its contents.

After wiping his mouth with the back of his hand, he smiled and passed the pail to his right. As the pail began its second trip around the circle, some followed Ray's leading, and some passed. By the time it reached me, I was sipping my third seven and seven and was beginning to feel no pain. I went to the bar, returned with a glass of water, threw in two minnows, watched them swim a moment then drank them down without a flinch. Feat accomplished, I passed the pail to my right and took a large sip of my drink. I had survived round two with flying colors.

Once more the pail arrived back at Ray's feet. To the surprise of many and horror of a few, round three began. Three minnows to a beer, and Ray was the first to indulge himself. By now, most of those in the circle were feeling the effects of their beers, as I was my seven and sevens. However, most were still in touch with reality enough to balk at round three and passed the pail without participating. I was not so fortunate. My drinks were clouding my mind, my senses, and my actions. When the pail reached me, I already had a glass of water ready. Almost joyfully, I sent three more minnows to join the previous three. I was beginning to enjoy this ritual.

By the time the pail finished the third cycle, very few had participated, and Ray did not even suggest a fourth. However, I was rather drunk by then and continued the ritual by myself. I rose to my feet, had a large glass of water and the pail brought to me, put four of the little "fishes" into the glass and watched them swim around as best they could. Then, with all eyes focused on me, I raised the glass into the air, shouted, "Cheers!" lowered the glass to my lips and began drinking. However, I had trouble drinking its contents down without pausing for air. When I paused, I could feel minnows in my mouth trying to swim in water that wasn't there. For a brief moment, I panicked, then quickly gulped more water out of the glass and swallowed, sending those final minnows to their doom.

As I sat down and reached for my chaser, Ray quieted the crowd and announced that I had set a new record at this ceremony by downing ten minnows. An ovation and words of congratulation followed. I was too drunk to fully appreciate them.

Once again fame had come to me, and I owed it all to my seven and sevens. Had I remained sober, I'm sure I would have downed one minnow, maybe three, but never ten, not on a bet.

After the ceremony was over, several onlookers, including staff and tourists, tried downing one minnow. Some found it easy, and others didn't. Some gagged and a few almost vomited. But everyone, who wanted to participate, did. Once the last minnow was taken from the pail and consumed, the bar returned to its normal sanity, and I returned to my room with the help of some friends.

The next day several people asked me how I felt. My pat answer was, "Apart from the hangover, I feel pretty good. However, every now and then, I get this terrible urge to go swimming."

A few days later, the first three inches of snow fell, and the clouds that brought it hung around for a week. This weather brought activities on the lake to a virtual standstill. More boats were taken out of the water by their owners, thus, many of the bright colors, that added to the beauty of the bay, were gone.

The water level continued to drop in the bay. The daily depth measurement from the end of the main dock was an indication that the two tour boats would soon have to be taken out. Without cruises, business would drop off rapidly. But without sufficient water, there was no other choice.

As September was drawing to a close, the few remaining staff members worked very hard. There were many jobs to be done to secure the marina for the long winter months ahead. The strain on my back from lifting canoes, rowboats, and motors caused me much pain and some spinal problems that only a chiropractor could correct at a later date. On October 2 the work was finally completed, the last trip to the John Colter Bar was taken, and the end-of-the-season, dress-up dinner was held.

The next day I loaded my belongings into my station wagon and said my good-byes. I took a final stroll to the marina, sat several minutes enjoying the fall colors, then returned to my wagon and headed toward Jackson. The scenery was as pretty as ever, only now the golden leaves on the aspens and the other fall colors on all the vegetation added a new dimension to the scenic beauty.

It had been a great four and a half months in many ways. However, with winter weather approaching, I was happy to be heading home. I knew in my heart that I would return the following year, and that realization warmed my soul.

Chapter XXV
Diets: I Could Write My Own Book and Get Rich

During my senior year of college, I received an unsigned greeting card in the mail. On the outside it read, "Do you want to lose ten ugly pounds?" I whispered, "Yes," to myself and quickly opened it to the inside and read, "Then cut your head off!" Funny? Yes, in a way—insulting in another. I knew it came from someone at the college, but over thirty years later, the sender remains a mystery. However, the culprit must have been someone who knew I was on one of my diets at the time and wanted to add a little humor to the drudgery of losing weight.

During a graduate course a few years later, I wrote a paper entitled, "The Place of Food in a Children's Institution." One important fact came out of my research: eating is a form of security for many children. Once food is in their stomachs, no one can take it away from them. Maybe that's the reason I enjoy eating and not because most foods, I eat, taste good.

Since the age of sixteen, when I began working summers at Mulcahey's Fish Fry stand, I've gained and lost well over 1,000 pounds of unwanted fat. I've tried virtually every diet that has been extolled in magazine articles and books, and they've all worked. I remember my protein diet of the early 1970s. I had to drink at least ten large glasses of water plus eat only protein foods. I lost a great deal of weight in a short time, but I'm sure I walked the weight off going back and forth to bathrooms.

My biggest problem has been keeping the weight off, not taking it off. My fear of gaining back lost weight is one reason I bite my fingernails. At times, when dining at a nice restaurant, I've been so afraid of gaining weight, I've mistakenly asked the waiter, "What wine goes well with fingernails?"

So many times in my life, I've wished that foods such as lettuce and carrots tasted as good as chocolate cake and apple pie. Why is it that the better something tastes the more fattening it is? Doesn't God have taste buds too? Why would a loving, caring God provide so many delicious foods and then cram them full of calories? Is He sadistic or did He do it to develop our will power? We'll never know here on earth.

Magazine and TV ads are thorns in the flesh to any weight conscious person. Talk about Pavlov's dogs! It should be against the law to show any food commercials on TV after 6:00 P.M. And all food ads in magazines should be presented in black and white. Maybe then people like me would have a fighting chance against gaining weight. The only other solution, I see, is to chain myself to my chair evenings while watching TV, and let someone else in the room keep the key. Obviously, this would prevent me from getting up and securing those ever present, always fattening snacks, the stimulation for which comes from TV food commercials.

Since my weight goes up and down like a YoYo, I have three wardrobes: one for thin, one for medium and the third for heavy. I learned years ago not to throw away clothes from any of the three, unless they're worn out, knowing I'd probably need them again. The ever-changing fashion scene is not my concern. It's the changing, fattening scene that is. One consolation is the fact that my sock, shoe, and glove sizes remain the same.

To solve the three-wardrobe problem, I'm waiting for the day clothing manufacturers come out with a full line of elastic clothes: one size fits all. Then I'll be able to keep up with the current styles at a fraction of the cost. Until then, I'll continue to wear mostly out-of-style clothes.

Over the past many years, friends have given me many pieces of advice. One told me, "Dave, eat anything you want but don't swallow." I've considered this on occasion but spitting chewed food into a pail sounds revolting—especially in restaurants. Another suggested that I eat all my meals off a dessert plate. I tried this, even one Thanksgiving Day, and it works, especially if you eat only one plateful, and it's not piled high like one of Dagwood Bumstead's sandwiches. Another admonished me to "Eat breakfast like a king, lunch like a queen, and supper like a pauper." This one works well too, but eggs, bacon, toast, and other such breakfast foods just don't taste as good as steak, mashed potatoes with lots of gravy, hot biscuits, and apple pie with ice cream.

A couple of years ago, I read that Mickey Rooney lost twenty pounds in a short time by eating anything he wanted any day until 2:00 P.M. Then he'd eat only an apple until the next morning. At the time, I weighed 204 pounds. I had fat in places some people don't even have places.

I decided to modify the king, queen, pauper suggestion and combine it with Rooney's diet plan. It was April 21, and my diet would end on my granddaughter's birthday, June 28. I was hoping to lose twenty pounds by then. I set up a routine and stuck to it most of the time. I allowed myself an ice cream cone once a week and, if invited to lunch or dinner, I accepted but ate modest portions, including dessert, no matter how fattening it was.

For breakfast, I'd eat like a queen. I'd eat a bowl of Total with nonfat milk and no sugar. I'd include fresh fruit if I had any. Two pieces of honey wheat-berry toast with a wee bit of oleo or jam and black coffee would round out the meal. I'm not much of a calorie counter, so I don't know how many were contained in my breakfast.

After breakfast, I'd hurry to the golf course nearby, walk the eighteen holes as fast as play would allow, and finish most days before noon. Then I'd head for Mr. T's Family Restaurant in downtown Riverside, California, and have my main meal. I'd eat like a king, consuming a seven-course feast: cup of soup; tossed salad; entree; baked potato with a little oleo; vegetable; roll with a little oleo; dessert, either pudding or Jell-O with whipped cream; black coffee and two glasses of water. While sitting at the circular counter eating, I'd enjoy the fellowship of other regulars from all walks of life. By 1:00 P.M. at the latest, my king's meal would be eaten, and I'd be full.

For supper around 6:00 P.M., I'd eat like a pauper. A wedge of lettuce, some green beans and two ounces of tuna fish in water were mixed together and topped with a small amount of low calorie salad dressing. This was my total fare. The total calories were 150, yet I would feel full. Of course the ever-present water and a cup of black coffee were also consumed.

After supper, I'd walk an hour at a fast pace. I'd wear enough clothes to make me sweat. I'm sure some people would say I was jolking: a happy medium between jogging and walking. I'd cover three to four miles.

Several evenings a week, while watching TV, I'd use two plastic, gallon-sized, antifreeze containers filled with water, as eight-pound dumbbells. Such exercise would strengthen my stomach and arm muscles as well as burn up calories.

On Saturdays and Sundays my routine changed a little. Instead of playing golf, I'd walk an hour each morning at a rapid pace. The rest of each day remained the same.

Once a week I'd step on the scale and record my weight on my calendar. I did this ritual at the same time each week, before breakfast in the morning. I was losing about four pounds a week, yet I was never hungry.

By June 28, I had lost thirty-six pounds. My waistline had gone from a forty-two to a loose thirty-six, and my stomach was flat. I did not look or feel like a fifty-four-year-old man. I had the appearance and energy of a man much younger. I felt terrific!

My thin wardrobe fit loosely. Some items were a little outdated, but I didn't care. Who'd notice anyway considering what many people were wearing in this "anything goes" society? However, to celebrate, I bought some new size thirty-six walking shorts.

I'd like to end this chapter here, but I must be honest and confess that I've gained twenty pounds back during the past three years. Two of those years have been spent writing this book. I'm now wearing my heavy wardrobe, but I'm on the same diet and losing fast. I've lost fourteen pounds in a month, and I'm getting thinner. I do not want to hear a doctor tell me, "You have the body of an eighteen-year-old. Unfortunately, it's encased in the fat of a fifty-seven-year-old."

The only difference between the two diets centers on the place where I eat my king's meal. I'm now eating it at the King's Table Buffet in Riverside. It has a wide range of foods including rich desserts. Believe it or not, I eat there six or seven noons a week, and I'm still losing weight. How do I manage? I eat only low calorie items. At times this is difficult, especially when my good friend and fellow diner, John Mac Afee, sits across from me eating mashed potatoes and gravy, chocolate cake, ice cream loaded with syrup and other such calorie-filled foods. In the end, I'll reach my goal then reward myself with a large piece of chocolate cake topped with soft ice cream. I'm waiting patiently for that day to come. Hmmmmm.

Chapter XXVI
The Hitchhiker: Drifter or Convict?

It was April 1986. I had been in Sparks, Nevada, visiting my son and his family for a few days. Then I headed for the mountains and beautiful Lake Tahoe. I stayed there a couple of days during which I celebrated my birthday. Now I was on way back to my apartment in Riverside.

I left Stateline, Nevada, on Tuesday morning, April 8. As usual, I took the steep, curvy Kingsbury Grade down into the valley and was soon on route 395 heading south. I hadn't gone far when I passed a seedy-looking man with a beard. He was hitchhiking. Shortly thereafter, I took a short detour off 395 to check out the golf course and the surrounding area just south of Gardnerville.

Satisfied, I headed back to 395 and continued south. I hadn't gone far when I saw the same man. I figured he must have caught a short ride after I passed him the first time. This time I decided to stop and give him a lift. He needed a ride, and I would enjoy some company. I picked him up and stored his backpack in the rear of my wagon.

Once underway, we exchanged first names and began a conversation. I offered him some of the cookies that Kim, my daughter-in-law, had baked for me, and he readily accepted. He gobbled up each cookie as if he hadn't eaten for a week.

In the course of our chitchat, Bill began to talk about Idaho. He mentioned how good the hunting and fishing were, and how he had spent a lot of time there doing both. He also mentioned how much he liked to backpack into the woods in Idaho away from civilization and people. He came across as a loner, but one skilled in living and surviving in the great outdoors. We continued talking until he fell asleep.

As I drove, I thought about our conversation. Every so often, I looked over at my sleeping passenger. He needed a bath, a shave, a clean set of clothes and, I'm sure, a few good meals. All of a sudden, my thoughts turned to a newspaper article I had read several days before.

The article was about a man who had been convicted of killing two game wardens in Idaho and had been given a thirty-year sentence for manslaughter. On Easter Sunday, March 30, 1986, he had escaped and was being sought by law enforcement officers in several states. Since reading that article, I hadn't read or heard, on radio or TV, that he had been recaptured. Suddenly a thought hit me like a bolt of lightning. Could this hitchhiker be that convict?

During the next several minutes, I kicked this question around in my mind. After all, he had talked about Idaho and activities the convict enjoyed. And both were the outdoor type. But, if he were the convict, why would he be hitchhiking? Especially on a fairly busy highway. Then I tried to recall the convict's name and what he looked like from the picture that had accompanied the article. But I couldn't. The only thing I felt sure about was the fact that the convict had no beard in the picture. Perhaps he felt safe hitchhiking, now that he had one, even though it was not fully grown. At any rate, if Bill were the escaped killer, I decided to treat him as nicely as I could. After all, I didn't want him to get angry at me.

We reached Bishop, California about lunchtime. I stopped for gas and food at an AM/PM Mini-Mart. I bought two hot dogs for Bill and two for me. I bought Bill a large soda, and I had coffee. He accepted both and thanked me. It didn't take him long to down both hot dogs, some more cookies, and his soda. We topped lunch off with large, soft ice-cream cones.

After lunch, we resumed our trip and talked some more. Bill mentioned that he had been in Idaho recently then in South Lake Tahoe visiting friends. Now he was headed for Las Vegas to visit more friends. After downing a few more cookies, he thanked me again for lunch and the cookies. He confessed that he had little money for food and appreciated my generosity. Then he put his head back on the seat and fell asleep.

Thinking about what he had said this time made me even more suspicious. I finally asked myself, "If he is the wanted convict, what can I do to protect myself, yet contact the authorities?" Since route 395 runs through miles and miles of desolate countryside, I decided to do nothing to arouse his suspicions. Once I dropped him off at his desired stop at the intersection of routes 395 and 58, I'd head for the nearest police station. Until then, I'd remained cool, calm, and collected. I'd also pray that he'd continue sleeping.

It was late afternoon and getting dark when we finally reached his point of departure. By then, he had eaten all my cookies and had gotten several hours of sleep. I handed him his backpack and bade him good-bye. He thanked me again then asked me for some change for coffee. I gladly handed some over, then reentered my wagon and pulled back onto the road. I took a final look at Bill in my rear view mirror as he headed across route 395 to route 58 east. Then I breathed a huge sigh of relief and headed for Adelanto and the police station there.

It was dark when I drove into the police parking lot. I quickly parked and walked into the building. A lone officer was sitting behind the counter. Seeing me enter, he asked, "Can I help you?" I replied that I hoped so and told him my story. He listened attentively then looked through a pile of the latest wanted posters and came up empty. If only I could have remembered the convict's name, it might have made a difference. The officer finally admitted he did not have anything on this nameless person and suggested that I stop at the State Highway Patrol office in San Bernardino.

As I drove to San Bernardino, I tried and tried to think of the convict's name but couldn't. With or without a name, I was hoping the Highway Patrol office would have some information at hand, but they didn't. In fact, the person behind the counter didn't seem overly interested in what I had to say. She acted very nonchalant about the entire matter, so I left, a little hot under the collar.

What to do? What to do? I kept asking this question to myself as I drove down the freeways into Riverside. Was I making a mountain out of a molehill? Should I forget the entire episode? Or should I try again?

I finally opted to try again. I exited the freeway at Seventh Street and drove to the Riverside Police Department. Once again my story was not taken seriously. I was encouraged to try the Sheriff's Department across the street. Perhaps they had some information on this man.

I headed that way and soon found the man in charge. I told him my story. Like the others before him, he listened then said he was sorry, but there was nothing he could do at that time. He suggested I return the next day and see one of the "higher ups." I thanked him and left.

As I walked back to my wagon, I felt deflated. Not only had none of the officers shown any real interest in my information, none asked for a description of Bill or any other pertinent questions. This bothered me.

I pulled away from the curb and headed home. As I approached University Avenue, I looked at my wrist watch and suddenly another idea popped into my mind. Since the main library would still be open, I could check back issues of *The Press-Enterprise* newspaper and see what I could find. So I turned left and headed for the library.

I quickly parked, walked to the entrance, went in, and made a beeline for the newspaper section. I found the copies that had been published for several days after his escape. In a short time, I hit the bull's-eye. I saw an article and his picture beside it. The picture confirmed my earlier recollection. The convict, Claude Dallas, Jr. had no beard. Thus, I could not tell if Bill was the convict in the picture or not.

I decided to read the article. There were similarities between the printed words and what Bill had said. However, there were not enough to convince me that my passenger was the wanted convict. I returned the newspapers to the proper shelf and headed home. As I drove, I decided to drop the matter and not pursue it any further.

The next morning, I told Sarge, a retired marine who lived in the same apartment complex, the entire story. He found a bit of humor in it and chuckled several times. When I finished, we both agreed that I should forget it. And I did.

On March 9, 1987, I took my newspaper down by the pool to read. I sat in a chair, shaded by an umbrella, and opened my folded paper. I started to read the first page when my eyes fell on a headline that caused my heart to skip a beat. Claude Dallas, Jr. had been captured the day before by the police not far from where I lived.

The Riverside Police had received an anonymous tip and had a motel under surveillance. The day of the capture, Dallas had walked to the nearby Stop-N-Go Market. As he was walking back, a positive ID was made, and he was captured in the parking lot of the market. A photo of the bearded Dallas accompanied the article, but I could not positively identify him as Bill.

The article also mentioned that he was using the alias, Al Schrank, when captured, and that he had been put on the FBI's "Ten Most Wanted List" forty-seven days after his escape. However, Dallas's whereabouts, during his year of freedom, was not known by the authorities, thus I didn't learn if he had been in South Lake Tahoe or Las Vegas.

Since his capture, I've tried to find out where he spent his year of freedom. I even wrote to him personally, but received no answer. Therefore, I'm still wondering if the hitchhiker named Bill was a drifter or a convict. I may never know for sure one way or the other.

Chapter XXVII
Epilogue

As noted in the beginning chapters, my brothers, sisters, and I were raised in rather primitive conditions. However, these conditions have not prevailed. Through hard work, determination and perseverance we have overcome, and life has been good to each of us.

The Reverend Doctor Courtney (Corky) Furman is a full professor at the School of the Ozarks, Point Lookout, Missouri. He teaches religion and philosophy courses and is Chairman of the Humanities Division. He also pastors the Hollister Presbyterian Church. He and his second wife, Jody, live in Branson, Missouri. They have six grown children.

Rose Marie Hess is a dental hygienist. She and her husband, Paul, reside in Norfolk, Virginia. They have two grown children.

Marilyn Kinnison is a remedial mathematics and reading teacher in Urbana, Ohio. She and her husband, Mel, reside in Urbana. They have three grown children and one (Stacy) in high school.

Paul (Paddy) Furman is a shift foreman at the ALCAN Corporation plant in Oswego, New York. He and his wife, Pat, have four grown children. They reside in Oswego.

The desire to drive tractor trailers was sown in my son, Mark, while in junior high school and grew over the years. During his senior year in high school, he and his cousin, Evelyn Phykitt, decided to start their own trucking company. They had business cards printed with the name GEM Trucking Company. GEM stood for God, Evelyn and Mark, since they wanted to put God first in their business. Their company remained a dream and never became reality. However, Mark did have his own truck for several years and made several trips each week between Reno, Nevada and Sacramento, California. Now he works for another trucking company and drives from Reno to Las Vegas and back.

Mark and his wife, Kim, reside in Sparks, Nevada. They have one daughter, Melody.

My daughter, Bonnie Jean Tarricone, has completed her Ph.D. degree in medical neurobiology at the Indiana School of Medicine, Indianapolis. She does brain research. She and her husband, Lee, reside in Indianapolis. They have a baby daughter named Lydia.

Shelley is teaching first grade in Ridgewood, New Jersey. Her second love is writing, and she hopes to make a name for herself writing children's literature.

Dr. George (Pit) Pitluga, Jr. is a professor of art history at Edinboro State College, Edinboro, Pennsylvania. His dad is retired and lives in North Carolina. His mom passed away several years ago.